Reorientations/Arabic and Persian Poetry

# Reorientations/Arabic and Persian Poetry

EDITED BY

SUZANNE PINCKNEY STETKEVYCH

INDIANA UNIVERSITY PRESS
*Bloomington and Indianapolis*

The paper used in this publication meets the minimum requirements of American National Standard for Information Sciences—Permanence for Paper for Printed Library Materials, ANSI Z39.48-1984.

Manufactured in the United States of America

**Library of Congress Cataloging-in-Publication Data**

Reorientations: Arabic and Persian poetry / edited by Suzanne Pinckney Stetkevych.
p. cm.
Includes bibliographical references and index.
ISBN 0-253-35493-5 (alk. paper)
1. Arabic poetry—History and criticism. 2. Persian poetry—History and criticism. I. Stetkevych, Suzanne Pinckney. II. Title.
PJ7541.R46 1993
892'.7109—dc20
93-6900
1 2 3 4 5 98 97 96 95 94

# CONTENTS

PREFACE vii

I. Pre-Islamic Panegyric and the Poetics of Redemption 1
*Mufaḍḍalīyah 119* of ʿAlqamah and *Bānat Suʿād* of Kaʿb ibn Zuhayr
*Suzanne Pinckney Stetkevych*

II. Toward an Arabic Elegiac Lexicon 58
The Seven Words of the *Nasīb*
*Jaroslav Stetkevych*

III. Guises of the *Ghūl* 130
Dissembling Simile and Semantic Overflow in the Classical Arabic *Nasīb*
*Michael A. Sells*

IV. "No Solace for the Heart" 165
The Motif of the Departing Women in the Pre-Islamic Battle Ode
*Hassan El-Banna Ezz El-Din*

V. The Earliest Demon Lover 180
The *Ṭayf al-Khayāl* in *al-Mufaḍḍalīyāt*
*John Seybold*

VI. "Tangled Words" 190
Toward a Stylistics of Arabic Mystical Verse
*Th. Emil Homerin*

VII. The Rise and Fall of a Persian Refrain 199
The *Radīf "Ātash u Āb"*
*Franklin D. Lewis*

VIII. "The Allusive Field of Drunkenness" 227
Three Safavid-Moghul Responses to a Lyric by Bābā Fighānī
*Paul E. Losensky*

NOTES ON THE CONTRIBUTORS 263
INDEX 265

# PREFACE

This volume presents the work of eight members of what has come to be called "the Chicago School" of Arabic and Persian literature. The studies represent a broad spectrum of Arabic and Persian poetry, ranging from the pre-Islamic ode of the sixth century C.E. to the seventeenth-century Safavid-Moghul ghazal, and address a similarly broad spectrum of literary critical issues. The sobriquet "Chicago School" denotes not so much a distinct theoretical or methodological approach, as a group of shared literary critical assumptions. Primary among these is the conviction that the classical literary traditions of the Islamic Middle East are fully "literatures" in the same sense of the term as we apply it to Western literary traditions. In whatever ways they differ from Western literatures, they are nevertheless not to be relegated to mere fodder for philological, sociological, or anthropological pursuits. And however impenetrable they may seem from a Western stance, Arabic and Persian poems are works of art and are regarded as such by the cultures that produced them.

What we are urging is not, however, a double standard, but rather a reexamination, refinement, and redefinition of our own literary sensibilities and critical methods. Having defined these traditions as fully literatures in their own right, it follows that they cannot be evaluated or interpreted solely according to critical standards and analytical methods derived exclusively from Western literatures.

With regard to contemporary literary critical trends, it appears to us that the reflexive and decontextualized application of these to understudied and undervalued classical traditions is more facile than fruitful. Above all, for the study of non-Western literatures to be perpetually following the latest critical trends of New York or Paris guarantees that it will always be fashionable, but never original. This is not to say that the studies offered here are not informed by the most recent critical thinking—for indeed they are—but rather that, taking a broader, longer-term view of literary critical concerns, our tendency is to let our choice of critical method be determined by issues generated by the literature itself.

In keeping with our conviction that the Arabic and Persian poetic traditions should be granted their due positions among the great classical world literatures, the studies in *Reorientations* address issues of broad literary cultural concern. In addition, the studies contain original translations of the poems under discussion that strive to capture the power and poeticity of the Arabic and Persian texts.

*Reorientations/Arabic and Persian Poetry* opens with an exploration of the ritual form and function of the Arabic ode (*qaṣīdah*) of the pre-Islamic period in Suzanne Pinckney Stetkevych's "Pre-Islamic Panegyric and the Poetics of Redemption." This study offers an analysis of two renowned classical Arabic odes, "A Heart Turbulent with Passion" by the pre-Islamic poet ʿAlqamah and "The Mantle Ode" composed by Kaʿb ibn Zuhayr for the Prophet Muḥammad. Employing the theory of gift exchange first formulated by Marcel Mauss and the paradigm of the "seasonal pattern" proposed by Theodor Gaster, the author argues that the panegyric ode functions as a ransom payment and as a pledge of fealty. Further, in proposing that "The Mantle Ode" itself generated the story of the Prophet's donation of his mantle to the poet Kaʿb ibn Zuhayr, the author reveals the mythogenic, as well as mythopoeic, power of the poem. Through establishing the ritual form and function of these two paradigmatic odes, the author provides a theoretical base for the reevaluation of the panegyric genre in classical Arabic as well as other literatures.

The *nasīb*, or opening section of the classical Arabic ode, with its recurrent elegiac motifs—the ruined abodes, the lost mistress, etc.—has traditionally been categorized as concretely descriptive of the realities of Bedouin life. In "Toward an Arabic Elegiac Lexicon," by contrast, Jaroslav Stetkevych argues through the analysis of seven key items of nasīb diction that its poetic intent and value lie not in its descriptive realism but in its deeper archetypal symbolism and, further, that this deeper level can be reached only through uncovering what Muṣṭafā Nāṣif terms "the myth behind the word." The analysis of the selected words—words which are repeated in a seemingly obligatory way in countless classical Arabic odes—proceeds on the basis of etymology, semantic range, mythopoeic and metaphorical association to reveal cultural, as well as more closely literary, connections with Ancient Near Eastern ritual, myth, and poetry. The method developed and employed in this study goes beyond the new philology inspired by Leo Spitzer into the realm of myth and archetype. In recognizing the true source of the nasīb's power, the study thus definitively refutes the traditional notion that the "Bedouin nasīb" which persisted throughout the urban and urbane periods of Islamic culture was an awkward conceit that had survived only because of formalist inertia.

Michael A. Sells's study of the simile in the classical Arabic nasīb, "Guises of the *Ghūl*," takes as its guiding metaphor the Protean self-transformations of a pre-Islamic mythical creature, the *ghūl*, a species of Jinn. The ghūl's fascination is to be found in the tension between the extraordinarily compelling nature of each guise and the elusive play of symbolic transformations out of which it emerges and into which it disappears. So too, the author argues, must the simile of the classical Arabic ode be understood. Traditional scholarship has emphasized the descriptive aspect of the Arabic ode and its dense texture of similes. But, the author argues, what occurs is often not description at all—description is but one guise among many. The similes dissemble: they promise a description, but deliver something that is not, or not only, descriptive, and sometimes not even a likeness. Thus, the similes involving the beloved outrun the descriptive point and flow into a chain of similes, or an extended simile, that ends in a metonymic evocation of an underlying archetype: the beloved as the lost garden.

In "'No Solace for the Heart,'" Hassan El-Banna Ezz El-Din treats one of the major motifs of the nasīb, the departure of the women of the tribe, termed the *ẓaʿn*. Typically the womenfolk, enclosed in howdahs and mounted upon male camels, are compared to ships at sea or desert trees, or are seen at their point of disappearance on the horizon. This study first examines the context of the word ẓaʿn as it occurs both in the nasīb and in its "countercontext" in the *fakhr* (boast) section of the ode. It then places this motif within the broader elegiac context of the nasīb with its dominant themes of loss and sorrow. Further, however, it demonstrates that the ẓaʿn bears both a structural and a semiotic connection to the theme of war, that is, that it functions as a key element in the pre-Islamic battle poem. In this respect, the author goes beyond the current level of discussion of battle poetry in the classical Arabic corpus, which up until now has limited itself merely to literal battle description within the ode. He proposes instead a structural model for a "battle poem" that does not merely take "battle" as a major theme of its boast section, but rather controls the structure and choice of motifs for the entire ode, even in the introductory elegiac section. The case of the ẓaʿn should prove paradigmatic for unlocking the structural and semiotic interdependence of classical Arabic poetic motifs traditionally considered to be merely paratactically concatenated.

In keeping with the critical directions of the earlier studies, John Seybold explores in "The Earliest Demon Lover" yet another of the traditional motifs of the nasīb, that of the night visit by the phantom of the beloved. Through the examination of this motif as it occurs in odes contained in the renowned classical anthology, the *Mufaḍḍalīyāt*, the author first establishes that the motif of the night phantom is cognate to the predominant elegiac nasīb motif, that of the *aṭlāl*, or ruined abode. He then poses the critical riddle: how is the phantom like a ruin? Both are figments of lost happiness, both conjure up for the poet an idyllic memory. Finally, the author speculates that the two images combined describe the practice of incubation—of sleeping in a sacred place for oracular purposes—and that the phantom thus may signal the onset of an oracle.

Arabic mystical poetry has always drawn heavily on the conventions and motifs of nonmystical verse, employing apparently worldly images, of wine, the beloved, etc., to express inner, spiritual experiences. As a result, this verse is often very ambiguous, to the extent that, when read out of context, it is difficult to discern whether the intention behind the images is carnal or spiritual. In "'Tangled Words'" Th. Emil Homerin reads back from accusations leveled at the celebrated panegyrist al-Mutanabbī that he employed convoluted expressions resembling the "tangled words" of the Ṣūfī poets, to begin to define stylistic characteristics peculiar to mystical verse.

The phrase "fire and water" burst onto the scene as a popular refrain in the Persian odes of the late eleventh and early twelfth centuries C.E. Masʿūd-i Saʿd

Salmān borrowed this refrain from a lesser-known poet, employing it in three odes, so that the refrain made quite an impression upon the literary scene and was borrowed by a number of other poets, including Sanā'ī, Abū al-Faraj Rūnī, and Rashīd al-Dīn Vaṭvāṭ, before gradually fading from the scene in the next century. In "The Rise and Fall of a Persian Refrain" Franklin D. Lewis takes this corpus of poems with the "fire and water" refrain to examine the sources and patterns of influence in the highly traditional art form of classical Persian court poetry. On this basis he then discusses the Arabo-Persian concepts of *istiqbāl* (imitation), *taḍmīn* (quotation), and *sariqah* (plagiarism) to offer a reassessment of current Western critical thought concerning poetic influence and the anxiety thereover.

Paul E. Losensky notes in "'The Allusive Fields of Drunkenness'" that the historians of Persian poetry have described in lengthy detail the departures in imagery and language of the so-called Indian, or "New," Style that flourished during the Safavid-Moghul period. Far less attention has been given to the practice of answering an earlier poem with another in the same meter and rhyme scheme, termed *istiqbāl* or *javāb-gū'ī*. Yet the collected works of the poets of this period are filled with odes and lyrics modeled after those of the "old masters." The emphasis placed on originality and innovation by Safavid-Moghul poets can be understood only in light of their thorough knowledge and appreciation of their literary past. To maintain the vitality and relevance of the tradition, these "late" poets could neither blindly mimic nor heedlessly disregard it, but needed, rather, to creatively interpret and rewrite it. After a discussion of the literary critical terminology employed in the Arabo-Persian tradition for a full range of concepts between *imitatio* and *creatio*, the author demonstrates, through close readings of three Safavid-Moghul responses to a lyric by the Timurid master Bābā Fighānī, that imitation and originality are not necessarily opposites, but are interdependent—and can even be identical.

It is the goal of these studies to demonstrate that Arabic and Persian poetry, when approached in fresh ways, can yield new literary critical insights and generate new critical concepts that cannot so easily be derived from within the Western tradition. In other words, in such areas as the ritual and sacrificial aspects of literature, the transition from orality to literacy, the iconographical and mythic dimensions of philology, *imitatio* as a form of *creatio*, etc., Arabic and Persian literary studies should be able to take their place in contemporary literary critical discourse. Finally, through reorienting our critical approach to classical Middle Eastern literatures we will gain a new vantage point on our own tradition that will lead us to a more profound and multidimensional new poetics.

# Reorientations/Arabic and Persian Poetry

# I

# PRE-ISLAMIC PANEGYRIC AND THE POETICS OF REDEMPTION

## *MUFAḌḌALĪYAH 119* OF ʿALQAMAH AND *BĀNAT SUʿĀD* OF KAʿB IBN ZUHAYR

*Suzanne Pinckney Stetkevych*

### Introduction

The classical Arabic ode, or *qaṣīdah*, sprang from the deep recesses of the pre-Islamic Arab autochthony (the Jāhilīyah or Age of Ignorance) to reign as the dominant Arabo-Islamic poetic form down through the first half of our own century.* Yet however vast and mighty its literary dominion, we find in the literary critical tradition—both Arab and Orientalist—two issues which appear to have dogged the qaṣīdah throughout the centuries. The first relates to the fact that the panegyric mode (*madḥ*), developed by the poet-courtiers of the Jāhilīyah alongside the tribal boast (*fakhr*), gained a position of preeminence in the Islamic period. With the lavish compensation accorded the panegyrists of the caliphal and princely courts came the accusation that the poet's encomia were mere sycophantic blandishment, thereby raising the issue of "sincerity." Concomitant to this attack on the integrity of the poet was an attack on the integrity of the poetic form. Thus we find in the well-known formulation of the ʿAbbasid critic Ibn Qutaybah (d. 276/889) that the "goal" or "purpose" of the qaṣīdah is the third and final *madīḥ* (panegyric) section, whereas the *nasīb* (amatory prelude) and *raḥīl* (desert journey) perform only a preambular rhetorical function.[1] To challenge these assertions, I have posited first a function for the panegyric qaṣīdah, that of a commodity in ritual exchange, and second, a ritual form or structure, that of the seasonal rite.

This argument for ritual function, however, generates a further literary critical problem. For the predominant Modern and preeminently Romantic concept of poetry posits in its "art for art's sake" dictum an inverse ratio between value and function; this study proposes—for pre-Islamic poetry, at least—a direct ratio. To argue this I have selected two well-known and highly esteemed classical

Arabic qaṣīdahs which on the basis of both internal evidence in the poem itself and external evidence, the *akhbār* (historical-anecdotal materials) that accompany the poems in the classical Arabic literary corpus, are associated with cases of ransom or redemption. The crux of my argument is that these two poems, the *Mufaḍḍalīyah 119* by ʿAlqamah ibn ʿAbadah and *Bānat Suʿād* (the Mantle Ode) of Kaʿb ibn Zuhayr, are not merely eloquent rhymed and metered appeals and panegyrics, but function in fact as exchange commodities in the redeeming of a human life—that is, as ransom payments. I propose that in light of this premise we can achieve a new understanding, first of all of the ritual function of poetry in premodern societies, a role fundamentally at odds with our Romantic and post-Romantic notions of poetry, poetics, and aesthetics, and second, a new estimation of the structure of the qaṣīdah. Above all, I hope to show that the functional aspect of poetry, far from reducing it to a demeaned and servile status, endowed it with a value and power unknown to our Romantic and post-Romantic poetry, which is by comparison not merely chaste, but impotent. Moreover, I would like to demonstrate that the aesthetic aspects of the poem are ultimately determined by its function.

The two poems to be analyzed have been selected on two grounds that are essential to the argument propounded: (1) both are traditionally regarded as superior examples of the poetic art; and (2) both have been handed down in a context of anecdotal materials (akhbār) that testify to their role in a redemptive transaction, or, more broadly speaking, their role in a multifaceted ritual exchange. It should be noted from the outset that for the modern literary critic the value of the akhbār is not so much *historical*, for their historicity is often doubtful and, in any case, difficult or impossible to substantiate, but *exegetical*, suggesting how the poem was traditionally perceived and interpreted. The first poem, the work of the renowned pre-Islamic poet ʿAlqamah ibn ʿAbadah,[2] who for his masterful poetry was awarded the sobriquet ʿAlqamah al-Faḥl ("the Stallion"), is associated with a straightforward ransom of captive kinsmen. The second is the celebrated *Qaṣīdat al-Burdah* ("Mantle Ode"), which the great poet and scion of great poets, Kaʿb ibn Zuhayr,[3] is said to have presented to the Prophet Muḥammad on the occasion of his conversion to Islam, and for which the Prophet conferred upon the poet his *burdah* (mantle). The first thus redeems a mortal soul, the second an immortal one. The first step of the argument will be to establish the function of the qaṣīdah as a commodity in a ritual exchange; the second will be to determine how a work of art comes to be worth a human life. The final step will be to demonstrate how the pagan poetic tradition redeemed itself.

## Part I. From Politics to Poetics: ʿAlqamah's *Mufaḍḍalīyah 119*, "A heart turbulent with passion"[4]

> Ḥammād al-Rāwiyah [d. 155/772 or 156/773] said: The Arabs used to present their poems to Quraysh and what they accepted was accepted

> and what they rejected, rejected. So ʿAlqamah ibn ʿAbadah came before them and recited the qaṣīdah that goes: "Is what you knew and safeguarded kept secret?"[5] They said: "This is the necklace string of time [*simṭ al-dahr*]!" Then he came again to them the next year and recited: "A heart turbulent with passion has borne you off," and they said, "These are the two necklace strings of time!"[6]

However suspect Ḥammād's probity, his taste has always been considered unimpeachable, and this attempt to attribute Jāhilī esteem to ʿAlqamah's poems must be read above all as an expression of his own estimation. Speaking on his own authority, the critic al-Jumaḥī (d. ca. 232/847) said of ʿAlqamah that he had composed three superb qaṣīdahs that were unsurpassed in Arabic poetry: "You have departed from al-Hijrān without direction," "A heart turbulent with passion has borne you off" (*Mufaḍḍalīyah 119*); and "Is what you knew and safeguarded kept secret" (*Mufaḍḍalīyah 120*).[7]

*Mufaḍḍalīyah 119* is said to have been composed after the battle of ʿAyn Ubāgh in 554 C.E.[8] On this day the Ghassanid King al-Ḥārith ibn Jabalah defeated and slew the Lakhmid King al-Mundhir ibn Mā' al-Samā' of al-Ḥīrah. Of the poet's tribe, the Banū Tamīm, who were clients of the latter, a number were taken prisoner, including the poet's brother (or nephew) Sha's. The poet is said to have addressed this poem to the victorious King al-Ḥārith on this occasion to plead for the release of his brother. The question that must be asked before the argument can proceed any further is: Is this qaṣīdah merely an eloquent request, rhymed and metered, for the prisoner's release, or does it function as a commodity in a ritual exchange, in particular, as a ransom payment? The evidence to support the latter interpretation is found in the commentary of al-Anbārī to the penultimate line of the poem:

> Sha's was ʿAlqamah's brother. . . . When al-Ḥārith heard him say "Then Sha's too deserves a bucket of your bounty's flood," he exclaimed, "Buckets and more buckets!" and then ordered the release of Sha's and all the prisoners of the Banū Tamīm. But ʿAlqamah said to al-Ḥārith, "Don't release the prisoners of the Banū Tamīm until I've gone to see them." When he went to see them he said, "I have asked the king for you as a gift and he has given you to me [*istawhabtukum min al-maliki fa wahabakum lī*]. Now he is going to clothe you and bestow gifts upon you; so, if you give me whatever clothes and gifts he bestows upon you, I will have you released, otherwise, I'll leave you here." So they vouchsafed him what he asked, and when they were led out he took what was with them and released them. . . .[9]

To this he adds a variant version:

> Sha's was ʿAlqamah's brother or some say his brother's son. He was

> taken captive on that day, so he came seeking his release. . . . When he reached the line "Then Sha's too deserves a bucket of your bounty's flood!" al-Ḥārith exclaimed, "Yes, and many bucketfuls!" and said to him, "Choose between a generous gift [*al-ḥibā' al-jazīl*] and the captives of the Banū Tamīm." ʿAlqamah replied, "You have exposed me to the calumny of the tongues of the Banū Tamīm. Give me today to consider the matter." Then he went to them and informed them of the king's offer, and they said to him, "Woe to you! Will you leave us and go?" He replied, "Surely the king will clothe you, mount you, and provision you. So, when you reach the tribe, then the mounts, clothes, and the rest of the provisions will be mine." They agreed to this, and the king released them.[10]

This anecdote, in its two slightly variant forms, reveals, above all, that ʿAlqamah's *bā'īyah* was not perceived as merely an "occasional poem" to celebrate the release of his brother, nor to either plead for or thank the king for his release. Rather, the supposition upon which the anecdotes rest is that the poet has presented the king with a valuable commodity and expects something of value in return. They further indicate that the poet so valued the poem that he felt the lives of his kinsmen were hardly adequate compensation. Moreover, as is clear from the diction employed in the anecdote, the transaction is presented as an exchange of gifts.

Having made this initial identification of the poem as ransom payment, we will look to the seminal findings of Marcel Mauss in his study *The Gift* (*Essai sur le don*) on the characteristics and functions of ritual exchange.[11] The akhbār reveal in the first place a striking correspondence between this ransom of prisoners and Mauss's definition of his subject as

> prestations which are in theory voluntary, disinterested, spontaneous, but are in fact obligatory and interested. The form usually taken is that of the gift generously offered; but the accompanying behaviour is formal pretense and social deception, while the transaction itself is based on obligation and economic self-interest. . . .[12]

In the case at hand, the primary obligation is that of ʿAlqamah to ransom/redeem his brother and other kinsmen. The anecdote reveals the obligatory nature of the gift/qaṣīdah by exposing the poet's ambivalence toward parting with a valuable commodity to no personal profit, and more explicitly by the poet's remark that the king will have exposed him to the calumny of his kinsmen should he opt for personal gain, the "generous gift," rather than the release of his kinsmen. "Obligation" and "economic self-interest" seem to be at odds with one another until the poet devises his ruse and thereby manages to "have his cake and eat it too."

The question may then arise as to why King al-Ḥārith gave all the prisoners in return for the poem instead of merely releasing Sha's and demanding the usual cash/cattle (*māl*) payment for the rest. Mauss provides an explanation for this too. The ritual exchange, in Mauss's formulation, subsumes three obligations: giving, receiving, and repaying.[13] "Failure to give or receive," Mauss remarks, "like failure to make return gifts, means a loss of dignity."[14] Further, accepting a gift entails accepting the challenge to repay that it implies. The picture becomes increasingly clear: to maintain his prestige among the Banū Tamīm, ʿAlqamah must ransom Sha's *et al.*; to maintain his royal dignity, al-Ḥārith must accept the gift/challenge and repay it *with interest*, or else face loss of rank. Mauss states: "No less important is the role which honor plays in the transactions. . . . Nowhere else is the prestige of an individual as closely bound up with expenditure, and with the duty of returning with interest gifts received in such a way that the creditor becomes the debtor."[15] This suggests that to have merely exchanged Sha's for the poem would have debased the king; it is precisely his generosity that establishes his royalty. For, in Mauss's words:

> Between vassals and chiefs, between vassals and their henchmen, the hierarchy is established by means of these gifts. To give is to show one's superiority, to show that one is something more and higher, that one is *magister*. To accept without returning or repaying more is to face subordination, to become a client and subservient, to become *minister*.[16]

It must have been precisely this realization that moved King al-Ḥārith to exclaim, when the poem asked for "a bucketful," "Buckets and more buckets!"

Having identified the presentation of the panegyric qaṣīdah as part of a ritual exchange, we will now examine other aspects and implications of this identification. E. E. Evans-Pritchard's summary of Mauss's conclusions makes a useful starting point: "The exchanges of archaic societies . . . are total social movements or activities. They are at the same time economic, juridical, moral, aesthetic, religious, mythological and socio-morphological phenomena. Their meaning can therefore only be grasped if they are viewed as a complex concrete reality. . . ."[17] It is our argument that in the poem too, inasmuch as it is at the heart of this "total social phenomenon," "all kinds of institutions will find simultaneous expression."[18]

The ritual function of the poem having been established through the akhbār, I would like to posit as the basis for the analysis of the qaṣīdah itself the ritual form of the poem. Most useful in this regard is the application of Theodor Gaster's formulation of the "seasonal pattern" in his *Thespis: Ritual, Myth, and Drama in the Ancient Near East*.[19] This will be done, however, with the provision that we are dealing with a Bedouin variant of the Ancient Middle Eastern agrarian pattern in which the "harvest" is not the seasonally determined one of grain, but the metaphorical "harvest" of human lives on the battle "field." The argument then is that Gaster's conclusions concerning the structure and function of ritual (and myth and drama) are *mutatis mutandis* applicable to the classical

Arabic qaṣīdah. We will therefore claim for the qaṣīdah, as Gaster does for the public ceremonies that usher in years and seasons, that they "are neither arbitrary nor haphazard, nor are they mere diversions. On the contrary, they follow everywhere a more or less uniform and consistent pattern and serve a distinctly *functional* purpose. They represent the mechanism whereby . . . society seeks periodically to renew its vitality and ensure its continuance."[20] The structure of the qaṣīdah will therefore be analyzed in accordance with the structural divisions that Gaster has determined for seasonal ritual:

> The activities fall into two main divisions which we may call, respectively, rites of Kenosis, or Emptying, and rites of Plerosis, or Filling. The former portray and symbolize the eclipse of life and vitality at the end of each lease, and are exemplified by lenten periods, fasts, austerities, and other expressions of mortification or suspended animation. The latter, on the other hand, portray and symbolize the revitalization that ensues at the beginning of the new lease, and are exemplified by rites of mass mating, ceremonial purgations of evil and noxiousness (both physical and "moral"), and magical procedures designed to promote fertility, produce rain, relume the sun, and so forth.[21]

These two sections are subdivided to produce four major elements:

> First come rites of *mortification*, symbolizing the state of suspended animation that ensues at the end of the year, when one lease on life has drawn to a close and the next is not yet assured. Second come rites of *purgation*, whereby the community seeks to rid itself of all noxiousness and contagion, both physical and moral, and of all evil influences which might impair the prosperity of the coming year and thereby threaten the desired renewal of vitality. Third come rites of *invigoration*, whereby the community attempts, by its own concerted and regimented effort, to galvanize its moribund condition and to procure that new lease on life which is imperative for the continuance of the topocosm. Last come the rites of *jubilation*, which bespeak men's sense of relief when the new year has indeed begun and the continuance of their own lives and that of the topocosm is thereby assured.[22]

The logic of the present enterprise then requires that these ritual divisions be aligned with the structural divisions of the classical Arabic qaṣīdah, which traditionally, in accordance with Ibn Qutaybah's (d. 276/889) formulation,[23] is considered tripartite. It is quite possible, however, to see in the nasīb, which comprises a description of the abandoned encampment, the lost mistress, the complaint against old age, etc., an expression of *mortification*, "suspended animation"; in the raḥīl which comprises the recounting of the hardships of the desert crossing and the description of the poet's mount, the she-camel, *purgation*;

the third and final section, in this case madīḥ (panegyric), must then be understood as encompassing both aspects of Filling, *invigoration* and *jubilation*, as such common elements as the battle or hunt followed by the feast would certainly allow.

Inasmuch as the seasonal pattern is a ritual and sacrificial one, we will expect to find expression of the change of status, from polluted to pure, symbolic death and rebirth, etc., that rites of passage and sacrifice normally entail. At one level, at least, ʿAlqamah's poem deals with a change of political allegiance, or an act of submission to a new liege lord. Thus the seasonal pattern of the agricultural cycle of mortification → purgation → invigoration → jubilation serves as a metaphorical foundation upon which to construct a ritual oath of allegiance: the lease on life that has drawn to a close is that of the poet's former liege lord, King al-Mundhir, who has been slain; the new lease is obviously that of the victorious King al-Ḥārith. The poem thus functions as a document of surrender. This is clear if we consider that, had a state of war continued, an act of military aggression would have been called for to rescue the captives. Instead we have an act of ritual submission in which the poet forswears his former allegiance to the Lakhmids and declares his new allegiance to the Ghassanids. Thus, precisely as Mauss has claimed, the ritual exchange is not merely a *quid pro quo* transfer of goods, but a complex phenomenon in which many institutions find simultaneous expression. With this in mind we can begin to examine ʿAlqamah's qaṣīdah.

*Mufaḍḍalīyah 119 of ʿAlqamah* [24] [1]

1. A heart turbulent with passion
       has borne you off,
   Long after youth has passed
       and the time of old age come.

2. Thoughts of Laylā trouble me
       though her dwelling is now far,
   Though there have come between us
       hostile fates and grave events.

3. She lives in guarded luxury,
       all talk with her forbidden;
   At her door a guard wards off
       all visitors.

4. When her husband is away
       no secret is divulged;
   Delightful is his homecoming
       when he returns.

5. Then do not compare me
with an untried youth—
May laden rain clouds water you
when they let down their loads,

6. May low-lying Yemeni clouds water you,
and clouds spread out on the horizon
Borne on the southwind in the evening
when the sun inclines to set.

7. What good is it to remember her
when she is of Rabīʿah's clan
And a well is being dug for her
in Tharmadāʾ?

8. If you ask me about womankind,
I am indeed
Discerning in their ailments,
eminently skilled:

9. Should a man's head hoary
or his wealth decrease,
He will find no share
in their affections;

10. They seek abundant wealth
wherever they know it's found,
In youth's first bloom alone
they take delight.

* * *

11. So leave her and dispel your cares
with a tall mount, bold as your resolve,
That even with a second rider
keeps up a lively trot,

12. To al-Ḥārith the Munificent
I hastened my she-camel
At such a pace her chest
and end ribs throb,

13. A fleet one whose
rib-riding hump and hump-front
The midday heat and constant journey
have consumed.

14. The morning after two-nights' journey
    she is like
A full-grown stripe-legged oryx doe
    that fears the hunters,

15. That takes refuge in
    the arṭā tree
After men, whose arrows she escaped,
    and dogs have sought her,

16. That she might bring me
    to the abode of one once distant,
Till, heading for one-night-distant water,
    she brought me to your generosity.

17. To you—may you repel all curses!—
    did she direct her gait
Through signless wayless wastes,
    their terror dreaded.

18. The twin polestars guided me to you,
    and a clear road
Above the rockmounds of whose stony tracts
    worn traces showed the way,

19. Upon which lay the corpses
    of abandoned beasts,
Their bones blanched, stiff
    their desiccated skin.

20. At a dung-fouled waterhole
    she's stopped to drink;
If it disgusts her, she has no nearby pasture
    but the journey and the ride.

***

21. Do not withhold your favor from me,
    a foreigner,
For amidst the king's domed tents
    I am a stranger.

22. You are the man in whom
    I place my trust,
For lords before have ruled me,
    then I was lost.

23. For the Banū Kaʿb ibn ʿAwf
restored their king,
While in the armies' midst another king
was left for dead.

24. By God were it not for the knight
on the black steed
They would have gone home in disgrace,
though homecoming is loved.

25. Into the fray you advance with him,
until his pasterns' white is black with blood,
And all the while you smite the casques
of foemen armor-clad.

26. You were clad in double coats of mail
from which are hung
Two choicest of blades—
the Slicer, the Gasher.

27. Then you fought them until
they warded you off with their ram,
When the sun of day had reached
the time to set.

28. The rustling of the chain mail
that they wore was like
Dry grainfields rustling
in the south wind.

29. The guardians of the Banū Ghassān
battled there,
Hinb, Qās, and Shabīb fought
with the sword.

30. As if above the men of al-Aws
beneath his charger's breast
And those of the Banū Jall that gathered
and of ʿAtīb

31. The sky's camel calf roared,
till one lay jerking like a slaughtered beast,
His weapons undespoiled,
another lay despoiled.

32. As if there poured down on them
        a storm cloud
    Whose thunderbolts left the vultures
        creeping on the ground.

33. None escaped except a tall mare
        still in her bridle,
    And a spirited blood stallion
        slender as a spear,

34. And an ironclad warrior
        possessed of perseverance,
    As if hennaed with the moisture
        of the blades' edge.

35. You are the one whose traces
        on the enemy,
    Of harm and benefit,
        leave lasting scars.

36. On every tribe you have bestowed
        a boon;
    Sha's too deserves a bucket of
        your bounty's flood.

37. To Ḥārith's high rank none draws nigh
        except his prisoner,
    His kinsman likewise
        is not abased.

Lines 1 through 10, what would normally be termed the nasīb, correspond to the mortification phase of Gaster's "seasonal pattern." The ostensible subject is a traditional one, the less-than-youthful poet still tormented by youthful passion. Though he should by this time be staid and even-tempered, he is still troubled by thoughts of Laylā, his long-gone mistress, and prays that rain, cleansing and life-giving, might fall on her now-distant dwelling. He then chides himself for his foolishness— he is not a boy in love for the first time, but a man of experience in affairs of the heart and the fairer sex. All the more reason that he should recognize that the past, however much he might call down new life on it, is irretrievable. Not only is Laylā gone, but his own youth too is fled: other "Laylās" will spurn him in favor of the younger and wealthier.

It is of course possible to read this "amorous introduction," along Ibn Qutaybah's line of thinking, as an enticement into the qaṣīdah—the lure of the prurient should never be underestimated—but, given ʿAlqamah's obligation to

Sha's and the danger to his own person in going before one who has just recently slain the poet's liege lord, it is unlikely that the poet is primarily interested in discussing with the king his *affaires de coeur*, or that the monarch has much interest in them. On the metaphorical level this passage is far more significant, for the "eclipse of vitality," the failed relationship with the mistress and the hoarying of the poet's head then express the demise of al-Mundhir, failed alliance, and misplaced allegiance. The "conceit" of the lost mistress thus functions as a metaphorical pre-statement of the explicit statement of the poet's political situation in lines 22 and 23.

The raḥīl (desert journey), comprising lines 11 through 20, then corresponds to the purgation phase of the seasonal pattern. Lines 11 and 12, in which the poet abandons the memory of Laylā and mounts his she-camel to seek solace with the munificent monarch, make sense only if the poet's "lost love" is taken to be a metaphorical expression of the slain liege lord. From the very beginning of the raḥīl the goal is explicitly stated as al-Ḥārith al-Wahhāb ("the Munificent"), so that the monarch's thoughts, as well as the poet's, are guided in the desired direction. The elements of the desert journey express purgation as part of a ritually determined progression. The "description," here as in the nasīb, is a metaphorical displacement rather than a naturalistic depiction: first from the poet to his mount, whose perseverance and determination are essentially his. She is driven till her chest and ribs throb from exertion (line 12), her hump is emaciated, consumed by heat and journey (line 13), her only drink is at a "dung-fouled waterhole." The sense of a liminal journey, a ritual test or contest, is expressed in lines 14 and 15, where the she-camel is likened to the oryx doe that escapes the hunters and their hounds, and further in line 19 in the image of the desiccated cadavers and bleached skeletons of beasts that failed to complete the crossing. The momentum of the ritual sequence is preserved in the images of unerring and instinctive sense of guidance and direction on the part of both the poet and his mount: the poet heads for al-Ḥārith's munificence as unerringly as a she-camel through the dark of night to water (line 16). The poet's moral instinct finds expression in the she-camel's sure sense of direction in the wayless desert (line 17), in the guidance of the Dioscuri and way markers (line 18), and in the overarching image of the inexorable journey. That his transit expresses above all a transfer of allegiance from the Lakhmid al-Mundhir to the Ghassanid al-Ḥārith may explain a curious detail that the classical commentators have not failed to remark upon. That is, that in line 17 the poet addresses his new Ghassanid liege lord with the ritual address of his former Lakhmid lords, "May you repel all curses!" (*abayta al-laʿna!*), rather than that of the Ghassanids, "O best of youths!" (*Yā khayra al-fityāni*).[25]

At line 21 the poet reaches King al-Ḥārith and the madīḥ section of the poem which, according to our chosen paradigm, should express Filling (replenishing) with its two subsections *invigoration* and *jubilation.* At this pivot point in the poem the poet states his case in two masterfully concise lines (21 and 22) that combine rhetorical complexity with simplicity of diction. This semantic core of the poem is expressed in completely straightforward terms that make it stand out from the dense weave of poetic diction, simile, and metaphor of the rest of the poem. The structure admirably conveys the change of allegiance sworn here. The poet enters with a dramatic negative imperative, "Do not withhold your favor from me, a foreigner," by which he invokes the law of hospitality that no monarch can transgress. This is followed by two parallel phrases in which, through the double antitheses of I/you and stranger/king, "For amidst the king's domed tents *I* am a *stranger* / *You* are the man in whom I place my trust" (*fa innī imru'un wasṭa al-qibābi gharībū / wa anta imru'un afḍat ilayka amānatī*), the poet throws himself upon the mercy of the king and declares his allegiance to him. In the final hemistich of the couplet the poet forswears his allegiance to his former masters, declaring that "lords before have ruled/owned me, then I was lost." The Emptying/Filling pattern thus forms the semantic and ritual core of the poem: the Emptying in this case referring to the demise of the Lakhmids, their "eclipse of vitality" taking a rather explicit form, and the poet's renouncing his allegiance to them; the Filling taking the form of the victory of al-Ḥārith and the poet's oath of allegiance to the victor.

The ancient seasonal ritual pattern of a king deposed and slain and a new king instated is found here too.[26] The *mortification* of the Lakhmids and *invigoration* of the Ghassanids is succinctly reiterated in line 23 in the "restoration" of al-Ḥārith (*addat . . . rabībahā* "they restored their king") and concomitant "abandonment" of al-Mundhir (*ghūdira . . . rabībū* "a king was abandoned"), the antithesis made all the more emphatic by the contrast of the active and passive voices. What follows (lines 24 through 34) is a "battle description" whose function in our proposed ritual paradigm is evident from Gaster's remark: "Rites of *invigoration* take various forms, of which the most common is the Ritual Combat, or mimetic battle between Life and Death, Summer and Winter, Old Year and New Year."[27]

The ritual form and function of this poetry should make us wary of employing it as history, and cautious as to the authenticity of its ascription to a particular historical event. The contents of the "battle description" are ultimately ritually, not factually, determined. The effect of this mimetic recounting of al-Ḥārith's victory over al-Mundhir is symbolically to renew life through blood sacrifice.[28] Of crucial importance to our reading of this passage is that what has commonly been termed "descriptive" in classical Arabic poetry, although grounded in the concrete, in physical appearance, ultimately expresses metaphysical concepts. The concept of battle as a form of sacrifice and redemption is expressed through a variety of images. Thus in line 23 the Banū Kaʿb ibn ʿAwf restore al-Ḥārith (the verb *addā* refers to restitution, payment of bloodwite, and performance of ritual), whereas al-Mundhir lies dead and abandoned on the battlefield: victor/victim. King al-Ḥārith is portrayed as slayer/sacrificer, bathed in blood as his black steed's white legs disappear when he wades into the blood of battle (line 25). In line 27, al-Mundhir, the vanquished king and champion, is termed *kabsh*, "hero, champion," but also "ram,"[29] with the sacrificial association of *kabsh al-fidā* (scapegoat).[30] Line 28 perpetuates the sacrificial imagery, changing the terms of the battle metaphor from animal to cereal sacrifice, and the apparent objective correlative from the visual to the acoustic: *takhashkhashu abdānu al-ḥadīdi ʿalayhimū / kamā khashkhashat yubsa al-ḥiṣādi janūbū* (The rustling of the chain mail that they wore was like / Dry grainfields rustling in the south wind). The key to understanding classical Arabic poetry is to realize that the apparent basis for comparison—the similar rustling sound of windblown grainfields and chain mail—is not the ultimate one. Rather, the poet is trying to convey an abstract analogy: that the slain on the field of battle serve to reinvigorate the warrior Bedouin populace just as the harvesting of grain reinvigorates the agrarian populace. This concept is an ancient one, and one more often conveyed in classical Arabic poetry through the common epithet for the heat of the battle, *raḥā al-ḥarb* "the handmill of war."[31]

The cosmic and sacrificial come together in the double reading of line 31. The "camel calf of the sky" (*saqbu al-samā'i*) is taken by the scholiasts to refer to the calf of the she-camel of Ṣāliḥ, the spurned prophet of the people of Thamūd. As al-Tibrīzī puts it: "He likens the troops that he counted after the army had plundered them and they had come under his charger's breast, then perished, to the people of Thamūd when they hocked the she-camel and its calf roared among them, then God destroyed them."[32] Then, reading the well-attested variant *dāḥiṣ* (kicking or thrashing like a slaughtered beast), the slain themselves are depicted as sacrificial victims. At the same time, the roar of the sky's camel calf in the context of the following line must, as Lyall reads it, refer to the thunderstorm, and *dāḥiḍ* (slipping) to those slipping and falling on the rain- (blood-) soaked earth.[33]

The cosmic element is perpetuated in line 32, in which the invigorating effect of blood shed on the battlefield is expressed through its resemblance to a mighty downpour that leaves the vultures with their feathers too drenched to take flight. This image combines two traditional ones: (1) the likening of bloodshed to rain and flashing swords to thunderbolts; and (2) the description of vultures feasting on the corpses of the slain, too bloated on flesh and blood to fly. The *locus classicus* of the latter is the line attributed to Ta'abbaṭa Sharran:

At morn the ancient vultures [2]
with bloated bellies stumble;
Unable to take flight they tread
upon the dead.[34]

As I have argued elsewhere,[35] the vulture is best understood as a *Seelenvogel*, equivalent to the owl (*hāmah*) form that the soul of the unavenged warrior was believed to assume to cry for the blood of vengeance. In this case, the recurrent image of the carrion-sated vultures too full of flesh to fly can be nothing other than an image of the *reincarnation*, in a rather literal sense of spirits filled with flesh—a striking image of reinvigoration. Line 32 makes sense only when read in this double metaphorical sense of vegetable revitalization through rain and animal revitalization through blood. This reading then connects line 32 to both lines 28 and 31.

Only the fittest survive this contest, the tall mare, her bridle still intact, the spirited blood stallion, and, as if the poet is likening the best breed of men to the best-bred battle steeds, the ironclad warrior, his hand stained with blood as if with henna (lines 33–34). Since staining the hands with henna is part of the marriage ritual, the effect of the latter simile is to identify the reinvigoration achieved through bloodshed on the battlefield with that associated with marriage and sexual fertility. In other words, as we see in the sacred marriage (*hieros gamos*) of the seasonal ritual, the deflowering of the bride is perceived as a form of bloodshed or sacrifice that produces new life.

If at this point we gather the elements employed by ʿAlqamah in what has traditionally been termed a "battle description," we will find that there is a striking degree of coincidence between them and the elements Gaster presents as a "typical seasonal ceremony": "The king, as representative of the topocosmic spirit, is deposed or slain." "A temporary king, or interrex, is appointed." "The king is ceremonially purified or performs penitential rites." "The king engages an antagonist in mock combat." "The king undergoes a 'sacred marriage.'" "The king is ceremonially reinstated." "Finally, the ceremony issues in a joyous celebration of the new-won life." "A frequent concomitant of the seasonal ceremony is a feast of the dead, the spirits of departed ancestors being believed to rejoin the community at moments of topocosmic crisis." There are ". . . magical rites to stimulate rainfall and fertility."[36] It appears above all that three aspects of "vitality" are metaphorically—and hence ritually—identified with one another: the *agrarian* that perceives "vitality" as the seasonal cycle of dry and rainy seasons, and death and rebirth in terms of the harvesting of grain; the *military* that perceives death and rebirth in the slaying of the enemy in battle; and the *sexual*, as expressed in the *hieros gamos*.

The same mythic-symbolic components are evident if we examine the etymological dimensions of royal nomenclature. The name of the victorious king, al-Ḥārith, itself derives in the first place from the Ancient Middle Eastern agrarian concept of fertility and invigoration. For the verb *ḥaratha* means to till, to sow, to cast seed, to plow the land for sowing. But it carries as well a sexual component, as witnessed in the Qur'ānic *nisā'ukum ḥarthun lakum*, "Your wives or women are your tillage, the place you sow your seed" (Qur'ān 2:223), or, indicating a surfeit of vigor, as in *ḥaratha imra'atahu*, "he went in to his wife a lot, or immoderately." Finally, the term is associated with bloodshed, for the form *ḥārith* itself or *abū al-ḥārith* is used as an epithet for the lion, because it is the most rapacious or predacious of beasts.[37] And we should bear in mind that the lion is, in the Arabic poetic metalanguage, virtually synonymous with the warrior.[38] Thus for the Ghassanid Bedouin king the name "al-Ḥārith" combines precisely those metaphorically, mythically, and ritually connected expressions of invigoration that are found in the "seasonal ritual": the cereal, sexual, and blood-sacrificial aspects of fertility.

After the mythopoeic intensity of the battle scene, line 35 turns to direct address of the king. The first effect of this is to identify him with the "ironclad warrior" of the previous line; the second is to arrest the royal attention for the poet's plea. This line is revealing in its juxtaposition of harm and benefit (*al-bu's, al-nuʿmā*), for in the context of the present argument—that of ritual exchange, and in particular of the gift as a challenge that must be met—the line produces multivalent readings. The first is that al-Ḥārith's gifts leave, in a positive sense, as lasting an impression upon his enemy as his attacks do in a negative sense. But the understanding that Mauss has provided for us of the baleful effect of the gift that cannot be reciprocated suggests that the sense of "traces" and "lasting scars" (*āthār, nudūb*) should be taken in the literal/negative sense for both: al-Ḥārith vanquishes/overwhelms his foe both in battle and in generosity. The mighty ruler is a two-edged sword, dealing death and dealing life.

In light of this reading we can begin to appreciate the full import of the poet's first mention of the Ghassanid king in line 12 as al-Ḥārith al-Wahhāb ("the Munificent"). Al-Ḥārith's prowess in battle has been established in the preceding twelve lines; his generosity, it is hoped, will be substantiated in his response to the coming line (36), "Sha's too deserves a bucket of your bounty's flood!"

Following his plea, the poet retreats from the personal tones of the second person to close the qaṣīdah with a final objective assessment of al-Ḥārith (line 37). The power of the closing line derives, like that of the lines that we have termed the semantic/ritual core of the poem (lines 21–22), from its combination of simple diction with rhetorical complexity: *wa mā mithluhū fī al-nāsi illā asīruhū / mudānin wa lā dānin li-dhāka qarībū* (To Ḥārith's high rank none draws nigh except his prisoner, / His kinsman likewise is not abased). The line plays with the antithesis of prisoner and kinsman (*asīr, qarīb*) and the pun (*jinās*) on *mudānin* (III a.p of *d-n-w*) (measuring up, being equal, drawing near) and *dānin* (I a.p. of *danā* or *daniya*) (near, drawing near, akin or lowly, base, contemptible). The first hemistich is fairly clear; it should mean "No one is his equal, or close to being so, except his prisoner." This is meant to surprise in its surface meaning, but is otherwise intended as a *kināyah* (allusion) to the king's munificence: so generously does he treat his prisoner that the latter's rank almost approaches his own. The second hemistich may be something of a *double entendre*, its multivalence compounded by the fact that *dānin* and *qarīb* can be synonymous, each meaning both "kinsman, relative" and "near, drawing near." Among the possibilities are "And no lowly man comes close [to treating his prisoner so well]," "no relative of his approaches [his rank, or that of his prisoner, or his generosity to his prisoner]," "no lowly/base man is a kinsman of his," and/or "and thus [likewise] his kinsman is not abased." Whatever reading we choose, the basic message is clear and in precise agreement with Mauss's findings: that high rank is achieved by munificence to those under one's protection; that prestige is acquired by generosity.

Returning to the seasonal paradigm, if the battle scene is taken as an expression of *invigoration*, then the plea for generosity, or rather the act of generosity for which the poet pleas, must be perceived as holding the place of *jubilation*. And indeed the release of prisoners and granting of amnesty on holidays and festivals is well known even up to our own day.

I would like to turn at this point to Mauss's statement that in rituals of exchange many institutions find simultaneous expression, and examine how these relate to the form and content of the qaṣīdah.

In light of the circumstances reported in the akhbār, as well as internal evidence, this qaṣīdah and the ritual exchange of which it forms a part, have a pronounced sociomorphic component: that of effecting the submission of ʿAlqamah to King al-Ḥārith, the abrogation of the poet's erstwhile allegiance to the Lakhmid al-Mundhir, and his oath of fealty to the Ghassanid ruler. The exchange of gifts—the qaṣīdah and the prisoners—thus marks the formation of a sociopolitical bond. The poem also amounts to a ritual prostration: the poet declares himself powerless, defeated, a stranger, and throws himself on the mercy of the king. Of course, it is one of the rules of the game that the monarch's rank and dignity are in direct proportion to his liberality to the supplicant.

Each phase of the "seasonal pattern" has a structural role in this transfer of allegiance. In the Emptying phase, *mortification* (the nasīb) constitutes the abrogation of the former allegiance whose vitality is on the wane; *purgation* (the raḥīl) expresses the abandonment of the failed former loyalties, a sort of penance for them, and, at the same time, the sense of new resolve and aspiration. In the Filling phase, *invigoration* is expressed in that part of the panegyric (madīh) that describes the potency and vigor of the new liege lord who will replace the moribund one; *jubilation* in the celebration of the new allegiance and the sealing of the pact through the exchange of gifts implied in the presentation of the poem and the request for Sha's's release. In this respect the battle scene functions as an expression of the poet's submission to his liege lord, his recognition that the king has power over life and death, specifically over that of the supplicant-poet and his captive brother/nephew. The poet's fealty consists of his thus placing his life in al-Ḥārith's hands, while placing his trust in the king's magnanimity. The idea is that in sparing his supplicant's life the king has, in effect, given him life (invigoration); and, conversely, that the poet, in showing his willingness to risk/sacrifice his life, is redeemed, and further (the other half of the bargain) now owes his liege lord his life. In this qaṣīdah, jubilation consists above all of ʿAlqamah's call for al-Ḥārith to signal his acceptance of the proposed contract by sealing it with the exchange of gifts, which thus perform the function of sacrifices or votive offerings. In other words, like the ritual exchanges that Mauss describes, the ransoming of a prisoner was by no means a simple economic transaction.

From the point of view of the poet, we can analyze the poem as well according to the tripartite rite of passage[39] or initiation and trace the poet's passage from *separation*, the loss of the beloved / of the former liege lord, through *liminality*, a transitional phase outside of society, encountering hardship and death in the desert crossing, and *aggregation*, the reentry into society with a new status and its attendant privileges and obligations. The advantage of this paradigm is that it highlights the change in status, the transition, of the ritual passenger—in this case the poet's transfer of allegiance from the vanquished al-Mundhir to the victorious al-Ḥārith.

The mythological aspect of the qaṣīdah is exhibited in the mythic "seasonal pattern" that forms its deep structure. As for content, we must keep in mind that classical Arabic literature in its most pristine forms, poetry and the Qur'ān, is characterized not by narrative myths, but by a "mythic residue" that takes the form of simile or metaphor, or what appears at first to be a merely descriptive passage. For example, the Emptying of the nasīb, the separation of lovers, the fading of youth, already calls for Filling in the poet's prayer for rain (lines 5–6). In the Arabic context the poetic and religious diction are here the same: *istisqā'*, the prayer for rain in time of drought. The effect in the nasīb then is to situate the apparently personal/intimate elegiac experience within the larger mythic/religious seasonal pattern.

Likewise the raḥīl (desert crossing) is not, as has traditionally been claimed, a showcase wherein the poet displays his skill in naturalistic description, but an expression of fasting and penance, of the sojourn in the wilderness that purges and purifies, the encounter with death in which the weak perish and from which the strong emerge with renewed strength, with the knowledge of their own mortality and the secret of immortality. The she-camel must then be understood as the poet's own psyche, the embodiment of resolve and right guidance whom emaciation makes all the fleeter, who knows to take refuge from death in the tree of life, who finds her way to water even at night, who ultimately conveys the ritual passenger to his goal: a new and permanent prosperity.

It is in these terms too that the battle scene must be read. The purpose of the poem is not (merely) to flatter al-Ḥārith with the description of his valor in battle, but to produce a poem that, by casting that battle in mythic/religious terms, incorporates it into a mimetic ritual act that serves, as all fertility ritual does, to guarantee the continued/renewed prosperity/fertility/victory of realm and ruler. Above all, the madīḥ celebrates the foremost attribute of the (divine) ruler: the power over life and death, the power to revive the realm through sacrifice; and second, the concept of the divine appointment of his victory. The king is therefore champion and hero, mounted on a mighty battle steed, bathed in blood, clad in double armor, girt with twain swords (lines 25–26). The harvest of battle (line 28) assumes cosmic proportions in the allusions to the divine scourge of line 31 and the likening of the blood shed by the flashing blades to a life-giving thunderstorm (line 32). The effect of this simile, too, is to fulfill the *istisqā'* (prayer for rain) of the nasīb (lines 5–6). If the first part of the madīḥ presents the ruler's power over death, it culminates by alluding to his power over life. Again the liquid element—of the *istisqā'* of the nasīb, the storm clouds of sacrificial blood (line 32), and the "moisture [*mā ibtalla*] of the blades' edge" (line 34)—is the vessel of expression, through a play on the Arabic *nadā*, "light rain, dew," but also, "generosity."

A final appraisal of the poem involves at once the above aspects, but also the economic and aesthetic ones. For if we accept the premise that ʿAlqamah's qaṣīdah is a ransom payment, a commodity in a ritual exchange, we are obliged to explain what it is that makes a poem worth a human life. It is the "poet's gift" in both senses that is crucial here, for if the hero can be victorious in battle, only the poet can transform that single event into a mimetic form capable of infinite repetition. The historical battle occurs but once and is ended; the poetic one is infinitely repeatable and, in ritual terms, repeatedly efficacious. Moreover, the poet is giving something of himself, sacrificing, as it were, something of his own life force to ransom his brother. For if poetry immortalizes, it is clear that the poet's voice/art is above all his own renown or immortality and that of his tribe, as expressed in the dominant Jāhilī genre of fakhr (boast or praise of self and tribe), and in *rithā'* (elegy for the fallen kinsman).[40] To divert this voice/gift to perpetuate the renown of nonkin is indeed to sacrifice something of one's own renown and immortality, one's own soul. This concept, too, was noted by Mauss in the archaic exchange:

> We can see the nature of the bond created by the transfer of a possession. . . . it is clear that . . . this bond created by things is in fact a bond between persons, since the thing is a person or pertains to a person. . . . It follows clearly from what we have seen that in this system of ideas one gives away what is in reality a part of one's own nature and substance, while to receive something is to receive part of someone's spiritual essence.[41]

And Mauss states further of "the power of objects of exchange": "Each of these precious things has, moreover, a productive capacity within it. Each, as well as being a sign and surety of life, is also a sign and surety of wealth, a magico-religious guarantee of rank and prosperity."[42]

What must finally be recognized is that it is precisely the aesthetic aspect of the qaṣīdah that makes it "immortal" and "immortalizing." For the function of the poem is not merely to record the battle, to document ʿAlqamah's oath of allegiance and al-Ḥārith's generous release of the prisoners of Tamīm, for then it would have only historical value, but to serve as a sociomorphic paradigm for the relation of all his subjects to al-Ḥārith, and of all Arab (and later Islamic) subjects to their ruler. The first explains why it was of value to al-Ḥārith, the second why the Arab-Islamic poetic tradition preserved and celebrated it.

The art of the qaṣīdah consists above all in effecting this metamorphosis from event to ritual/myth, from the ephemeral to the permanent. As recent studies in the field of orality and literacy have demonstrated, the function of poetry, and all those devices which we term "poetic," is essentially mnemonic, for in nonliterate societies the only way to preserve information is to memorize it. As Eric Havelock has shown, rhyme, meter, assonance, alliteration, antithesis, parallelism, etc., all serve to stabilize and preserve the oral "text."[43] The same holds true for simile, metaphor, and pun.[44] Furthermore, we can add to these rhetorical elements the ritual structure of the classical Arabic qaṣīdah and the sequence themes that traditionally occur within the structural units. That is, that Havelock's words, "Ritualization becomes the means of memorization,"[45] are applicable to structure as well.

The ritualization and mythicization of the historical event does not, however, merely endow it with mnemonic stability, but, what is more important, it imbues it with suprahistorical significance. In order for al-Ḥārith's name to survive, in order to produce a commodity that would be the equivalent of a human life, ʿAlqamah had to transform the events of his day into a "text" so laden with meaning that future generations would commit it to memory. It thus functions, as Havelock has shown for poetry in oral cultures, as "the instrument for the establishment of a cultural tradition."[46] In this ʿAlqamah succeeded, and, what is more, some two hundred years later the renowned Kufan philologist, al-Mufaḍḍal al-Ḍabbī (d. ca. 170/786), would include this qaṣīdah among the 130-odd poems of the anthology that he compiled, it is said, at the bidding of the Caliph al-Manṣūr for the instruction of his son Muḥammad, the future Caliph al-Mahdī.[47]

The exchange of poem for prisoner appears to be a fair one if we accept the equivalence of biological and poetic perpetuity. How appropriate then that one of the few anecdotes about ʿAlqamah that have come down to us is concerned precisely with the identity of sexual and poetic potency, that is, the etiological anecdote of how ʿAlqamah received the sobriquet "al-Faḥl" ("the Stallion"). Both the intent and humor of this anecdote revolve around the double entendre of "steed" (*faras*), by which the poets intend the description of their battle steeds in their respective qaṣīdahs, but through which the Ṭā'ī woman alludes to their respective sexual organs or abilities.[48]

The story goes that ʿAlqamah was a friend of the renowned prince and poet of the Jāhilīyah, Imru' al-Qays. One day the two debated which of them was the better poet, until Imru' al-Qays said, "You describe your she-camel and horse and I'll describe mine." ʿAlqamah agreed and proposed that Imru' al-Qays's wife, a woman from the Banū Ṭayyi' who hated her husband, judge between them. Imru' al-Qays composed his qaṣīdah that opens, "O my two companions, pass by Umm Jundub with me / that we may fulfill the need of a tormented heart!" and ʿAlqamah his that begins, "You have departed from al-Hijrān without direction, / it is not right to keep away so long." When they had finished the two qaṣīdahs they presented them to the Ṭā'ī woman and Imru' al-Qays asked her, "Which steed is better, mine or ʿAlqamah's?" To which she replied, "ʿAlqamah's." "Why?" inquired the irate husband. "Because," she replied [paraphrasing lines from their respective poems], "you cry out and thrash your legs and hit, whereas he goes straight for the game/prey [*jāhara al-ṣayda*]." When Imru' al-Qays heard this he divorced her and ʿAlqamah married her, thus acquiring the sobriquet "al-Faḥl."[49]

## Part II: From Mythopoesis to Mythogenesis: Kaᶜb ibn Zuhayr's *Bānat Suᶜād*, "Suᶜād has departed"[50]

In the discussion of ᶜAlqamah's *Mufaḍḍalīyah 119* the role of the qaṣīdah as a ransom payment for the poet's captive kinsmen and, further, as an oath of transfer of allegiance from the vanquished Lakhmid to the victorious Ghassanid monarch was established. An attempt was then made to examine the ritual, mythic, and poetic features associated with the societal function of the poem. On the basis of the conclusions drawn from the analysis of ᶜAlqamah's pre-Islamic panegyric qaṣīdah, I would like to propose a new reading of the celebrated *Bānat Suᶜād* ("Suᶜād has departed") that is said to have been presented to the Prophet Muḥammad by the renowned scion of Jāhilī poets, Kaᶜb ibn Zuhayr. An analysis based on the external evidence of the akhbār and the internal evidence in the qaṣīdah itself reveals that this poem too served as a redemption payment, this time for the poet's own life, and likewise served as a pledge of fealty marking the poet's transfer of allegiance from the moribund tribal ethos of the Jāhilīyah to the triumphant Prophet of Islam. Again, it is the akhbār that first alert us to the ritual function of the qaṣīdah, virtually providing a prose narrative of what the poem is ultimately about.

> Bujayr ibn Abī Sulmā al-Muzanī converted to Islam, and his people, including his full brother Kaᶜb, got angry with him. Bujayr met the Prophet during the Hijrah. Then Kaᶜb sent the following message to him:

1. Take, you two, a message [3]
 to Bujayr from me,
"Did you receive what I said at al-Khayf,
 did you?

2. You drank with al-Ma'mūn
 a thirst-quenching cup,
He gave you a first draught,
 then a second.

3. You abandoned the ways of right guidance
 and followed him,
To what was it, woe to you,
 that he guided you?

4. To a religion no father or mother of yours
 ever followed,
Nor any one
 of your kinsmen!"

When these verses reached Bujayr he recited them to the Prophet who exclaimed, "He speaks the truth, I am al-Ma'mūn [the trustworthy one] and he is a liar; and certainly he found no father or mother of *his* following Islam." Then Bujayr replied to his brother:

1. Who will take Kaᶜb a message, "Will you accept the religion for which [4]
You falsely blame me, though it is the more judicious course?

2. So to God alone, not to al-ᶜUzzā nor al-Lāt,
Make for safety, while you can, and submit,

3. Before a day when no one is safe or escapes from the Fire,
Except the submissive Muslim, pure of heart.

4. To me the religion of Zuhayr —and it is nothing—
And the religion of Abū Sulmā are now forbidden."

When the Apostle of God returned to Medina from al-Ṭā'if, Bujayr wrote to Kaᶜb: "The Prophet is intent upon killing all of the polytheist poets who attack him,[51] and Ibn al-Zabaᶜrā and Hubayrah ibn Abī Wahb [two Qurashī poets] have fled. So if you have any use for your life, then turn to the Messenger of God, for he does not kill anyone who comes to him repentant. If you won't do this, then flee to safety." When Bujayr's message reached him, Kaᶜb became greatly distressed and anxious, and those in his tribe spread alarming news about him, saying, "He is as good as dead," and the Banū Muzaynah refused to shelter him. So he made his way to Medina and stayed with an acquaintance of his there. Then he came to the Apostle of God. The Prophet did not know him, so he sat down before him and said, "O Apostle of God, if Kaᶜb ibn Zuhayr were to come to you repentant and submitting to Islam, would you accept him, if I brought him to you?" "Yes," he replied. Then he said, "I am Kaᶜb." Suddenly one of the Anṣār leapt up and cried, "Let me cut off his head!" But the Prophet restrained him, whereupon Kaᶜb recited his panegyric to the Prophet.[52]

The story of the conversion of Kaᶜb and Bujayr, the two sons of the master poet of the Jāhilīyah and paradigm of pre- or proto-Islamic virtue, Zuhayr ibn Abī Sulmā, is one that points to the inner conflict involved in conversion. For embracing Islam involved the transfer of loyalties from the inherited ancestral ethos of the Jāhilīyah, of which Zuhayr ibn Abī Sulmā had been the noblest embodiment, to a new religion founded by an orphaned upstart from the politically powerful Quraysh. The akhbār and the poetic exchange that they contain first indicate that it is virtue, not inherent viciousness, that holds Kaᶜb back from Islam: *pietas*, piety and devotion to the ways and religion of his ancestors. A closer look at the first poem indicates that, from the traditional point of view, Bujayr's conversion is nothing but opportunistic treachery. For whereas from the Islamic point of view to be given a drink by or share a cup with the Messenger of God suggests the cup of immortal life, from Kaᶜb's perspective, it is the commensal cup of tribal membership. In drinking from it Bujayr has denied his own kin and the right guidance (*hudā*) of the ancestral ways (lines 3–4). Nor does Bujayr deny this in his reply: he has abandoned the goddesses of the Jāhilīyah to worship the one God; the religion of his kinsmen is nothing to him, the religion of Abū Sulmā he considers forbidden. His reason: that only the Muslim, pure of heart, will escape perdition. That this is treachery by Jāhilī standards is clear if we compare it to the celebrated statement of that ethos by the last of the great Jāhilī *fursān al-ᶜArab* (Arab knights), who refused to convert to Islam, Durayd ibn al-Ṣimmah:

I gave my orders at the twisted sand dune, [5]
but they did not see that I was right
till the morning of the morrow.

When they defied me, I went along with them,
although I saw their error and that I
was not well-guided.

For am I not of the Banū Ghazīyah?
If they err, I err with them,
if they are rightly guided,
so am I.[53]

The prose part of the akhbār is a sort of prosaic or literalist version of the poem. The Messenger of God has outlawed Kaᶜb; his choice is to flee or convert/submit. The situation becomes clear to him when his own tribesmen consider him "as good as dead" (*maqtūl*) (which is the equivalent of disowning him, since it implies that they will neither defend nor avenge him), and, finally, his own clan, the Muzaynah, refuse him shelter and protection. Kaᶜb does not betray the ancestral ways, his kinsmen do. And it is only when he sees that the "religion of Abū Sulmā" is no more, that the old social order is extinct, that he heads for Medina to embrace the new one, Islam, and submit to its Prophet.

Inasmuch as the akhbār can be said to serve as a sort of *sharḥ* (commentary) to the qaṣīdah, this much explains the poem as an expression of transfer of allegiance, as an oath of fealty to the Prophet of Islam. That the poem is likewise a redemption payment is apparent from Muḥammad's outlawing the poet and his kinsmen's disowning him and declaring him *maqtūl* (already slain, as good as dead). It is the poem that then redeems Kaᶜb (both in this world and the next). To make the point more explicit, the akhbār, again presenting a "prosaic" (in both senses of the word) version of salvation, depict Muḥammad as saving Kaᶜb's mortal as well as immortal soul by restraining the zealous Anṣārī who would behead him on the spot. As if to make the exchange of his life for his poem explicit, it is at precisely this point, according to the akhbār, that Kaᶜb recites his renowned ode.

*"Bānat Suᶜād" of Kaᶜb ibn Zuhayr*[54] [6]

1. Suᶜād has departed and today
   my heart is sick,
   A slave to her traces,
   unransomed and enchained.[55]

2. On the morning of departure
   when her tribe set out
   Suᶜād was but a bleating antelope
   with languid gaze and kohl-lined eye.

3. When she smiles she flashes
   side teeth wet
   As if with a first draught of wine
   or with a second,

4. Mixed with cool water from a wadi's bend,
   in a pebbled streambed limpid
   And sparkling in the noontime sun,
   chilled by the northwind,

5. Cleansed by the winds
   of all dirt and dust,
   And by white cumuli left overflowing
   with a night cloud's rain.

6. Alas! what a mistress, had she been true
   to what she promised,
   Had true advice not gone
   unheeded.

7. But she is a mistress
in whose blood are mixed
Calamity, mendacity,
inconstancy and perfidy,

8. She never stays the same
but is as mutable
As the *ghūl* in her garb
ever-changing.

9. Nor does she hold fast love's bond,
once she has claimed it,
Except as sieves
hold water.

10. The false promises of ʿUrqūb
were her model,
Her promises were nothing except
empty prattle.

11. I hope and pray that in the end
they'll be fulfilled,
But they will remain forever
unfulfilled.

12. Don't be deceived by the desires
she aroused, the promises she made,
For hopes and dreams
are a delusion.

13. Suʿād alit at nightfall in a land
unreachable
But by the best of she-camels
of noble breed and easy pace,

14. Never to be reached but by a she-camel
huge and robust
That despite fatigue sustains
her amble and her trot,

15. Sweat gushing from the glands
behind her ears,
Eager for the nameless road,
its waymarkers effaced,

16. With the eyes of a lone white antelope
  she pierces the unknown
 When roughlands and sand dunes blaze
  in high noon's sun,

17. Stout where the pendant hangs,
  full where the shackle binds,
 Her build the best of all
  the stallions' daughters,

18. Huge as a mountain, her sire her sibling,
  by a dam blood stallion bred,
 Her uncle by sire and dam the same,
  She is long-necked, brisk-paced.

19. The tick walks on her hide,
  but then the smoothness
 Of her breast and flank
  makes it slip.

20. Sturdy as the onager,
  her sides piled with meat,
 Her knees set wide, clear of
  the breastbone's daughters,

21. As if her muzzle and
  the two sides of her jaw
 Between her eyes and throat
  were an oblong stone.

22. She brushes with a tail
  like a stripped palm branch, tufted
 Over a dry udder,
  its milk ducts unimpaired,

23. Hook-nosed, in her ears the expert eye
  discerns nobility of breed,
 In her two cheeks,
  great smoothness.

24. Overtaking others, she speeds
  on legs lance-like and nimble,
 Like an oath annulled they barely
  touch the ground,

25. Brown their sole sinews, they scatter
 pebbles in their wake,
So tough no shoes protect them
 on the hilltops

26. On a day when the chameleon
 is as burnt as if
His sun-scorched parts were bread
 baked on hot rock.

27. As if the repeating motion of her forelegs
 when she is drenched in sweat
And when the narrow mountain peaks
 are cloaked in the mirage,

28. And the camel driver, his song their goad,
 says to the tribe
When ashen locusts kick up pebbles,
 "Stop and rest,"

29. At high noon were the arms of a woman
 tall and middle-aged,
Risen in lament, then others,
 near-barren and bereft, respond,

30. Wailing, arms flailing,
 when the heralds announced
The death of her firstborn,
 bereft of reason,

31. Tearing her clothes from her breast
 with her bare hands,
Her woolen shift ripped from her collarbone
 in shreds.

32. My slanderers at her two sides
 denounced me saying,
"You, o Son of Abū Sulmā, are
 as good as dead."

33. And every trusted friend in whom
 I put my hopes
Said, "I cannot help you, I am occupied
 with other things."

34. So I replied, "Out of my way,
you bastards!"
For all that the All-Merciful decrees
will come to pass!

35. For every man of woman born,
though he be long secure,
Will one day be borne
on humpbacked bier.

36. I was told God's Messenger
had threatened me,
But from God's Messenger
pardon is hoped.

37. Go easy, and let Him be your guide
who gave to you
The gift of the Qur'ān in which
are warnings and discernment!

38. Don't hold me to account for what
my slanderers have said,
For, however great the lies against me,
I have not sinned!

39. I stood where I saw and heard
what would have made
The mighty pachyderm,
had it stood in my stead,

40. Quake with fear unless
the Messenger of God,
By God's leave,
granted it protection,

** I kept on across the wasteland,
clad in coat of mail,
Beneath the wing of darkness,
and the curtain of the night,[56]

41. Until I placed my right hand,
without contending,
In the hand of an avenger,
his word the word.

42. He is more dreaded by me
    when I speak to him
And I am told, "You will be questioned
    and must answer,"

43. Than a lion,
    snapping and rapacious,
Its lair in ʿAththar's hollow,
    thicket within thicket,

44. Who in the morning feeds flesh
    to two lion whelps
That live on human flesh,
    flung in the dust in chunks,

45. Who when it assaults its match
    is not permitted
To leave its match
    unnotched,

46. For whom the braying onager
    falls silent,
In whose wadi no hunters
    stalk their prey,

47. In whose wadi lies an honest man,
    his weapons and torn clothes
Flung in the dust,
    his flesh devoured.

48. The Messenger is surely a sword
    from whose flash light is sought,
One of the swords of God,
    an Indian blade unsheathed,

49. In a band of Qurashis whose spokesman
    said to them in Mecca's hollow
When they submitted to Islām,
    "Depart!"

50. They departed, but no weaklings
    departed with them,
None who flee the battle,
    none unsteady in the saddle, none unarmed.

51. Haughty high-nosed champions,
    who on battle day
Don shirts
    of David's weave,

52. White, ample, their rings
    interlocking
As if they were the qafʿā' plant's
    interlocking rings.

53. They walk as the white camels walk
    when kept in check by blows,
While the stunted black ones
    go astray.[57]

54. Neither jubilant when their spears
    strike down a tribe,
Nor distraught when
    they are struck,

55. The spear does not pierce them
    except in the throat,
Nor do they shrink from
    death's water troughs.

Kaʿb's nasīb (lines 1–12) is constructed of the traditional motif of the bereft lover describing his departed mistress, Suʿād. If we note the derivation of the name Suʿād (which Hidayat Hussain aptly translates as "Beatrice") from the root *s-ʿ-d*, whence *saʿādah*, prosperity, good fortune, happiness, felicity,[58] it is possible to read this passage as an elegy to a bygone Golden Age, an elegy to the Jāhilīyah. Suʿād and all her etymological baggage—prosperity, happiness, good fortune—have departed. The forlorn poet is left behind, raving over the traces of the now-empty encampment. In the context of our argument, this must be read as a metaphor for the poet's political situation: the ethos of the Jāhilīyah is obsolete, the poet has been abandoned and betrayed by his kinsmen. He is "unransomed, unredeemed" (*lam yufda*), or, as another version has it, "unrequited" (*lam yujza*). On the surface this diction refers metaphorically to Suʿād's failure to return his affections in kind; on a deeper level the literal usage suggests the treachery of kinsmen who have failed in their reciprocal obligations to him, which are, above all, to ransom and to avenge.

In the description of the lost "felicity" that ensues, two aspects of the beloved are emphasized: first, in lines 2–5, her beauty, fertility, and purity: her glance like the antelope's, her flashing teeth that taste of the finest wine mixed with the cool limpid waters of rain-fed mountain streams. In lines 6–12, however, purity gives way to perfidy: beautiful as the promise of "felicity" may have been, it was ultimately a broken one. It is *ghūl*-like inconstancy, the broken promise, betrayed hopes and desires, deception and delusion that complete the nasīb.

Given the Islamic context in which this qaṣīdah has come down to us, the closing lines of its nasīb are striking for two elements of diction that have an eminently Qur'ānic resonance. These are *abāṭīlū* ("empty prattle," rhyme word, line 10) which occurs in the Qur'ān principally in the form *bāṭil* (false, falsehood, vanity, lie) in association with *kufr* (disbelief) and in opposition to *ḥaqq* (truth) and *niʿmat Allāh* (God's blessing) (Qur'ān 31:30; 22:62, etc.) and *taḍlīlū* ("delusion," rhyme word, line 12, from form II *ḍallala*, to lead astray, into error), which occurs most often in the first form *ḍalla/yaḍillu* (to stray, err) and in association with *kufr* (unbelief), *shirk* (polytheism), and *ẓulm* (oppression, injustice) and in opposition to *hudā* (right guidance) (Qur'ān 41:1; 13:14; 34:24; 4:116; 19:38; 53:30, etc.). The effect of employing Qur'ānic diction is to point out the analogy between Qur'ānic and poetic discourse, to alert the audience to the poet's true intent. For in the poet's mind his kinsmen's failure to fulfill the obligations of Jāhilī *virtus* (*murū'ah*) reveals the bankruptcy, the ultimate falsehood and error, of the ancestral ways, and is thus equatable with the Qur'ānic *kufr* and *shirk* (unbelief and polytheism). In terms of Gaster's seasonal pattern, then, this nasīb constitutes an expression of the *mortification* phase. The seasonal breakup of the transhumant tribes marks the end of one "lease on life," and the "new lease" is not yet assured; at the same time the broken vow and unfulfilled promise mark the dissolution of the Jāhilī "social contract."

Most curious in this qaṣīdah, and yet what most confirms our reading, are the transitional lines from the nasīb to the raḥīl (lines 13–14). Whereas we normally find the poet eschewing the distant and unattainable mistress and declaring his intention to seek his fortune elsewhere (as in ʿAlqamah's qaṣīdah), line 13 of Kaʿb's poem states quite precisely that it is to regain "Suʿād" that he undertakes the desert journey. This only makes sense, both poetically and politically, if we take this to mean a "new Suʿād," the "prosperity, good fortune, and felicity" of Islam.

The entire raḥīl of this poem (lines 13–31) is devoted, not to the recounting of any particular journey, but to the description of that certain she-camel of line 13 that alone can reach the distant dwelling of Suʿād. In the context of our reading, this ostensibly realistic and visual depiction of the physical and instinctual attributes of the poet's mount must be understood as ultimately referring to the poet's own resolve, his inner moral fortitude. For the poet's passage, the transition from the pagan *pietas* of the Jāhilīyah to Islam, is primarily a spiritual, not a physical, journey. His camel mare is thus described as being "the best," "of noble breed and easy pace" (line 13), huge, indefatigable (line 14). The *himmah*, goal, aspiration, usually attributed to the poet himself at the end of the nasīb or at the beginning of the raḥīl, appears in line 15 as an attribute of his mount. For *ʿurḍah* (suited to, fit for) is taken by the commentators to mean *himmah* (ambition, aspiration, zeal).[59] "Fit" or "eager" for the unknown road whose waymarkers are obliterated then indicates an instinctive sense of direction (as in ʿAlqamah, line 17), or, as we would say, a "moral compass." Undaunted by the midday heat, her glance pierces the unknown (line 16).

Line 17 describes the she-camel in terms that define her domestication, for if she combines the attributes of wild animals—the gazelle's piercing glance (line 16), the onager's sturdiness (line 19)—these have been tamed to serve mankind: her neck is thus termed *muqallad* (II pass. part. as noun of place), the place-where-the-halter (*qilādah*, more precisely, what is hung about the neck of beasts being brought to Mecca for sacrifice)[60] -goes; her pastern *muqayyad*, the place-where-the-shackle (*qayd*) -goes. The best qualities of the natural world have been harnessed to serve the cultural, or even sacrificial, one. The same idea is given voice in line 18, where the natural law of survival of the fittest is displaced by the cultural laws of animal husbandry. This camel mare is "in and inbred twice" (Sells's translation), so inbred that she was sired on her dam by her brother, and her maternal uncle is her paternal uncle too (line 18). Line 22 seems likewise to allude to nature serving culture: her tail is likened to a stripped palm branch, that is, a plant domesticated; her dry udder indicates perhaps first of all that she is barren, and such she-camels make sturdier mounts, but further that she serves to transport humans: she is not a milch camel, nor has she perpetuated her own species. By contrast it is her animal strength that is emphasized in line 25: her pads are so tough that even on the roughest ground they need no shoes (a preeminent symbol of "culture").

Most curious here is line 24. As a simple simile it is quite appropriate: so nimble is the she-camel's pace that her feet look as though they are about to touch the ground, but are raised again so quickly that it seems they never do—like an oath about to be fulfilled, then suddenly annulled. Read in the context of lines 6 through 12, however, it seems that what speeds the poet on his "journey" is the annulment or abrogation of the obsolete ethos of the Jāhilīyah. In all, the mixture of natural and cultural attributes amounts to an apt characterization of the she-camel as "betwixt and between" categories and classes: the most domesticated of the beasts, she is yet the most beast-like of the domesticated animals in physical power and strength of instincts. She thus embodies the "liminal" qualities of the poet/passenger himself who must make the transition from the law of the Banū Muzaynah to the law of God's Messenger. Line 26 alludes, in the Lévi-Straussian language of "the raw and the cooked," to the purifying, purgative aspect of the liminal journey through a transubstantiation from living flesh to baked bread, from nature to culture. The effect of heat and hardship is to weed out the weak and unfit; the strong survive, but transformed and reborn. The raw (= nature) chameleon scorched by the sun is metaphorically metamorphosed into the cooked (= culture) (*mamlūl* refers to bread or meat baked in embers or on heated rocks).

The final section of the raḥīl (lines 27–31) consists of an unusual simile which likens the relentless motion of the she-camel's forelegs in the hottest part of the day—when camel caravans normally stop to rest, when locusts, lest they burn their feet, kick aside the scorching pebbles to find cooler ground—to that of the bereaved mother's arms as she frantically tears at her clothes. The more common simile in the raḥīl is, as for example in the *Muʿallaqah* of Labīd,[61] the likening of the she-camel to the oryx doe whose calf the wolves have killed. The pathos of Labīd's simile is here replaced by an image of grief and loss that is at once instinctual and ritual: the mythic dementia of the Middle Eastern female lamentation. This culturally conditioned hysteria triggered by loss and despair endows the female mourners with the strength to shred their clothes with their bare hands, to tear their hair and scratch their faces. It is precisely the "unnatural" strength that the ritual dementia of female mourning unleashes that is likened to the unflagging energy of the she-camel. And it is ultimately the poet's own relentless drive, spurred on by the bereavement of the nasīb, that is implicit in this simile and explicitly expressed in the coming lines (32–33). As is evident from the diction of line 29, what is being mourned is, above all, the failure of fertility, here of the human rather than cereal reproductive cycle. The bereft woman is "middle-aged" (*naṣaf*), which implies that she is no longer of (prime) childbearing age—the smaller cycle failed—and (line 30) her firstborn is dead—the larger cycle failed, too. Her sister mourners are likewise "near-barren" (*nukd*) and "bereft" (*mathākīl*).

The ritual wail or lament for the dead youth is well known in the Ancient Near East. Gaster relates the practice of howling and lamenting at seasonal ceremonies of Mortification. Among the many instances attested among ancient civilizations he mentions the Egyptian laments for Isis at the first harvesting of grain, the lamentations for Osiris, the ritual dirges of Demeter and Kore among the Greeks, those for Attis in Asia Minor and Adonis in Syria; and likewise the mention in *Gilgamesh* of the annual weeping for Tammuz, the lord of fertility. Gaster argues, however, that the ritual weeping is a homeopathic method of producing rain, and may not originally have been an expression of mourning at all.[62] He concludes:

> If these arguments are correct, the practices of howling and wailing at seasonal ceremonies need not be interpreted as acts of mourning, but rather as mere expressions of excitement or as functional procedures designed to promote fertility through the magical properties of tears. In the latter case, they would fall into the category of rites of Invigoration rather than of Mortification. This is not to deny that a certain element of mourning must always have been present.[63]

The point with regard to the poem at hand is that, coming as it does at the end of the raḥīl, the lamentation simile has the effect of simultaneously mourning what has been lost and, as though through that very mourning, reviving it—for it is essentially, as it operates here, an image both of loss (Mortification) and, inasmuch as it describes the vigor of the she-camel, of Invigoration.

At line 32 there occurs a sudden break in subject and style. The poet abruptly shifts from the lexically rich and metaphorically dense poetic metalanguage of the nasīb and raḥīl to a stripped-down, univocal, apparently "prosaic" narrative discourse. This "prosaic" style dominates the entire midsection of the qaṣīdah, from lines 32–42, until, at line 43, the poet reimmerses himself once more in the poetic metalanguage of allusion, metaphor, etc. It is the apparent "simplicity" of this section that gives it its power; its striking effect is due precisely to its contrast to the "poeticity"—the richness of specifically poetic diction, the allusiveness, the multivalence—of the traditional nasīb and raḥīl that precede it. But its very simplicity is, of course, nothing but a poetic conceit. It is not really "prosaic" at all, but a brilliant rhetorical construct. If we keep in mind that the akhbār have no provable factual/historical basis, it does not seem unlikely in this case that they are a secondary derivation from the qaṣīdah itself. Kaᶜb ibn Zuhayr's conversion is, most probably, his own literary construct—a literary construct so convincingly realistic that it generated the "historical" construct. In other words, the akhbār that traditionally accompany the poem in the literary sources are not the record of actual events, but most likely a narrative fleshing-out of the semantic crux of the poem, which has then been prefaced to the qaṣīdah by way of commentary. My argument, then, is that this passage (lines 32–41) is not necessarily any more factual or historical than any other passage in the poem, but, rather, that it is a meticulously crafted literary construct whose historicity may well be a conceit. Kaᶜb ibn Zuhayr's conversion may well be his own creation. It is, in fact, precisely structured according to the ritual paradigm of sacrifice and redemption, and is as rigidly ritually controlled as the nasīb and the raḥīl. And, of course, this passage is far more rhetorically and semantically complex than a first "prosaic" reading suggests.

The first part (lines 32–36) forms the structural and semantic core of the entire qaṣīdah and is therefore, ultimately, the key to reading the entire poem. This section is set off not only by the abrupt change in style (diction, etc.) between lines 31 and 32, but also by the maintenance throughout the five lines of the I passive participial form (*mafᶜūl*) as the rhyme word. The effect of this morphological repetition is rendered especially emphatic by the fact that the penultimate rhyming vowel is interchangeably *ī* or *ū* and is apparently randomly varied throughout the poem, except in this passage. Here the rhyme functions semantically as well as acoustically, for it brackets the conversion that generated the entire qaṣīdah from *maqtūl* (slain) in line 32 to *ma'mūl* (hoped for) in line 36; from death to hope. The transition from lost hope (line 33, cf. also lines 11–12) to hope renewed, from death—as portrayed in the bereft woman simile and the denunciation of Kaᶜb's calumniators (lines 29–32)—to rebirth, points once again in the direction of the ritual form and antecedents of Kaᶜb's qaṣīdah, and also to its ultimate intent. Referring to two formulations of ritual patterns, the rite of passage, or initiation, and the seasonal pattern, Gaster remarks:

> The connection between Initiation and Invigoration is brought out especially by the fact that the former is frequently identified with *rebirth*. The

> most obvious illustration of this lies, of course, in the very word "neophyte" (lit., "newly implanted") by which initiants are commonly known, as well as ideas of regeneration (and even immortality) which are invariably associated with admission to the mysteries in ancient cults. Thus, in the mysteries of Attis, the candidate was looked upon as "one about to die"; when he had performed the required rites, he emerged to a new life.[64]

The poet begins by claiming that he was falsely accused; it is his calumniators that would see him dead (line 32). He then presents himself before the Prophet as a helpless supplicant, betrayed by friends in whom he had put his hope and trust (line 33). In both lines the poet is portrayed as passive victim—he hopes "in whom I put my hope" (*āmuluhu*) (active), but is rebuffed. This is in contrast to lines 34–35 in which the forceful active voice of line 34, "So I said (*fa-qultu*) 'Out of my way! . . .'" makes it clear that the poet has some hand in his own salvation—i.e., that he is in some sense worthy. But—and this is the essence of "Islam"—the poet's forceful act is to submit to God's will, to admit his own mortality. Moreover, he must be willing to sacrifice his own life, and this is precisely the intention of line 34: that he will face possible death and leave the outcome in God's hands. It is this "sacrifice" that is the necessary requirement for the poet's redemption. To put it more clearly, the "drama" of Kaʿb's "submission," *islām*, and its moral value as well, requires that he face the risk of death to do it. This, as pointed out above, is made abundantly, if prosaically, clear in the akhbār by the attack of the Anṣārī zealot. Without this element of risk, of putting his life in God's or his Messenger's hands, Kaʿb's conversion would have been mere opportunism. The poet does make some attempt to positively dispose the Almighty when, in line 34, he chooses of the ninety-nine names of God "al-Raḥmān" (the Merciful).

It is the poet's act of *islām*, of submission, that is with masterful concision expressed in line 36: *unbi'tu anna rasūla Allāhi awʿadanī / wa al-ʿafwu ʿinda rasūli Allāhi ma'mūlū* (I was told God's Messenger had threatened me / But from God's Messenger pardon is hoped). The first hemistich expresses Muḥammad's power, the second Kaʿb's submission to it. Line 36 thus functions as lines 21–22 do in ʿAlqamah's qaṣīdah as a statement of supplication, prostration, and declaration of allegiance. It also shares its stylistic characteristics: simplicity of diction combined with rhetorical complexity. In Kaʿb's line this takes the form of antithesis imbedded in chiastic structuring. The chiasmus proceeds from a passive configuration of soft consonants *n,b,n*, then "Rasūl Allāh" (Messenger of God), to climax with the harsher and active *w,ʿ,d* of the threat; its antithesis, pardon, also in *ʿ,w,d*, begins the countermovement, followed by another "Rasūl Allāh," and the chiasmus then concludes as it opened with the passive in soft *m* and *l*. "Islam" as willing self-effacement is conveyed through the use of the passive voice. Whereas in line 33 the poet says, "I hope" (*āmulu*) in the first-person active, in line 36, when confronting the Messenger of God, the poet hardly dares to hope, but employs instead the passive participle *ma'mūl* (to be hoped for). "I was informed that the Messenger of God had threatened me" (*unbi'tu . . . awʿadanī*)—the poet is passive subject (*nā'ib fāʿil*) and direct object, but no longer actor/agent.

Through the parallel placement of Rasūl Allāh (Messenger of God) in the middle of each hemistich this line expresses both recognition and submission. The rhetorical power of this repetition is all the more striking in that no mention has been made of Muḥammad up till now. The way was perhaps prepared by the mention of the All-Merciful in line 34, but it is only with line 36 that the poet's *shahādah* (creed) is completed. The religious message, the essence of Islamic faith, is also stated here: God, as represented by his Messenger, threatens perdition—an expression of might—but at the same time is capable of pardon, forgiveness. It is the submission to this divine power and authority and the hope for his mercy that constitutes Islam. Line 36 is thus rhetorically, acoustically, and semantically the crux of the qaṣīdah.

Returning to the original hypothesis of this essay, it is evident that this core passage of Kaʿb's qaṣīdah, inasmuch as it offers a concise statement of the ritual paradigm that informs the whole work, is, like Mauss's "ritual exchange," a total social phenomenon. Simultaneous expression is given to all kinds of institutions: the poet redeems himself (economic), he swears his fealty to the new order (sociopolitical), he recognizes God's Messenger and submits to Islam (religious, moral) through a qaṣīdah whose power, value, and durability are functions of its artistry (aesthetic). The mythological aspect is expressed in the mythic/ritual pattern of death and rebirth (*maqtūl* → *ma'mūl*); its mythogenic aspect, as will be discussed further on, in its creation of the conversion of Kaʿb ibn Zuhayr as a mythopoeic expression of the transition of Arab society from the Jāhilīyah to Islam.

The tension of the climax of line 36 is broken in line 37 by its opening word *mahlan* ("Go easy") and equally by a relaxation of the rhetorical intensity and the alteration of the rhyme from the fivefold repetition of *mafʿūl* to a *tafʿīl* (*tafṣīlū*), after which an apparently random morphological variation in the rhymeword sets in. The poet exhorts the Prophet to follow the guidance of God and the Qur'ān and to go easy on him. Lines 38–41 constitute a reiteration of the ritual pattern of the poet's *islām*/conversion. The message is bracketed in rhymewords from the same root (*q-w-l*, to speak), each made more emphatic by *tajnīs* (paronomasia) within the line: *aqwāl* and *aqāwīl* in line 38 refer to the fabrications and false accusations of the poet's calumniators; in line 41 *qīluhu al-qīlū* refers to the veracity and authority of the Prophet's speech, his power and intention to carry out what he says. The direction of the passage is thus from falsehood to truth. The terror and danger of the transition is expressed in the "fear and trembling" of the poet, or pachyderm, before God's Messenger (lines 39–40). As in ʿAlqamah's qaṣīdah, the point here is that the *mamdūḥ* (recipient of the panegyric), Muḥammad, has power over life and death, and only by his granting him protection does the poet's fear abate. Line 40 reiterates in *yurʿadu . . . tanwīlū* (quake with fear . . . granting [protection]) the same antithesis as line 36 between the threat of punishment and hope for forgiveness.

The closing line of this passage, line 41 is, like line 36, an expression of submission to (divine) authority. As for the meaning of the poet's placing his hand in that of the Prophet without contending (*waḍaʿtu yamīnī lā unāziʿuhū fī kaffi . . .*), al-Sukkarī explains: "That is, 'I placed my right hand in his by way of submission, not contention.' I.e., he surrendered himself to him and acknowledged him. For the Arabs, when they swore an oath to something, would strike each other on the right hand."[65] The intent of "exacting vengeance" (*dhī naqimātin*) (*naqimah* = vengeance, penal retribution, punishment)[66] is to indicate that Muḥammad is a man to be feared.

This entire passage (lines 32–41) must be read in light of lines 6–11 of the nasīb. For there Emptying is expressed as the failure or breakdown of trust, the abrogation of the Jāhilī social contract: mendacity, inconstancy, perfidy, the failure to fulfill promises. Of special interest here is the antithesis between "her promises were nothing except empty prattle" (*mā mawāʿīduhā illā al-abāṭīlū*) of line 11 and "his word the word" (*qīluhu al-qīlu*), i.e., who keeps his word, whose word is law, of line 41; failed hope as opposed to hope fulfilled; the seduction and misguidance (*taḍlīl*) of misplaced trust (line 12) as opposed to the right guidance (*hadā*, to guide aright), exhortation and the discernment of right from wrong (*tafṣīl*) (line 37). The section from line 32 to 41 thus constitutes a ritual kernel whose form is thus the key to that of the qaṣīdah as a whole and whose conclusions thus provide the fulfillment of the nasīb. The movement from Emptying to Filling is expressed in a variety of ways, but especially in the movement from unfulfilled promise to fulfilled promise, and—in the most Qur'ānic of terms—from *taḍlīl* (misguidance) to *hadā/hudā* (right guidance). The effect is to identify the "falsehood" of Suʿād in the nasīb section with the falsehood of the poet's slanderers and calumniators. At the same time, the Filling phase of this section creates a bridge to its fuller development in the final sections of the poem.

In the following section (lines 42–47) the subject is the fear engendered by the Messenger of God; the ritual function is that of Invigoration. The fear of the temporal judgment of Muḥammad when Kaʿb revealed himself and his identity and had to answer for his deeds (line 42) was bound to generate an "Islamic" reading, as indeed we find cited in the *sharḥ* of al-Tibrīzī.[67] For both temporal and divine judgment are involved here, both the mortal and the immortal soul. The elative form "He is more dreaded" (*la-dhāka ahyabu*) serves as a pivot point for the poet to modulate from the "prosaic" style of the poem's semantic core via the simile back into the imagery and diction of the poetic world.

The description of the warrior, by metaphor or simile, as a lion is a traditional one. The effect of the elative here is rhetorically to magnify the Prophet and the fear he inspires. In terms of the present argument, this has the effect of intensifying both sides of the fear/hope equation. For the value of a man's mercy is directly commensurate with the power of his wrath: the mercy or pardon of a weakling is worthless. We might, begging the pardon of the Muʿtazilites, term this the principle of "the promise and the threat" (*al-waʿd wa al-waʿīd*). This principle might also explain much of the Meccan *sūrahs* of the Qur'ān. Unless Muḥammad could inspire in his fellow Arabs the dread of divine chastisement, he could not induce them to seek divine mercy. Moreover, it must be kept in mind that the dominant image of Invigoration in Kaʿb's poem—the lion that feeds flesh to its cubs—is simply a metaphorical variant of the Invigoration of ʿAlqamah's qaṣīdah, that of the warrior revitalizing his kin group by slaying the enemy, expressed there in the "reincarnation" of the vultures. The diction of line 44, *ʿayshuhumā laḥmun* (literally, "their life is meat"), is to be taken on an ultra-literal level as an expression of blood sacrifice and redemption, of Invigoration. Whereas in ʿAlqamah's qaṣīdah the connection between the Bedouin battle pattern and the agricultural seasonal pattern was established by means of simile—the likening of the rustling of chain mail to that of ripe grainfields (line 28) and of the bloodbath of the battlefield to a thunderstorm (line 32)—in Kaʿb's poem we must look beyond the rhetorical to the etymological. If we note that in Hebrew *leḥem* means bread, we obtain a reverse transubstantiation. In other words, we can trace in the semantic shift of *l-ḥ-m* from cereal to carnal the cultural shift from agrarian to Bedouin.

A change from the object to the subject of the simile occurs in line 45 in the change from the bestial to the martial. Line 46 appears to shift back to the lion, describing the terror, both instinctual and rational, that both beast (the onager) and man feel for the formidable lion. But the barrier between the subject and the object of the simile is becoming more and more attenuated. In the context of the qaṣīdah, the ravaged corpse of line 47 suggests what the poet's own fate might have been had he contended with Muḥammad rather than converted.

The closing section of the poem (lines 48–55) opens with a final military metaphor that depicts the Prophet as a sword of God, an image that would later achieve great popularity in Islamic military and caliphal panegyric.[68] Lines 48–50, like lines 32–36, constitute a semantic core of the poem and display the rhetorical features that we have come to associate with such sections. In line 48 we find the structuring of very simple, straightforward diction in chiastic form—*inna al-rasūla la sayfun yustaḍā'u bihī / muhannadun min suyūfi Allāhi maslūlū*—to reiterate the Islamic message of right guidance and divine might. This leads into a description of the Muhājirūn, Muḥammad's early Meccan supporters who emigrated with him to Medina. This migration or *hijrah* is presented here as a spiritual one, for these are the true core of Muḥammad's followers. The "passage" that they make is thus identified with "Islam" itself. Four words from lines 49–50, *aslamū zūlū / zālū fa mā zāla* (whose spokesman [Muḥammad?] said when *they submitted to Islam*, "*Depart!*" *They departed*, but the weaklings, etc., *did not depart*), constitute a remarkably concise definition of Islam and, at the same time, a separation of the wheat from the chaff: those who obey the Prophet's command are Muslims and heroes; those who do not are "damned" cowards. The *hijrah* too thus functions as a "passage" from the Jāhilīyah to Islam, and, as in all such rites, only the morally and physically strong complete the passage.

In the ensuing description of the Muhājirūn that closes the poem (lines 51–55), the poet once more reimmerses himself in the diction and imagery of the classical qaṣīdah. They are high-nosed, clad in chain mail of David's weave (lines 51–52). In line 53 the Muhājirūn in their battle ranks are described as a troop of majestic white camels that are kept in line by the stick, whereas the scrawny black ones, traditionally said to refer to the Medinese Anṣār (Helpers), "stray from the road" (*ʿarrada*), i.e., flee the battlefield.[69] Despite the apparent Jāhilī imagery and diction, the allusion must certainly be to the antithesis in Sūrat al-Fātiḥah of the Qur'ān between those that God blesses and guides on "the straight path" (*al-ṣirāṭ al-mustaqīm*) and the misguided (*al-ḍāllīn*) with whom He is angry. Finally, Kaʿb ibn Zuhayr seals his qaṣīdah with two lines of praise for the Muhājirūn that are as purely Jāhilī as those that opened it. Both closing lines combine antithesis with litotes to express in the understated tone of the negative the equanimity of the hero in battle, and in death. And yet, however purely Jāhilī in diction and imagery, the Islamic context has utterly transformed the meaning of the closing line. For the draught from death's water troughs (*ḥiyāḍi al-mawti*) in pre-Islamic times expressed devitalization or mortification, most often of the enemy. But for the Muhājirūn, as for any Muslim, death in battle "in the way of God" (*fī sabīl Allāh*) is an act of self-sacrifice and martyrdom that guarantees salvation and life everlasting. That is, in terms of the ritual patterns herein employed, the death of a martyr constitutes revitalization and invigoration.

## From Poesis to Mythopoesis

Returning to the critical premises upon which our analysis was based, we can begin to draw together the various aspects of the poem. First of all, in terms of ritual exchange, we find in Kaʿb's poem a "total social movement" in which multiple institutions find simultaneous expression. The institution of redemption itself is an economic, legal, and sociomorphic one. Through the payment—in Kaʿb's case, of the qaṣīdah—the outlawed poet is admitted as a legal member of society, the legally "dead" Kaʿb is "alive" to society once more and assumes all the rights and obligations entailed in that membership. This in and of itself indicates the poem's function in a rite of passage in which the ritual passenger changes from one social status to another. With the addition, in Kaʿb's case, of the Islamic element, the residual mythic aspects already apparent in ʿAlqamah's qaṣīdah are reactivated; the poem takes on a moral and religious aspect. The transfer of allegiance is not from one Bedouin liege lord to another, but from the poet's natal tribal society to a radically new social order, from the Jāhilīyah to Islam. It is not merely Kaʿb's mortal life that is redeemed, but his immortal soul. It is at this point that the poesis becomes mythopoesis, and, insofar as this poem appears to have generated its akhbār and in doing so to have made the conversion of Kaʿb ibn Zuhayr paradigmatic for all Muslims, mythogenesis.

At this point, too, Kaʿb's poetic pedigree enters the picture. Kaʿb was the scion of one of the Jāhilīyah's premier poetic families: his father, Zuhayr, was one of the most celebrated poets of the Jāhilīyah; Zuhayr's father was a poet, as were his maternal uncle, Bashāmah, his stepfather, Aws ibn Ḥajar, and his sisters, Salmā and al-Khansā'.[70] Kaʿb's redemption by means of a qaṣīdah therefore represents as well the redemption of the Jāhilī poetic tradition in Islam. His composing of an "Islamic" qaṣīdah so fully in the tradition of the Jāhilīyah has the effect of rendering the pre-Islamic "pagan" qaṣīdah, not anti-Islamic, but proto-Islamic. It is thus especially appropriate that he is the son of Zuhayr, who was renowned for the celebration of the virtues of peace, and in whose *Muʿallaqah* is found the mention of Allāh and of the Day of Reckoning.[71] This certainly must be the intent of the story of the testament of Zuhayr ibn Abī Sulmā to his sons Kaʿb and Bujayr:

> [Zuhayr] is said to have frequented the society of men learned in the various religions then existing, and he thus became aware of the impending appearance of a great Apostle who would unite mankind in the pure worship of one sole God. He is said to have seen in a vision a rope let down from heaven, which he tried to catch, but which he found to be beyond his reach. This he interpreted to himself as a revelation that the advent of the long expected Apostle was at hand, but that he himself would not live long enough to see and hear him. He told all these things to his two sons, and advised them to accept the teachings of the new Apostle if he should appear in their time. Zuhair died.[72]

The second of our critical propositions, the seasonal pattern of ritual and myth, will go far in explaining how the salvation of poetry was effected. First of all, the pattern of Emptying → Filling that shaped the qaṣīdah itself is essentially a ritual model designed precisely to accomplish cultural transitions. The ritual pattern allows for a multivalent layering of meaning, and hence enables the poem to give simultaneous expression to a variety of institutions. The "seasonal" pattern as embodied in the nasīb → raḥīl → madīḥ form of the classical qaṣīdah thus expresses first Kaʿb ibn Zuhayr's political conversion from his tribe to Muḥammad, in terms analogous to that of ʿAlqamah's transfer of allegiance from the Lakhmids to the Ghassanids; then the religious conversion of Kaʿb from the ancestral religion of the Banū Muzaynah to Islam; this in turn becomes paradigmatic of the conversion of Arab society from the Jāhilīyah to Islam and, further, of the subjugation of the pre-Islamic poetic tradition to Islam.

If the theory of ritual exchange explains how and why the qaṣīdah was composed, the ritual pattern explains why it was preserved and repeated. The difference between the composition of the poem and its preservation and repetition (these last two being identical for orally transmitted poetry) is that between the Last Supper and Holy Communion. Walter Burkert's remarks on ritual will provide some insight here:

> Since the work of Sir Julian Huxley and Konrad Lorenz, biology has defined *ritual* as a behavioural pattern that has lost its primary function—present in its unritualized model—but which persists in a new function, that of communication. . . . this communicating function reveals the two basic characteristics of ritual behaviour, namely repetition and theatrical exaggeration. For the essentially immutable patterns do not transmit differentiated and complex material information but, rather, just one piece of information each. This single piece of information is considered so important that it is reinforced by constant repetition so as to avoid misunderstanding or misuse. The fact of understanding is thus more important than what is understood. Above all, then, ritual creates and affirms social interaction.[73]

If the primary function of Kaᶜb's poem is to redeem the poet, to save his mortal skin and immortal soul, its new ritual function is then to convey that single most vital piece of information in the Islamic culture that preserved and ritualized it, that is, the Islamic message of spiritual redemption and salvation. Just as the fertility ritual, as evidenced in ᶜAlqamah's qaṣīdah, is reenacted to ensure the renewed prosperity of the ruler and the realm, so the recitation of Kaᶜb ibn Zuhayr's qaṣīdah serves as a reaffirmation of Islamic faith. Furthermore, Burkert's remarks on repetition in ritual, especially when coupled with the phenomenon of redundancy that is characteristic of orally transmitted poetry, go far in explaining the numerous reiterations of the ritual pattern *within* the qaṣīdah—first in the overall structure, then in the series of shorter repetitions (lines 32–36, 37–42, 44, 49–51, 53)—and through a variety of metaphors. That is, the internal repetition of the ritual pattern functions to ensure that even if parts of the text are lost, corrupted, or misunderstood, the qaṣīdah's vital message of sacrifice and redemption will not be lost.

I would like to close with some remarks on the mythogenic capabilities of the Arabic qaṣīdah, a generative power of the poem itself which *Bānat Suᶜād* seems to exemplify. Given what current theory tells us about the preservation of "texts" in societies of primary orality, that is, the relatively greater stability of poetry over prose,[74] we must assume that Kaᶜb's qaṣīdah is more "authentic" than the akhbār associated with it. Furthermore, internal evidence (lines 32–36) suggests that the qaṣīdah may be the source of the akhbār. That is, that the apparently discursive section (lines 32–41) that we have termed the "semantic core" of the poem generated a prose narrative, equally ritual in structure, that was prefixed to the poem to function as a sort of commentary that directs the reader to read the poem as an Islamic one. In other words, the akhbār make explicit the message of sacrifice and redemption that is implicit in the poem (as sort of *ḥall al-manẓūm*—prosification of verse). The akhbār must thus be understood primarily as literary constructs, as prose narrative restatements of the poetic "message." Their function is therefore reiterative—an external redundancy to reinforce the internal redundancy of the ritual and oral qaṣīdah—and exegetical.

## Conclusion: From Mythopoesis to Mythogenesis

No discussion of Kaᶜb ibn Zuhayr's *Bānat Suᶜād* would be complete without the mention of the Mantle (*burdah*) of the Prophet. So closely is this story associated with this qaṣīdah, that the poem is commonly referred to as The Mantle Ode (*qaṣīdat al-burdah*). The story goes that when Kaᶜb recited this qaṣīdah to the Prophet Muḥammad, he conferred upon the poet a mantle which is said to have been purchased by the Caliph Muᶜāwiyah from Kaᶜb's heirs for 20,000 dirhams and worn by the caliphs on feast days.[75] Here, too, what is of concern in terms of the present argument is not the historicity of the event that is the subject of the *khabar*[76] but, as with the interpretation of al-Sukkarī's *khabar*, the analysis of the text *qua* text and its relation to the poetic text.

The donation of the mantle must be understood above all in the context of the conferring of a symbolic gift, that is, as part of a ritual exchange. In this light it functions in two ways. First, as Karl Brockelmann and Georg Jacob noted, the conferring of a robe of honor (*ḥullah*) upon poets as a reward for their verse was a well-established custom among the Arabs.[77] In the Arabic literary context, to have one's poetry rewarded with a royal robe of honor (*ḥullah*) was, as al-Farazdaq attests in a line about ᶜAlqamah, a distinction tantamount to having one's verse immortalized in the hearts or on the tongues of the people:

The Stallion ᶜAlqamah upon whom
kings' robes were bestowed
Was proverbial among the people
for his words.[78] [7]

In the context of this essay, we must understand the donation of the mantle above all as an act of ritual exchange: the qaṣīdah functions as a symbolic gift in a ritual of allegiance or fealty, and the robe or mantle then functions as the symbolic countergift. In the discussion of ᶜAlqamah's qaṣīdah I argued that in such rituals of allegiance the supplicant offers his life or something of himself to the ruler, and the ruler, in accepting his allegiance grants him his protection and virtually confers life, or new life, upon his vassal. The gift and countergift of the fealty ritual, especially when we keep in mind Mauss's remark that the gift contains something of the giver or soul of the giver, embody the essence of fealty: that each owes the other his life, that each will protect the other with his life. The mantle thus symbolizes the Prophet's protection, and, inasmuch as the garment is a symbol of the soul, the gift of immortal life. The robe or mantle functions likewise as a symbol of legitimacy.[79] Rudi Paret, giving the biblical example of the miraculous mantle of the Prophet Elijah (II Kings 2:13–15), thus quite correctly explains the interest of the Umayyads in obtaining and retaining this relic. Moreover, by expanding Paret's citation back to II Kings 2:8, it is clear that the "mantle" of Elijah that Elisha takes up is identified with the "spirit" of Elijah.[80]

The symbolic function of the mantle conferred upon the poet "saved" by Islam becomes all the clearer when contrasted with the function of garments in the story of the Jāhilī poet whom the Prophet is said to have condemned as "the leader of the poets into Hellfire,"[81] Imru' al-Qays. Unable to find supporters among the Arabs to aid him in his quest for extravagant vengeance for his slain royal father, Imru' al-Qays abandons his suits of ancestral armor (hereditary legitimacy) and seeks support from the Byzantines. When a slanderer at Caesar's court informs the emperor that Imru' al-Qays has an illicit liaison with his daughter, Caesar, who had sent the Arab prince forth with an army, sends him an embroidered robe interwoven with gold, but also "laced" with poison. The overjoyed prince no sooner dons it than his skin breaks out in sores and sloughs off, and he dies.[82] If his ancestral armor symbolizes hereditary legitimacy, then surely the lethal foreign robe of honor symbolizes illegitimacy. And if the Byzantine Christian robe brings perdition to the renegade Arab who dons it—surely the true sense of Imru' al-Qays's sobriquet *al-malik al-ḍillīl* (the errant/erring king),[83] then surely the Mantle of the Prophet must confer salvation. If Kaʿb, as the scion of Zuhayr ibn Abī Sulmā, represents that aspect of the Jāhilīyah that was proto-Islamic, Imru' al-Qays is perceived as the embodiment of all that was anti-Islamic.

For Kaʿb, then, the mantle was not merely a sign of recognition of his poetic achievement or of the legitimacy of poetry under Islam. Rather, the submission (*islām*) of the poet to the prophet as expressed in the ritual exchange of poem for mantle became paradigmatic of the submission of the poetic to the prophetic in Islamic culture. And just as the poet had to submit to be saved, so too did the poetic tradition.

We concluded our discussion of ʿAlqamah's qaṣīdah by attempting to equate biological and poetic perpetuity. The issue for Kaʿb ibn Zuhayr's qaṣīdah is one of prophetic and poetic immortality. The Islamic promise of immortality is well known; as for poetry, we close with the following anecdote recorded in *Kitāb al-Aghānī:* The Caliph ʿUmar said to [Kaʿb?] ibn Zuhayr, "Whatever became of the robes of honor that Harim bestowed upon your father?" "The passage of time wore them out," he replied. "But," said the Caliph, "the robes [i.e., qaṣīdahs] that your father bestowed upon Harim time has not touched."[84]

# Notes

* This paper was first presented at the 200th meeting of the American Oriental Society, Atlanta, Georgia, March 25–28, 1990. The research for this study was funded by an Outstanding Young Faculty Award and Summer Research Fellowship from the Indiana University Office for Research and the Graduate School (1990).

1. The full passage is quoted below, note 23.
2. Fuat Sezgin, *Geschichte des arabischen Schrifttums: Band III: Poesie bis ca. 430 H.* (Leiden: E. J. Brill, 1975), 120–122.
3. Ibid., 229–235.
4. For the poem and the akhbār I have relied mainly upon Lyall's edition of al-Anbārī's recension and commentary in Charles James Lyall, ed. and trans., *The Mufaḍḍalīyāt: An Anthology of Ancient Arabian Odes compiled by Al-Mufaḍḍal son of Muḥammad, according to the Recension and with the Commentary of Abū Muḥammad al-Qāsim ibn Muḥammad al-Anbārī.* Vol. I: *Arabic Text*; Vol. II: *Translation and Notes* (Oxford: Clarendon Press, 1918), 1:762–786. I have also consulted al-Tibrīzī's recension and commentary in Abū Zakarīyā Yaḥyā ibn ʿAlī al-Tibrīzī, *Sharḥ al-Mufaḍḍalīyāt*, ed. ʿAlī Muḥammad al-Bijāwī (Cairo: Dār Nahḍat Miṣr, n.d.), 1304–1323, in which the poem appears as no. 120; and Aḥmad Muḥammad Shākir and ʿAbd al-Salām Muḥammad Hārūn, eds., *al-Mufaḍḍalīyāt*, 6th printing (Cairo: Dār al-Maʿārif, 1979), 390–396; and Lyall's English translation and notes in Lyall, *Mufaḍḍalīyāt*, 2:327–333. Abdulla El Tayib has selected this poem as a paradigmatic example of the eulogistic qaṣīdah in the Ibn Qutaybian sense and of its "overall unity," but offers no substantiation for this but a brief glossing of the motifs. See Abdulla El Tayib, "Pre-Islamic Poetry," in A. F. L. Beeston et al., eds., *The Cambridge History of Arabic Literature: Arabic Literature to the End of the Umayyad Period* (Cambridge: Cambridge University Press, 1983), 104–109.
5. *Mufaḍḍalīyah 120* follows directly the qaṣīdah under discussion in that collection. It is translated with notes in Lyall, *Mufaḍḍalīyāt*, 2:333–341; a new translation with introduction appears in Michael A. Sells, *Desert Tracings: Six Classic Arabian Odes* (Middletown: Wesleyan University Press, 1989), 11–20. And see below, Ch. 3.
6. Shākir and Hārūn, *al-Mufaḍḍalīyāt*, 390.
7. Muḥammad ibn Sallām al-Jumaḥī, *Ṭabaqāt fuḥūl al-shuʿarā'*, ed. Maḥmūd Muḥammad Shākir (Cairo: Maṭbaʿat al-Madanī, n.d.), 1:139 (Shākir and Hārūn, *al-Mufaḍḍalīyāt*, 390). See above, note 4.
8. See al-Tibrīzī, *Sharḥ al-Mufaḍḍalīyāt*, 1304; Lyall, *Mufaḍḍalīyāt*, 1:328. In this case the battle of ʿAyn Ubāgh would seem to be identical with Yawm Ḥalīmah, and not the 570 C.E. battle when al-Ḥārith's son Mundhir defeated the Lakhmid Qābūs and conquered al-Ḥīrah. See Irfan Shahid, arts. "Ghassanids," "al-Ḥārith ibn Djabalah," and "Yawm Ḥalīma," in *The Encyclopaedia of Islam*, 2nd ed., ed. H. A. R. Gibb et al. (Leiden: E. J. Brill, 1960-).
9. Lyall, *Mufaḍḍalīyāt*, 1:786 and 2:333.
10. Ibid.
11. Marcel Mauss, *The Gift: Forms and Functions of Exchange in Archaic Societies*, trans. Ian Cunnison (New York: Norton and Co., 1967) (*Essai sur le don, forme archaïque*

*de l'échange* [1925]). Hamori has compared certain elements *within* the qaṣīdah—the beloved, the she-camel—to Mauss's description of ritual objects, but has not treated the poem itself as a ritual-exchange object. See Andras Hamori, *On the Art of Medieval Arabic Literature* (Princeton: Princeton University Press, 1974), 26–27. Mauss's work has generated numerous derivative studies. Of these the most recent and the closest to the matter at hand is Leslie Kurke, *The Traffic in Praise: Pindar and the Poetics of Social Economy* (Ithaca: Cornell University Press, 1991). In it, the author analyzes Pindar's epinician odes as objects in a ritual exchange. Parts I and II contain much that is, *mutatis mutandis*, applicable to the present study and should provide a basis for the reevaluation of Arabic panegyric of later periods as well. Chief among the points of interest with regard to the present argument are the recognition of poetry as conferring immortality (Part I *passim*); praise as part of a gift-exchange system (Part II *passim*); and the reckoning of the poem as among the *agalmata* (precious objects used in gift exchange) (94–95, 105–106, 155–159).

12. Mauss, *Gift*, 1.
13. Ibid., 37.
14. Ibid., 40.
15. Ibid., 35.
16. Ibid., 70.
17. Ibid., vii.
18. Ibid., 1.
19. Theodor H. Gaster, *Thespis: Ritual, Myth, and Drama in the Ancient Near East* (New York: Norton and Co., 1977). Again, Hamori has employed Gaster's *kenosis/plerosis* in discussing the relation of some elements within the qaṣīdah, but in a manner quite different from the present discussion. See Hamori, *Medieval Arabic Literature*, 11–19 *passim.* More germane are Haydar's and Sperl's analyses of the qaṣīdah structure. See Adnan Haydar, "The *Muʿallaqa* of Imru' al-Qays: Its Structure and Meaning, I and II," *Edebiyât* 2 (1977): 227–61 and 3 (1978): 51–82; Stefan Sperl, "Islamic Kingship and Arabic Panegyric Poetry in the Early Ninth Century," *Journal of Arabic Literature* 8 (1977): 20–35; and Stefan Sperl, *Mannerism in Arabic Poetry: A Structuralist Analysis of Selected Texts* (Cambridge: Cambridge University Press, 1989), esp. Ch. 1, "The Islamic Panegyric," 9–28. See also Suzanne Pinckney Stetkevych, "Structuralist Interpretations of Pre-Islamic Poetry: Critique and New Directions," *Journal of Near Eastern Studies* 42, no. 2 (1983): 85–107. The most important critical result of these studies, as Sperl has pointed out with respect to his own "strophe/antistrophe" formulation, is to establish all the thematic sections of the qaṣīdah as equally weighted parts of a balanced structure, rather than to subordinate, as Ibn Qutaybah did, the nasīb and raḥīl, as being merely preambular to the *gharaḍ*, the "goal" of the poem. See Sperl, *Mannerism*, 25; and Ibn Qutaybah, below, note 23.
20. Gaster, *Thespis*, 23.
21. Ibid.
22. Ibid., 26.
23. "I have heard from a man of learning that the composer of Odes began by mentioning the deserted dwelling-places and the relics and traces of habitation. Then he wept and complained and addressed the desolate encampment, and begged his companion to make a halt, in order that he might have occasion to speak of those who had once lived there and afterwards departed; for the dwellers in tents were different from townsmen or villagers in respect of coming and going, because they moved from one water-spring to another, seeking pasture and searching out the places where rain had fallen. Then to this he linked the erotic prelude (*nasīb*), and bewailed the violence of his love and the anguish of separation from his mistress and the extremity of his passion and desire, so as to win the hearts of his hearers and divert their eyes towards him and invite their ears to listen to him, since the song of love touches men's souls and takes hold of their hearts, God having put it in the constitution of His creatures to love dalliance and the society of

women, in such wise that we find very few but are attached thereto by some tie or have some share therein, whether lawful or unpermitted. Now, when the poet had assured himself of an attentive hearing, he followed up his advantage and set forth his claim: thus he went on to complain of fatigue and want of sleep and travelling by night and of the noonday heat, and how his camel had been reduced to leanness. And when, after representing all the discomfort and danger of his journey, he knew that he had fully justified his hope and expectation of receiving his due meed from the person to whom the poem was addressed, he entered upon the panegyric (*madīḥ*), and incited him to reward, and kindled his generosity by exalting him above his peers and pronouncing the greatest dignity, in comparison to his, to be little" (trans. Nicholson). Reynold A. Nicholson, *A Literary History of the Arabs* (Cambridge: Cambridge University Press, 1956), 77–78 (Abū Muḥammad ʿAbd Allāh ibn Muslim Ibn Qutaybah, *Kitāb al-shiʿr wa-al-shuʿarā'*, ed. M. J. de Goeje [Leiden: E. J. Brill, 1904], 14–15).

24. I have followed al-Anbārī's recension, except where otherwise noted. Lyall, *Mufaḍḍalīyāt*, 1:762–786. See above, note 3.

25. Al-Anbārī in Lyall, *Mufaḍḍalīyāt*, 1:776.

26. Gaster, *Thespis*, 60–61.

27. Ibid., 37.

28. See Sperl, "Islamic Kingship," 30.

29. See Lyall, *Mufaḍḍalīyāt*, 2:332.

30. That is to say that the slaying of al-Mundhir is understood as a sacrifice to reinvigorate al-Ḥārith. Cf. Gaster's remark concerning the mysteries of Attis in Roman times: "The reinvigoration of the king is indicated by the fact that, in Roman times, the slaughter of the bull was regarded at the same time as a sacrifice for the health and welfare of the emperor (*pro salute imperatoris*)." Gaster, *Thespis*, 68.

31. See Suzanne Pinckney Stetkevych, "Ritual and Sacrificial Elements in the Poetry of Blood-Vengeance: Two Poems by Durayd ibn al-Ṣimmah and Muhalhil ibn Rabīʿah," *Journal of Near Eastern Studies* 45, no. 1 (1986): 42–43; and Suzanne Pinckney Stetkevych, *The Mute Immortals Speak: Pre-Islamic Poetry and the Poetics of Ritual* (Ithaca: Cornell University Press, 1993), ch. 2.

32. Al-Tibrīzī, *Sharḥ al-Mufaḍḍalīyāt*, 1320.

33. There is some lexical confusion between *dāḥiṣ* and *dāḥiḍ*. According to Ibn Manẓūr, the former means to kick like a slaughtered beast, and ʿAlqamah's line is cited to attest this. The latter means primarily to slip, but is also used synonymously with the former. See Abū al-Faḍl Jamāl al-Dīn Ibn Manẓūr, *Lisān al-ʿArab* (Beirut: Dār Ṣādir, n.d.), s.v. *d-ḥ-ṣ* and *d-ḥ-ḍ*; and al-Anbārī and Lyall, in Lyall, *Mufaḍḍalīyāt*, 1:784, 2:332–333.

34. Abū Zakarīyā Yaḥyā ibn ʿAlī al-Tibrīzī, *Sharḥ al-Tibrīzī ʿalā Dīwān ashʿār al-ḥamāsah* (Cairo: Būlāq, 1879), 2:161.

35. See Suzanne Pinckney Stetkevych, "The Rithā' of Ta'abbaṭa Sharran: A Study of Blood-Vengeance in Early Arabic Poetry," *Journal of Semitic Studies* 31, no.1 (1986): 40–42; and S. Stetkevych, *Mute Immortals*, ch. 2.

36. Gaster, *Thespis*, 61–62, 65.

37. Edward William Lane, *Arabic-English Lexicon*, 8 vols. (New York: Frederick Ungar, 1956); and Ibn Manẓūr, *Lisān*, s.v. *ḥ-r-th*.

38. See the discussion of *Bānat Suʿād* by Kaʿb ibn Zuhayr, below, Part II.

39. The analysis of the classical Arabic qaṣīdah in this light has been proposed in S. Stetkevych, "Structuralist Analyses of Pre-Islamic Poetry," 98–107, and is developed in S. Stetkevych, *Mute Immortals*. And see below, pp. 34–35.

40. On this point see, for example, al-Baghdādī's remark that "the perpetuation of the mention of a person after his death takes the place of his life. Have you not seen the poet's line: 'So praise us, you sons of bastards, / for our deeds, for indeed praise is immortality.'" ʿAbd al-Qādir ibn ʿUmar al-Baghdādī, *Khizānat al-adab wa lubb lubāb lisān al-ʿArab* (Cairo: Maktabat al-Khānjī, 1987) 5:46. See also S. Stetkevych, *Mute Immortals*, chs. 5 and 6.

41. Mauss, *Gift*, 10.
42. Ibid., 43.
43. Eric A. Havelock, *The Literate Revolution in Greece and Its Cultural Consequences*, (Princeton: Princeton University Press, 1982), 116–117; and S. Stetkevych, *Mute Immortals*, chs. 5 and 6.
44. See S. Stetkevych, "Ritual and Sacrificial Elements," 37–38.
45. Eric A. Havelock, *The Muse Learns to Write: Reflections on Orality and Literacy from Antiquity to the Present* (Princeton: Princeton University Press, 1986), 70.
46. Ibid., 71.
47. Sezgin, *Poesie*, 53–54; Lyall, *Mufaḍḍalīyāt*, 2:xiv.
48. That this is what is intended here is clear from the variant versions of this anecdote, see esp. al-Anbārī, in Lyall, *Mufaḍḍalīyāt*, 1:764. Precisely this sort of anecdote in which the woman's voice is employed to draw attention to the sexual aspect of a double entendre is analyzed in Fedwa Malti-Douglas, *Woman's Body, Woman's Word: Gender and Discourse in Arabo-Islamic Writing* (Princeton: Princeton University Press, 1991), ch. 3.
49. This anecdote exists in a number of versions, several of which I have conflated here. Al-Anbārī and Lyall, in Lyall, *Mufaḍḍalīyāt*, 1:763–764, 2:327–328.
50. Of the many recensions of and commentaries on *Bānat Suʿād,* I have relied primarily on Abū Saʿīd al-Ḥasan ibn al-Ḥusayn al-Sukkarī, *Sharḥ Dīwān Kaʿb ibn Zuhayr* (Cairo: Dār al-Qawmīyah, 1965), 3–25; Yaḥyā ibn ʿAlī al-Tibrīzī, in Fritz Krenkow, "Tabrīzī's Kommentar zur Burda des Kaʿb ibn Zuhair," *Zeitschrift der Deutschen Morganländischen Gesellschaft* 65 (1911): 241–279; and Abū Muḥammad ʿAbd al-Malik ibn Hishām, *al-Sīrah al-nabawīyah*, 4 vols. (Cairo: Dār al-Fikr, n.d.), 3:1353–1366. English versions of the qaṣīdah and its akhbār are found in M. Hidayat Husain, "Banat Suʿad of Kaʿb bin Zuhair," *Islamic Culture* 1 (1927): 67–84; and A. Guillaume, trans., *The Life of Muhammad: A Translation of Isḥāq's Sīrat Rasūl Allāh* (Lahore and Karachi: Oxford University Press, 1974), 597–601 (which quotes Nicholson's translation). A new translation by Michael A. Sells has appeared as "*Bānat Suʿād*: Translation and Interpretative Introduction," *Journal of Arabic Literature* 21, no. 2 (1990): 140–154. For further sources, see Sezgin, *Poesie*, 230–235. See also Sells's discussion of the nasīb section below, ch. 3.
51. Indeed, the *Sīrah* version states that Muḥammad had alread killed some poets who had composed invective against him. See Ibn Hishām, *al-Sīrah al-nabawīyah*, 3:1353.
52. Al-Sukkarī, *Sharḥ Dīwān Kaʿb ibn Zuhayr*, 3–5. For the translation, analysis, and politico-historical interpretation of the rich body of variant versions (*riwāyāt*) of Kaʿb ibn Zuhayr's encounter with the Prophet Muḥammad (without, however, any discussion of the *Bānat Suʿād* qaṣīdah itself), see Michael Zwettler, "The Poet and the Prophet: Towards an Understanding of the Evolution of a Narrative," *Jerusalem Studies in Arabic and Islam* 5 (1984):313–87. Of particular interest is his discussion of *al-ma'mūr* (the bidden one) as a variant of *al-ma'mūn* (the entrusted one) (pp. 330–334). See also the sources cited above, note 50.
53. Abū al-Faraj al-Iṣbahānī, *Kitāb al-aghānī*, 31 vols., ed. Ibrāhīm al-Abyārī (Cairo: Dār al-Shaʿb, 1969), 10:3470.
54. I have followed al-Sukkarī's recension, except where otherwise noted.
55. Reading *lam yufda*. See al-Sukkarī, *Sharḥ Dīwān Kaʿb ibn Zuhayr*, 6.
56. Ibn Hishām, *al-Sīrah al-nabawīyah*, 3:1363.
57. As the commentarists read it this line would translate:

> They walk as the white camels walk,
> and their sword's blow
> Protects them when
> the black runts flee the field.

See al-Sukkarī, *Sharḥ Dīwān Kaʿb ibn Zuhayr*, 24–25; Krenkow, "Tabrīzī's Kommentar," 278. See discussion below, this chapter.

58. Lane, *Lexicon*, s.v. *s-ʿ-d*.

59. Al-Sukkarī, *Sharḥ Dīwān Kaʿb ibn Zuhayr*, 10; Ibn Hishām, *al-Sīrah al-nabawīyah*, 3:1358.

60. Lane, *Lexicon*, s.v. *q-l-d*.

61. Lines 36–46; see Abū ʿAbd Allāh al-Ḥusayn ibn Aḥmad al-Zawzanī, *Sharḥ al-Muʿallaqāt al-sabʿ*, ed. Muḥammad Muḥyī al-Dīn ʿAbd al-Ḥamīd (Cairo: Maktabat Muḥammad ʿAlī Ṣabīḥ, n.d.), 202–208. See the translation and discussion in S. Stetkevych, *Mute Immortals*, ch. 1.

62. Gaster, *Thespis*, 30–34.

63. Ibid., 34.

64. Ibid., 43.

65. Al-Sukkarī, *Sharḥ Dīwān Kaʿb ibn Zuhayr*, 21, note 2.

66. Lane, *Lexicon*, s.v. *n-q-m*.

67. Krenkow, "Tabrīzī's Kommentar," 273.

68. See Suzanne P. Stetkevych, *Abū Tammām and the Poetics of the ʿAbbasid Age* (Leiden: E. J. Brill, 1991), chs. 7 and 8.

69. See al-Sukkarī, *Sharḥ Dīwān Kaʿb ibn Zuhayr*, 24–25.

70. Al-Iṣbahānī, *Kitāb al-aghānī* 10:3778; A. J. Arberry, *The Seven Odes: The First Chapter in Arabic Literature* (London: George Allen and Unwin, 1957), 98.

71. Zuhayr's *Muʿallaqah*, lines 26–27; see al-Zawzanī, *Sharḥ al-Muʿallaqāt al-sabʿ*, 155.

72. Husain, "Banat Su'ad," 67. For the Arabic text of this and a related *khabar* see Muḥmūd Shukrī al-Ālūsī, *Bulūgh al-arab fī maʿrifat aḥwāl al-ʿArab*, 3 vols., ed. Muḥammad Bahjat al-Atharī (Beirut: Dār al-Kutub al-ʿIlmīyah, n.d.) 3:101.

73. Walter Burkert, *Homo Necans: The Anthropology of Ancient Greek Ritual and Myth*, trans. Peter Bing (Berkeley: University of California Press, 1983), 23. See also S. Stetkevych, "Ritual and Sacrificial Elements," 37–38.

74. See Havelock, *The Muse Learns to Write*, 63–78.

75. Versions of this anecdote are found in al-Jumaḥī, *Ṭabaqāt*, 1:103; Ibn Qutaybah, *al-Shiʿr wa-al-shuʿarā'*, 60; and Abū ʿAlī al-Ḥasan Ibn Rashīq al-Qayrawānī, *al-ʿUmdah fī maḥāsin al-shiʿr wa-ādābih wa-naqdih*, 2 vols., ed. Muḥammad Muḥyī al-Dīn ʿAbd al-Ḥamīd (Beirut: Dār al-Jīl, 1972), 1:23–24, etc. See Rudi Paret, "Die Legende der Verleihung des Prophetenmantels (*burda*) an Kaʿb ibn Zuhair," *Der Islam* 17 (1928): 9–14; and Sezgin, *Poesie*, 229–230. The most extensive study of the sources, variants, and politico-historical significance of the *burdah* report is that of Zwettler, which serves as an update and corrective of Paret. Of particular interest is his tracing its development into a "Prophetic *ḥadīth*" in the early third century H. See Zwettler, "The Poet and the Prophet," 334–372.

76. Sezgin, *Poesie*, 230, and Zwettler, "The Poet and the Prophet," 345–347.

77. Cited in Paret, "Die Legende," 13.

78. Cited by al-Anbārī in Lyall, *Mufaḍḍalīyāt*, 1:764.

79. On the "witness value of symbolic objects" see Walter J. Ong, *Orality and Literacy: The Technologizing of the Word* (London: Methuen, 1982), 97.

80. Paret, "Die Legende," 12–13.

"Then Elijah took his mantle, and rolled it up, and struck the water, and the water was parted. . . . When they had crossed, Elijah said to Elisha, 'Ask what I shall do for you, before I am taken from you.' And Elisha said, 'I pray you, let me inherit a double share of your spirit.' . . . behold a chariot of fire and horses of fire separated the two of them. And Elijah went up by a whirlwind into heaven. And Elisha saw it and cried, 'My father, my father! The chariots of Israel and its horsemen!' And he saw him no more. Then he took hold of his own clothes and rent them in two pieces. And he took up the mantle of Elijah that had fallen from him, and went back and stood on the bank of the Jordan.

Then he took the mantle of Elijah, . . . and struck the water, saying, 'Where is the Lord, the God of Elijah?' And when he had struck the water, the water was parted . . . and Elisha went over. Now when the sons of the prophets who were at Jericho saw him over against them, they said, 'The spirit of Elijah rests on Elisha.'" II Kings 2:8–15 (Revised Standard Version).

81. Ibn Qutaybah, *al-Shiʿr wa-al-shuʿarā'*, 51.

82. Al-Iṣbahānī, *Kitāb al-Aghānī*, 9:3219–3221.

83. See the discussion of *ḍ-l-l* above.

84. Al-Iṣbahānī, *Kitāb al-Aghānī*, 10:3769.

# Appendix of Arabic Texts

## [1] قَال عَلْقَمَةُ بْنُ عَبَدَةَ

١ طَحَا بِكَ قَلْبٌ فِي الْحِسَانِ طَرُوبُ
بُعَيْدَ ٱلشَّبَابِ عَصْرَ حَانَ مَشِيبُ

٢ يُكَلِّفُنِي لَيْلَى وَقَدْ شَطَّ وَلْيُهَا وَعَادَتْ عَوَادٍ بَيْنَنَا وَخُطُوبُ

٣ مُنَعَّمَةٌ مَا يُسْتَطَاعُ كِلاَمُهَا عَلَى بَابِهَا مِنْ أَنْ تُزَارَ رَقِيبُ

٤ إِذَا غَابَ عَنْهَا الْبَعْلُ لَمْ تُفْشِ سِرَّهُ
وَتُرْضِي إِيَابَ الْبَعْلِ حِينَ يَؤُوبُ

٥ فَلاَ تَعْدِلِي بَيْنِي وَبَيْنَ مُغَمَّرٍ سَقَتْكِ رَوَايَا الْمُزْنِ حِينَ تَصُوبُ

٦ سَقَاكِ يَمَانٍ ذُو حَبِيٍّ وَعَارِضٌ تَرُوحُ بِهِ جُنْحَ الْعَشِيِّ جَنُوبُ

٧ وَمَا أَنْتَ أَمْ مَا ذِكْرُهَا رَبَعِيَّةً يُخَطُّ لَهَا مِنْ ثَرْمَدَاءَ قَلِيبُ

٨ فَإِنْ تَسْأَلُونِي بِالنِّسَاءِ فَإِنَّنِي بَصِيرٌ بِأَدْوَاءِ النِّسَاءِ طَبِيبُ

٩ إِذَا شَابَ رَأْسُ الْمَرْءِ أَوْ قَلَّ مَالُهُ فَلَيْسَ لَهُ مِنْ وُدِّهِنَّ نَصِيبُ

١٠ يُرِدْنَ ثَرَاءَ الْمَالِ حَيْثُ عَلِمْنَهُ وَشَرْخُ الشَّبَابِ عِنْدَهُنَّ عَجِيبُ

١١ فَدَعْهَا وَسَلِّ الْهَمَّ عَنْكَ بِجَسْرَةٍ كَهَمِّكَ فِيهَا بِالرِّدَافِ خَبِيبُ

١٢ إِلَى الْحَارِثِ الْوَهَّابِ أَعْمَلْتُ نَاقَتِي لِكَلْكَلِهَا وَالْقُصْرَيَيْنِ وَجِيبُ

١٣ وَنَاجِيَةٍ أَفْنَى رَكِيبَ ضُلُوعِهَا وَحَارِكَهَا تَهَجُّرٌ فَدُؤُوبُ

١٤ وَتُصْبِحُ عَنْ غِبِّ السُّرَى وَكَأَنَّهَا        مُوَلَّعَةٌ تَخْشَى الْقَنِيصَ شَبُوبُ
١٥ تَعَفَّقُ بِالْأَرْطَى لَهَا وَأَرَادَهَا        رِجَالٌ فَبَذَّتْ نَبْلَهُمْ وَكَلِيبُ
١٦ لِتُبْلِغَنِي دَارَ ٱمْرِئٍ كَانَ نَائِيًا        فَقَدْ قَرَّبَتْنِي مِنْ نَدَاكَ قَرُوبُ
١٧ إِلَيْكَ أَبَيْتَ اللَّعْنَ كَانَ وَجِيفُهَا        بِمُشْتَبِهَاتٍ هَوْلُهُنَّ مَهِيبُ
١٨ هَدَانِي إِلَيْكَ الْفَرْقَدَانِ وَلَاحِبٌ        لَهُ فَوْقَ أَصْوَاءِ الْمِتَانِ عُلُوبُ
١٩ بِهَا جِيَفُ الْحَسْرَى فَأَمَّا عِظَامُهَا        فَبِيضٌ وَأَمَّا جِلْدُهَا فَصَلِيبُ
٢٠ تُرَادُ عَلَى دِمْنِ الْحِيَاضِ فَإِنْ تَعَفْ
فَإِنَّ الْمُنَدَّى رِحْلَةٌ فَرُكُوبُ
٢١ فَلَا تَحْرِمَنِّي نَائِلًا عَنْ جَنَابَةٍ        فَإِنِّي ٱمْرُؤٌ وَسْطَ الْقِبَابِ غَرِيبُ
٢٢ وَأَنْتَ ٱمْرُؤٌ أَفْضَتْ إِلَيْكَ أَمَانَتِي        وَقَبْلَكَ رَبَّتْنِي فَضِعْتُ رُبُوبُ
٢٣ فَأَدَّتْ بَنُو كَعْبِ بْنِ عَوْفٍ رَبِيبَهَا        وَغُودِرَ فِي بَعْضِ الْجُنُودِ رَبِيبُ
٢٤ فَوَاللّٰهِ لَوْلَا فَارِسُ الْجَوْنِ مِنْهُمُ        لَآبُوا خَزَايَا وَالْإِيَابُ حَبِيبُ
٢٥ تُقَدِّمُهُ حَتَّى تَغِيبَ حُجُولُهُ        وَأَنْتَ لِبَيْضِ الدَّارِعِينَ ضَرُوبُ
٢٦ مُظَاهِرُ سِرْبَالَيْ حَدِيدٍ عَلَيْهِمَا        عَقِيلَا سُيُوفٍ مِخْذَمٌ وَرَسُوبُ
٢٧ فَقَاتَلْتَهُمْ حَتَّى ٱتَّقَوكَ بِكَبْشِهِمْ
وَقَدْ حَانَ مِن شَمْسِ النَّهَارِ غُرُوبُ
٢٨ تَخَشْخَشُ أَبْدَانُ الْحَدِيدِ عَلَيْهِمُ
كَمَا خَشْخَشَتْ يُبْسَ الْحِصَادِ جَنُوبُ
٢٩ وَقَاتَلَ مِنْ غَسَّانَ أَهْلُ حِفَاظِهَا        وَهِنْبٌ وَقَاسٌ جَالَدَتْ وَشَبِيبُ

٣٠ كَأَنَّ رِجَالَ ٱلْأَوْسِ تَحْتَ لَبَانِهِ      وَمَا جَمَعَتْ جَلٌّ مَعًا وَعَتِيبُ

٣١ رَغَا فَوْقَهُمْ سَقْبُ السَّمَاءِ فَدَاحِصٌ

بِشِكَّتِهِ لَمْ يُسْتَلَبْ وَسَلِيبُ

٣٢ كَأَنَّهُمُ صَابَتْ عَلَيْهِمْ سَحَابَةٌ      صَوَاعِقُهَا لِطَيْرِهِنَّ دَبِيبُ

٣٣ فَلَمْ يَنْجُ إِلاَّ شَطْبَةٌ بِلِجَامِهَا      وَإِلاَّ طِمِرٌّ كَالْقَنَاةِ نَجِيبُ

٣٤ وَإِلاَّ كَمِيٌّ ذُو حِفَاظٍ كَأَنَّهُ

بِمَا ٱبْتَلَّ مِنْ حَدِّ الظُّبَاتِ خَضِيبُ

٣٥ وَأَنْتَ الَّذِي آثَارُهُ فِي عَدُوِّهِ      مِنَ الْبُؤْسِ وَالنُّعْمَى لَهُنَّ نُدُوبُ

٣٦ وَفِي كُلِّ حَيٍّ قَدْ خَبَطْتَ بِنِعْمَةٍ      فَحُقَّ لِشَأْسٍ مِّنْ نَدَاكَ ذَنُوبُ

٣٧ وَمَا مِثْلُهُ فِي النَّاسِ إِلاَّ أَسِيرُهُ      مُدَانٍ وَلاَ دَانٍ لِّذَاكَ قَرِيبُ

•

## [2] قَالَ تَأَبَّطَ شَرًّا

٢٦ وَعِتَاقُ الطَّيْرِ تَغْدُو بِطَانًا      تَتَخَطَّاهُمْ فَمَا تَسْتَقِلُّ

•

## [3] قَالَ كَعْبُ بْنُ زُهَيْرٍ

١ أَلاَ أَبْلِغَا عَنِّي بُجَيْرًا رِسَالَةً      فَهَلْ لَكَ فِيمَا قُلْتُ بِالْخَيْفِ هَلْ لَكَا

٢ شَرِبْتَ مَعَ الْمَأْمُونِ كَأْسًا رَوِيَّةً      فَأَنْهَلَكَ الْمَأْمُونُ مِنْهَا وَعَلَّكَا

٣ وَخَالَفْتَ أَسْبَابَ الْهُدَى وَتَبِعْتَهُ      عَلَى أَيِّ شَيْءٍ وَيْبَ غَيْرِكَ دَلَّكَا

٤ عَلَى خُلُقٍ لَمْ تُلْفِ أُمًّا وَلاَ أَبًا      عَلَيْهِ وَلَمْ تُدْرِكْ عَلَيْهِ أَخًا لَكَا

[4] **قَالَ بُجَيْرٌ**

١ مَنْ مُبْلِغٌ كَعْبًا فَهَلْ لَكَ فِي الَّتِي    تَلُومُ عَلَيْهَا بَاطِلاً وَهْيَ أَحْزَمُ

٢ إِلَى اللهِ لاَ الْعُزَّى وَلاَ اللاَّتِ وَحْدَهُ    فَتَنْجُو إِذَا كَانَ النَّجَاءُ وتَسْلَمُ

٣ لَدَى يَوْمِ لاَ يَنْجُو وَلَيْسَ بِمُفْلِتٍ    مِنَ النَّارِ إِلاَّ طَاهِرُ الْقَلْبِ مُسْلِمُ

٤ فَدِينُ زُهَيْرٍ وَهْوَ لاَ شَيْءَ دِينُهُ    وَدِينُ أَبِي سُلْمَى عَلَيَّ مُحَرَّمُ

•

[5] **قَالَ دُرَيْدُ بْنُ الصِّمَّةِ**

١ أَمَرْتُهُمْ أَمْرِي بِمُنْعَرَجِ اللِّوَى

فَلَمْ يَسْتَبِينُوا الرُّشْدَ إِلاَّ ضُحَى الْغَدِ

٢ فَلَمَّا عَصَوْنِي كُنْتُ مِنْهُمْ وَقَدْ أَرَى    غَوَايَتَهُمْ وَأَنَّنِي غَيْرُ مُهْتَدِ

٣ وَهَلْ أَنَا إِلاَّ مِنْ غَزِيَّةَ إِنْ غَوَتْ    غَوَيْتُ وَإِنْ تَرْشُدْ غَزِيَّةُ أَرْشُدِ

•

[6] **قَالَ كَعْبُ بْنُ زُهَيْرٍ**

١ بَانَتْ سُعَادُ فَقَلْبِي الْيَوْمَ مَتْبُولُ    مُتَيَّمٌ إِثْرَهَا لَمْ يُفْدَ مَكْبُولُ

٢ وَمَا سُعَادُ غَدَاةَ الْبَيْنِ إِذْ رَحَلُوا    إِلاَّ أَغَنُّ غَضِيضُ الطَّرْفِ مَكْحُولُ

٣ تَجْلُو عَوَارِضَ ذِي ظَلْمٍ إِذَا ابْتَسَمَتْ

كَأَنَّهُ مُنْهَلٌ بِالرَّاحِ مَعْلُولُ

٤ شُجَّتْ بِذِي شَبَمٍ مِنْ مَاءِ مَحْنِيَةٍ

صَافٍ بِأَبْطَحَ أَضْحَى وَهْوَ مَشْمُولُ

٥ تَجْلُو الرِّيَاحُ الْقَذَى عَنْهُ وَأَفْرَطَهُ     مِنْ صَوْبِ سَارِيَةٍ بِيضٌ يَعَالِيلُ
٦ يَا وَيْحَهَا خُلَّةً لَوْ أَنَّهَا صَدَقَتْ     مَا وَعَدَتْ أَوْ لَوَ اَنَّ النُّصْحَ مَقْبُولُ
٧ لَكِنَّهَا خُلَّةٌ قَدْ سِيطَ مِنْ دَمِهَا     فَجْعٌ وَوَلْعٌ وَإِخْلاَفٌ وَتَبْدِيلُ
٨ فَمَا تَدُومُ عَلَى حَالٍ تَكُونُ بِهَا     كَمَا تَلَوَّنُ فِي أَثْوَابِهَا الْغُولُ
٩ وَمَا تَمَسَّكُ بِالْوَصْلِ الَّذِي زَعَمَتْ     إِلاَّ كَمَا تُمْسِكُ الْمَاءَ الْغَرَابِيلُ
١٠ كَانَتْ مَوَاعِيدُ عُرْقُوبٍ لَهَا مَثَلاً     وَمَا مَوَاعِيدُهَا إِلاَّ الْأَبَاطِيلُ
١١ أَرْجُو وَآمُلُ أَنْ يَعْجَلْنَ فِي أَبَدٍ     وَمَا لَهُنَّ طَوَالَ الدَّهْرِ تَعْجِيلُ
١٢ فَلاَ يَغُرَّنْكَ مَا مَنَّتْ وَمَا وَعَدَتْ     إِنَّ الْأَمَانِيَّ وَالْأَحْلاَمَ تَضْلِيلُ
١٣ أَمْسَتْ سُعَادُ بِأَرْضٍ لاَ يُبَلِّغُهَا     إِلاَّ الْعِتَاقُ النَّجِيبَاتُ الْمَرَاسِيلُ
١٤ وَلَنْ يُبَلِّغَهَا إِلاَّ عُذَافِرَةٌ     فِيهَا عَلَى الْأَيْنِ إِرْقَالٌ وَتَبْغِيلُ
١٥ مِنْ كُلِّ نَضَّاخَةِ الذِّفْرَى إِذَا عَرِقَتْ
عُرْضَتُهَا طَامِسُ الْأَعْلاَمِ مَجْهُولُ
١٦ تَرْمِي الْغُيُوبَ بِعَيْنَيْ مُفْرَدٍ لَهِقٍ     إِذَا تَوَقَّدَتِ الْحُزَّانُ وَالْمِيلُ
١٧ ضَخْمٌ مُقَلَّدُهَا فَعْمٌ مُقَيَّدُهَا
فِي خَلْقِهَا عَنْ بَنَاتِ الْفَحْلِ تَفْضِيلُ
١٨ حَرْفٌ أَخُوهَا أَبُوهَا مِنْ مُهَجَّنَةٍ     وَعَمُّهَا خَالُهَا قَوْدَاءُ شِمْلِيلُ
١٩ يَمْشِي الْقُرَادُ عَلَيْهَا ثُمَّ يُزْلِقُهُ     مِنْهَا لَبَانٌ وَأَقْرَابٌ زَهَالِيلُ
٢٠ عَيْرَانَةٌ قُذِفَتْ فِي اللَّحْمِ عَنْ عُرُضٍ
مِرْفَقُهَا عَنْ بَنَاتِ الزَّوْرِ مَفْتُولُ

٢١ كَأَنَّ مَا فَاتَ عَيْنَيْهَا وَمَذْبَحَهَا
مِنْ خَطْمِهَا وَمِنَ اللَّحْيَيْنِ بِرْطِيلُ
٢٢ تُمِرُّ مِثْلَ عَسِيبِ النَّخْلِ ذَا خُصَلٍ
فِي غَارِزٍ لَمْ تَخَوَّنْهُ الأَحَالِيلُ
٢٣ قَنْوَاءُ فِي حُرَّتَيْهَا لِلْبَصِيرِ بِهَا   عِتْقٌ مُبِينٌ وَفِي الْخَدَّيْنِ تَسْهِيلُ
٢٤ تَخْدِي عَلَى يَسَرَاتٍ وَهْيَ لاحِقَةٌ   ذَوَابِلٍ وَقْعُهُنَّ الأَرْضَ تَحْلِيلُ
٢٥ سُمْرِ الْعُجَايَاتِ يَتْرُكْنَ الْحَصَى زِيَمًا
لَمْ يَقِهِنَّ رُءُوسَ الأُكْمِ تَنْعِيلُ
٢٦ يَوْمًا يَظَلُّ بِهِ الْحِرْبَاءُ مُصْطَخِمًا   كَأَنَّ ضَاحِيَهُ بِالنَّارِ مَمْلُولُ
٢٧ كَأَنَّ أَوْبَ ذِرَاعَيْهَا وَقَدْ عَرِقَتْ   وَقَدْ تَلَفَّعَ بِالْقُورِ الْعَسَاقِيلُ
٢٨ وَقَالَ لِلْقَوْمِ حَادِيهِمْ وَقَدْ جَعَلَتْ
وُرْقُ الْجَنَادِبِ يَرْكُضْنَ الْحَصَى قِيلُوا
٢٩ شَدَّ النَّهَارِ ذِرَاعَا عَيْطَلٍ نَصَفٍ   قَامَتْ فَجَاوَبَهَا نُكْدٌ مَثَاكِيلُ
٣٠ نَوَّاحَةٍ رُخْوَةِ الضَّبْعَيْنِ لَيْسَ لَهَا   لَمَّا نَعَى بِكْرَهَا النَّاعُونَ مَعْقُولُ
٣١ تَفْرِي اللَّبَانَ بِكَفَّيْهَا وَمِدْرَعُهَا   مُشَقَّقٌ عَنْ تَرَاقِيهَا رَعَابِيلُ
٣٢ يَسْعَى الْوُشَاةُ بِجَنْبَيْهَا وَقَوْلُهُمُ   إِنَّكَ يَابْنَ أَبِي سُلْمَى لَمَقْتُولُ
٣٣ وَقَالَ كُلُّ خَلِيلٍ كُنْتُ آمُلُهُ   لا أُلْفِيَنَّكَ إِنِّي عَنْكَ مَشْغُولُ
٣٤ فَقُلْتُ خَلُّوا طَرِيقِي لاَ أَبَا لَكُمُ   فَكُلُّ مَا قَدَّرَ الرَّحْمٰنُ مَفْعُولُ
٣٥ كُلُّ ابْنِ أُنْثَى وَإِنْ طَالَتْ سَلاَمَتُهُ   يَوْمًا عَلَى آلَةٍ حَدْبَاءَ مَحْمُولُ

٣٦ أُنْبِئْتُ أَنَّ رَسُولَ اللّٰهِ أَوْعَدَنِي     وَالْعَفْوُ عِنْدَ رَسُولِ اللّٰهِ مَأْمُولُ
٣٧ مَهْلاً هَدَاكَ الَّذِي أَعْطَاكَ نَافِلَةَ الـ     قُرْآنِ فِيهَا مَوَاعِيظٌ وَتَفْصِيلُ
٣٨ لاَ تَأْخُذَنِّي بِأَقْوَالِ الْوُشَاةِ وَلَمْ     أُذْنِبْ وَلَوْ كَثُرَتْ عَنِّي الأَقَاوِيلُ
٣٩ لَقَدْ أَقُومُ مَقَامًا لَوْ يَقُومُ بِهِ     أَرَى وَأَسْمَعُ مَا لَوْ يَسْمَعُ الْفِيلُ
٤٠ لَظَلَّ يُرْعَدُ إِلاَّ أَنْ يَكُونَ لَهُ     مِنَ الرَّسُولِ بِإِذْنِ اللّٰهِ تَنْوِيلُ
** مَا زِلْتُ أَقْتَطِعُ الْبَيْدَاءَ مُدَّرِعًا     جُنْحَ الظَّلاَمِ وَثَوْبُ اللَّيْلِ مَسْدُولُ
٤١ حَتَّى وَضَعْتُ يَمِينِي لاَ أُنَازِعُهُ     فِي كَفِّ ذِي نَقِمَاتٍ قِيلُهُ الْقِيلُ
٤٢ لَذَاكَ أَهْيَبُ عِنْدِي إِذْ أُكَلِّمُهُ     وَقِيلَ إِنَّكَ مَسْبُورٌ وَمَسْئُولُ
٤٣ مِنْ ضَيْغَمٍ مِنْ ضِرَاءِ الأُسْدِ مُخْدَرُهُ     بِبَطْنِ عَثَّرَ غِيلٌ دُونَهُ غِيلُ
٤٤ يَغْدُو فَيَلْحَمُ ضِرْغَامَيْنِ عَيْشُهُمَا     لَحْمٌ مِنَ الْقَوْمِ مَعْفُورٌ خَرَادِيلُ
٤٥ إِذَا يُسَاوِرُ قِرْنًا لاَ يَحِلُّ لَهُ     أَنْ يَتْرُكَ الْقِرْنَ إِلاَّ وَهْوَ مَفْلُولُ
٤٦ مِنْهُ تَظَلُّ حَمِيرُ الْوَحْشِ ضَامِزَةً     وَلاَ تُمَشِّي بِوَادِيهِ الأَرَاجِيلُ
٤٧ وَلاَ يَزَالُ بِوَادِيهِ أَخُو ثِقَةٍ     مُطَرَّحُ الْبَزِّ وَالدِّرْسَانِ مَأْكُولُ
٤٨ إِنَّ الرَّسُولَ لَسَيْفٌ يُسْتَضَاءُ بِهِ     مُهَنَّدٌ مِنْ سُيُوفِ اللّٰهِ مَسْلُولُ
٤٩ فِي عُصْبَةٍ مِنْ قُرَيْشٍ قَالَ قَائِلُهُمْ     بِبَطْنِ مَكَّةَ لَمَّا أَسْلَمُوا زُولُوا
٥٠ زَالُوا فَمَا زَالَ أَنْكَاسٌ وَلاَ كُشُفٌ     عِنْدَ اللِّقَاءِ وَلاَ مِيلٌ مَعَازِيلُ
٥١ شُمُّ الْعَرَانِينِ أَبْطَالٌ لَبُوسُهُمُ
مِنْ نَسْجِ دَاوُدَ فِي الْهَيْجَا سَرَابِيلُ
٥٢ بِيضٌ سَوَابِغُ قَدْ شُكَّتْ لَهَا حَلَقٌ     كَأَنَّهَا حَلَقُ الْقَفْعَاءِ مَجْدُولُ

٥٣ يَمْشُونَ مَشْيَ الْجِمَالِ الزُّهْرِ يَعْصِمُهُمْ

ضَرْبٌ إِذَا عَرَّدَ السُّودُ التَّنَابِيلُ

٥٤ لَا يَفْرَحُونَ إِذَا نَالَتْ رِمَاحُهُمُ

قَوْمًا وَلَيْسُوا مَجَازِيعًا إِذَا نِيلُوا

٥٥ لَا يَقَعُ الطَّعْنُ إِلَّا فِي نُحُورِهِمْ

مَا إِنْ لَهُمْ عَنْ حِيَاضِ الْمَوْتِ تَهْلِيلُ

# II

# TOWARD AN ARABIC ELEGIAC LEXICON

## THE SEVEN WORDS OF THE *NASĪB*

*Jaroslav Stetkevych*

The *nasīb,* or opening section of the classical Arabic ode, with its recurrent elegiac motifs—the ruined abodes, the lost mistress, etc.—has traditionally been categorized as concretely descriptive of the realities of Bedouin life. This study, by contrast, argues through the analysis of seven key elements of *nasīb* diction that the poetic intent and value of the *nasīb* lies not in descriptive realism but in deeper archetypal symbolism. And, further, that this deeper level can be reached only through uncovering what Muṣṭafā Nāṣif terms "the myth behind the word." The analysis of the selected words—words which are repeated in a seemingly obligatory way in countless classical Arabic odes—proceeds on the basis of etymology, semantic range, mythopoeic and metaphorical association to reveal cultural, as well as more closely literary, connections with Ancient Near Eastern ritual, myth, and poetry. The method developed and employed here goes beyond the new philology inspired by Leo Spitzer into the realm of myth and archetype.

### ***Ṭalal*** **(Ruin)**

*ʿŪjā ʿalā ṭ-ṭalali l-muḥīli la'annanā*
*nabkī d-diyāra kamā bakā -Bnu Khidhāmī*

Halt over the ruin of yesteryear, perhaps there
We shall weep over abodes Ibn Khidhām's way![1]

In a "traditionalist" and ultimately also mythopoeic sense, we may accept Imru' al-Qays's invocation of the distant poetic ways of the legendary bard Ibn

Khidhām—his halting at the campsite ruin and apostrophizing his two companions—as the instance when the Bedouin poet first became aware of his own reenactment of a topos. We accept furthermore that that topos was also capable of exerting upon him and upon his poetics its legitimizing force.

From then on, too, with the same poetically efficient sense of balance between licence and legitimacy, poet after Arab poet felt the compulsion to stop over his chosen or fated, real or figurative, ruined "site." Thus Suwayd Ibn Kurāᶜ al-ᶜUklī calls upon his two companions:[2]

*Wa ḥuṭṭā ᶜalā l-aṭlāli raḥlī wa innahā*
*la-awwalu aṭlālin ᶜaraftu bihā l-ᶜishqā*

And set down upon the ruins my camel's saddle,
For these are the first ruins where I knew
love's passion.

Over such ruinous sites time flows in seasonal streams, making them reappear, resiliently, as ancient sacred writs. Thus in the *Muᶜallaqah* of Labīd:[3]

*Wa jalā s-suyūlu ᶜani ṭ-ṭulūli ka'annahā*
*zuburun tujiddu mutūnahā aqlāmuhā*

And flooding streams brought back to sight ruinous sites,
Like writings traced anew.

Even the rather studiedly non-elegiac ᶜUmar Ibn Abī Rabīᶜah of the Umayyad period feels comfortable with the topos of the ruins—enough so to group them in a tightly knit, kindred topical cluster with *dār* and *diman*:[4]

*Hal taᶜrifu d-dāra wa l-aṭlāla wa d-dimanā*
*zidna l-fu'āda ᶜalā ᶜillātihī ḥazanā*

Do you know the abode, the ruins and "dung-droppings,"
What grief they added to the heart's ills!

And so forth, and so forth. The mere quoting of the textual occurrences of the topos of the *ṭalal* from the main anthologies and *dīwāns* of Arabic poetry would fill quite inordinate numbers of pages.

Such fealty to a specific topos must sooner or later leave in the mind of a critic or historian of classical Arabic poetry the suspicion that the Arabic poetic *ṭalal* is not to be understood merely on the level of surface semantics that is dealt with by the kind of textual exegesis called *sharḥ*, for even a careful consultation of a lexicon will reveal in it aspects of meaning that point beyond such exegesis. We may, therefore, find that the word *ṭalal* can mean "remains of walls and of places of worship," or that it may refer to "elevated places," as well as to all that "appears," or "looms," from the distance—such as a hill with a settlement upon it.[5] Thus in a fragment kept anonymous in the classical anthology of the Arabian elegiac mood, *Al-Manāzil wa al-Diyār* of Usāmah Ibn Munqidh:[6]

*Thawā māthilan bayna ṭ-ṭulūli l-mawāthilī*
*fa hal balla min dā'i l-jawā l-balābilū*

Erect he stood among the upright looming ruins—
But has he recovered from love's consumption
and sorrows?

When we look into the etymological possibilities of the word *ṭalal*—and thus into the possibilities of its broader semantics—we come up with the realization that in the "matter" of *ṭalal* the lexicon itself has accumulated quite a layering of debris which lies there in need of its own archaeology; for, aside from the meanings already mentioned, which represent only one of the archaeological layers of this lexical debris, we have such other, not at all marginal semantic as well as root potsherds as *ṭall*, meaning "dew"; *ṭull*, meaning (unavenged) "blood"; *ṭill*, meaning "serpent"; and other, more complex nominal forms—some recognizably deverbal, others not. If to this so-called root entry which could not possibly claim the quality of etymology we add other, indirect etymological convergencies such as *tall* with the plural form of *tilāl/tulūl/atlāl*, meaning "hill of rubbish," and such verbal roots as *ṭalaʿa* ("to rise," "to grow," "to go up"), and *talaʿa* ("to erect," "to lift," etc.), we emerge above all with the conviction that the real pre-Islamic poetic *ṭalal* as "ruin" could not quite belong into its pro forma lexicographic entry space, but that it is rather related to such "separate" root entries as *ṭalaʿa* and *talaʿa*—not even to the verbal *talla*—at least not in Arabic—unless we accept here the principle of "antonymy" (*taḍādd*), for in Arabic *ṭalla* implies downward intent or movement, not upward as in *ṭalaʿa/talaʿa*, most unlike the would-be deverbal *tall* (hill; heap of rubbish).

It is thus the etymology that leads us *outside* the Arabic lexical pale which gives us more certainty as to where we are in the lexical archaeology of the Arabic *ṭalal*; and so it is through the avenues of Hebrew and Aramaic (and even Coptic) that we can easily divest ourselves of much burdensome "stratographic" pileup of would-be roots and thus separate the Arabic poetic *ṭalal* in the first degree from its emphatic consonantal sound alikes such as "dew," "unavenged blood," and "serpent," among others. The latter three, however, may exercise their connotative poetic effect regardless of their etymology. What thus remains by elimination is the Arabic *tall* as "hill of rubbish" and the Hebrew *tell*—according to Wilhelm Gesenius "commonly derived from the root *t-l-l*."[7] At this point we then have to face more the image quality—the visualization—of the *ṭalal* than its sound, and for that image we must go no further than to the region through which the earliest Arabian caravans would have passed even centuries before the first Arabian bard, such as Imru' al-Qays's legendary model, Ibn Khidhām, had ever stopped over ruins and sung his song.

### *Dār* (Abode)

At this point we should more profitably move to our second key word, that of *dār*, which, with great frequency, is found in pre-Islamic *nasīb* openings with reference to deserted habitation placed upon heights or hilltops. Thus in the familiar ode rhyming in *dāl* by al-Nābighah al-Dhubyānī:[8]

*Yā dāra Mayyata bi l-ʿalyā'i fa s-sanadī*
*aqwat wa ṭāla ʿalayhā sālifu l-abadī*

O abode of Mayyah, upon height and peak,
It lies deserted, its old days long since past.

Or in the opening verse of Zuhayr Ibn Abī Sulmā's ode in *rā'*:[9]

*Li man id-diyāru bi qunnati l-Ḥijrī*
*aqwayna min ḥijajin wa min dahrī*

Whose are the abodes on the rise of al-Ḥijr?
They grew deserted with the passage
of years of pilgrimage and turns of time.

The location of such abodes was not altogether clear to the earliest, already Islamic, exegetes of this poem. When asked about it, the great scholiast Abū ʿAmr answered hesitantly: "I do not know of any 'place of interdicted access'—for that is otherwise the meaning of *al-ḥijr*—other than the Ḥijr of the Thamūd, nor do I know whether this is the one or not."[10] The Thamūdic-Nabataean caravan city of al-Ḥijr, in its monumentality a worthy extension of Petra, is, of course, the Islamized Madā'in Ṣāliḥ of the vicinity of al-ʿUlā—thus another rock city of "high places." It is in this context that we may understand Zuhayr's poem's verse three:[11]

*Qafran bi mundafaʿi n-naḥā'iti min*
*ḍafaway ulāti ḍ-ḍāli wa s-sidrī*

Laid waste by the torrent in rock-hewn water beds,
From both sides, where the *ḍāl* and the lote grow.

Putting all referential indicators together, there thus emerges from the opening verses of Zuhayr's poem an image of the *diyār* (abodes) on the "high places" of that al-Ḥijr which had become legendary for its mysterious habitations cut out of and into rock. What the poet adds to this as he draws upon an entirely archetypal tradition, are the two sides, or slopes, of this extraordinary place, representing them as overgrown with trees of no lesser symbolic presence than the two varieties of the Arabian lote tree: one archaic Bedouin, at home on native mountain slopes of Najd (*al-ḍāl*), the other (*al-sidr*), brought in from a domain/abode, that is both at the beginning and at the end of all archetypal legend making.

The contact between *dār* and *ṭalal* thus made, we are also told *what* the meaning of the Bedouin sense of loss and melancholy might be: that the source of all of Bedouin poetic melancholy is the awareness of *happiness lost*—happiness both ancient and remote, for which the abode/*dār* is only a figure, and that other happiness, one that was taken from the poet when the *khalīṭ* (tribal throng) dispersed and in its seasonal centrifugality took away the poet's beloved as *ẓaʿīnah*. Remaining alone in the void of the *dār*, the poet issued his "question," although aware of the futility of his pose. Thus once again al-Nābighah al-Dhubyānī:[12]

*Ṭāla l-wuqūfu ʿalā rusūmi diyārī*
*qafrin usā'iluhā wa mā -stikhbārī*

*Dāran taʿaffat lā anīsa bi jawwihā*
*illā baqāyā dimnatin wa awārī*

................

*Dārun li-Mayyata idh humū laka jīratun*
*hayhāta minka manāzilu l-aḥwārī*

Long was the halting over desolate abodes' traces.
I questioned them, but to what avail was my query

Of abode effaced, and no soul inside—
None but remains of droppings, pegs
to fasten beasts?

................

An abode of Mayyah, when they dwelled nearby,
But now how remote are the halting sites
of white oryx cows!

Both in its immediacies and in its hesitations, such melancholy blends all that is close and distant, personal and communal of the appetites for happiness that the poet once possessed. Thus for al-Jaʿdī, the other al-Nābighah of bardic fame, the *dār* of melancholy contemplation is not that of the "beloved" but of the *qawm*, his comrades in arms:[13]

*Li man id-dāru ka anḍā'i l-khilal*
*ʿahduhā min ḥiqabi d-dahri l-uwal*

*Dāru qawmī qabla an yudrikahum*
*ʿanatu d-dahri wa ʿayshun dhū khabal*

Whose is the abode—like worn-out scabbard thongs,
Its time of pledged bond—the first of all time.

Abode of my folk, before it was seized
By contrary fate and life's disarray.

And stepping into a time that lies between the historical and the legendary—which in the *nasīb* is the time of the objectivization of the elegiac stance—we find al-Aswad Ibn Yaʿfur intoning his *ubi sunt* elegy over the adversities of the once sovereign Sassanians, "the people of al-Khawarnaq and al-Sadīr," who, too, succumbed to the fate of the abodes (*diyār*):[14]

11. *Jarat ir-riyāḥu ʿalā makāni diyārihim*
*fa ka'annamā kānū ʿalā mīʿādī*

14. *Fa idhā n-naʿīmu wa kullu mā yulhā bihī*
*yawman yaṣīru ilā bilan wa nafādī*

12. *Wa la qad ghanū fīhā bi anʿami ʿīshatin*
*fī ẓilli mulkin thābiti l-awtādī*

With winds speeding over abodes' sites,
They were as though bound by appointed time.

Then, one day, all bliss and all
distracting enterprise
Pass into decay and waste—

And yet they had once reveled in life most blissfully,
Secure in royal power's shade.

The ultimate meaning of such abodes/*diyār* becomes then even clearer in the hermeneutically relevant *tradition* attributed to ʿAlī Ibn Abī Ṭālib, who, while passing by the newly conquered Ctesiphon, had overheard one of his troop recite the above verse (*Jarat ir-riyāḥu*). "What was it you had said?" he turned to the man, who then proceeded to declame to him the poem. But ᶜAlī spoke: "Hadn't you said 'How many paradisical gardens and fountains they left behind!'"; then adding: "My boy, but they failed to acknowledge Divine bounty, so heaven's blows befell them. Beware, therefore, of denying heaven's bounty, lest heaven's blows befall you!"[15]

ᶜAlī Ibn Abī Ṭālib had thus consciously identified the semiotics and contextualization of the archaic Arabian repository of bliss—specifically of lost bliss. *Diyār* and *jannāt/jinān* (gardens) were to him kindred concepts with the difference that, belonging to the Jāhilīyah, the *niᶜam* (graces) of the *diyār* had been false and were *lost*, whereas the *niᶜam* of the eschatological *jannāt*, i.e., the *diyār* now claimed by Islam, were not at the "lost" beginning but at the "gained" end. On the other hand, *dār* is an adequately attested word in the Qur'ān, although with a restricted symbolic range. Thus in the Sura of the Story, verse 81, it is used in the story of Korah/Qārūn in a quite concretized way: "So we made the earth to swallow him and his *dwelling*" (*fa khasafnā bihi wa bi dārihi l-arḍa*). So, too, is verse 84 (and 85) of the Sura of the Cow: "You shall not shed your own blood, neither expel your own from your *dwellings*" (. . . *wa lā tukhrijūna anfusakum min diyārikum*), although here al-Qāḍī al-Māwardī's "third level of interpretation" (*ta'wīl*) proposes an equation between the two "abodes" (*min al-jannati llatī hiya dārukum*).[16] Only in the Sura of Yūsuf, verse 25, and in that of "The Cattle," verse 127, is the expression *dār as-salām* a clear reference to Paradise. Even more literal is verse 30 of the Sura of the Bee: "And surely the *abode* of the world to come is better—excellent is the *abode* of the god-fearing" (*wa la dāru l-ākhirati khayrun wa la niᶜma dāru l-muttaqīna*), for there the mention of *dār* is immediately followed (v. 31) by the invocation of the Gardens of Eden (*jannātu ᶜAdnin yadkhulūnahā*).

Then, in a manner close to the poetic domain of the use of *dār/diyār*, where, as we had seen, it is linked to the meaning of *ṭalal*, and where an expression such as *ahlu ṭ-ṭulūli* would equal that of *ahlu d-diyāri*, is the equation in a Prophetic *ḥadīth* of *ahlu l-maqābiri* with *ahlu d-diyāri*: "The Prophet would instruct [his followers] that, when they enter the burial grounds (*al-maqābir*), they should say: 'Peace be upon you, O people of the abodes (*ahlu d-diyāri*) from among the believers and the Muslims. Truly, we shall follow in your wake. Of God we ask well-being for us and for you'."[17] On the other hand, the rhetorical function of *al-maqābir* in the Sura of Rivalry (*al-takāthur*), verse 2, is merely that of impressing the fear of death and the presence in the mind of the fragility of all earthly business. It is a *memento mori* on an ascetic rather than symbolic level.

Having thus reviewed the textualities of *dār* as *ṭalal*, then as *jannah*, and even as *qabr*, we come to the question of the quiddity of the space that is the *dār*. Already al-Khalīl Ibn Aḥmad had defined it as to its shape: "Any place taken up as settlement by a people is a *dār*, even if there not be in it any construction; and it was named *dār* because it forms a circle around (*li dawrihā*) those who inhabit it, just as the wall (*al-ḥā'iṭ*) was named wall because it 'blocks in' (protectively) that which it contains."[18] The root *d-w-r* itself is thus etymologically "instantly revealing." It *says* so much in one breath, as it were. But it is also a very complex root, since it even resists being unequivocally characterized as Semitic. In Hebrew it is not richly attested as a verb (Ps. 84:11) but is instead more common when used nominally (*dūr*). As already noted by Nöldeke, it points semantically (*Geschlecht, Generation, Zeitraum*) toward the related root (and meaning) of the Arabic *dahr.*[19] Al-Khalīl Ibn Aḥmad's semantic association of *d-w-r* with *al-ḥā'iṭ* (wall) is also strengthened through the Assyrian *dūru/dūrā* (Aramaic form), meaning "wall" as well as "duration," "eternity."[20]

This solid Semitic attestation is, however, disturbed by the parallel root—and semantic range—of the Indo-European *ter/turn/drehen/tornare/truia* (Etruscan). Also compare the Slavic *dwir/dwór/dwor* as "inner (or outer) yard," "enclosure," "court," with the Arabic *dār* and the classical as well as postclassical *dawār* ("precinct of an idol," "precinct of a shrine," "communal house or hall." And who knows what to think of the "walls of Troy" as these have been symbolically re-created in the spiral-like labyrinths known as *Trojaburgen.*[21]

Attempting clarification by contrast, there has to be brought out at this point the difference between *dār* and *bayt.*[22] Certainly in the Islamic period, *bayt* has acquired rich cultic connotations. Its reference to the Kaᶜbah, however, would necessarily give it a rectangular, or square, form, as opposed to the roundness of the *dār*. Otherwise, in the earliest Arabic usage, it is a term for the tent and, by extension, habitation under one roof. The further meaning of *bayt* as "family" or "household" (*ahl*) is thus implicitly present in the structure's function and even in its verbal etymological base: *bāta* meaning "to stay through the night." Furthermore, those who stay in the *bayt* through the night, its *ahl*, point equally back to that Bedouin domicile and social unit determined by the "tent"—which in Hebrew is none other than *ohel.* This leads us to the linguistically tautological, privileged social designation of *ahl al-bayt*, "the tent-community of the tent." At this junction, however, the cultic link between the specific *ahl* and the specific *bayt* is made, and "nobility" approximates itself semiotically (more than narrowly semantically) to "priesthood."

The squareness of the Kaᶜbah as *al-Bayt*, or vice versa, needs no further insistence in its Arabic visualization. As *Bayt Allāh*, however, it leads us to its closest linguistic and cultic antecedent, the Hebrew *bet el*, equally the "House of God" and equally rectangular in its main form. This *bet el*, also known in Greek as *baitylos*, is iconographically represented as a conoid stone set upon a rectangular base. The ancient god of the Nabataeans, Dushara, was also called "Lord of the House," and was represented as a conical, or rather *domical*, stone raised upon a square chamber, platform, or altar. If the divinity component of the iconographic structure is thus the domic/conic stone and the square part is the actual *bayt/bet*, it is interesting to note that that divine stone in the form of a dome-like roof had also been recognized as being of black color and an asteroid.[23]

### Rabʿ (Vernal Encampment)

Opposite the Arabic poetic *dār* in its roundness which it always insinuates as an ultimate perception of form—the form of the lost "circle" of bliss and perfection, and therefore always of *only erstwhile* habitation—we find the poetically almost wholly inefficacious *bayt*, which in turn suggests undisrupted habitation and ultimately a concretized cultic function independent of the *qaṣīdah*. If, however, there is the possibility in the classical Arabic poem of a juxtaposition of these two basic forms—round and square—that possibility is realized not through the markedly infrequent textual coincidence of *dār* and *bayt*, but rather through the full textual balance in the opening verses of the *nasīb* of *dār* and *rabʿ*. The lexicon lists the latter term as meaning primarily "a spring encampment," then also as "a house," "a tent," and last but not least, "a bier."

Instances illustrating the uses in the classical Arabic poetic corpus of *rabʿ* when it is in contextual proximity to *dār* are numerous indeed. Zuhayr Ibn Abī Sulmā salutes the *rabʿ* of his *dār* in the sixth verse of his *Muʿallaqah*:[24]

> *Fa lammā ʿaraftu d-dāra qultu li rabʿihā*
> *alā -nʿam ṣabāḥan ayyuhā r-rabʿu wa -slamī*

> And when I recognized the abode,
>     I said to its *rabʿ*:
> "Good morrow to you, O *rabʿ*, and be well!"

And al-Nābighah al-Dhubyānī laments its desolation in his ode in *dāl*:[25]

> *Waqaftu fīhā uṣaylālan usā'iluhā*
> *ʿayyat jawāban wa mā bi r-rabʿi min aḥadī*

> There [*dār*] I halted at evening time to question it.
> There was no answer, and in the *rabʿ*
>         there was no one.

And once again al-Nābighah al-Dhubyānī:[26]

> *Waqaftu bi rabʿi d-dāri qad ghayyara l-bilā*
> *maʿālimahū wa s-sāriyātu l-hawāṭilū*

> I halted at the *rabʿ* of the abode,
>     its markers altered by decay
> And by night-traveling clouds pouring down.

Or the already Abbasid poet, al-Buḥturī:[27]

*Fa lam yadri rabʿu d-dāri kayfa yujībunī*
*wa lā naḥnu min farṭi l-asā kayfa nas'alū*

But the *rabʿ* of the abode knew not how to answer me,
And we, from sorrow's excess, knew not how to ask.

As well as a poet from the anthology *Al-Manāzil wa al-Diyār* of Usāmah Ibn Munqidh:[28]

*Wa lā siyyamā dārun wulidta bi rabʿihā*
*wa kunta bihā jadhlāna fī khayri āhilī*

And especially an abode in whose *rabʿ* you were born
And where you were lighthearted, living amidst
the best of folk.

Even though in the above examples of the poetic occurrence of the term *rabʿ* it is certainly not against the respective verses' lyrical grain to understand *rabʿ* as implying a vernal camping ground, what strikes the receiving sensibility is nonetheless the insistent juxtaposition of *dār* and *rabʿ*—or *dār* within *rabʿ*. Thus particularly in the last example of *dārun wulidta bi rabʿihā*. It is at such points of contextualized reading that further massive subtextuality of the Arabic *qaṣīdah* tradition begins to impress itself conjointly upon the levels of understanding of its poetic language. To return to the classical Arabic lexicon once again, we remind ourselves that *rabʿ* is "a place where people abide in the season called *rabīʿ*." As such it knows the variants of *marbaʿ* and *murtabaʿ*. But it also has the meaning of "a settled place of abode or constant residence *whenever and wherever it be*"; so, too, *murtabaʿ* comes to mean "a place where a camel beats the ground with its *four (arbaʿ) legs* while alighting," thus generating descriptively the meaning of "a halting place." Furthermore, the meaning of "bier" ought to have attached itself to *rabʿ* because a bier is "raised" and because it is of "rectangular shape." Also, *rabʿ* designates "a large number" (probably forty); and in its form of *rabʿah* it is "a vessel of *four* sides" and also "a chest" in which copies of the Qur'ān are kept.[29]

Like most roots, especially in languages that structure themselves lexically according to highly form-bound—and thus oversimplified—systems, the Arabic root *r-b-ʿ* is as much that which it claims to be—that is, a consonantal core of legitimate morphology-based etymology—as also a *mélange* of would-be derivatives stemming from semantic attraction. Ultimately, however, even homonymic chance and semantic attraction do not entirely escape a sort of semantic pollination. Thus *rabʿ*, the vernal campsite, is also the "site of alighting"—as the Aramaic *r-b-ʿ*, the Hebrew *r-b-ṣ*, and the Arabic *r-b-ṭ/r-b-ḍ* should permit. *Rabʿ* is, however, also a place of alighting during the "fourth month" of the solar calendar—*rabīʿ* in Arabic, but also, much more specifically in Hebrew, *harebīʿī* (Ezek. 1:1); and that "fourth month" is also a month of the renewal of vegetation and of growth (*r-b-w*).

Above all, it is the time of "four" and the place of the "four-edged" or "four-sided" geometry of surface that, together, determine the semiotics and the poetic presence of the Arabic *rabʿ*; and it is this four-ribbed poetic presence of *rabʿ* that we find in the *nasīb* of the Arabic *qaṣīdah* in juxtaposition to *dār*, the space of roundness and the circular time of mutability. What is in the horizontal sense of the poetic line a juxtaposition, however, is in the visual and conceptual sense an overlaying or "in-scription"—a quadrature of the circle: the *rabʿu d-dāri* of poet after Arabian poet. Others have expressed this proposition through the favorite symbolically and mythopoeically defining means of their respective cultures: the *paradisus claustralis*, the Byzantine dome over its four arches, the myth of the foundation of city and a civilization in the Roma Quadrata with its central pit (*mundus*) from which the wider *circumference* was drawn, and its "first" central square building, the actual Quadrata Roma, in which the sacralized tools for the ritual (mythic) "foundation" of the city were kept. Out of it all we emerge with a multifaceted but symbolically intimately interlaced cosmological view of "original," or "primal," habitation.

## *Nu'y* (Trench)

In further retracing the poetic "ground plans" and circumferences of archaic Bedouin habitation, we shall now turn to the textually only slightly less ubiquitous references to the *nu'y* as the "trench," or "fosse," that was dug around the *dār*/abode. Its practical function was to prevent floodwaters from inundating the inhabited space. As part of the elegiac whole of the opening scene of the *nasīb*, however, it too contributes to that scene's sense of long abandonment and desolation—especially since it comes accompanied by the rich semiotics and imagist quality of further Bedouin accouplements of melancholy such as *al-awārī*, the abandoned "ropes to tie down riding beasts in an encampment," or *al-athāfī*, "the [three] hearthstones on which is placed a cauldron."

Thus ʿAbīd Ibn al-Abraṣ expresses his sorrow over his people's abodes of which nothing remains but ashes and old animal droppings,[30]

*Wa awāriyya qad ʿafawna wa nu'yan*
*wa rusūman ʿurrīna mudh aḥwālī*

And withered ropes to tie down beasts, and a trench,
And traces laid bare of years that rolled by.

Here, too, al-Nābighah al-Dhubyānī's ode in *dāl* maintains its position as the *locus classicus*: in vain did the poet question the abandoned abode (*al-dār*) of his beloved Mayyah.[31]

*ᶜAyyat jawāban wa mā bi r-rabᶜi min aḥadī*

*Illā l-awāriyya la'yan mā ubayyinuhā*
*wa n-nu'ya ka l-ḥawḍi bi l-maẓlūmati l-jaladī*

There was no answer, and in the *rabᶜ*
there was no one,

But ropes to hobble beast, that I barely espy,
And the *trench*, trough-like in hard,
compacted ground.

In another ode, with the rhyme in *rā'*, the same poet conjures up the *nu'y* linked elegiacally to "stones" that imply the referent of the *athāfī*. In a lyrically efficacious paradox, explicitness thus turns into circumvention:[32]

*ᶜŪjū fa ḥayyū li Nuᶜmin dimnata d-dārī*
*mādhā tuḥayyūna min nu'yin wa aḥjārī*

Alight and greet the remains of Nuᶜm's abode—
But what shall you greet of trench and stone?

Equally lyrically condensed is the contextualization of the *nu'y* in the fifth verse of the *Muᶜallaqah* of Zuhayr Ibn Abī Sulmā:[33]

*Athāfiyya sufᶜan fī muᶜarrasi mirjalin*
*wa nu'yan ka jidhmi l-ḥawḍi lam yatathallamī*

Fire-blackened hearthstones where a cauldron stood
of an overnight halting place,
And a trench, not flood-washed,
like a trunk-hewn trough.

Even though the impression that Zuhayr Ibn Abī Sulmā gives of the departure from the encampment is one of haste, or almost as if the presence of those who had camped there were still lingering over things left behind, this is itself only a melancholy illusion that pursues its own lyrical purposes. Otherwise the *nu'y* is inseparable from the waste and ruination that is brought about by an almost unqualifiable "pastness," or if that pastness is qualified at all, it may be associated in meaning with the enigmatic palimpsestic antiquity of the remains of a writing[34] that yet strikes the eye so vividly—as in the opening verse of an ode by Ḥātim Ibn ᶜAbd Allāh al-Ṭā'ī:[35]

*A taᶜrifu aṭlālan wa nu'yan muhaddamā*
*ka khaṭṭika fī raqqin kitāban munamnamā*

Do you recognize the ruins and a crumbled trench
That are like writing over parchment penned
in ornate hand?

But ultimately, defying the newness of their palimpsestic epiphany as writ, such ruins and such a *nu'y* are no more than the frailest of illusions, for the poet continues in his ode (v. 4):[36]

*Wa ghayyarahā ṭūlu t-taqaddumi wa l-bilā*
*fa mā aʿrifu l-aṭlāla illā tawahhumā*

Time's long procession and decay
have changed them,
And I know no ruins, only pretense.

Similarly in an ode by ʿAbīd Ibn al-Abraṣ, where the linear writ of the *nu'y* appears as it were "dotted" by a *dimnah* still in its surface semantics as "dung remains of the encampment":[37]

*Li man id-dāru aqfarat bi l-janābī*
*ghayra nu'yin wa dimnatin ka l-kitābī*
*Ghayyarathā ṣ-ṣabā wa nafāḥu janūbin*
*wa shamālin tadhrū duqāqa t-turābī*

Whose abode is this that wasted in the yard,
But for a trench and dung spots, writing-like,
Faded by the east wind and by south wind's gusts,
And by the north wind that winnows fine dust?

This iterated presence of the *nu'y* in the poetic visualization of Bedouin habitation forces the modern sensibility—lest it become an outright interloper—not to ask further questions about the conceivable graphic veracity of the image, for in critical terms that image would at best amount to a description of that which already *stands* depicted, but rather to try to proceed past the described to the "in-scribed"—in our case, to that which bespeaks what is "inside" while itself being the circumscription and the outer limit.

An exploration of the etymology of *nu'y*—direct or associative, but poetically productive in either case—ought to be among the most hazardous tasks to undertake. Here the initial simplicity and accessibility of result offered by the classical Arabic philological approach of deverbal derivation will all too soon cast us into a tangle of root associations and overlappings that appear to counteract the very purpose of semantically productive lexicography. This, however, must not be viewed as poetically inoperative. To start with, *nu'y*, the "trench," is presented lexicographically as having only a very limited verbal "base" in *na'ā/an'ā/inta'ā*, "to dig (a trench) around a tent." Here ends the "attested" etymological scope of the word. The remainder of the lexical entry under *na'ā* refers itself to the general range of meaning of "distance": either of "removing" or of "being remote," or of being, or keeping, "aloof," and to "averting" (an evil), etc. Turning to associative roots, which are then separate lexical entries, we obtain the richly productive verbal root of *nawā*, with the meaning of "to intend," "to purpose," but also "to emigrate," and "to go off, be remote from." Here the most indicative noun ought to be *nawan* as "absence," "remoteness," but also as "course," "direction," "end of journey"—and thus "intention."

If the *nu'y* of the Arabic poetic domain is a trench, it is also, as attested by the *locus classicus* of al-Nābighah al-Dhubyānī's ode in *dāl*, "trough-like" (*wa n-nu'ya ka l-ḥawḍi*)[38] and thus perceivable as a containing "vessel," *inā'*. The latter, however, is itself found forcibly displaced into the unrelatable root *'a-n-y/'a-w-n* that denotes "time," "duration," and "patience." Through pure alliteration and lexicographic rigor, which, however, are themselves not wholly devoid of poetically efficacious overtones, *nu'y* conjures ultimately not only a sense of distance-as-space but also that of distance-as-time.

Finally, through the semantics of *na'ā/nawā* we also come up against the root *n-h-w/n-h-y*, denoting "end," "extreme," "limit," "prohibition"; but there, too, we find the word/words *nahy/nuhy* with the meaning of "pond (of stagnating water)," which should bear more closely on our search for the true poetic *nu'y*.

To sort out such a confusing overflow of relations and associations, we must once again turn to the specific textual *nu'y* of the *nasīb* in its most poignant classical contextualization. Thus in the already familiar ode in *dāl* by al-Nābighah al-Dhubyānī:[39]

*Yā dāra Mayyata bi l-ʿalyā'i fa s-sanadī*
*aqwat wa ṭāla ʿalayhā sālifu l-abadī*

*Waqaftu fīhā uṣaylālan usā'iluhā*
*ʿayyat jawāban wa mā bi r-rabʿi min aḥadī*

*Illā l-awariyya la'yan mā ubayyinuhā*
*wa n-nu'ya ka l-ḥawḍi bi l-maẓlūmati l-jaladī*

*Ruddat ʿalayhī aqāṣīhī wa labbadahū*
*ḍarbu l-walīdati bi l-misḥāti fī th-tha'adī*

*Khallat sabīla atiyyin kāna yaḥbisuhū*
*wa raffaʿathū ilā s-sijfayni fa n-naḍadī*

*Aḍḥat qifāran wa aḍḥā ahluhā -ḥtamalū*
*akhnā ʿalayhā lladhī akhnā ʿalā Lubadī*

O abode of Mayyah upon height and peak,
It lies deserted, its old days long since past.

There I halted at evening time, to question it.
There was no answer, and in the *rab*$^{c}$
there was no one,

But for ropes to hobble beasts, that I barely espy,
And the trench, trough-like
in hard compacted ground,

Its outer edges propped, pounded into moist soil
By the slave-maid's strokes of hoe.

She cleared the trench of obstructions
before a coming torrent,
And extended it up to the tent-flaps
and the piled up goods.

It lies deserted now, its folk all packed and gone.
What once brought ancient Lubad down,
ravaged it too.

The poet's elegiac apostrophe to the abandoned abode of his beloved Mayyah (v. 1) leads to his brief "narration" of his halting at the desolate place and to his "questioning" it (v. 2).[40] The narration turns into an equally brief description, or visualization, of the scene (v. 3), and it is there that the *nu'y*, the sole sufficiently discernible relic of the melancholy site, is mentioned—for the hobbling-ropes or nooses to which the former inhabitants' mounts had once been tied (*al-awārī*) are now barely visible. In the subsequent two verses (vv. 4 and 5) the descriptive mode once again changes, becoming a digressive narration in which the "story" of the *nu'y* is told: how it was built, who built it, and what purpose it served. Then, as if stressing that the dynamism of detail of the *nu'y* excursus was not at all meant to interfere with melancholy contemplation but was itself part of an elegiacally contextualized re-creative imagination, the poet, in a clear sweep that signals a closure (v. 6), takes us back to the poem's opening apostrophe, objectivizing it in the manner of an answer and an explanation—and also as a conclusive reinstatement of the elegiac stance. Of the six verses of this elegiac opening section of a pre-Islamic ode, the specific motif with the images of the *nu'y* thus claims the three central ones. The formally framing opening and closing verses of the whole thematic unit are then a reminder that it, the *nu'y* itself, functions only as part of the circle of the poetic meaning that is the *dār*, or more concretely, that it itself is the textually "visible" circumscription of that meaning.

In image after image, poet after poet thus insists on drawing the outer line of the *nu'y* around the inner circle of the *dār*. At some point such iconic repetitiveness must begin to reveal its implicit meaning, not merely its explicit functionality. To approach that implicit meaning we may have to reach out to other functional, and then ultimately symbolic, analogies between the Arabic poetic *nu'y* and its equivalents in other material cultures and in other physical climes.

The first analogy to consider is that between the *nu'y* and the "eaves," or the German *Traufe/Dachtraufe*. In the English, as in the German-Teutonic sense, "eaves"/*Traufe* are the border of the roof that overhangs the wall of the house. As such they are in their "first," visible sense the outer delineation of the inhabited space. From that the archaic northern European concept of protected space may be said to have taken its point of departure. As the word "eaves" reveals through its composite derivative of to "eavesdrop"—which in its modern semantics has brought about a second, associative folk etymology—it represented not only a protected line but also one of *danger*, through which the invasion of the space of protected privacy could occur. The eaves (as pointed out by "eavesdrop"), or the Teutonic *Traufe*, was above all, however, a line of demarcation made visible by the rainwater running down from the roof's edges and drawing a discernible line on the ground; and it was the protective magic force of that drawn line, or of the resulting drain, that was perceived both as the line of safety toward the interior and of danger toward the outside. Physically as well as symbolically, the fall of rainwater about the inhabited space—and the line at which that rainwater was contained—thus had to do with the magic demarcation of protected space.[41] In this respect, Hans Peter Duerr, basing himself largely on the Germanic folklorist Will-Erich Peuckert, notes that "the line demarcated by the water dripping from the eaves delineates the Teutonic homestead, the living space of the extended family, and also the line beyond which demons could not go."[42] But he goes beyond Peuckert's Teutonic scope, adding that "in the Mediterranean region, a furrow was often made around the settlement as a border against demons"[43]—which takes us again back to the myth of the foundation of Rome with its characteristic Plutarchian mythopoeic confusion between, or fusion of, the two symbolic shapes, circular and square, as well as the superposition of the two principal sites, Comitium and the Palatine, one the site of the circular trench *mundus*, which semantically and symbolically is both heaven and earth, and the other the site of Roma Quadrata, which is somehow equally inseparable from the *mundus*. Resigned to the absence of a fully congruous image in Plutarch,[44] but accepting the centrality of his *mundus* with or without Roma Quadrata, we follow him for reasons relevant to us:

> Then, taking this [the *mundus*] as a centre, they marked out the city in a circle round it. And the founder, having shod a plough with a brazen ploughshare, and having yoked to it a bull and a cow, himself drove a deep furrow round the boundary lines, while those who followed after him *had to turn the clods, which the plough threw up, inwards towards the*

> *city, and suffer no clod to lie turned outwards* [my italics]. With this line they mark out the course of the wall, and it is called, by contraction, <pomerium>, that is <post murum>, *behind* or *next the wall.* And where they purposed to put in a gate, there they took the share out of the ground, lifted the plough over, and left a vacant space. And this is the reason why they regard all the wall as sacred except the gates.[45]

According to Plutarch there were thus two circular trenches—or a trench and a furrow—marking the foundation of Rome: one, the *mundus*, forming the center, the other, the furrow, drawing the circumference; furthermore, the first one was meant to be cultic, the second apotropaic[46]—the one "the innermost," the other "the outermost": the magic center and the magic limit.

There should be little doubt that the Arabian *nu'y* dug around the tent corresponds physically to the line of the eaves/*Traufe*, and that its recurrence in a specific poetic context in which every word, as term, possesses a highly concentrated symbolic potential must give to it of its function- and placement-derived symbolism. Especially its apotropaic power is to be assumed—since it is also the abode's, or the settlement's, "limit." One should be able to go even further: into the kind of textual comparison that would reveal in the extended functionality of *nu'y* traits of magical-symbolic specificity. Thus we shall be reminded that in the Plutarchian story of the foundation of Rome the founder "himself drove a deep furrow round the boundary lines, while those who followed after him had to turn the clods, which the plough threw up, inwards towards the city, and suffer no clod to lie turned outwards." Here we must entertain no doubt that the turning of the clods *from the outside of the deep furrow to the inside*, facing the city, has its somehow decisive magical-apotropaic, or symbolic, meaning. We may then proceed and ask ourselves why al-Nābighah al-Dhubyānī, a poet of archaic Arabia, would insist on the *nu'y*'s "outer" ends or edges being propped back in the manner of "being turned back upon it" before being beaten into the moist soil. Is this the so lightly proposed and generalized assumption of "detail consciousness" and "naturalism" of the archaic Arabian poet, or is there in the procedure of building a *nu'y* an element of established custom, a ritual itself not too distant from the apotropaic magic of "founding"?

At this point we should then return to those diverse, false and not so false, concrete as well as only poetically associative, semantic confluences that exist in the ancient *nu'y*: of remoteness, removal, averting evil, migration, purpose, intention, end of journey, and even a vessel that, trough-like, may be both full and empty of water, or one that may even be "on" water.[47]

## *Dimnah* (Dung)

To anyone coming from outside the fold of the Arabic linguistic and literary "in-culturation," no word of the classical Arabic poetic lexicon is more difficult to approach and to tolerate aesthetically, or even in the broadest sense appreciatively, than *dimnah*. The word's *prima facie* semantics clash most frontally with any contextually induced presumption that in it and around it there may cohabit some exquisitely fine strains and echoings of Arabic elegiac lyricism. It invariably strikes in the culturally ill-attuned, literalist, and hastily objectivizing reader's sensibility the kind of discordant tone that threatens to preclude through irony, or to banalize, all supposed poetic intent and all the intimacy of lyricism—for, in an inescapable way, according to all the lexicographical authorities, *dimnah*, with its plural form *diman*, refers itself most stubbornly to dung and, more precisely, to the dung left behind at the site of an encampment. It is lexicographically further specified as the dung of horses or other solid-hoofed animals; but it is also broadened to mean a place "blackened" by human habitation with marks, or traces, left of dung of cattle.[48] The verbal forms of its consonantal "root" are clearly denominative to the extent to which they refer themselves to the meaning of *dimnah* as "dung." Otherwise they pursue what appears to be their own highly strained etymology that through *damala* leads ultimately to *zabala*, now really meaning "to dung." Beyond that, in its verbal meanings, the root *d-m-n* links up with *ḍ-m-n/ḍ-m-r*, with their variations upon the meaning of "hiding," "concealment," "harboring" (negatively as well as positively), and "containing." All of this, and especially the etymologically unencumbered, or unmitigated, meaning of the nominal form *dimnah/diman* as "dung," seems to have little bearing on the elegiacally lyrical presence and efficacy of the word. The poetic transmutation of meaning in *dimnah*, away from every demystifying semantic concretization, is so complete that even its translation, which all too easily would undo its lyrical aura, is best avoided—at least for the purposes of much of the present discussion. Only a few examples from the most nearly archaic Bedouin poetic repertory will suffice to lead us into the otherwise already familiar world of the elegiac *nasīb* opening through this, perhaps the most lyrical of all the Arabic poetic gateways, which is the *dimnah/diman*.

Thus, beginning with Imru' al-Qays,[49] we already have a *nasīb* with an implicitly full elegiac scope of the meaning of *dimnah*:

*Li man id-diyāru ghashītuhā bi suḥāmī*
*fa ʿAmāyatayni fa haḍbi dhī Aqdāmī?*

Whose abodes are these, there where I stood perplexed
—At Suḥām, and at ʿAmāyatayn, and at the rise
of Mount Aqdām?

Over these, first unknown (v. 1) and then barely recognized (v. 3) abodes/*diyār*, the poet calls upon his two companions to halt and weep with him as had once done the legendary Ibn Khidhām (v. 4). For the litter-borne maidens (*ẓaʿāʾin*) have long since departed (vv. 5 and 6). Only the poet stands there as if intoxicated (v. 7). We are thus at the point of a recapitulation of the poet's *wuqūf* (halting), or at its culmination; and here, too, i.e. in verse 7, occurs the poetically not at all awkward but clearly somehow unique word *diman*:

*Fa ẓaliltu fī dimani d-diyāri ka'annanī*
*nashwānu bākarahū ṣabūḥu mudāmī*

And among the abodes' *diman* (dung remains)
I stayed on
As if I were inebriate of morning wine.

Another early poet, al-Nābighah al-Dhubyānī, will even favor the mentioning of *dimnah* in his odes' opening verses. Thus in the ode whose *nasīb* is devoted to Nuᶜm, the beloved that bears the name that suggests no less than celestial grace:[50]

*ᶜŪjū fa ḥayyū li Nuᶜmin dimnata d-dārī*
*mādhā tuḥayyūna min nu'yin wa aḥjārī*

Turn off the road, then halt and greet
the *dimnah* of Nuᶜm's abode—
But what trench and what hearthstone
shall you greet?

Or in the opening of his *nasīb* for the "tyrannous" Ẓallāmah, whose name could also have been an epithet for the same woman that he had once called Grace and Happiness (Nuᶜm):[51]

*A min Ẓallāmata d-dimanu l-bawālī*
*bi murfaddi l-Ḥubayyi ilā Wuᶜālī*

Are these Ẓallāmah's faded *diman*,
Where sands spread at Ḥubayy, toward Wuᶜāl?

A further, elegiacally effective early characteristic of the *dimnah* was the perception of its ancientness, as when the equally pre-Islamic Bishr Ibn Abī Khāzim implies that his poetic *dimnah* is an *ᶜādiyyah*, that is, as ancient as the lost race of ᶜĀd:[52]

*A min dimnatin ᶜādiyyatin lam ta'annasī*
*bi siqṭi l-liwā bayna l-kathībi fa ᶜasᶜasī*

There, at the drifting crest,
between sand-dune and mirage,
Is there an ancient *dimnah* to kindness mute?

But the semanticity of *dimnah/diman*—and of its variants such as *dimn*—may also be mixed and overlapping with its other true, or false, etymologies. For instance, the presence in verse 15 of ʿAntarah's *Muʿallaqah* of the verb *taḍamm-ana* with its meaning of "to comprise," "to comprehend," or "to secure"—just as the loins of a stallion "comprise" progeny—should indicate a perception on the part of the poet of the existence of a semantic bond between the connotative yields of *ḍ-m-n* and *d-m-n* that goes beyond mere alliteration, particularly since in that case, *dimn*, as "dung," finds itself in an insinuating antithesis to its *fructifying* context:[53]

*Aw rawḍatan unufan taḍammana nabtahā*
*ghaythun qalīlu d-dimni laysa bi maʿlamī*

Or an untrodden meadow, its verdure sheltered,
its grass rain-grown,
Of few remains of dung [*dimn*], to man unknown.

ʿAntarah's verse thus points to the actual, poetically effective possibility of a textually attested occurrence of our term in question as "dung." And yet, even in the context of that verse we are told that such dung "is rare" (*qalīlu d-dimni*), and that its rarity may be due to its being excluded, as it were, from the interdicted and privileged space which the poet perceives as *rawḍatan unufan*, but which we know is also the poet's beloved in her quality of metaphor for the archetypal *locus amoenus*—or vice versa. The specific context of *nasīb* lyricism thus retains its meaning-forming hold over the connotative depth of *dimnah* even there where it is intentionally kept recognizable as "dung." A further, for the etymologist perhaps disconcerting, but poetically possible, meaning of *dimnah/diman* is that of "long and deeply harbored grudge" or "deep-rooted hatred," as in the verse of Zuhayr Ibn Abī Sulmā:[54]

*Yaṭlubu bi l-witri aqwāman fa yudrikuhum*
*ḥīnan wa lā yudriku l-aʿdā'u bi d-dimanī*

He seeks out men to find revenge,
and he attains them in due time,
But never do the enemies effect
their hatred's depth.

Here, however, *diman* is etymologically relatable only to the consonantal root *ḍ-m-n*, as we had encountered it in the above-mentioned verse by ʿAntarah. We could also take into consideration the further implied variant of *ḍ-m-r* (cf. *ḍamīr*). As such it speaks of something "contained," "hidden," "buried," and "re-pressed." Once there is added to such a basic semantic grid the negative burden of *diman* (whose "unpleasantness" must in some manner vent itself perceptually as well), together with the additional verbal root of *damara* that denotes "destruction" and "ruin"—and which is a negative semantic mirror image of *ḍ-m-n/ḍ-m-r*—there becomes possible the composite meaning of the "hidden, repressed, and long-standing grudge." Especially the long duration of such a state of mind is stressed by scholiasts. Thus in al-Aṣmaʿī's comment regarding this meaning of *dimnah* as it bears on Zuhayr's verse, we read that "enmity shall not be a *dimnah* unless extended time passes over it."[55] Even "grudge" and "hatred," therefore, when seen as *dimnah*, share in the common denominator of the word's elegiac, *nasīb*-rooted meaning, which is the necessary perception of time as "old" or as "antiquity." We may then, ultimately, not have strayed that far afield from the *dimnah ʿādiyyah* of Bishr Ibn Abī Khāzim. In this central respect, too, *dimnah* may be further identified as being characteristic principally of the usage of the poets of the Jāhilī period—in contrast to the word's expanded connotative properties in the poetry of the Umayyad and Abbasid periods.

This latency of the sense of antiquity in the Jāhilī elegiac *dimnah* may be contextualized poetically in diverse ways—some pointing to that condition directly, some indirectly. ʿAbīd Ibn al-Abraṣ, in whose verse *dimnah* is a frequently recurring topos, sees in it once the "remains of the *dimnah* of ruins" (*baqāyā min dimnati l-aṭlālī*) within an old encampment's "tracings laid bare over the passage of years" (*wa rusūman ʿurrīna mudh aḥwālī*);[56] then again as the futility of "an old man's weeping at a *dimnah*, while already total hoariness crowns his head";[57] and even more saliently, ʿAbīd Ibn al-Abraṣ epitomizes the oldest Bedouin poetry's frequent, imagist as well as conceptual, association of the abandoned encampment's *dimnah* with traces of ancient writing:[58]

*Li man id-dāru aqfarat bi l-janābī*
*ghayra nu'yin wa dimnatin ka l-kitābī*

Whose abode is this that wasted at the yard,
But for a trench and a *dimnah*, writing-like?

And elsewhere he dwells on this motif again in a recognizably paraphrastic way, making such *dimnah* writing appear as though it were a retraced palimpsest:[59]

*Li man dimnatun aqwat bi ḥarrati Ḍarghadī*
*talūḥu ka ʿunwāni l-kitābi l-mujaddadī*

Whose *dimnah* is this, that lies deserted
at the black basalt track of Ḍarghad,
Emerging like a book's border lettering redrawn.

In his *Muʿallaqah*, Labīd,[60] too, builds the abandoned abodes (*diyār*) of the ode's verse 1 together with the *diman* of verse 3 into a palimpsest-like double image of retrieved ancient writing, first as the product of the hand of nature imitating that of man (v. 2): "as stone slabs guard the written word" (*kamā ḍamina l-wuḥiyya silāmuhā*), where the verb *ḍamina* seems to signal the phonetically inverted *diman* that opens verse 3:

*Dimanun tajarrama baᶜda ᶜahdi anīsihā*
*ḥijajun khalawna ḥalāluhā wa ḥarāmuhā*

*Diman*—after their turn of life in concord,
Yet more years passed and ran their course—
of months sanctioned and proscribed.

Then, in verse 8, those faded traces of habitation come to resemble to the poet's eyes "scrolls of writing penned anew by writing reeds" (*ka'annahā zuburun tujiddu mutūnahā aqlāmuhā*). Likewise the poet Thaᶜlabah Ibn ᶜAmr al-ᶜAbdī begins a *qaṣīdah*:[61]

*Li man dimanun ka'anna hunna ṣaḥā'ifū*
*qifārun khalā minhā l-Kathību fa Wāḥifū*

Whose are the *diman* like parchment written on:
A desolation, Kathīb and Wāḥif, their people gone!

This pre-Islamic, and also *mukhaḍram* (transitional), perception of *dimnah/diman* as referential to a "pastness" which is abstracted from a personal or experiential sense of time and which tries, as it were, to reach out to still graspable archetypes, or merely icons, of that receded domain of time, changes rather abruptly with the advent of the Umayyad age. From there on *dimnah* becomes a purely lyrical "time-place," not unlike M. M. Bakhtin's *chronotope*,[62] with a fully internalized referentiality of meaning as well as of a more expressedly personal poetic validity. As such, the *dimnah* finds its place within the Bedouinizing poet's sensibility with great pervasiveness. It is as part of that development that the accommodation of the dictionary meaning of the word *dimnah* becomes uncompromisingly challenging to a new, internalizing sensibility, and with it to any hermeneutics of Arabic lyricism. If the *dār* of the *nasīb* opening of the *qaṣīdah* is now on its way toward becoming the poet's heart, what will then be the place of the lexicographer's *dimnah*—both in the *dār* and in the heart?

The ᶜUdhrī poet ᶜUrwā Ibn Ḥizām represents very closely the textual dividing line of the passage from still archaic pastoral semiotics to the semiotics of the new internalized sensibility:[63]

*Alā yā ghurābay dimnati d-dāri khabbirā*
*a bi l-bayni min ᶜArfā'a tantaḥibānī*

*Fa in ḥaqqan mā taqūlāni fa -nhaḍā*
*bi laḥmī ilā wakraykumā fa kulānī*

O you two crows of the abode's *dimnah*, tell me:
Is it ʿAfrā''s departure that you bemoan?

For, if what you say is true, then
To your nests carry my flesh—and gorge on me!

In these verses the poet apostrophizes the two "crows of separation" indirectly through another studiedly archaizing motif: because of the introduction of the number two from an equally *nasīb*-derived topos of the "two companions" that console, or berate, the poet for his self-indulgence in melancholy. But the two crows are here in the first degree "the two crows of the *dimnah* of the abode." Only with these implied notions in mind are we given to entertain the visually "direct" image of two actual crows hopping over plausibly concrete "dung remains" (*dimnah*) of an abandoned Bedouin abode. Poetry and folklore, however, have added to such a scene the further semiotics of "broadcasting a message of separation"—this on top of the archaic meaning of "witnessed destruction," or of an even more deeply set latency of ill omen. In the sensibility of the no-longer-archaic poet, the first connotative meaning of the motif of the two crows at the *dimnah* may thus have been very skillfully employed, but for that, too, it may be almost perfunctory in its taken-for-granted implication. A weightier, or more "active," second sense is undoubtedly being here communicated as well—but only to the degree to which the two crows of ill omen are to be understood as also representing the two doves of primarily post-Jāhilī Arabic lyrical poetry, where they empathetically bemoan, rather than premonitorily signal or announce, the lovers' separation. Even though the paired—but poetically fated to be separated—doves are birds which in their archaic semiotics are no less tragic[64] than the crow, in the poetry of the Umayyad period their elegiac-idyllic connotation of meaning was already conveniently attuned to the ambiguities—and even polarizing tensions—of a love lyric: between the bittersweetness of the language of accommodated, melancholy-mellowed sorrow and the quickened rhetoric of the conceit of pathos.

Past the Umayyad period the contrast, and indeed the incompatibility, between the *dimnah* of the lexicographers and that of poetic usage comes to the foreground even more. To the Abbasid poet al-Buḥturī, the *diman* fully replace the enunciation of the *dār*/abode as the elegiac contours of habitation—and even the elegiac mood itself, centered in the *diman*, becomes easily modulated into idyll:[65]

*Dimanun janaytu bihā l-hawā min ghuṣnihī*
*wa saḥabtu fīhā l-lahwa saḥba l-muṭrafī*

*Diman*—where I cropped
love's passion from its bough,
And where I strutted in pleasure's silken robe.

Or again, in an almost exploratory reiteration of phrasing that comes even closer to the archetypal core that *diman* now reveals:[66]

*Dimanun raḍaʿtu bihinna akhlāfa ṣ-ṣibā*
*law lam yakun baʿda r-raḍāʿi fiṭāmuhū*

*Diman*, where I sucked from the breast of youth—
O would that after nursing weaning had not come!

Also in al-Buḥturī, it may at times be the editors, or the copiers, or perhaps even the poet himself who will fail to distinguish, or will lightheartedly hasten to restore, the "textual correctness" of a "*dimnah* of their tribe" (*dimnatun min ḥayyihim*), when it appears as "a *dimnah* of their love" (*dimnatun min ḥubbihim*). This will be attempted even in a highly abstraction-bent, metaphorizing context in which "parting" itself has become the poet's "native soil":[67]

*Alifū l-firāqa ka'annahū waṭanun lahum*
*lā yaqrubūna ilayhi ḥattā yabʿudū*

*Fī kulli yawmin dimnatun min ḥayyihim*
*tuqwī wa rabʿun minhumū yata'abbadū*

They grew familiar with separation as though
parting were their native ground:
No sooner approaching than it is time to part.

Each day a *dimnah* of their tribe [of their love]
Lies waste, and after them a spring abode
turns wild.

Furthermore, also in al-Buḥturī, we find *diman* turned into no less than the guiding stars of travelers lost in the space of love:[68]

*Dimanun mawāthilu ka n-nujūmi fa in ʿafat*
*fa bi ayyi najmin fī ṣ-ṣabābati nahtadī*

*Diman*, looming before us like stars—
but should they fade,
By what star then, in love's ways,
shall we be led?

To another eminent Abbasid lyricist, al-Sharīf al-Murtaḍā, *diman* are star-like as well. He looks at them through the tears in his eyes, and they turn into stars, prism-refracted:[69]

*Dimanun law ranat ilayhinna ʿaynā /*
*ka qubayla l-firāqi qulta: nujūmū*

*Diman*—had your eyes gazed on them
On the eve of parting, you'd have said: Stars!

And to throw a studiedly discordant, pessimistic note into the elegiac serenity of Abbasid *dimnah* lyricism, there comes al-Sharīf al-Murtaḍā's contemporary and aestheticist follower, Mihyār al-Daylamī:[70]

*Dimanun ka masḥabati l-azim /*
*mati musḥalan imrāruhā*

*Mātat ḥaqā'iquhā wa khul /*
*lida zūruhā wa muʿāruhā*

*Diman*, as faint as traces left
By trailing single-stranded reins.

Whatever truth was in them died,
And what was false and borrowed
withstood time.

It is, however, once again al-Sharīf al-Murtaḍā who helps us most of all to grasp the extent, and also the simplicity, of the independence of the Abbasid lyrical *dimnah* from extrapoetic semantic entanglements. To him—as poet and, we should be able to say, as aesthete—there is an intrinsic bond of relationships between elegiac melancholy, *diman*, and happiness:[71]

*Fa immā shi'tumā an tusʿidānī*
*fa murrā bī ʿalā d-dimani l-bawālī*

But if you wish to make me happy,
Take me to where the wasted *diman* are.

Such a verse stands out as a quintessential statement on the Arabic poetic meaning of *dimnah/diman*. In the Arabic context of the producing as well as of the receiving sensibility it is as strong, lyrically direct, and simple as is Goethe's *Kennst du das Land, wo die Zitronen blühn*[72] in the context of that poet's, and that poetic culture's, straddling of an already escaping Classicism and a not yet arrived Romanticism.

But in Arabic poetry the yearning that is capable of harboring its own paradoxical objectivization of the scene of happiness in the capsule of one word is also, through that word, directly linked to the presence of something that is dark, remote, and incubating—all the things which the word *dimnah* comprises somehow within, and beyond, its known semantics and origin. Such things are not easily explained or touched upon by even the most pristine lyrical stances of other poets in other poetic cultures born of other matrices of sensibility.

As one steps sufficiently far back, however, into precisely those darknesses, distances, and incubatory recesses of words—of a word such as *dimnah*—one may just possibly find one's way to older, stranger, but nonetheless culturally bridging poetic and symbolic stances. Let us thus return to the poetic-semantic conundrum of *dimnah* through a number of seemingly unrelated but nevertheless hermeneutically converging avenues.

1. Mindful of the difficulty of defining the meaning of *dimnah* positively, perhaps we should find it easier to propose for it a *negative*, antonymic pairing through which to gain further insight—or perhaps only an added circumspection. The antonym to the whole connotative scope of *dimnah* in the poetry of the *nasīb* is the Arabic term, and concept, *wiṣāl* ("amorous union"); for *dimnah* excludes *wiṣāl* as much as *wiṣāl* excludes *dimnah*. Where *dimnah* lives, *wiṣāl* dies. And yet, as we had seen in our primary attempt at establishing a likely etymological range for *dimnah*, one of the indirectly active meanings in the word's "root" might well be that of "to contain," and thus "to bring together." Conversely, *wiṣāl* bears the burden of its own clearly antinomic connection with the root *f-ṣ-l*, denoting "separation."[73] Broadly connotatively, we may thus be dealing here with only one idea: that of rejected, or unfulfilled, love. As such, in poetry's erotic realm, this idea of *dimnah* is reflected as one of the strongest archetypes, and as such, too, it ought to be found translated into the realm of the myth. Admittedly, we have a notorious difficulty with that latter realm in our ways of looking at Arabic poetry. We shall, therefore, avail ourselves in a seconding manner of a Greek antonymic/synonymic, decidedly mythical analogue, namely that of Mintha/Iunx.

Mintha, or Mint, was a nymph who, in her chthonic quality, was the concubine of the god of the underworld, Hades. Her relationship with the god was thus distinctly *illicit*. Displaced in Hades's favors by Persephone, the god's *licit* wife, she vainly threatened recourse to spells of seduction. For that she was punished by being changed into the aromatic plant *mint*. In classical Greek erotic pharmacology this plant was believed to have the property of making women sterile or of preventing them from conceiving when applied before intercourse. In that it had a negative effect on sperm and, as Marcel Detienne points out in the same context of ancient Greek pharmacopoeia, "While it excites sexual desire, mint prevents that desire from being productive."[74] This imputed enfeebling characteristic of mint is also reflected in the interdiction to eat or grow mint during wartime.[75] Marcel Detienne also notes "the links established by Greek lexicographers between the name of the plant *míntha* and the word *mínthos* which is its synonym but which also denotes goat's dung, human excrement and other equally foul-smelling substances."[76]

Significantly to us, this mint/Mintha that stimulates erotically as both concubine and aromatic plant, but that also leads to infertility or abortion, and which even displays an etymology that connects it with substances such as "dung" and "excrement," is then also linked by Zenodotus of Ephesus, the first librarian of the Museum of Alexandria, to the nymph/bird Iunx, by whose name Mintha was also known.[77] The nymph Iunx, herself transformed into the bird iunx, which is the wryneck, was then used in ancient Greek seduction magic—originally as spread crosswise and tied to a whirling wheel, and then as that wheel itself. The magic of that iunx/wheel was believed to have the power to *join* lovers together. It is here that the combination of Mintha and Iunx as one mythological and symbolic syncresis should enable us to contextualize symbolically in Arabic poetry the mutual exclusion, and at the same time attraction, of *dimnah* and *wiṣāl*—of their consension and their paradox: of a *dimnah* that in its poetic semantics is so strongly metathetically attracted to Mintha, and a *wiṣāl* that is not just a symbolic equivalent of Iunx but a semantic one as well—even if the resulting etymology of *iunx*, though capable of producing the meaning of *wiṣāl*, may be merely one of "attraction." Otherwise there is the Arabic specific term for the plant "mint." It is *naʿnaʿ* or *naʿnāʿ*, and in Arab folklore today, especially in Iraq, it remains a plant that instills the fear of male impotence. Men decidedly refuse to add it to their tea whenever they expect to have sexual intercourse.

2. A wholly recessive further avenue to explore is that of the ambivalent quality of putrefaction that is latent in *dimnah* as part of the paradox of its poetic use—a quality in which Piero Camporesi would certainly detect those "micro-demons of transformatory growth, of transmogrified matter" that lead to "reproduction *ex putri*," the "will-o'-the-wisp whose habitual lair was a dung-heap, . . . or the moist and frothy warmth of manure."[78] Even the sacred place of the "solar" Apollo's oracles is a "place of putrefaction" before the god's seasonal summer return from the Hyperboreans.[79] And shall we otherwise be shocked or repelled by the Arabic poetic exaltation of their campsite *dimnah*, knowing that already the ancient Egyptians had seen in it a substance worthy of symbolizing the sun itself? They connected the dung beetle's "nesting" of its eggs inside dung, and then the rolling of that dung up into a ball and pushing it with vigor and patience to a hatching place, with their idea of the sun's being kept on its course by a cosmic scarab. The sun's energy and the sun's movement were associated with the vital regenerative energy of the "fertilized" dung ball and with that dung ball's inherently purposeful, "chartered" movement along the ground.

The mystifying association of a dung ball with the life-giving sun and the bestowing of cosmic properties upon the dung beetle is then also given its precarious symbolic equilibrium by associating dung heaps with death and with places of burial. The most interesting such association comes to us from Strabo's *Geography* (16.4.24), in which that classical author records a report on some funerary customs of the Nabataeans of Petra. "They," Strabo relates, "have the same regard for the dead as for dung . . . , and therefore they bury even their kings beside dung-heaps."[80] Since, as historical and archaeological scholarship affirms, such a custom could not be said to have had general validity in Nabataean Petra,[81] we must attribute even greater attention to the statement that it was the kings of the Nabataeans who were deserving of such a distinct form of burial, even if that be no more than an archaizing continuation, or resumption, of the funerary practice of 'Ritual Exposure' of the dead—itself most likely of Iranian origin—that must have reached Petra with the Parthian incursions into Syria.[82] On the other hand, already in 1885, Charles Simon Clermont-Ganneau had suggested that in Strabo's reference to dead kings and dung heaps we may have an underlying confusion between the Nabataean word for "tomb" and the Greek word for "dung heap," that is, between *kfr* (Aramaic *kafār*, *kafrā*), both "village" and "tomb" in Nabataean usage, and *kopron*, the Greek "dunghill."[83]

Between the suggestion of a Nabataean 'Ritual Exposure' theory and the possibility that Strabo's report may reflect his own, or his source's, lexical superposition of a purely philological nature, we might propose—on the basis of our literary experience with the ancient, as well as the semantically evolving but still "classical" Arabic, *dimnah*—that, even if there had been a homographic or homonymic conflux of "grave" and "dung heap" in Strabo's text, this must not necessarily be considered as philological confusion that calls for an emendation. Here, as in many literary-textual instances, associative "misprision" may be the bearer of its own meaning, with even an ultimate tantalizing philological validation. For, as much as *kafr/kafār/kafrā* can legitimately lead phonetically to an Arabic/Semitic *ghafara* ("to cover," "to hide," "to conceal"), as well as to *qabara* (to bury), beyond the narrowest substantivization of "village," it can also point in the semantic-symbolic direction of a self-renewing, chthonic process, whose issue is precisely a chthonic reemergence of "life." It thus contains the characteristic semantic circularity of the paradox: of having to die in order to live and of having to live in order to die.[84] On that level we may accommodate, with some ease, even the cultural-anthropological phenomenon of 'Ritual Exposure' and, of course, the Egyptian cosmic scarab/dung beetle as well. Here, too, Shakespeare's Henry V makes further sense, even beyond the level of that magnificent rhetorical bravado, as he responds to the French herald Montroy before the battle on St. Crispin's day:

> And those that leave their valiant bones in France,
> Dying like men, though buried in your dunghills,
> They shall be fam'd; for there the sun shall greet them.
>
> [*Henry V* iv.3 (99)]

This once again takes us back to the Arabic dichotomy between the literalist lexicographic semanticity of *dimnah* and its poetic denial of the exclusivity of such semantics. This dichotomy tolerates and even welcomes the generative semantics of sublexicographic etymology. It thus arrives at meanings such as "hiding," "concealing," "harboring," and "containing" and, through them, comes full circle to those royal Nabataean "burials by the dung-heaps," that are called not villages but graves and dunghills and that should not be philologically "emended" but rather supplemented by eventual Greek homonyms which, at some levels of the "disease of language," may not even be mere homonyms. So, too, somewhere between the semiotics of those reported Nabataean burial customs and the semantic diapason of the Arabic poetic *dimnah*, there may be placed the "idiom" *khaḍrā' al-diman* with its still strong inner dynamics of metaphor. Thus, in a *ḥadīth*, the Prophet Muḥammad is reported to have said: "Beware of the green shoot of the dung heap," adding, "that is, the beautiful woman of bad stock."[85] In a metaphor/idiom such as this we are given both fascination and refusal, beauty and corruption—a biological corruption, however, out of which beauty comes to life through a morally neutral process. Upon this moral neutrality that is somehow as inseparable from beauty as it is from life, a nonbiological, that is, moral, rigor of subordinated life is then imposed by "usage." At that point we forget the richer metaphor and are left with the semantically snug idiom.[86]

3. No matter how reluctantly, here we should also take cognizance of the metathetic homonym of *dimnah/diman* which is the Scandinavian/Danish, and ultimately English, *midden*, also meaning "dung," "dunghill," "an accumulation of refuse about a dwelling place: a refuse heap": also "kitchen *midden*"; and "the highly organic soil deposited by an earthworm about its burrow," etc. It also occurs in compounds such as *middenhead* ("the top of a dunghill") and *middenstead* ("the site of a dunghill").[87] Here the organic *putri* associated with habitation and with chthonic renewal of life (note the etymologically relatable *muck*) comes as close to the Arabic *dimnah* as does its homonymic phonetics.

4. To pursue further some suggestive ambiguities, we shall return to "concrete" Semitic root relationships of *dimnah*, such as those found between Arabic and Hebrew. Thus in the latter we have the familiar root *d-m-n*, "to prepare," "to improve," "to manure land." Derivations are here denominative, not unlike in Arabic. Their nominal form/matrix ought to be that of *domen*, meaning "dung," which, however, was apparently originally a reference to corpses lying on the ground as offal.[88] It should not be too farfetched to feel reminded at this point of what we already know of the Nabataean royal burials. Then, attested in biblical Hebrew, there are several place names, or rather names of towns, of *d-m-n* etymology. Thus *Dimnah*, a Levitical city in Zebulun;[89] then also *Madmenah*, a town/place near Jerusalem[90]—a word which otherwise means "dung place" or "dung pit";[91] and *Madmannah*, a city of southern Judah.[92]

The fact that the root underlying *dimnah/domen* could produce in Hebrew a number of names of cities or designations of inhabited places ought to be of some further semiotically triggering relevance to us; for it is perhaps also worth looking into the nonetymological but, because of its metathetic homonymity, still strongly associative, firstly Aramaic, then also Hebrew as well as Arabic, term *madīnah* as "city"/"province"/"district." In Hebrew we come across it as a rule—and only with one exception in I Kings 20:14—in texts from the Persian period: Esther 1:1, 3; Ezra 2:1; Nehemia 1:3. The fact of its distinct lateness in the biblical text and of its connection with specifically Persian administrative terminology may, furthermore, be helpful in relating it to its earliest textual evidence in Arabic poetry as well as in the Qur'ān, although in the latter it receives not a Persian contextualization but an anecdotal Egyptian pharaonic one that is nonetheless stylistically kindred.[93]

The term *madīnah* itself, as shared semantically by Hebrew, Aramaic, and Arabic, claims its derivation from the root *d-y-n*, however, meaning both "to judge" and "to plead one's case (in court)." As such, it corresponds in its morphology to the feminine of the Arabic passive participial form. It would thus be a "judged," or "administered," social or political unit of inhabited space—only then lexicographically noted as a province, district, or city. This Arabic passive participial derivation, however, may not be easily applied to either Aramaic or Hebrew, because in those languages the form *mafᶜūl(ah)*, which is the Arabic morphological mold for *madīnah*, does not exist. A nonparticipial nominal Aramaism (of place) is thus to be assumed. The difficulty in an all too facile Arabization of the term also comes to the surface when we consider its specifically Arabic plural form, *madā'in*, which does not conform to the passive participial root derivation from *d-y-n*, but which suggests rather the hypothetical singular *faᶜīlah/madīnah*, based on the consonantal root *m-d-n*, thus offering a familiarly "associative" semantic and semiotic perception in spite of its quarrel with a philological correctness that appears poetically and symbolically unreceptive.

So much we may obtain chiefly from the term's Hebrew, and also Aramaic (Dan. 2:48, 49; 3:1–3, 12, 30), usage. In the Arabic case we observe above all the absence of the word *madīnah* from the pre-Islamic poetic lexicon altogether. The first poets to incorporate it into their verse are of the transitional period between Jāhilīyah and Islam, called the *mukhaḍram* generation. Thus ᶜAbdah Ibn al-Ṭabīb will refer to it in his ode from the first Islamic campaigns of the conquest of Sassanid Iraq. His beloved, Khawlah, had followed the warring expedition and had settled in a camp "neighboring the people of the city domains," or *al-madā'in*, the Sassanid palace-capital of Ctesiphon.[94] For us to notice is the fact that *al-madā'in* in this ode is mentioned in the second verse of the *nasīb*—precisely there where most other poems would have in evidence their archaic elegiac *dimnah/diman*.

Otherwise, too, an unmitigated archaic sense of the elegiac, and even of the tragic, is supportively projected in Arabic legend and mythopoesis—but not quite in poetry—by the same plural form of *madā'in* ("city domains"), when used toponymically, as Madā'in Ṣāliḥ to designate the old Nabataean-Thamūdic mercantile and mortuary rock city of al-Ḥijr.

Accordingly, even when in the first Islamic decades poets actually begin to mention the newly Islamic city of Medina itself, it is as a place of little cheer. Thus the *mukhaḍram* Ḍābi' Ibn al-Ḥārith Ibn Arṭāh al-Burjumī complains of his imprisonment in Medina:[95]

*Man yaku amsā bi l-Madīnati raḥluhū*
*fa innī wa Qayyārun bihā la gharībū*

If there are those who with the evening
set down their saddles in Medina,
I and my mount Qayyār are strangers there.

Throughout the Umayyad period the occurrence of *madīnah* remains infrequent in poetry, restricted to traditional *nasīb* or *nasīb*-like contexts, as, for instance, when the panegyrist al-Akhṭal places it in one of his odes' *nasīb* extension in which the careful tillage of a vineyard is described. That description is then still worded in a manner reminiscent of al-Nābighah al-Dhubyānī's careful digging of a *nu'y* trench, although al-Akhṭal places it into the further, strongly evocative context of *ḥajir/ḥijr*, which, as a place-name, had itself come to be called Madā'in (Ṣāliḥ):[96]

*Rabat wa rabā fī ḥijrihā -bnu mudaynatin*
*yaẓallu ʿalā misḥātihī yatarakkalū*

It grew, and in its [interdicted] fold there grew
a borough's son [*-bnu mudaynatin*],
His tilling foot constantly on the spade.

Ruins of campsites, ruins of cities, and always dunghills—decay all, but seemingly of two natures: of the melancholy of memory and the stubborn latency of culture's endurance, and then, again, of the greater and even more stubborn latency of self-regenerating biological force and joy of life. *Khaḍrā'u d-dimani* sounds different then. And from Shakespeare's Henry V, with the defying pathos of heroic bones lying buried in dunghills, one can walk in a straight line to the eighteenth-century Ukrainian poet Ivan Kotlarevs'kiy, whose double-edged travesty of Vergil's *Aeneid*, although no longer pathos-laden, remains symbolically unscathed in the reverberations of its image and diction:[97]

But when the Greeks burned Troy to ash
They turned it into middenstead.

Did Troy, then, really perish when it fell?—And thus, through this philologically admittedly venturesome excursus into etymologies that are semantic reechoings, we may yet return to the Arabic poetic *dimnah* with a sense of unpremeditated, perhaps undeserved, comfort.

### *Athāfī* (Hearthstones)

Compared with the multiple difficulties of finding much needed hermeneutical assistance to unlock the poetic semantics of *dimnah/diman*, our next Arabic lyrical key word, the *athāfī*, should appear almost devoid of complications—at least as regards the word's immediate fitting into a "poeticity" of meaning. It means "hearthstones"—but only such as are three in number. It purveys, therefore, a rudimentary idea of the tripod, and its morphological "plurality" may be said to fall formally into the category of *pluralia tantum*, although lexicographically as well as in isolated prose instances—but hardly ever textually-poetically[98]—it possesses the singular form, or forms, of *uthfīyah/ithfīyah*. In its textual attestation, *athāfī* is a word as firmly part of the most archaic Arabic poetic diction as is its contextual companion, *dimnah*. It does not, however, present any problems of taste adjustment and aesthetic sufferance—the sort *dimnah* cannot but presuppose. Linked to the image of desolation which pervades the opening stance of the *nasīb*, the *athāfī*, with all their primary semantic clarity, are, however, not a semiotically "neutral" or in a rough sense denotative lexical item either. Their mere enunciation brings up strong images and sensations of emptiness, loss, melancholy, and even tragedy. The sense of melancholy, or nostalgia, is even present in those rare instances when the *athāfī* are found in primarily narrative prose texts—such as the retelling of the otherwise quite mundane circumstances of the Prophet Muḥammad's encamping during the Raid of al-ʿUshayrah.[99] In the first degree this is the case because of the presence in the mind of the store of textual echoes that the word leaves behind through its ubiquitousness in the most elegiac of classical Arabic *nasīb* openings. But as "tripod," the *athāfī* also strike more archetypal echoes—among them being the symbolically generated inevitable implicitness of the number three. Even as a proverb, *thālithatu l-athāfī* (the third one of the *athāfī*) means the final stroke of ill fortune, supreme affliction, or impending death.[100] To a degree, it thus implies something which the tripod of the hearth has in common with the tripod of the oracle. Then, too, without going beyond purely Arabic etymology, we recognize the connection not only between the "root" of *al-athāfī* (*th-f-y*) and the antonymic pair *dafi'a* (to be warm) and *ṭafi'a* (to be extinguished [fire]), but also between it (*th-f-y*) and the metathetic root *t-f-th*, as in *tafitha* (to abandon oneself to filth), or rather as in the textually firmer qur'ānic and subsequently ritual-terminological nominal form *tafath* (filth [bodily]),[101] and also as in *taffatha* (to stain, contaminate, [a place] with blood).[102] Finally, not to be excluded is the associative onomatopoeia of expectoration (*taffa*), denoting disgust, as in *tuffan laka* (Fie! Shame on you!).

But before venturing further into semantic and etymological ramifications of the *athāfī* when they are textually and referentially increasingly extrapoetic—and ultimately also other-than-Arabic—we should appeal to the testimony of the word's unmitigated Arabic poetic currency in the context of the elegiac opening scene of the abandoned abode in the *nasīb*. Also, we shall proceed from a literal enunciation of the term *athāfī* to its figured substitutes. Thus we find in the *Muʿallaqah* of Zuhayr Ibn Abī Sulmā:[103]

*Waqaftu bihā min baʿdi ʿishrīna ḥijjatan*
*fa la'yan ʿaraftu d-dāra baʿda tawahhumī*

*Athāfiyya sufʿan fī muʿarrasi mirjalin*
*wa nu'yan ka jidhmi l-ḥawḍi lam yatathallamī*

There I stopped, twenty seasons past,
But the abode, although surmised, I hardly knew:

Fire-blackened hearthstones where a cauldron stood
of an overnight halting place,
And a trench not flood-washed,
like a trunk-hewn trough.

Or in what remains as the opening verse of a poem by another pre-Islamic bard, al-Muraqqish the Elder:[104]

*Hal taʿrifu d-dāra ʿafā rasmuhā*
*illā l-athāfiyya wa mabnā l-khiyamī*

Do you know the abode, its trace effaced,
But for hearthstones and tent base?

So, too, in the already *mukhaḍram* al-Ḥuṭay'ah:[105]

*Yā dāra Hindin ʿafat illā athāfīhā*
*bayna ṭ-ṭawiyyi fa ṣārātin fa wādīhā*

O abode of Hind, effaced but for its hearthstones,
There with the stone-cased well,
the mountain-ridges, the dry riverbed.

And yet, already in the pre-Islamic *qaṣīdah* it is possible to find the *athāfī* appearing far removed from the *nasīb*—and thus hermeneutically out of the binding reach of that section's image-evoking and melancholy quality. Precisely then, however, a certain degree of abstraction takes place in the connotative range of the word. A certain quintessentiality remains. Thus in the apostrophic section of the *qaṣīdah* rhyming in *mīm* by ʿAlqamah:[106]

*Bal kullu qawmin wa in ʿazzū wa in kathurū*
*ʿarīfuhum bi athāfī sh-sharri marjūmū*

Yet every tribe, though it be mighty, though numerous,
Its chief shall not escape ill fortune's
hearthstones' blows.

The inevitability of fate, the inexorable pronouncement of the ill designs of fortune, these are literally the "hearthstones of evil"; and in the total phrasing of *ʿarīfuhum bi athāfī sh-sharri marjūmū* we even discover an oracular quality. Beginning with the word *ʿarīf*, we are already introduced to the ambiguity of the phrasing. The word should mean "chief," as in our translation. Still, the scholiast Abū Muḥammad al-Qāsim Ibn Muḥammad Ibn Bashshār al-Anbārī, the father of the more commonly remembered commentarist of the *Muʿallaqāt*, Abū Bakr Muḥammad Ibn al-Qāsim al-Anbārī, purposefully introduces uncertainty into the word's surface meaning. In his explanation of *ʿarīf* he cites a hermeneutically supportive verse (*qāla al-ākhar*), in which a tribe's *ʿarīf* performs what is termed *yatawassamu*, i.e., "he engages in prognostication," which, in turn, harkens back to the "anticipation of spring rain," or to "search for spring grass." An *ʿarīf* is thus understood to be a "knower" of what is to come. In ʿAlqamah's verse, however, the *ʿarīf* does not prognosticate. Instead, he is himself "stoned" (*marjūm*), as it were, by the three hearthstones/*athāfī*. This, assisted by the further meaning of *rajama/marjūm* as "to conjecture"/"conjectured," infers also a "reading of ill fortune" through "casting stones" (*al-ṭarq bi al-ḥaṣā*) and through the "flight of birds," i.e., through "augury," such as is called technically *ʿiyāfah*. After all, one of the more frequent metaphoric ramifications of the motif of the "three" *athāfī* is, as we shall see, "the three doves" (*al-ḥamāmāt al-thalāth*). Who, then, is the archaic "chief" referred to as *ʿarīf?* In much later Arabic terminology he is also known as the "master builder" or "master mason." But in archaic Arabic he was still closer to being, if not a shaman or medicine man, the one who could read fate's signs. Through such an understanding of the components of ʿAlqamah's image—i.e., of *ʿarīf* and *marjūm*—we may then intimate that the three stones of the *athāfī* are somehow the focus from which fate's pronouncement emanates; for the poet quite clearly lets the meaning of both *ʿarīf* and *marjūm* be conditioned by the semiotics of the *athāfī* as an oracular tripod.

In post-Jāhilī poetry, especially in the Abbasid period, there is observable an added freedom in the way in which the image of the *athāfī* is constructed. But there is also the strong insistence on an archaizing Bedouin anchoring of diction that is easily mistaken for conservatism. The poet al-Buḥturī will combine both trends:[107]

*Wa athāfin atat lahā ḥijajun dū /*
*na laẓā n-nāri muththalin ka l-athāfī*

And hearthstones (*athāfin*), year after pilgrims' year
By fire's blaze untouched, pitched up
like the Athāfī stars.

With al-Buḥturī we are already in an age of complex, polyfaceted construction of the image. We are also facing a new concept of poetic semantics. Thus, on the one hand, the poet harkens back to the archaic *ḥijaj* of a time count that revolves around the rites of pilgrimage.[108] That is where his equally archaic first *athāfī* belong. His second *athāfī*, now the name of a grouping of three stars, he sees as *muththalin*, i.e., both "effaced" (archaic) and standing up: "pitched up" as would pertain to a star or a constellation. It is of further interest that the *three* stars called al-Athāfī are those that are at the head of the star cluster called Qidr (cauldron)—with which they form part of the constellation al-Tinnīn/Draco. This makes them not only the projection of a familiar Bedouin perception of the firmament, but also a chthonic concept of access to earth center—as it were through the hearth which is the center of the *dār*.

Vis-à-vis such a play of poetic fancy, the even later, only sentimentally archaizing poet, al-Sharīf al-Murtaḍā, may yet take us with unperturbed ease back to the *athāfī*'s simplest elegiac beginnings:[109]

*Waqafnā ʿalā rabʿi l-aḥibbati waqfatan*
*fa lam nara illā ramdadan wa athāfiyā*

We stopped for awhile at our loves' vernal grounds,
But saw there none but fine ash dust
and hearthstones.

It is not uncommon, however, for already pre-Islamic references to the *athāfī* to be figurative or otherwise oblique; and that this phenomenon should occur more frequently during the Umayyad and Abbasid periods. Thus al-Nābighah al-Dhubyānī is the more oblique the more direct he appears, when, meaning the *athafī*, he nevertheless only speaks of the abandoned encampment's "stones" (*al-aḥjār*):[110]

*ʿŪjū fa ḥayyū li Nuʿmin dimnata d-dārī*
*mādhā tuḥayyūna min nu'yin wa aḥjārī*

Alight and greet the remains of Nuʿm's abode!
But what shall you greet of trench and stones?

The already early Umayyad, ʿUbayd Allāh Ibn Qays al-Ruqayyāt, qualifies those stones further as "fire-blackened ones" (*sufʿ*):[111]

*Yā sanada ẓ-ẓāʿinīna min Uḥudī*
*ḥuyyīta min manzilin wa min sanadī*

*Mā in bi mathwāka ghayru rākidatin*
*sufʿin wa hābin ka l-farkhi multabidī*

O mountain rise of those who from Uḥud went their way,
Hail to you—as halting place, as mountain rise!

Nothing but yawning stillness in your dwelling place,
Nothing but windblown ashes and
*fire-blackened stones* puckered like chicks asquat.

In such cases we realize that, rather than weakening the elegiac effect of the "presence" of the *athāfī*, an oblique reference to them, especially one that draws upon symbolically efficacious qualifiers, may strengthen that effect. Such is the case of the adjectival, and even nominal, way in which the word *khawālid* (plural of *khālidah*) stands for the *athāfī*. Its accepted "literal" meanings are: "those that last long or remain for ever," "those that retain their youthful appearance"; but also "those that abide in their place"; and then, as an epithetic replacement, the *khawālid* figure as the *athāfī* themselves, and also as "immovable rocks" that are earth-riveted, as it were. With those meanings in mind it is possible to approach verses such as Labīd's:[112]

*Fa waqaftu as'aluhā wa kayfa su'ālunā*
*ṣumman khawālida mā yabīnu kalāmuhā*

There I stood and asked them, but how do we ask
The mute, immovable ones, whose speech
yields no sense?

Or much later, Abū Nuwās's[113]

*Li man ṭalalun ʿāfī l-maḥalli dafīnū*
*ʿafā āyuhū illā khawālidu jūnū*

*Kamā -qtaranat ʿinda l-masā'i ḥamā'imun*
*gharībātu mumsan mā lahunna wukūnū*

Whose ruins are those of the erased halting place,
dust-buried,
Their signs effaced but for the earth-riveted,
unchanging, black ones,

Clustered together like doves at evening time,
Strangers to night shelters, without nests?

Here the words *khawālidu jūnū* are used both epithetically and metaphorically to stand for the *athafī*. To these, then, is joined the simile of the doves gathering into a covey as the evening begins to fall: strangers to the place, not finding their nests. The total image has an extended double referentiality; for the presence of doves as simile to the first metaphor of *khawālidu jūnū* is not merely strengthening the first metaphor/epithet but has rather the further effect of splitting the double image of the implied *athāfī* into a chthonic one (first: *khawālid* as earth-riveted) and an etherial one (second: the covey of doves), thus providing together the "hesitancy" of a perfect elegiac mood piece.

Already in their pre-Islamic formulaic model, the doves of Abū Nuwās's expanded image of the *athāfī* are either specified or strongly suggested by context as being three in number. Their image is then linked to the epithet of *khawālid*. This is brought out clearly in Zuhayr Ibn Abī Sulmā's evocation of the wind-swept, empty abode of Umm Maʿbad, of which but little remains,[114]

*Ghayru thalāthin ka l-ḥamāmi khawālidin*
*wa hābin muḥīlin hāmidin mutalabbidī*

Only a threesome clasping the ground, like doves,
And year-old ashes—cold, encrusted.

And another pre-Islamic bard, Bishr Ibn Abī Khāzim, compresses into one verse almost the full scope of the epithetic and metaphoric representations of the *athāfī*:[115]

*Ka'anna khawālidan fī d-dāri sufʿan*
*bi ʿarṣatihā ḥamāmātun wuqūʿū*

As though some earth-riveted ones, fire-blackened,
Were doves that in the abode's courtyard
came to rest.

Here the commentary proposes that the *khawālid* represent the *athāfī* because of the length of time that the abode lies deserted; as for the doves, they resemble the *athāfī* because the latter are blackened by the hearth's fire, not unlike the flanks of the doves that become blackened when they come to "fall" in the courtyard of the *dār*. We shall soon see, however, that, especially as regards the "doves" (*ḥamāmāt*), such commentary may yet contain in its own oblique way not only a transparently connotative and imagist realness, but also a vestigial access to etymologically more deeply implanted meaning.

As poetry thus tends to turn upon itself hermeneutically, we find already one of the earliest Jāhilī poets, Abū Du'ād al-Iyādī, insisting further on the soot-blackness of the doves-as-*athāfī*—that is, if Usāmah Ibn Munqidh's reading is to be preferred over that of von Grunebaum[116]—but his more interesting addition to the dove simile is his calling such *athāfī*/doves *al-firād*, "those that are single, apart, unmatched, unpaired":

*A min rasmin taʿaffā aw ramādī*
*wa suḥmin ka l-ḥamāmāti l-firādī*

Is this an effaced trace of abode—or ashes
And soot-blackened [hearthstones]
like unpaired doves?

We thus know with sufficient inferential certainty that the soot-black doves are three in number. Moreover, we also know that in Abū Du'ād al-Iyādī's verse that number is called "unpaired." With any other group of birds this would not mean much, but speaking of doves as being unpaired necessarily implies loss and a sense of melancholy if not of tragedy. Of course, the poet is speaking of the meaning of the *athāfī*.

Later poets, Umayyad as well as early Abbasid, will not hesitate to add increased articulation to the already highly accentuated formalism of their diction as that diction engages the motif of the doves of the *athāfī*. Thus al-Ṣimmah al-Qushayrī actually counts his doves to be three, stressing further their analogy to the "tripod" of the abode:[117]

*Wa ghayru thalāthin fī d-diyāri ka'annahā*
*thalāthu ḥamāmātin taqābalna wuqqaʿā*

Only a threesome in the abodes,
Like three doves that swooped down and met.

So, too, Abū Ḥayyah al-Numayrī, to whom the traces of the abandoned springtime abode are[118]

*Ka'anna ḥamāmātin thalāthan bi rabʿihā*
*waqaʿna fa mā yas'amna ṭūla wuqūʿī*

As though three doves in those vernal quarters
Alighted and never wearied of long stay.

None of the oblique references to the *athāfī*, however, is elegiacally more intense than that of the *aẓ'ār*, the [three] she-camels bereft of their own nurslings, searching to nurse, as foster mothers, an orphaned foal. In the image the *aẓ'ār* create there is, therefore, tragedy on both sides, on that of the bereft mothers—especially when, with added pathos, these figure poetically always as three in number—and on the side of the motherless foal. Into this the Arabic poet will pour his own elegiac pathos, as does the *mukhaḍram*, or rather "Companion" poet, Mutammim Ibn Nuwayrah al-Yarbūʿī:[119]

*Wa mā wajdu aẓ'ārin thalāthin rawā'imin*
*aṣabna majarran min ḥuwārin wa maṣraʿā*

*Yudhakkirna dhā l-baththi l-ḥazīna bi baththihī*
*idhā ḥannat il-ūlā sajaʿna lahā maʿā*

*Idhā shārifun minhunna qāmat fa rajjaʿat*
*ḥanīnan fa abkā shajwuhā l-barka ajmaʿā*

*Bi awjada minnī yawma qāma bi Mālikin*
*munādin baṣīrun bi l-firāqi fa asmaʿā*

No passion of three foster-nursing,
love-bonded she-camels is as strong,
When of an unweaned foal they find
the dragged trail, the death place.

The sorrowful, the sad one they remind
of his great pain:
When plaintively the first one calls,
the others groan in unison.

When the eldest of them lets resound
her yearning moan,
Her anguish makes the whole alighting herd
moan too.

No, none was more stricken than I, on the day
When the herald of Mālik's death
spoke his word of fatal parting!

In contrast to this poetic use of the three *aẓ'ār*, a single she-camel bereft of her foal and presented instead with a substitute, even if that substitute be a taxidermically prepared one (*baww*), will in poetry be referred to not as *ẓi'r* but as *ʿajūl*.[120] The fact that the foster-mothering she-camels remain referred to as the "three *aẓ'ār*" even when there is no eliciting of the *athāfī* motif should point in two directions, both having to do with symbolic meaning: one, that, although having detached themselves from the hearth tripod in image, the *aẓ'ār* nevertheless carry over from the implicit presence of the *athāfī* the conversive impulse that leads from the presumed realistic singleness of *ẓi'r/baww* to a vestigial, referential threesomeness; and second, that that very threesomeness of the *aẓ'ār* may also have its own symbolic-elegiac reason of being and be parallel to, superimposed upon, but not otherwise generated by, the sphere of meaning of the hearth tripod. As reflecting the latter property, one may consider the story of the Three Marys, the elegiac accolade to the story of the Passion of Christ. The analogy begins at the appropriate point of vagueness and even outright uncertainty as to the provenance of the number three in the story—for none of the four Gospels evidences adequate clarity about the matter. Only if we accept forcedly some exegetic adjustment or other of the tradition that the Salome of the scenes of Christ's Passion is also a Mary, do we obtain three Marys in Mark 15:40—Mary Magdalene, Mary the mother of James the younger, and Salome; so too in Matthew 27:56, if, once again, we follow the exegetic tradition that Salome, "the mother of the sons of Zebedee," was the third Mary. Otherwise, according to the *Legenda Aurea* and the apocryphal "acts" of the Three Marys, the three were Mary Cleophae, Mary Salome, and Mary the mother of Jesus; whereas the French and Spanish devotional tradition recognizes as the Three Marys Mary Magdalene, Mary Cleophae, and Mary Salome—once again to the exclusion of Mary the natural mother of Jesus.[121] To go one step further, we shall also suggest that in the symbolic construct of the Three Marys there is an undeniable element of "adoption" that brings the trio close to being a symbolically unified version of the Mater Dolorosa, Jesus being not only their bewailed God but also their sorrow-nurtured son. And thus, in spite of other distances, we still remain here close to the symbolic circumscription of the *aẓ'ār*, even though these be viewed without an immediate regard to their connection to the *athāfī*.

A different angle of vision is obtained in the case of the fateful Judgment of Paris, in which Hera, Athena, and Aphrodite vie for the prize of the apple. The fruitfulness of the apple[122] won in the contest by Aphrodite is, in Aphrodite's possession, an illicit fruitfulness that leads to the abduction of Helen, the Trojan War, and the destruction of Troy. Above all, symbolically, there is perceptible in the Judgment the language of the oracular inevitability of fate. But there is no sorrow at the source of the oracle. Fate is wholly indifferent at the point of its inception. The appearance of the Three Witches in Shakespeare's *Macbeth* (I:1,3), on the other hand, is then quite explicit as to its oracular purport, although here, too, the particular, never explicit language of the oracle depends on the meaning of the seeming cacophony of the three voices that are, however, as much three as they are one, and that are ultimately as clear as they are veiled.

Aspects of the *aẓ'ār/athāfī* are also reflected in the myth of Perseus and the Graiae, the daughters of the strongly chthonic Phorkys and Keto. The first characteristic of the Graiae was that they were three with only one eye among them.[123] It was through obtaining that eye that Perseus could force them to reveal to him the way to the Gorgons. In their ability to "reveal" a secret (clearly a characteristic of the oracular), the three Graiae were archetypally chthonic. But they were also an incarnation of "old age." They were gray-haired from birth. In a sense, they were *khawālid* not in the qur'ānic exegetic sense but in that of the pre-Islamic elegiac setting.

In some respects closer to the topos of the Arabic *aẓ'ār*—but also to the *athāfī*—are the three cows of the Celtic myth of the death of the magician Cu Roi. These three cows, which were the object of a destructive strife over the succession to the kingship of Ulster, had the property of filling every day with their milk an enormous cauldron. This cauldron they called their calf.[124] If in the Arabic mythological context this piece of Celtic lore evokes perhaps most directly the tragic outcome of the story of the She-Camel of Ṣāliḥ and of the destruction of the people of Thamūd,[125] it also belongs to the symbolic context of the *aẓ'ār/athāfī* and, with them, as we shall duly see, to that of the archaic Arabic symbolism of the cauldron/*qidr*.

A concise but representative illustration of the way the motif of the three *aẓ'ār* stands fully for that of the *athāfī* will at this point suffice. Thus Bishr Ibn Abī Khāzim produces a mixed, or layered, metaphor, in which the shift of referential meaning between *aẓ'ār* and *athāfī* is already on its way to being accomplished:[126]

*Ramādun bayna aẓ'ārin thalāthin*
*kamā wushima r-rawāhishu bi n-nawrī*

Ashes, amidst three foster-mothering camel mares
of nurslings bereft,
Like wrist veins tattooed with indigo-black.

The poet's deserted encampment has literally "ashes lying amidst the three *aẓ'ār*." Only in the second half of the verse, through his use of *rawāhish*, which primarily means "veins on a riding animal's fore feet," will we be reminded of the still enduring metaphoric presence of the three *aẓ'ār* as not wholly the *athafī*. But in the poetic reality of the verse—in something like Dante's "first reading"[127]—Bishr Ibn Abī Khāzim's *aẓ'ār* are already the sadness-awakening, elegiac hearthstones, and the tattooed wrists are only the memory, perhaps quite old, of a woman who once squatted by the camp's hearth.

The Umayyad al-Kumayt Ibn Zayd al-Asadī, on the other hand, is already obliged to do the opposite: to reclaim the metaphor latent in the *aẓ'ār/ẓu'ār* from the setting-in of its unidimensional semantic equivalency with the *athāfī*. His elegiac *ẓu'ār* she-camels still kneel, "though without knees":[128]

*Wa lam tuhijnī ẓ-ẓu'āru fī l-manzili l-*
*qafri burūkan wa mā lahā rukabū*

Nor did the foster-mothering she-camels disquiet me
At the bleak campground, kneeling down
though without knees.

Ultimately, it is not only the tragic sense or the deepened elegiac mood in the *nasīb* that is conveyed through the motif of the *athāfī*, for, when occurring—albeit rarely—in non-elegiac sections of the *qaṣīdah*, its tone is modulated to reflect the larger tone of the respective section or theme. Thus the same al-Kumayt of the elegiac *ẓu'ār* endows the *athāfī* motif with all the sense of warlike threat and danger once he displaces it into the *qaṣīdah*'s structural section of tribal pride (*fakhr*) and retributive admonition—for such must be the rhetorical tone of that section:[129]

*Ta'allaqa barqun ᶜindanā wa taqābalat*
*athāfin li qidri l-ḥarbi akhshā -qtibālahā*

*Fa dūnaka qidra l-ḥarbi wa hya muᶜirratun*
*li kaffayka wa -jᶜal dūna qidrin jiᶜālahā*

A lightning flash! and the hearthstones
of war's cauldron fell in place.
O how I fear their fortuitous junction!

So beware that war's cauldron
not defile your hands—
Handle a cauldron with a pot rag!

Here the poet speaks of the lightning flashes on the horizon foreboding war among the clans, and of the fires of uncontrolled temper—of the old *jahl*—flaring up, and of the ominous, still oracular, hearth tripod of the cauldron of war. Not much in the symbolic semantics of the *athāfī* has changed. Only a circumstantial semiotic adjustment to the new mood and theme took place. Also, as part of the thematic dislodgment, the corollary symbol of the cauldron of war has been introduced. In itself, the cauldron is a symbol of strong mythopoeic resonances, whose elucidation in Indo-European mythology must at this point suffice as reference only.[130] Purely in the Arabic poetic context, it is important to note further, however, that the cauldron (*qidr*) may only become a "cauldron of war," or otherwise of ill omen, when it is associated with the *athāfī*. Without that semiotic link, as may be seen in the encomiastic verse of al-Nābighah al-Dhubyānī, it will be a cauldron of nobility and generosity:[131]

*Baqiyyatu qidrin min qudūrin tuwurrithat*
*li āli l-Julāḥi kābiran baᶜda kābirī*

A cauldron's remains, of cauldrons
where long since fires burned,
Of the house of Julāḥ, elder after elder.

After this review of the "textuality" of the Arabic poetic *athāfī*, we are left not only with the confirmation of their "belonging"—as one component among many—to a broadly elegiac opening scene of the classical Arabic *qaṣīdah*'s *nasīb*, in which a uniformity of mood subsumes and explains it all, but also with a strong symbolically discrete component characterized by a never quite subsumable individuation that defines the manner in which it enters into what may be called "the general meaning." The general meaning is the one that is modulated by it into particular instances. Only as it proceeds from text to text does it reveal its own meaning. And, furthermore, it, too, has its own "generals" and "particulars."

The first, most general aspect of the *athāfī* as hearthstones—not even as three hearthstones yet and not yet a tripod—is that they belong in a house, where they are "central" even if they are not in any concrete middle point of the inhabited structure. They are the inhabited structure's organizing "focus" of social belonging and togetherness. As we are told by the poetic semiotics of the *athāfī*, they form an inseparable part of the imaginary spacial-geometric notion that is the *dār*. Never are they even part of a *bayt*. Irrespective of any concrete realities of archaic Bedouin habitation—the eventual *bayt* rectangularity of a tent, for instance—the *athāfī* are, therefore, to be imagined not merely as a point within a circular space but as the focal point of that space. And, once again irrespective of social changes and accommodations, the fire of the *athāfī*, as it reflected an archaic social order, remained in the classical Arabic poem a domain of the woman. As a symbolic configuration, the Bedouin *dār* with its *athāfī* may thus well be said to correspond to other, similar, symbolic configurations, such as the circularity of the Roman *aedes* devoted to Vesta, the goddess-keeper of the sacred hearth both domestic and civic—as much as she, herself, is also that hearth. Etymologically,[132] ritually, and symbolically, this Roman hearth goddess is also predated by, or merely runs parallel to, the Greek hearth goddess, Hestia, who, although not tied to the circularity of the symbolic space of Vesta, appears to point to a Delphic-oracular provenance of the flame of her hearth.[133] Both aspects of the resulting symbolic hearth are necessary to our full understanding of the three *athafī*. Furthermore, the circumstances of the extinction specifically of the domestic fire of Hestia are wholly those of the extinction of the hearth of the *athafī*. To quote Ginette Paris, "The Hestia of a home was always extinguished on an occasion of mourning, if the latter signified at the same time the end of a household, the death of a family, the abandonment of a location, and the dispersion of those who had formerly constituted the household."[134]

Going beyond the domestic hearth to the communal and even the customary-ritual, we cannot but visualize the *khalīṭ*, the seasonal motley of clans bent on departure and dispersal, or the tragic, and then simply proverbial, *tafarraqū aydiya Sabā*, the dispersal of the doomed Sabaeans. It is then that the *athāfī* stand out blackened, desolate. They are left behind immobile (*khawālid*), as the hearths of Hestia and Vesta, too, are to be left in their place, *unmoved.*

Before concluding our dissection of the meaning of the Arabic poetic *athāfī* by linking the word in its semantic history to concrete evidence drawn from outside the Arabic lexicon proper, it appears hermeneutically—not just philologically—useful to examine further one of its epithetic substitutes, namely, the already repeatedly broached *khawālid*, together with one metaphorization or, more often, simile, namely, that of *ḥamāmāt*. As we saw in the verse-examples already cited, both offer poetically important oblique approaches to the image and meaning of the *athafī*, and both may be found grouped into one compounded image, as in the case of the above cited verse by Bishr Ibn Abī Khāzim.[135]

We had translated the epithet *khawālid* in various ways: as "immovable ones," as "the earth-riveted, unchanging," as "clasping the ground," and we have also taken into consideration a scholiast's lexicographically representative understanding of *khawālid* as a reference to "the length of time since the abode was deserted." Then there are the word's, or its root's, extrapoetic meanings. For the most part these are tinted by qur'ānic exegesis, although to a lesser degree they have also found their way into poetry outside the *nasīb*. These revolve around "duration," and in a primary way around "duration of habitation," but also around "youthfulness" in the sense of "being slow in becoming hoary when advanced in years" (Lane, *kh-l-d*)—thus not so much to the moment or state of youthfulness itself as to its preservation.

There is apparent, therefore, a semantic uneasiness, or tension, between poetic and extrapoetic *kh-l-d* as it leads to *khawālid*. While one claims duration as preservation of youthfulness or protection from hoariness, the other invokes an almost predestined, if not preexisting, ancientness—a hoariness from birth as was the hoariness of the three Graiae. But then, we may not have been looking carefully enough at the use of the substantivized verbal noun *khuld* in the Qur'ān, where it is commonly understood as "eternity," both positively as reward and salvation (21:15) and negatively[136] as damnation (10:52; 32:14; 41:28), nor paid much attention in the same qur'ānic text to that root's equally polarized distribution of participial and verbal occurrences (2:82; 3:15; 3:107; 3:136; 4:13; 4:122; 5:85; 5:119; 9:75; 9:89; 9:100; 14:23; 18:109; 20:76; 23:11 [positive], and 25:69; 47:15; 4:14; 4:93; 9:63; 2:81; 2:275; 23:103; 4:169; 7:20 [negative]). For the most part, the above references reveal that the qur'ānic rhetoric of salvation and damnation thus shares remarkably equitably the sense of *khuld* in a rhythm that approaches rigorous alternation. The semiotic conclusion to be drawn from this might thus be that the eschatological sublimation of *khuld*, when counterbalanced that closely by the same *khuld*'s plumb downgrading to "hell's" damnation, is made rhetorically particularly efficacious because of the vertically structured, binary semantic tension that inheres in the word *khuld* itself. The resulting question is not so much one of semantic priority within the connotational choices of *khuld* as that of its etymology-bespeaking semantic matrix: Where did *khuld* begin—in "heaven" or in "hell," or rather: in the higher regions of the awareness of the self or in the lower ones? Is it an origin or an aspiration? And thus, translated into time, is it the future or the past? These are not abstract philosophical questions. They are questions about the meaning of a word.

In the prequr'ānic Arabic poetic contexts of the *qaṣīdah*'s motif of the *ʿādhilah*, *khuld* reveals its truth and its paradox: it is a perpetuation of the past, a survival of the name and its glory[137] through the "act" of memory, that is, through a return to the past. There is no "future" for such a *khuld* except through this continuous mnemonic archaeology. We shall be inclined to accept such semantics of *khuld* more readily if we reach its "lowest" level—which will reveal itself as chthonic, eschatologically wholly uncelestial. Already the Arabic lexicons put us on the alert by placing close to the *khuld* of Paradise and eternity the derivationally puzzling entry of another *khuld*—as well as *khald/khild/khuldah/khildah*—all of them meaning "mole," "a blind animal living underground." Then, too, we find in the same lexicons certain verbal forms of that root, such as Form IV, showing through the prepositions *bi* and *ilā* a distinct chthonic tendency of connotation: "to cleave, cling (to the ground)," "to incline to (the ground)." From here, it is then through the etymological linkage with Hebrew that we can comfortably confirm the chthonic origins of *khuld*, for there (recognizing that Hebrew does not differentiate between *ḥ* and *kh*) we find the verbs *ḥalad* and *ḥilled* clearly meaning "to dig," "to undermine," with *ḥoled* as the "digging animal" or, substantivally, as the "mole" (Lev. 11:29). So, too, is the case of the Aramaic *ḥūldā*. The Hebrew *ḥeled* will, however, have the familiar Arabic *khuld*-related meaning of "duration of life" (Pss. 36:6, 89:48, 49:9). Interestingly, the Hebrew *ḥeled* has also its other meaning of "world" (Pss. 17:14, 49:2, Is. 38:11), which would pair with the Arabic *dunyā*, itself "low" and chthonic.

Returning to the qur'ānic use of *khuld* and *khālid* [*ūn*], we recognize that even in the numerous instances in which *khuld/khālid* occur as eschatologically "positive," or heaven-turned, denotations, the very insistence of qur'ānic diction on the phraseological or formulaic coupling of *khuld/khālid* with *jannah*, as, for instance, in *jannatu l-khuldi* (25:15) ("the garden of eternal abode"), *jannātu ʿadnin tajrī min taḥtihā l-anhāru khālidīna fīhā* (20:76) ("gardens of Eden, underneath which rivers flow, [they] dwelling there forever"), etc., should alert us to the chthonic affinity between the two; for *jannah*, as much as the Hebrew *gen* and the Aramaic *ginnā*, may itself only be "projected" into the eschatological "heavenly" sphere out of its primary chthonic "hiddenness," "buriedness," "darkness," and also "protectedness." Thus the Arabic verb *janna* means "to veil," "to conceal," out of which *ajannat* (*waladan/janīnan*) becomes "she concealed, guarded, bore in her womb [a child, an embryo, or a fetus]"; and, as much as *janīn* is a fetus, the other-than-human (but not angelic) creature called by an etymologically kindred name is the necessarily chthonic *jinn*, but furthermore implying in Arabic a link with the "incubus." *Kanna* ("to conceal," "to keep secret") and other related roots reinforce further the chthonic hiddenness of *janna*, allowing the formation of the word *janan* for "grave."

*Jannatu khuldin* is thus an almost tautological chthonic construct burdened with all the residual meanings of both *jannah* and *khuld*. As Celestial Paradise in the Islamic qur'ānic sense, it is quite literally only the eschatological "upward" projection of the chthonic incubatory Garden on-Earth, or rather, in-Earth. The chthonic residue in qur'ānic eschatological visions is further perceivable in the formulaic, or iconic, insistence, verse after qur'ānic verse, that the blessed shall live forever in gardens *underneath* which there are rivers flowing: *jannātun tajrī min taḥtihā l-anhāru khālidīna fīhā* (3:15; also 3:136; 4:13; 4:122; 5:85; 5:119; 9:72; 9:89; 14:23; 20:76; 29:58).[138]

We come closer to the chthonic semiotics of the *athāfī*-as-*khawālid* in the qur'ānic references to damnation, where *khawālid* remains chthonic even beyond the "word about the end," i.e., beyond the eschatology of salvation/damnation. Thus the opposite of *jannah*-plus-*khuld* is *jahannam*-plus-*khuld* (4:93; 9:63; 23:103). *Jahannam*, however, is none other than the Valley of Ben Hinnom /*ge ben-hinnom* (Josh. 15:8, 18:16; II Kings 23:10; etc.), also shortened to Valley of Hinnom/*ge hinnom* (Josh. 15:8, 18:16; Neh. 11:30), whose precise position scholarship has failed to establish, but which may be either the Valley of Kidron or the deep ravine to the west and south of Jerusalem. It was there that children were burnt as offerings to Molek (II Kings 23:10). It is this valley which became the archetypal topos of damnation; but it was also the place where, quite literally, the closest biblical Hebrew precursor of the Arabic *athāfī* was to be found (see below). The *khuld* of *jahannam*/*ge hinnom* will put us thus semiotically in touch with the *khuld* of the *athāfī* themselves.

As for the "three doves," *al-ḥamāmāt al-thalāth*, which in the motif of the *athāfī* appear for the most part as a simile or as a further metaphorization within a simile, they are meant to resemble the *athāfī* as an image or otherwise point to something that is characteristic or connotatively significant in them. Following the scholiasts' primary exegetic reading, it would suffice to know that the color of the three doves/*athāfī* is black, or blackened, and that, as such, these doves are visually associated, or even confused, with age- and fire-tarnished hearthstones. Regardless of its unappealing simplicity, this approach to the image is, nevertheless, surprisingly valid at least on one, let us call it philological, level, for as such it also permits access to the image on other levels.

First of all, what we know of the bird—and the word—*ḥamāmah* (*āt*) as "dove" is that in classical Arabic poetic usage it means for the most part a wild dove, the ambiguity of the legend of Zarqā' al-Yamāmah in al-Nābighah al-Dhubyānī's ode notwithstanding.[139] As turtle dove, the *ḥamāmah* is found in poetry in pairs only, or else in the tragic, or melancholy, solitariness of bereavement. Only in the image of the *athāfī*, wholly motif-determined and not otherwise motivated or justifiable, does it appear in its iconic triality. A further characteristic of the *ḥamāmah* is its general ruddiness of color and a distinct black neck ring. All this considered, the scholiasts' association of the *ḥamāmah* with the *athāfī* would appear to be based on its associability with the extinguished fire of the hearth, albeit not only through the sooty color of the three stones upon which the three doves somehow alight ("fall"), thus blackening their plumage till they themselves resemble the hearthstones. Instead, we must consider here the likelihood that an act of associative, image-evoking false etymology has taken place—that, to begin with, there were no doves involved but the two principal conditions of a hearth with its stony trivet waiting to be put into language: the heat (red) of the burning fire and the charred sootiness covering that trivet upon the fire's extinction. In both respects the Arabic consonantal root *ḥ-m-m* applies fully. It conveys the sense of the heat of the fire as well as the state and coloration of that which remains charred by it. Thus it may speak of the charcoal when it is still hot, as *jamrah* (embers), as well as when it is extinguished, cold and black. By meaning "hot" and "fevered," it suggests a red coloration. Otherwise it points to that which is burnt out and has turned black. Where the dove fits into such a semantic scope is difficult to tell, unless one admits that it does not fit at all. The first rudimentary poetic perception of the *athāfī* must have been as the scholiasts tell us: as black, perhaps with emphasis on intense blackness. As such they were, therefore, *ḥumm*, the plural of *aḥamm/ḥammā'*; that is, their blackness was a variant of *sufᶜ* (black, tinged with redness), which, aside from being another poetic epithet of the *athafī*, is also a color-restating adjunct to, or variant of, the *ḥamāmāt*.

The three doves, we should thus infer, entered the semantic sphere of the *athāfī* in the first degree through the semantic door of color,[140] or rather because the possible word's semantic base of color was poetically too narrow and insufficient. Other potential inferences of the *athāfī* ring semiotically equally strong, or even stronger. Primarily, because of the mood determinant of the *nasīb*, poetic melancholy was breaking through concrete semiotic sutures ready to transform any realism of color into symbolism of distant associative provenance. The phonetic base of *ḥ-m-m*, which would have otherwise referred itself no more than to the existence or the absence of fire, red and black, had to transcend itself, generating, both falsely and legitimately, all in one, a word such as *ḥamāmāt*/doves. And, furthermore, the fact that the doves, too, had to be three in number was the expression of a complicating symbolic necessity: the necessity of the chthonic, oracular tripod as center of the fateful encounter in an inanimate oneness (*taqābalna wuqqaᶜā*). It was also the expression of that elegiac pathos that had made possible the fusion between the three foster-mothering she-camels (*aẓ'ār*) and the *athāfī*. Ultimately, therefore, it is possible to say that the scholiasts' and the exegetes' concern with the "color" of the *ḥamāmāt*-as-*athāfī* is an evasive hermeneutical maneuver that, although it quite conceivably implies a degree of knowledge of matters such as the ones above, nevertheless reveals the more radical flaw of the unwillingness of those interpretative channels to see in the *athāfī* themselves the kind of symbolic depth that would not be wholly absorbed into the "domestic" scenario of the *dār*-as-*ṭalal*. Such unwillingness also limits the symbolic range of the complex oblique images of the *aẓ'ār* or the *ḥamāmāt*.

To conclude our discussion of the *athāfī*, we shall now turn to where we might have begun. For we may safely claim to know which is, and where lies, the philologically as well as symbolically most pertinent, even if distant, antecedent of our Bedouin *athāfī*. It lies somewhere in, or near, the Valley of Kidron, on the outskirts of ancient Jerusalem, side by side with the Valley of Hinnom, the *ge hinnom* of child immolation and damnation that was itself damned to be eternal. There it is referred to by the Hebrew word *tofet*. W. Robertson Smith already saw a connection between it and the Arabic *uthfīyah/athāfī* and suggested that it may be of Aramaic origin, and that its primary meaning was that of "fireplace."[141] Otherwise, the word *tofet* is not found in any Punic or Canaanite source.[142]

In the Old Testament we first encounter *tofet* in II Kings (23:10), where it is said to be in the Valley of Ben Hinnom. There it has been defiled by the immolation of children to the underworld deity Molek. In Isaiah (30:33) it figures in the oracle concerning the destruction of Assyria. There, once again a *tofet* is a place of burning and abhorrence, as it has been in the unclean Valley of Hinnom, "and the breath of the Lord, like a stream of brimstone, kindles it." In Jeremiah (7:31, 7:32, 19:11–14) *tofet* is used to point to Judah's sin and to the fall of Jerusalem: *tofet* itself shall become a burial place. It and the Valley of Hinnom shall no more be known as such, but shall be called "the valley of slaughter." In this scene of the destruction of Jerusalem *tofet* shall be filled with dead bodies "till there be no place"; and the scene turns into one of final silence and desolation, almost changing from pathos to melancholy (Jer. 7:34): "Then will I cause to cease from the cities of Judah, and from the streets of Jerusalem, the voice of mirth and the voice of gladness, the voice of the bridegroom and the voice of the bride; for the land shall be desolate!"

Something more than the linguistic certainty of a sound etymology of the archaic biblical *tofet* has remained in the Bedouin *athāfī*. It is true that it is no longer the ominous altar-fireplace used to dispose of sacrificial victims. It has moved from the blood and the pathos of unmitigated ritual and myth into the much calmer and poetically controlled regions of the elegiac and melancholy reliving of Bedouin sorrow and sense of loss. But we may never be quite certain of how close such loss and sorrow in the mythopoeic space and time of the Bedouin poem are to, or how far from, those archaic "things of *tofet*," or how they meandered through that mythopoeic space till they found themselves in their new, now quite obvious-seeming, company of the reliquary of the archaic *nasīb*. There, with the *athāfī* in their place, we have, as it were, not only circumscribed the opening scene of the classical Arabic *nasīb* but have found its hub and allowed a distinctly symbolic world to fashion itself out of the physical remains of an "abandoned encampment" cast into poetic limelight.

## *Su'āl* (Question)

Our final key word will not come out of the reliquary of the "things" of the *nasīb* but will instead be one that will reflect the bewilderment of the Arabic poet as that poet stood in contemplation before that bleak repository, those elusive physical, or merely mnemonic, remains of an "encampment" that submitted as little to his sense of reality as they allowed themselves to be articulated beyond the presentiment of a symbol. It is at this point, therefore, that the Bedouin poet asks his question (*su'āl*).

There are several ways in which the classical Arabic *qaṣīdah* deals with the motif, or rather the poetic stance, of "questioning." Purely formally, much of what we are about to discuss is, in its own way, also a matter of poetic craft and genre: of how a poem starts, or of how a poet begins. Especially in a strong lyrical genre such as the Arabic *qaṣīdah*, which does not easily allow for the self-distancing narrative respite of the ballad, for instance, and which certainly would not tolerate the calm long-windedness of an epic *arma virumque cano*, the choices to begin a poem are limited. The poet has to break into the poem directly—for the most part either through the apostrophe of a question or through that of a command/request, or in an exclamation aimed at his inanimate surroundings. He asks: *li man id-diyāru* (Whose are the abodes?), *li man ṭalalun* (Whose ruin is it?), or *hal mā ᶜalimta . . . maktūmu* (Is that which you knew . . . kept hidden?), *hal ghādara sh-shuᶜarā'u* (Have the poets left [untouched]?), etc.; or else he voices his *qifā nabki* (Halt, you two, let us weep!) and *qif il-ᶜīsa* (Halt the amber-colored camels!), or *alā ᶜim ṣabāḥan* (Now good morrow to you . . . !) and *yā dāra Mayyata* (O abode of Mayyah!). All these are lyrical beginnings, and it is in such a genre-dictated context that we find that intrinsically differentiated, most melancholy, and to the poet most unsettling questioning as well; and that questioning will be spelled out always directly, repetitively, monotonously as *sa'altu/usā'ilu/su'āl*. Most of all, there must not be an answer to it. Only with the Umayyad period will the Arab poet begin to claim that he knows the answer, and only during the high Abbasid era of *badīᶜ* will such a pretense become another topos. But did the early Bedouin poet know it as he listened to the language of silence? He certainly never tired of repeating his question.

Thus the already familiar opening verses of al-Nābighah al-Dhubyānī's ode in *dāl*:[143]

*Yā dāra Mayyata bi l-ᶜalyā'i fa s-sanadī*
*aqwat wa ṭāla ᶜalayhā sālifu l-abadī*

*Waqaftu fīhā uṣaylālan usā'iluhā*
*ᶜayyat jawāban wa mā bi r-rabᶜi min aḥadī*

O abode of Mayyah, upon height and peak,
It lies deserted, its old days long since past.

I halted there at evening time to question it.
There was no answer, and in the vernal campsite
there was no one.

And even when the same poet does not explicitly counterbalance his question with the abandoned abode's silence, such fullness of context is to be regarded as poetically no longer necessary:[144]

*Waqaftu bi rabᶜi d-dāri qad ghayyara l-bilā*
*maᶜārifahā wa s-sāriyātu l-hawāṭilū*

*Usā'ilu ʿan Suʿdā wa qad marra baʿdanā*
*ʿalā ʿaraṣāti d-dāri sabʿun kawāmilū*

I halted at the abode's springtime grounds,
its semblance altered by decay
And by night-traveling clouds that poured down,

Asking questions about Suʿdā while, after us,
Full seven years had passed over the abode's yards.

And once again from the same poet as he muses over the desolation of the abodes:[145]

*Waqaftu bihā l-qalūṣa ʿalā -kti'ābin*
*wa dhāka tafāruṭu sh-shawqi l-muʿannī*

*Usā'iluhā wa qad safaḥat dumūʿī*
*ka'anna mafīḍahunna ghurūbu shannī*

*Bukā'a ḥamāmatin tadʿū hadīlan*
*mufajjaʿatin ʿalā fananin tughannī*

There I halted my young camel mare, gloomily,
Disarranged by yearning, overwhelmed.

I questioned them as my tears freely ran
As though their flow came from
a worn-out water skin,

As when a dove laments—calling out, cooing,
Dolefully singing on a bough.

When not abandoned by its inhabitants, the abode is to the poet ʿAntarah a body in possession of a live spirit. Abandoned, the spirit dwells there no more and only the body has remained:[146]

1. *Yā dāru ayna taraḥḥala s-sukkānū*
*wa ghadat bihim min baʿdinā l-aẓʿānū*

5. *Yā dāru arwāḥu l-manāzili ahluhā*
*fa idhā na'aw tabkīhimū l-abdānū*

6. *Yā ṣāḥibī sal rabʿa ʿAblata wa -jtahid*
*in kāna li r-rabʿi l-muḥīli lisānū*

1. O abode, where did your people take the road,
Where, with the morning, without us,
did the camel litters take them?

5. O abode, the souls of places are their folk.
When they are distant, the bodies weep for them.

6. My friend, do strive and ask
the springtime camp of ʿAblah—
If last year's springtime camp but had a tongue!

In still another poem, ʿAntarah acknowledges his perplexity before the mute abodes; but he refuses to accept their silence, or rather, he refuses not to ask:[147]

*Fa waqaftu fī ʿaraṣātihā mutaḥayyiran*
*asalu d-diyāra ka fiʿli man lam yadhhalī*

And I halted in [the ruins'] yards, perplexed,
Questioning the abodes like one
not willing to forswear.

As if epitomizing the topic in a succinct formulation, Labīd directs his questioning to the "mute, immovable [or time-defying] ones" (*ṣumman khawālida*). In this manner, however, aside from conjuring in our imagination the pathos of the "eternality" of the geological silence of massive rocks and boulders, the poet submits also to the topical circumscription of the early Bedouin *nasīb*, thus inviting our imagination to return to the *athāfī*:[148]

*Fa waqaftu as'aluhā wa kayfa su'ālunā*
*ṣumman khawālida mā yabīnu kalāmuhā*

There I stood and asked them, but how do we ask
The mute, immovable ones, whose speech
yields no sense?

The still pre-Islamic, or perhaps already *mukhaḍram*, ʿAwf Ibn ʿAṭīyah Ibn al-Kharīʿ al-Tamīmī al-Ribāʿī comes closer to defining the dialogics of the silence of the *diyār*. He calls the language of their meaning the speech of secrets, for their silences are in themselves riddles. They are not revealed but kept tantalizingly as presages and intimations. The poet is left standing as though receiving such hermetic silences/messages in a state of inebriation:[149]

*Waqaftu bihā uṣulan mā tubīnū*
*li sā'ilihā l-qawla illā sirārā*

*Ka'annī -ṣṭabaḥtu ʿuqāriyyatan*
*taṣaʿʿadu bi l-mar'i ṣirfan ʿuqārā*

There I stood at evening, an asker
Without clear answer, only secret words.

As though I had awakened to wine of long effect
That rises to the head, pure and strong.

And many more poets—then, in the Bedouin Jāhilīyah, and thereafter—still went on halting over the abodes of their abandonment to direct to them their outpour of questions, which, indeed, was like one large, cumulative question, time after time, poem after poem. Thus, from among the poets of the *Mufaḍḍalīyāt*, there was Muraqqish the Elder, Bashāmah Ibn ʿAmr al-Ghadīr, Rabīʿah Ibn Maqrūn, and ʿAbd Allāh Ibn ʿAnamah al-Ḍabbī, all pre-Islamic or *mukhaḍram*;[150] while of the Umayyad poets that still halted and questioned in the archaic manner, there may be mentioned Dhū al-Rummah,[151] or al-Walīd Ibn Yazīd.[152]

These poets asked but were not answered. There was only the burden of the question that would not be repressed. Gradually, however, the imagination of poets who were no longer Bedouin had begun to succumb to a new, demythologizing restlessness. Such an imagination was groping for lyrical and contemplative rather than symbolic answers. Non-canonic approaches to the ancient question began to multiply, turning into diversely mannered attempts to find a variant of the answer, or to escape from it altogether. Still of the Umayyad period, among the first departures, if not anomalies, should be ʿUmar Ibn Abī Rabīʿah's verses. There the *ṭalal* may still be jealous not to reveal its secret, but it is no longer mute:[153]

*Yā ṣāḥibayya qifā nastakhbir iṭ-ṭalalā*
*ʿan baʿḍi man ḥallahū bi l-amsi mā faʿalā*

*Fa qāla lī r-rabʿu lammā an waqaftu bihī*
*inna l-khalīṭa ajadda l-bayna fa -ḥtamalā*

O friends two, halt and let us hear
the campsite ruin's news
Of one who yesterday there had set camp:
What has she done?

But when I halted there, the springtime
campground said to me:
The clans had gathered only to depart!

A further noncanonic step is taken by the Abbasid al-Buḥturī, who finds himself "mute" in the presence of "mute" abodes. His inability to "ask" is as great as is the ruin's inability to answer:[154]

*Fa lam yadri rasmu d-dāri kayfa yujībunā*
*wa lā naḥnu min farṭi l-jawā kayfa nas'alū*

And the trace of the abode knew not how to answer us,
And we, too, for grief's excess, knew not
how to ask.

But a rigorous chronology of motif development becomes now less important. The openness of the motif is what matters. Archaic regressions are now as viable poetically as are conceptual advances that are strictly of the realm of *badīᶜ*. That way, too, because, as motif, it now faces as much backward as forward, we may obtain a hermeneutically valid clue to the understanding of the primary symbol of the archaic questioning itself. Thus, in one of his panegyric *qaṣīdah*s, Abū Tammām addresses his elegiac question, still from within the poem's *nasīb*, in the "obligatory" first person—and with self-conscious persistence (*ẓaliltu ul-ḥifu*)—to the traces of the abandoned encampment (v. 7). Then, however, only three verses later, it is the poet's eulogized patron, the vizier Muḥammad Ibn ᶜAbd al-Malik Ibn al-Zayyāt, who *asks*—still *sa'ala*—the rain-bringing star Spica Veneris[155] to pour rain generously over the desolate traces (*rusūm*), to which the star *responds* with all its vivifying bounty:[156]

7. *Wa ẓaliltu ulḥifu fī s-su'āli rusūmahā*
*wa l-manᶜu min tuḥafi s-su'āli l-mulḥifī*

10. *Sa'ala s-simāka fa jādahā bi ḥayā'ihī*
*minhū bi wablin dhī wamīḍin awṭafī*

7. On and on, with my question I beset its traces,
Though refusal be the rare gem
of importunate asking.

10. He asked Spica, and upon [the traces] it sent
its bounty for his blameless sake:
A downpour, a flash of lightning
through dark clouds.

Abū Tammām may thus have given us more than his personal clue to the understanding of the old questioning, for in his poem's verse 10 we hear the answer to his question: it is the fructifying rain from the propitious star that shall bring new life to the "encampment" and redeem the wasteland. Significantly, only this eulogized patron (*mamdūḥ*) may ask and expect such an answer; or rather, he is the executor of it. In the present case it is the powerful vizier whose implied intercession with the caliph/Spica will bring redemption. The vegetation symbolism of the return of welfare and abundance to the wasteland is thus brought to the surface in this Abbasid *badīʿ* poet's stubbornly archaizing question, which, in spite of its *badīʿ*-mannered answer, remains anchored in the symbol.

In one more poem Abū Tammām restates the motif of the question before the wasteland, and this time wholly within the elegiac strictures of the *nasīb*, thus *not* allowing for redemption:[157]

3. *Qad mararnā bi d-dāri wahya khalā'un*
   *wa bakaynā ṭulūlahā wa r-rusūmā*

4. *Wa sa'alnā rubūʿahā fa -nṣarafnā*
   *bi saqāmin wa mā sa'alnā ḥakīmā*

5. *Aṣbaḥat rawḍatu sh-shabābi hashīman*
   *wa ghadat rīḥuhu l-balīlu samūmā*

3. We passed by the abode as it lay empty,
   And we wept over its ruins and traces.

4. We questioned its vernal quarters, then departed,
   Bearing our malady, and no physician consulted:

5. The meadow of youth was arid,
   Its moisture-laden wind turned to simoom.

It is relevant to notice, however, that in another redaction the poem's verse 4 undergoes what is unquestionably a hermeneutically significant transformation: *bi saqāmin* is changed into *bi shifā'in*. "Malady" becomes "cure," and the question itself receives an implied answer in the verse's second hemistich: "Cured, though no physician was consulted." Verse 5 then falls necessarily by the wayside, for in the question the poet's inner wasteland has tasted redemption.[158] In all its apparent textual innocence, such a hermeneutically searching emendation thus approaches the threshold past which there lies the realm of the Orphic redemptive descent—and also the healing of the Fisher King.

A later Abbasid poet, Mihyār al-Daylamī, follows that road, although he chooses only to infer that his question reaches its target and that there exists an understandable answer:[159]

*Naʿam waqaftu ʿalā l-aṭlāli as'aluhā*
*mā kullu mustakhbarin tuṣghī masāmiʿuhū*

*Wa qad yujībuka waḥyan man tukhāṭibuhū*
*wa tafhamu l-qawla mimman lā turājiʿuhū*

Yes, over ruins, there I halted and questioned,
But not all that are asked have ears to hear.

Though one you speak to may yet *reveal* the answer,
And you may understand the speech of one
you do not query.

This is how Mihyār al-Daylamī understands the traditional language of the possibility of an answer: as a symbol revealed through *waḥy*, which is "revelation," or perhaps no more than "intimation." Mihyār's *waḥy*, however, is no longer the *wuḥiyy* of Labīd's *Muʿallaqah* (v. 2), that secret, time-resistant palimpsestic "writing" to which there still clings the memory of the physical existence of once-encountered ruins. To this Abbasid poet the answer can no longer lie—even initially—in the ascertainment of the remains of a tangible past. His *waḥy* will have to answer only the question about the meaning of that which is past.

Then, too, in another poem by the same Mihyār al-Daylamī, we hear that it is the poet's song, his poetry, which stirs up, or "infects," the ancient places and makes them speak. Such poetic power we shall without hesitation identify as Orphic. Also, the motif is now transformed into pure lyrical musing, in which the poet's dialogue (*muḥāwarah*) with the ruins is in the first place an internalized self-questioning monologue:[160]

*Kam waqfatin lī ʿalā Sharāfin wa fī t- /*
*turbi ʿiṭārun wa fī ṣ-ṣabā suqmū*

*Jarat maʿa r-rasmi lī muḥāwaratun*
*fahimtu minhā mā qālahū r-rasmū*

*Ka'anna shiʿrī aʿdā maʿāhidahū*
*fa aʿrabat lī ʿirāṣuhā l-ʿujmū*

Many a time have I stopped at Sharāf, when
The ground exuded perfumed redolence
and languidness was in the eastern breeze.

There I exchanged words with the camp's traces,
And I understood what the traces spoke—

As though my verses had stirred up sites
of old assignations,
And jumbly courtyards spoke with lucid tongue.

The strongest hermeneutical argument, however, that leads to the understanding of this so stubbornly insisted-upon "question" of the Arabic *aṭlāl/diyār* lyricism does not lie primarily in the self-commenting value of the historical development of that motif as we have traced it so far. It lies rather in the further fact that, without much change in its phrasing and semiotics, it is possible to view this motif in a manner that dispels whatever remains of its hermeneutical opacity—provided we step outside the formal genre context of the classical Arabic *nasīb* into that of the classical Arabic dirge-elegy, which, in its own right, is also genre-specific. Here it is Muhalhil Ibn Rabīʿah, the champion of the Banū Taghlib in their much-poeticised bloody feuds of vengeance with the Banū Bakr, who, both chronologically—for being one of the pre-Islamic bards with the most creditable claim to antiquity—and in matters of genre-identity—for having left us a number of the strongest and most genre-defined dirge-elegies in the classical Arabic poetic corpus—achieves a deepening of the symbol of the "question" that is its own cognitive paradox beyond the need of an answer. To know and not to know become equally important. Thus, in an elegy in which he weeps over the death of his brother Kulayb, Muhalhil Ibn Rabīʿah shouts out into the void of the "wasteland" (*al-baladu l-qifāru*) his call that insists on remaining a question; but the "wasteland," while still resounding with broadly elegiac echoes of the *nasīb*, has now become equated with the poet's brother, the fallen hero—or it is because of him that the land has turned into a waste:[161]

*Daʿawtuka yā Kulaybu fa lam tujibnī*
*wa kayfa yujībunī l-baladu l-qifārū*

I called you, O Kulayb, and you did not reply—
The wasteland, how will it answer me?

But the two genres, that of the structured heroic *qaṣīdah* and that of the dirge-elegy, have here more than one point of contact on the plane of diction and motifs; and so we know that the dead hero, having become the "wasteland," is, with full intertextual transparency, also the abandoned abode (*dār*) of the *qaṣīdah* and its ruin (*ṭalal*). To all these the poet issues his call/question. Beyond the *dār*, however, and beyond the "wasteland" of *al-balad al-qifār*—or in them both—as we also learn from Muhalhil Ibn Rabīʿah's elegy, there lies the grave, the ultimate wasteland and the ultimate abode. This becomes clear in the elegy's verse 20:[162]

*Sa'altu l-ḥayya ayna dafantumūhū*
*fa qālū bi safḥi l-ḥayyi dārū*

I asked the tribe: Where have you buried him?
There's an abode, down past the tribe, they said.

Here we would even seem to have received our much-expected "answer"; but that answer does not pretend to explain the ultimate enigma. It is only a guide. It leads the questioner back to where there will be his repeated encounter with the radical absence, or with the "wasteland" (v. 7). The "action" in the elegy might, therefore, be retold differently—that is, in proper sequence—which the poet has not chosen to do. The question remains unanswered, or answered only through the cognitive paradox of the symbol.

Outside this and other elegies by Muhalhil Ibn Rabīʿah, it is the legendary lore that grew around the poet and his brother Kulayb that has insisted further on the poet's tragic "question." Aside from its topical sketchiness in the Ayyām al-ʿArab, this lore is contained in the folk epic, or narrative romance, that for the most part has then spun its own vast digressive entwinement of myth and legend. The romance is known as the story, or *sīrah*, of *Al-Zīr Sālim*, after Muhalhil Ibn Rabīʿah's epithet *al-zīr*, meaning "the assiduous visitor," one who keeps the company of women. But in the romance the strongly archetypally constructed persona of the poet-as-hero even manages to change the semiotics of this epithet, for in his tragic-heroic transformation that follows his brother's death, al-Zīr, the erstwhile "visitor of women," becomes the unremitting visitor of his fallen brother's grave, and also the grave's "questioner." More often than not, however, popular romances simplify, and ultimately banalize, the archaic pathos of myth and symbol, explaining such matters in their own way. Here, too, Jassās of the Banū Bakr, the slayer of Kulayb, is being advised by his brother that

> day in, day out, in the morning al-Zīr visits the grave of Kulayb, greets it and says: "I have killed in vengeance for you such a one and such a one. Are you satisfied thereby, or not?" But no one answers him. In my view [Jassās's brother continues to advise him], you should choose a man whom you shall put inside the vault so that no one may see him, and when al-Zīr comes to visit the grave as is his custom and asks his brother that question, he [the hidden man] shall answer him with slight voice, faintly: "I am satisfied, O my brother, return your sword to the sheath and from this day forth abstain from giving battle to their men!"[163]

In the romance we are thus given a calculatedly false answer which, however, is not devoid of its own hermeneutic preoccupation. The vicarious redemption of the "value" of heroic life coined in the concrete terms of the archaic Bedouin ethos of blood vengeance, is here suggested, although clad in an antiheroic stratagem. In the scheme of poetic and symbolic justice of heroic romance, however, the banalizing stratagem will fail, and we revert to the non-banalizable realization that the "question"—even in the romance—remains as far from being answered as it has been in Muhalhil Ibn Rabīʿah's archaic dirge-elegy.

Again and again, after Muhalhil Ibn Rabīʿah, the "question" directed to the grave reappears in the classical Arabic elegiac poem. It is then also invariably contextualized as part of the "visitation." Thus, the sufi poet Aḥmad Ibn al-Mahdī al-Ghazzāl "visits," and "halts," and "asks," desiring to penetrate the secret of "the son of dust" and of "how things happen" in the nether world. Once again, we thus sense the Orphic impulse:[164]

*Yā zā'ira l-qabri qif bi l-qabri muʿtabirā*
*wa -s'alhu ʿan ḥālihī in kunta mukhtabirā*

*Wa qul lahū kayfa ḥālu -bni t-turābi wa mā*
*jarā lahū fīhi ḥaddithnī wa kayfa jarā*

*Wa ʿanhu yā qabru ḥaddithnī bi qiṣṣatihī*
*li anna ʿindaka min akhbārihī khabarā*

You who visit the grave, halt there and give thought,
Ask it how he fares, if to know you care!

To the grave say: How fares the son of dust,
And what befell him there? Speak,
how do things happen there?

Recount to me his story, grave,
For surely news of him you bear!

Or again, there is the voice of an anonymous woman-elegist:[165]

*Hal khabbara l-qabru sā'ilīhī*
*am qarra ʿaynan bi zā'irīhī*

*Am hal turāhu aḥāṭa ʿilman*
*bi l-jasadi l-mustakīni fīhī*

*Law yaʿlamu l-qabru man yuwārī*
*tāha ʿalā kulli mā yalīhī*

Did the grave yield news to questioners,
Or find solace in its visitors?

Or did it even comprehend
Whose body rests in it?

O, if the grave but knew whom it enshrouds,
It would not harbor those who pass on after him!

The stopping at the abandoned encampment and the questioning are thus symbolic stances kindred to those of the visitation of the grave and of its questioning; and in both cases we could state with the certainty of one of Michelangelo's epitaphs for Cecchino Bracci—where the tomb also speaks—that "*la sepoltura parla a chi legge questi versi.*"[166] There is here the promise to those who read the Orphic poets' verses that tombs shall speak to them as they first spoke to those poets themselves. The Arabic elegiac poets of the *nasīb*, reinforced by the poets of the genre-specific threnodic elegy, knew this the best way: the way poets "know" in their poetic praxis. Stubbornly unmindful of the abrading and banalizing effects of traditionality, it was always the poet as *faber* who, faithful to his Orphic, secret-probing impulse, managed to salvage his question's symbolic, and thus poetically live, core.

To reach out in another direction, outside of things immediately Arabic—although not outside a common semantic and semiotic referentiality that should bear on our understanding of the Arabic elegiac question—there lies the Hebrew word of *she'ōl*, the archaic "underworld," or "netherworld" of the Hebrew Bible. Several generations ago, there was still enough etymologizing curiosity present in Hebrew philology to have put forward suggestions of a possible origin, or "root," of this Hebrew equivalent of Hades. Then, however, without having reached much certainty in that domain, the inquiries appear to have come to a prevaricating standstill, clinging to the discouraging dictum that, concerning *she'ōl*, "most now refrain from positive etymology."[167] The problem may rest largely in the fact that, on the surface of things, there is little in biblical semantics and usage to bring together the specific term of *she'ōl* with the verbal root of *sha'al* ("to ask") as it occurs in the Hebrew text. Only a fleeting reference in Gesenius touches on the possibility that in *she'ōl* there may be etymologically imbedded the meaning of a "place of inquiry" and that it be somehow part of, or a reference to, "necromancy." To this we shall come later. The other two suggested etymologies that deserve to be considered are the Hebrew *sho'al*,[168] ("hollow hand")—and from there the etymologically possible "hollow place > *Hölle*/hell"—as well as the equally conceivable reference to a "low place" through the root *s-h-l*, such as in the Arabic *sahl*. The latter, however, presents us primarily with the meaning of "plain"/"plane," allowing for "low and smooth" only as an antonym of *ḥazn* ("high and rugged").

By virtue of its own contextualizations—not necessarily because of the preceding explorations in lexicographical etymology—the Hebrew *she'ōl* is also easily placed "below," however. Thus in I Samuel 2:6, God "lowers to *she'ōl* and raises"; so, too, in Isaiah 14:9, *she'ōl* lies "below" (*mittaḥat*); and, also in Isaiah (14:11), things (the pomp of life) are "brought down" to *she'ōl*. So, too, the world of forbidden sensuality, the house of perdition, where stolen waters are sweet and where bread eaten in secret is pleasant, is in the "depths" (*be ʿimqe*) of *she'ōl*. Equally in Isaiah 57:9, *she'ōl* is a place of moral downfall; as it is also the place of Israel's fall from grace and of exile in Hosea 13:14.

But it should be of significance that in the biblical *locus classicus* of the *she'ōl* as motif, the biblical writer, or redactor, chooses not to mention the term itself.

Nevertheless, that unelicited *she'ōl* is then the more strongly present in the mind as the "place of inquiry" for the purpose of necromancy. We are speaking here of I Samuel 28:6–25, where the story of Saul's night of agony before the battle with the Philistines is told.[169] Anxiety and dispiritedness have driven Saul to consult an *'eshet baᶜalat-'ob*, that is, a woman who is a conjurer of the dead, or one who can make them "return" from the underworld. The place where Saul finds such a woman is in itself semiotically revealing. It is ᶜĒn Dōr, the "well," and also the "eye" (the Arabic *ᶜayn*), of an "abode," the recognizable *dār* of the Arabic *nasīb*, but otherwise a word of rare occurrence in the biblical text—unless it carries the meaning of "generation." Such a place name, considering its context in I Samuel 28, is a strong reference to the omphalos as the sole point through which it is possible to enter the world of the dead.

While the term *she'ōl* does not occur in the story of Saul's consultation of the Sibyl, it does occur apart from that story in I Samuel 2:6, where the power to recall from *she'ōl* is given not to a Sibyl but to God. That in itself might be viewed as a case of a "redactor's" unwilling compensatory hermeneutics. In the story of Saul's agony and downfall, the king of the Israelites, conscious of his inability to face the Philistines, turns to Yahveh: "And Saul *asked* Yahveh, but Yahveh *did not answer* him—neither by dreams, nor by *'ūrīm* (lots of absolution [?]), nor through prophets" (*wayyish'al Sha'ūl ba Yehowā we lo ᶜanahū Yehowā*) (28:6). It is this passage, then, that introduces Saul's actually seeking out the Sibyl and asking her to bring from the nether world—which here, as it were, is no longer in need of further terminological specification as *she'ōl*—the phantom of Samuel; and furthermore, it is this passage, which, if translated into the Arabic idiom of the *nasīb*, would give us both the phrasing and the stance (*wuqūf*) of the Bedouin poet's questioning of the abandoned abode. As Yahveh fails to answer, so does the empty abode. The verses in I Samuel 28 that follow are then to be read almost as hermeneutical comments on both the Arabic *su'āl* and the Hebrew *she'ōl*. But, returning to verse 28:6, we register on that discreet level on which semiotics operates through the employ of style, that it is a questioner by the name of Saul/*Sha'ūl* who "asks"—*yish'al*—and that here *Sha'ūl*, the Asked One, becomes the morphologically hypothetical *sha'ūl*: the persistent, stubborn, if you will, "asker," to whom Yahveh, the *ṭalal*, did not "indicate," or "give to know" (*ᶜanahū*), an answer. Not unlike the perseverance, or the anxiety, of the archaic Arabian poet when that poet faces his *ṭalal* with his *su'āl* is the impulse behind the first Israelite king's search for archaic answers with the "woman of ᶜĒn Dōr," the holder of the secret of access to *she'ōl*.

Without leaving the chthonic domain, we may now entertain further our other "layer" of speculation, in which the Hebrew *she'ōl* may be at least brought near to the Hebrew root *sh-ᶜ-l*, which points to the meaning of "hollowness." From here a further inference, prompted by highly associative Arabic semiotics, should lead us not so much to the hollow of the underworld as rather make us halt at the underworld's gates, through which only the answered question of the chthonic password allows passage—a passage which, too, may in the end be fatal. At least such is the testimony of myth. By this we propose to relate the root phonetics, and even more firmly the scope of meaning of the *su'āl* of the *nasīb*, to the Arabic term—and mythopoeia—of the sphinx: the *siʿlāh*/*siʿlā'*/*siʿlā* of three equally valid pronunciations. There is, however, much ambiguity in this *siʿlāh*/sphinx. Its association with the chthonic root *sh-ʿ-l* is, for all we know, coincidental on that one level—although such a coincidence is semiotically formative and helpful. Then there is the undercurrent of etymologically founded synonymity between the Greek sphinx and the Arabic *siʿlāh*, for, as much as *siʿlāh* ought to be relatable to *suʿāl* ("cough"), in its Greek etymology, the sphinx conveys the meaning of the "asphyxiator" or "throttler." Both words, *siʿlāh* and sphinx, would thus reveal a common onomatopoeia first of all, which then were capable of leading to the complex semiotics of asphyxiation and the oppression of the chest by the incubus. We know furthermore, however, that the Greek incubus, itself of remote Egyptian origin, had been sent by Hera to Thebes, where it, or rather she, asked the Thebans the great riddle about the three ages of man, devoured those that failed to solve the riddle, and brought devastation to the city. Oedipus alone solves the riddle and redeems the wasteland. Oedipus facing the Sphinx is thus in the ultimate sense not different from the Arabic poet standing before the *ṭalal*. Both the Sphinx and the *ṭalal* contain the answer to their question/riddle; and, conveniently paraphrasing Paul Diel, the riddle/question, when it is solved/answered, will liberate the land from devastation and revert "ruinous life" to "renewed life."[170] And thus, not at all marginal to our mythopoeia, there is a further etymological connection of phonetic cause-and-effect between the expectoration of the cough and the question—or are we simply dealing with semiotically driven-together, discrete lexical superpositions? Is not speech as enunciation in Arabic also "expectoration," *lafẓ*?

To conclude our discussion of the stubborn repetitiveness of the Arabian poet's "questioning" of the *ṭalal*, we shall take notice of the mysterious centrality "questioning" possesses in the narrations of the legend of the grail. Thus, when Chrétien de Troyes's Perceval[171] finally finds himself in the Grail Castle, which is also the castle of his "infirm" host, the Fisher King, and witnesses the procession in which a mysterious bleeding lance, candelabra, and above all, the golden vessel called *á graal* are solemnly carried past him, he, Perceval, refrains from asking the "question" about the purpose of the *graal*, because of the knightly indoctrination in discretion he had received from his mentor, Gornemant.[172] For that, that is, for not "asking," he loses the vision of the grail, and when he wakes up in the morning, he finds the hall where he had witnessed the procession empty and the castle deserted. Repeatedly, it is then revealed to him that, had he "asked" concerning the grail, his host, the Fisher King, would have been healed of his infirmity, and fertility would have returned to the wasteland. Perceval's silence before the grail, however, was due not solely to his obedience to Gornemant, but, we are told, also to his tongue's having been tied once before when he had failed to express filial tenderness and consideration for his mother's suffering on the day he rode off in search of knightly fulfillment. "Though these explanations are different," writes the Chrétien scholar Jean Frappier, "it is possible to regard them as valid, each on its plane."[173] Both planes imply respective flaws. One is that of "formal" adherence to norm and of flawed practical judgment, while the other is a spiritual and religious flaw that manifested itself through lack of compassion. This explanation by Jean Frappier, although plausible within the immediate textuality of the Perceval romance, does not address itself to the symbol in the "question," however. We should, therefore, do better by following Northrop Frye's pondering over the "question" in Wolfram von Eschenbach's *Parzival*, and his recalling to mind T. S. Eliot, who, "as early as 'Prufrock' . . . is haunted by the theme of 'some overwhelming question,' which he associates with the return of Lazarus from the dead."[174] But it is above all through the archaic Arabian question before the *ṭalal* that we may give full justice to that symbol as it relates to the hermeneutical enigmas of the grail and the wasteland of the Fisher King—and to *why* they demand redemption through the "question."[175] One thing we can claim for the Arabic Bedouin poet: he did not have to say of himself what Wolfram von Eschenbach's Parzival was driven to confess: "He who rode to Munsalvaesche and saw the true grief there and failed to ask any question whatever, that am I, unfortunate man."[176]

In the opening scene of the classical Arabic ode/*qaṣīdah*, with the encampment's ruin and desolation, and then the poet's halting and questioning, there is thus made felt through all seven of our elegiac key words of the *nasīb* the symbolic resonance of an Arabian Orpheus standing at the gates to the underworld of his memory, of his recollection of most deeply submerged bliss. It is then, however, up to the rest of the poem to prove that the poet-singer's is an ability to charm, to create a spell that has the power to open the gates of the underworld—to establish and to validate the fullness of the Orphic act. The "question" before the *dār*-as-*ṭalal* may, therefore, be only the initial step in the presentation of the Orphic case in the Arabic *qaṣīdah*.[177] The poet's real spell is then the rest of the poem. In the opening scene of a *qaṣīdah* such as the great ode of Labīd, where we find the pathos of culture falling back and the idyll of nature taking its place, it is possible to view the compressed frames of the procession of poetic time: protracted, as it were, into a dreamy motion of renewal, self-renewal, or Orphic rebirth rather than destruction. Nature on its own terms, as it lives and gains, becomes the expression of the Orphic song. All objects, all things living, live their truest lives within the stillness of the closed Orphic frame of the poet's song, his paradoxical celebration of melancholy.

# Notes

1. Imru' al-Qays, *Dīwān*, ed. Muḥammad Abū al-Faḍl Ibrāhīm, 3rd ed. (Cairo: Dār al-Maʿārif bi Miṣr, 1969), 114.

2. Usāmah Ibn Munqidh, *Al-Manāzil wa al-Diyār*, ed. Muṣṭafā Ḥijāzī (Cairo: Dār al-Taḥrīr li al-Ṭabʿ wa al-Nashr [Al-Majlis al-Aʿlā li al-Shu'ūn al-Islāmīyah—Lajnat Iḥyā' al-Turāth al-Islāmī], 1387/1968), 127.

3. Abū Bakr Muḥammad Ibn al-Qāsim al-Anbārī, *Sharḥ al-Qaṣā'id al-Sab' al-Ṭiwāl al-Jāhilīyāt*, ed. ʿAbd al-Salām Hārūn, 3rd ed. (Cairo: Dār al-Maʿārif bi Miṣr, 1969), 526.

4. ʿUmar Ibn Abī Rabīʿah, *Dīwān*, (Beirut: Dār Ṣādir/Dār Bayrūt, 1385/1966), 432.

5. Edward William Lane, *An Arabic English Lexicon* (London: Williams and Norgate, 1865) (photo offset ed., New York: Frederick Unger Publishing Co., 1955), s.v. *ṭ-l-l*.

6. Usāmah Ibn Munqidh, *Al-Manāzil wa al-Diyār*, 111.

7. Wilhelm Gesenius, *Hebräisches und aramäisches Handwörterbuch über das Alte Testament* (Berlin/Göttingen/Heidelberg: Springer Verlag, 1954), 879.

8. Al-Nābighah al-Dhubyānī, *Dīwān*, recension Ibn al-Sikkīt, ed. Shukrī Fayṣal (Beirut: Dār al-Fikr, 1388/1968), 2.

9. Abū al-ʿAbbās Aḥmad Ibn Yaḥyā al-Shaybānī Thaʿlab, *Sharḥ Dīwān Zuhayr Ibn Abī Sulmā* (Cairo: Al-Dār al-Qawmīyah li al-Ṭibāʿah wa al-Nashr, 1384/1964) (photo offset of Dār al-Kutub ed., 1944), 86.

10. Ibid., 86.

11. Ibid., 87.

12. Al-Nābighah al-Dhubyānī, *Dīwān*, 96–97. Usāmah Ibn Munqidh (*Al-Manāzil wa al-Diyār*, 86) records a slightly different version of these verses. Other editions (W. Ahlwardt, L. Shaykhū, and Karam al-Bustānī) lack these verses altogether.

13. *Shiʿr al-Nābighah al-Jaʿdī* [*Dīwān*], ed. ʿAbd al-ʿAzīz Rabbāḥ (Damascus: Al-Maktabah al-Islāmīyah, 1384/1964), 97.

14. Charles James Lyall, ed. and trans., *The Mufaḍḍalīyāt: An Anthology of Ancient Arabian Odes compiled by Al-Mufaḍḍal son of Muḥammad, according to the Recension and with the Commentary of Abū Muḥammad al-Qāsim ibn Muḥammad al-Anbārī*. Vol. I: *Arabic Text*; Vol. II: *Translation and Notes* (Oxford: Clarendon Press, 1918), 1:449–450 (no. 44). In the present poem, I have adopted, however, the ordering of verses as 11/14/12, following Usāmah Ibn Munqidh (*Al-Manāzil wa al-Diyār*, 6).

15. Usāmah Ibn Munqidh, *Al-Manāzil wa al-Diyār*, 21.

16. Ibid., 55.

17. Muslim Ibn al-Ḥajjāj al-Qushayrī, *Ṣaḥīḥ Muslim*, commentary by al-Nawawī, 18 vols. (Cairo: Al-Maṭbaʿah al-Miṣrīyah, 1347/1929), 7:45.

18. Usāmah Ibn Munqidh, *Al-Manāzil wa al-Diyār*, 55.

19. "So möchte ich auch den engen Zusammenhang von *d-h-r* und *d-w-r* (vgl. *dahr* und *dor*) aufrecht erhalten," writes Nöldeke in his review of the Prolegomena of a Hebrew-Arabic dictionary for the Old Testament, by Friedrich Delitzsch (*Zeitschrift der Deutschen Morgenländischen Gesellschaft* 40 [1886]: 741).

20. Gesenius, *Hebräisches und aramäisches Handwörterbuch*, 159.

21. Hans Peter Duerr, *Sedna oder Die Liebe zum Leben* (Frankfurt am Main: Suhrkamp Verlag, 1984), 152–153.

22. Here it is also necessary to note that, aside from the principal *nasīb* references to *dār/diyār*, there is a related third term that occurs in the *nasīb* as well, albeit much less frequently. It is *dārah*, pl. *dārāt*. As a rule it forms part of names of place, such as, for instance, Dārat Juljul of the *Muʿallaqah* of Imru' al-Qays (*Dīwān*, 10 [v. 9]). See a discussion of this term in Nūrī Ḥammūdī al-Qaysī, *Al-Ṭabīʿah fī al-Shiʿr al-Jāhilī*, 2nd ed. (Beirut: ʿĀlam al-Kitāb/Maktabat al-Nahḍah al-ʿĀrabīyah, 1404/1984), 35–37.

23. Of this stone Herodianus wrote that it was *round*, of black color, and fallen from the sky. See E. Baldwin Smith, *The Dome: A Study in the History of Ideas* (Princeton: Princeton University Press, 1971), 72, quoting from I. Eckhel, *Doctrina numorum veterum*, VII, 1828, 250.

24. Al-Anbārī, *Sharḥ al-Qaṣā'id al-Sab'*, 243.

25. Al-Nābighah al-Dhubyānī, *Dīwān*, 2.

26. Ibid., 113.

27. Abū ʿUbādah al-Buḥturī, *Dīwān*, ed. Ḥasan Kāmil al-Ṣīrafī, 3rd ed. (Cairo: Dār al-Maʿārif bi Miṣr, 1977), 3:1788 (no. 686).

28. Usāmah Ibn Munqidh, *Al-Manāzil wa al-Diyār*, 14.
29. Lane, *Lexicon*, s.v. *r-b-ᶜ*.
30. ᶜAbīd Ibn al-Abraṣ, *Dīwān* (Beirut: Dār Ṣādir/Dār Bayrūt, 1384/1964), 113.
31. Al-Nābighah al-Dhubyānī, *Dīwān*, 2–3; see also above, p. 119.
32. Al-Nābighah al-Dhubyānī, *Dīwān*, 2–3.
33. Al-Anbārī, *Sharḥ al-Qaṣā'id al-Sabᶜ*, 241. The redaction of al-Shaybānī Thaᶜlab has the variant *ka ḥawḍi l-juddi* for *ka jidhmi l-ḥawḍi* (*Sharḥ Dīwān Zuhayr Ibn Abī Sulmā*, 7).
34. Cf. Labīd Ibn Rabīᶜah's *Muᶜallaqah*, v. 2: *kamā ḍamina l-wuḥiyya silāmuhā* ("as their stone slabs contained the writ")(al-Anbārī, *Sharḥ al-Qaṣā'id al-Sabᶜ*, 519).
35. Ḥātim Ibn ᶜAbd Allāh al-Ṭā'ī, *Dīwān Shiᶜr*, recension of Hishām Ibn Muḥammad al-Kalbī, ed. ᶜĀdil Sulaymān Jamāl, 3rd ed. (Cairo: Maktabat al-Khānjī, 1411/1990), 220.
36. Ibid.
37. ᶜAbīd Ibn al-Abraṣ, *Dīwān*, 41.
38. Al-Nābighah al-Dhubyānī, *Dīwān*, 3. Cf. the close formulaic phrasing of *ka jidhmi l-ḥawḍi* in ibid., 43; in Zuhayr Ibn Abī Sulmā's *Muᶜallaqah*, v. 5; and in the already early Islamic, ᶜUbayd Allāh Ibn Qays al-Ruqayyāt (*Dīwān*, ed. Muḥammad Yūsuf Najm [Beirut: Dār Ṣādir/Dār Bayrūt, 1378/1958], 75).
39. Al-Nābighah al-Dhubyānī, *Dīwān*, 2–6.
40. See further, Jaroslav Stetkevych, "Sīnīyat Aḥmad Shawqī wa ᶜIyār al-Shiᶜr al-ᶜArabī al-Kilāsīkī," *Fuṣūl* 7, nos. 1 and 2 (October 1986/March 1987): 24–25.
41. Both old and modern, now largely multicultural proverbs referring to "running away from the rain and ending up under a drainpipe, or under the eaves," too, are undoubtedly to be linked to very archaic warnings not to overstep the limit of the "eaves"/*Traufe*.
42. Hans Peter Duerr, *Dreamtime: Concerning the Boundary between Wilderness and Civilization*, trans. Felicitas Goodman (Oxford and New York: Basil Blackwell, 1985), 245. See more specifically, Will-Erich Peuckert, "Traufe und Flurgrenze," *Zeitschrift für Volkskunde* (Stuttgart: W. Kohlhammer Verlag) 50 (1953), esp. 66, 68–71.
43. Duerr, *Dreamtime*, 245.
44. Ludwig Deubner makes every effort at clarifying the Plutarchian confusion, albeit ultimately with limited success as well, especially since he leans too much toward the historicity and possible archaeological verifiability of the foundation myth rather than toward an anthropological interpretation that might be a more appropriate avenue of inquiry. See Ludwig Deubner, "Mundus," *Hermes. Zeitschrift für klassische Philologie* 68 (1933): 226–287.
45. *Plutarch's Lives*, trans. Bernardotte Perrin (London: William Heinemann/New York: The Macmillan Co., 1914), 1:118/119–120/121.
46. Deubner, "Mundus," 285.
47. This last etymological possibility I intend to explore separately, for my interest in it would lead me too far afield, away from Arabic, and even away from generally Semitic literary and linguistic spheres.
48. Lane, *Lexicon*, s.v. *d-m-n*.
49. Imru' al-Qays, *Dīwān*, 114.
50. Al-Nābighah al-Dhubyānī, *Dīwān*, 233; also quoted above, this chapter.
51. Al-Nābighah al-Dhubyānī, *Dīwān*, 136.
52. Bishr Ibn Abī Khāzim al-Asadī, *Dīwān*, ed. ᶜIzzat Ḥasan, 2nd ed. (Damascus: Manshūrāt Wizārat al-Thaqāfah, 1392/1972), 99.
53. Al-Anbārī, *Sharḥ al-Qaṣā'id al-Sabᶜ*, 311. See also in Dhū al-Rummah's poem no. 52, v. 57 (*Dīwān*, 2nd ed. [Damascus: Al-Maktabah al-Islāmīyah li al-Ṭibāᶜah wa al-Nashr, 1384/1964], 490), where *diman* means actually "dung." But also note that the verse in question is no. 57, thus no longer part of the *nasīb*.
54. Al-Shaybānī Thaᶜlab, *Sharḥ Dīwān Zuhayr Ibn Abī Sulmā*, 122.

55. Ibid., 123.

56. ʿAbīd Ibn al-Abraṣ, *Dīwān*, 113.

57. Ibid., 124.

58. Ibid., 41.

59. Ibid., 65.

60. Al-Anbārī, *Sharḥ al-Qaṣā'id al-Sabʿ*, 517–520.

61. Lyall, *Mufaḍḍalīyāt*, 1:559 (no. 74). See also ibid., 743 (no. 114, v. 5), for a *mukhaḍram* illustration of this topos.

62. Cf. M. M. Bakhtin, *The Dialogic Imagination*, ed. Michael Holquist, trans. Caryl Emerson and Michael Holquist (Austin: University of Texas Press, 1988), 84ff.

63. Abū al-Faraj al-Iṣfahānī, *Kitāb al-Aghānī*, ed. ʿAbd al-Sattār Aḥmad Farrāj (Beirut: Dār al-Thaqāfah, 1380/1961), 23:298. The cited verses do not occur in all the recensions of the *Aghanī*, however.

64. Thus in a Sumerian poem of sometime before 1500 B.C., in a description of the mythic land of Dilmun, consistently negative terms are found for what that *locus amoenus* "is not." There "the raven utters no cries . . . the lion kills not, the wolf snatches not the lamb, unknown is the kid-devouring wild dog," and "the dove droops not the head . . ." ("Enki and Ninhursag: A Paradise Myth," trans. S. N. Kramer, in James B. Pritchard, ed., *Ancient Near Eastern Texts Relating to the Old Testament*, 2nd ed. [Princeton: Princeton University Press, 1955, 38]). The tragic quality of the dove is brought out even in the contrivedly archaizing *qaṣīdah* by Khalaf al-Aḥmar, where that scholiast-poet allows the *qaṭāh* (sand grouse) to die because it is the substitute for the weeping turtle dove, which in turn is the metaphor for the sorrows of the poet-lover (W. Ahlwardt, *Chalef elahmar's Qasside.* Berichtigter arabischer Text, Uebersetzung und Commentar, mit Benutzung vieler handschriftlichen Quellen. Nebst Würdigung Josef von Hammer's als Arabisten [Griefswald, 1855], 391ff). R. B. Onians reviews the diverse, predominantly death-related semiotics of the dove in antiquity and in folklore: thus the evidence in Syria and Palestine of the belief that the "departed spirit" was a dove; the *columbaria* with niches for the urns or ashes of the dead; the presence of actual dovecots next to graves; etc. So, too, the association of the Erinyes with dark-colored doves (Aelian, X, 33). Cf. also the Old Testament references to the dove's joyless note : it "mourns" (Isa. 38:14; Isa. 59:11; Ezek. 7:16; Nah. 2:7) (*The Origins of European Thought: About the Body, the Mind, the Soul, the World, Time, and Fate. New interpretations of Greek, Roman and kindred evidence also of some basic Jewish and Christian beliefs* [Cambridge/New York/New Rochelle/Melbourne/Sydney: Cambridge University Press, 1988 (1951)], 500–501). In this context it is even possible to interpret the message of doom given by God to the prophet Jonah (1:1–2) as a message given to the dove, the bird that semiotically is not unrelated to the crow—for the Hebrew name for the prophet who, as messenger, was ordered to "rise and go to Nineveh . . . and cry against it [the cry of doom]" is itself the Hebrew word for "dove"/*yōnā*.

65. Abū ʿUbādah al-Buḥturī, *Dīwān*, 3:1411 (no. 555).

66. Usāmah Ibn Munqidh, *Al-Manāzil wa al-Diyār*, 142. This verse does not occur in the Dār al-Maʿārif edition of al-Buḥturī's *Dīwān*. There is a poem in the *Dīwān* (3: 2033–2036), however, that is of the same rhyme and meter.

67. Al-Buḥturī, *Dīwān*, 1:627. The editor of the *Dīwān* merely records the variant *min ḥubbihim*, whereas the editor of *Al-Manāzil wa al-Diyār* (p. 156) takes the trouble to remark that the above variant constitutes a corruption (*taḥrīf*). It is, however, easily understood how such a "corruption" could have occurred when it is otherwise part and parcel of a highly deconcretized metaphorical diction.

68. Al-Buḥturī, *Dīwān*, 1:544.

69. Al-Sharīf al-Murtaḍā, *Dīwān*, ed. Rashīd al-Ṣaffār et al. (Cairo: ʿĪsā al-Bābī al-Ḥalabī, 1958), 3:181.

70. Mihyār al-Daylamī, *Dīwān* (Cairo: Dār al-Kutub al-Miṣrīyah, 1344/1925), 1:398.

71. Al-Sharīf al-Murtaḍā, *Dīwān*, 3:106.

72. Johann Wolfgang von Goethe, *Werke*, 22 vols. (Mainz und Weimar, 1932), 1:107.

73. Cf. Jaroslav Stetkevych, "Arabic Hermeneutical Terminology: Paradox and the Production of Meaning," *Journal of Near Eastern Studies* 48 no. 2 (April 1989): 88–89.

74. Marcel Detienne, *The Gardens of Adonis: Spices in Greek Mythology*, trans. Janet Lloyd, intro. J. P. Vernant (New Jersey [Atlantic Highlands]: The Humanities Press, 1977), 74.

75. Ibid., 74—as reference to the Aristotelian *Problemata*, XX.2.923 a 9–13.

76. Detienne, *The Gardens of Adonis*, 74.

77. Ibid., 83.

78. Piero Camporesi, *Incorruptible Flesh: Bodily Mutation and Mortification in Religion and Folklore*, trans. from the Italian Tania Croft-Murray, Latin text trans. Helen Elsom (Cambridge/New York/New Rochelle/Melbourne/Sydney: Cambridge University Press, 1988), 204.

79. Walter Burkert, *Homo Necans: The Anthropology of Ancient Greek Sacrificial Ritual and Myth*, trans. Peter Bing (Berkeley/Los Angeles/London: University of California Press, 1983), 130.

80. Strabo, *The Geography of . . .* , trans. Horace Leonard Jones (London: William Heinemann Ltd/New York: G. P. Puṭnam's Sons, 1930), 5:366/367–368/369 (16.4.26) (Loeb Classics).

81. See the discussion of this question by G. R. H. Wright, "Strabo on Funerary Customs at Petra," *Palestine Exploration Quarterly*, July-December 1969, pp. 113–116. See also Gregory Nagy, *Greek Mythology and Poetics* (Ithaca and London: Cornell University Press, 1990), 174–177, on the Avestan *sairiia*, "the dried manure used as a proper funerary resting place for the corpse," and otherwise on Exposure.

82. Wright, "Strabo on Funerary Customs at Petra," 114.

83. Ibid., 113.

84. The secretary and poet of the court of Saladin, al-Qāḍī al-Fāḍil (d. 596/1200), brings out the symbolic circularity between the words "city" (*madīnah*) and "cemetery" (*maqbarah*) in verses that fall within our expanded argument of *dimnah/diman*—enabling us to further nourish the interpretative licence of associative etymologizing:

*Wa l-mudnu in rajaᶜa l-musā- / firu aw idhā kharaja l-musāfir*
*Fa bidāyatu mā yaltaqī / wa nihāyatu l-baladi l-maqābir*
*Mā -staqbalatka wa waddaᶜat- / ka l-mudnu illā bi l-maqābir*

The cities, if there the wayfarer returns,
Or when he leaves—

What he first meets,
And what is at the end, are cemeteries!

Cities do not come to receive you,
Except with cemeteries!

See al-Qāḍī al-Fāḍil (ᶜAbd al-Raḥīm Ibn ᶜAlī al-Baysānī) *Dīwān*, 2 vols., ed. Aḥmad Aḥmad Badawī and Ibrāhīm al-Abyārī (Cairo: Wizārat al-Thaqāfah wa al-Irshād al-Qawmī/al-Idārah al-ᶜĀmmah li al-Thaqāfah, 1961), 2:496 (no. 540).

85. Abū Muḥammad al-Qāsim al-Anbārī quotes this *ḥadīth* in his commentary on v. 20 of ᶜAlqamah's *qaṣīdah*, which figures as no. 119 in Lyall, *Mufaḍḍalīyāt*, 1:778. There the reference is to "polluted watering ponds" (*dimni l-ḥiyāḍi*). Here, however, we must also remember that *ḥiyāḍ* also means "menstruation," or the "*pollution* of menstruation."

86. Another challenging analogy to the *ḥadīth* semantics of the "idiom" *khaḍrā' al-diman* presents itself in the name of the Umayyad, or early Abbasid, poet ʿAbd Allāh Ibn al-Dumaynah—the son of the "little," or "dear," *dimnah*. This poet, one of the favorite lyricists of the Umayyad/Abbasid period, thus grew as a man of letters, and biologically, out of a morally unaffected *dimnah* that was at home in an undisrupted poetic tradition.

87. *Oxford English Dictionary*, s.v. midden.

88. Cf. II Kings 9:37; Jer. 8:2, 9:21, 16:4, 25:33; Ps. 83:11.

89. Josh. 21:35 (but to be read, perhaps, *rimmonah*).

90. Isa. 10:31.

91. Isa. 25:10.

92. Josh. 15:31; I Chron. 2:49.

93. The plural form *al-madā'in* occurs in the Qur'ān three times in a recognizably related manner (Al-Aʿrāf, 111; Al-Shuʿarā', 36, 54). In all three cases there is also a clearly perceptible similarity of diction and context with the aforementioned late biblical books of Esther 1:1, 3, Ezra 2:1, and Nehemiah 1:3, where the word's meaning is not that of "city" but rather of "province," or "district" as administrative unit. It is in the qur'ānic occurrences of *madīnah* in the singular form that, of the fifteen cases (Al-Aʿrāf, 123; Al-Tawbah, 101 [twice], 120; Yūsuf, 30; Al-Ḥijr, 67; Al-Kahf, 19, 82; Al-Naml, 48; al-Qaṣaṣ, 15, 18, 20; Al-Aḥzāb, 60; Yā Sīn, 20; Al-Munāfiqūn, 8), only Al-Aʿrāf, 123, may have the (older?) "administrative" meaning. In the other cases the meaning of town/city in the qur'ānic text, and in subsequent Arabic literary usage as a whole, appears to have crystallized.

94. Lyall, *Mufaḍḍalīyāt*, 1:268 (no. 26, v. 2).

95. Abū Saʿīd ʿAbd al-Malik Ibn Qurayb Ibn ʿAbd al-Malik al-Aṣmaʿī, *Al-Aṣmaʿīyāt*, ed. Aḥmad Muḥammad Shākir and ʿAbd al-Salām Hārūn, 3rd ed. (Cairo: Dār al-Maʿārif bi Miṣr, n.d.), 184 (no. 64, v. 1). To be noted, too, is that this poet is also a sensitive *dimnah* lyricist. See ibid., 180 (no. 63, v. 5).

96. *Sharḥ Dīwān al-Akhṭal al-Taghlibī*, ed. Īlīyā Salīm al-Ḥāwī (Beirut: Dār al-Thaqāfah, 1968), 263. See also Zuhayr Ibn Abī Sulmā's poem, where this verse is cited in the commentary to Zuhayr's use of *ibn bulaydah* (Al-Shaybānī Thaʿlab, *Sharḥ Dīwān Zuhayr Ibn Abī Sulmā*, 271 [v. 8]).

97. Ivan Kotlarevs'kiy, *Eneida* (Berlin: Olha Diakova, 1922), 17.

98. See such a highly exceptional case in Imru' al-Qays, *Dīwān*, 166 (v. 39 of a poem rhyming in "r"). There the singular *uthfīyah* occurs with the meaning of a "well-rounded rock," to describe the rump of a horse. It thus falls outside the scope of the *nasīb*, into the theme of "chivalrous hunt."

99. Abū Muḥammad ʿAbd al-Malik Ibn Hishām, *Al-Sīrah al-Nabawīyah* (Cairo: Dār al-Fikr, 1980), 2:635.

100. See a "late" classical poetic example in al-Sharīf al-Murtaḍā, *Dīwān*, 2:268. In more modern usage, however, *thālithatu l-athāfī* also acquires meanings of "firmness," "definitiveness," etc.

101. Al-Ḥajj (XXII), 29.

102. Thus in the *ḥadīth*: *fa taffathat al-dimā'u makānahu* (and blood [lit. "the" blood] stained/contaminated its place). Cited from Muḥammad Murtaḍā al-Ḥusaynī al-Zabīdī, *Tāj al-ʿArūs*, ed. Muṣṭafā Ḥijāzī (Kuwait: Maṭbaʿat Ḥukūmat al-Kuwayt, 1389/1969), 5:179. In his perusal of *Tāj al-ʿArūs*, Lane has the verb as *tafathat* (i.e., as a First Form), however (Lane, *Lexicon*, s.v. *t-f-th*).

103. Al-Anbārī, *Sharḥ al-Qaṣā'id al-Sabʿ*, 241.

104. Lyall, *Mufaḍḍalīyāt*, 1:470 (no. 49).

105. Al-Ḥuṭay'ah, *Dīwān*, Recension of al-Aʿrābī and Abū ʿAmr al-Shaybānī, Commentary by Abū Saʿīd al-Sukkarī (Beirut: Dār Ṣādir, 1387/1967), 240.

106. Lyall, *Mufaḍḍalīyāt*, 1:809 (no. 120, v. 31).

107. Al-Buḥturī, *Dīwān*, 3:1382 (no. 548).

108. Cf. Labīd, above, p. 141.
109. Usāmah Ibn Munqidh, *Al-Manāzil wa al-Diyār*, 142. This verse is not found in al-Sharīf al-Murtaḍā's *Dīwān*.
110. Al-Nābighah al-Dhubyānī, *Dīwān*, 233.
111. ʿUbayd Allāh Ibn Qays al-Ruqayyāt, *Dīwān*, ed. Muḥammad Yūsuf Najm (Beirut: Dār Ṣādir/Dār Bayrūt, 1378/1958), 75.
112. Al-Anbārī, *Sharḥ al-Qaṣā'id al-Sabʿ*, 528 (v. 10).
113. Abū Nuwās [al-Ḥasan Ibn Hāni'], *Dīwān*, ed. Aḥmad ʿAbd al-Majīd al-Ghazālī (Beirut: Dār al-Kitāb al-ʿArabī, 1402/1982), 68.
114. Al-Shaybānī Thaʿlab, *Sharḥ Dīwān Zuhayr Ibn Abī Sulmā*, 220.
115. Bishr Ibn Abī Khāzim, *Dīwān*, 130.
116. Usāmah Ibn Munqidh, *Al-Manāzil wa al-Diyār*, 185; and Gustav E. von Grunebaum, "Abū Du'ād al-Iyādī: "Collection of Fragments," *Wiener Zeitschrift für die Kunde des Morgenlandes* 51 (1948–52): 261. Von Grunebaum's edition of the fragment returns to the, in our textual contexts more common, choice of *sufʿ* over Usāmah Ibn Munqidh's *suḥm*. It also chooses *al-farādi* over *al-firādi*, as well as *yuʿaffā* over *tuʿaffā*.
117. Usāmah Ibn Munqidh, *Al-Manāzil wa al-Diyār*, 178. Al-Aṣmaʿī's recension of this short *ʿaynīyah* poem by al-Qushayrī (in Abū ʿAlī al-Qālī, *Kitāb al-Amālī*, 2nd ed. [Cairo: Dār al-Kutub al-Miṣrīyah, 1344/1926], 1:190–191) does not include the above verse.
118. Usāmah Ibn Munqidh, *Al-Manāzil wa al-Diyār*, 140.
119. Lyall, *Mufaḍḍalīyāt*, 1:541–542 (no. 67, vv. 41–44).
120. Al-Khansā', *Dīwān*, Commentary by Thaʿlab Abū al-ʿAbbās Aḥmad Ibn Yaḥyā Ibn Sayyār al-Shaybānī al-Naḥwī, ed. Anwar Abū Suwaylim (ʿAmmān: Dār ʿAmmār, 1409/1988), 381 (v. 11 of poem beginning *Mā hāja ḥuznaki am bi l-ʿayni ʿuwwārū*).
121. F. G. Holweck, *A Biographical Dictionary of the Saints—With a General Introduction on Hagiography* (St. Louis and London: B. Herder Book Co., 1924) (Detroit: Gale Research Company, 1969), 679.
122. *Der kleine Pauly. Lexikon der Antike auf der Grundlage von Pauly's Realencyclopädie der Classischen Altertumswissenschaft*, ed. Konrat Ziegler and Walter Sontheimer (Munich: Alfred Bruckenmüller Verlag, 1972), 4:514.
123. In his essay "*Märchen—Mythos—Sage*," Lutz Röhrich further relates to the myth of the Graiae a fairy tale of three women with only one eye. In a manner characteristic of fairy tales, however, instruments of magic take the place of the search of and guidance along the way to that which is desired (*Antiker Mythos in unseren Märchen*, ed. Wolfdietrich Siegmund [Kassel: Erich Röth-Verlag, 1984], 14).
124. Jarich G. Oosten, *The War of the Gods: The Social Code in Indo-European Mythology* (London/Boston/Melbourne/Henley: Routledge and Kegan Paul, 1985), 76–78.
125. Qur'ān, 7: 73–79; 11: 61–68; 26: 141–158; 54: 23–32; 91: 11–14; and 17: 59.
126. Bishr Ibn Abī Khāzim, *Dīwān*, 95.
127. Dante Alighieri, *Il Convivio* (Turin: Collezione di Classici Italiani, 1927), 4: 35, 39. In his discussion of the four levels of meaning of a text, Dante concludes "that the literal sense should always come first as the one in which the other meanings are included, and without which it were impossible and irrational to attend to the others. . . ." See *The Convivio of Dante Alighieri*, (London: The Temple Classics, 1903), 64–65.
128. Al-Kumayt Ibn Zayd al-Asadī, *Hāshimīyāt*, Commentary by Abū Riyāsh Ibn Ibrāhīm al-Qaysī, ed. Dāwūd Sallūm and Nūrī Ḥammūdī al-Qaysī (Beirut: ʿĀlam al-Kitāb/Maktabat al-Nahḍah al-ʿArabīyah, 1404/1984), 101.
129. Abū al-Faraj al-Iṣbahānī, *Kitāb al-Aghānī*, ed. Ibrāhīm al-Abyārī (Cairo: Dār al-Shaʿb, 1390/1970), 17:6282.
130. Oosten, *The War of the Gods*, 72–90.
131. Al-Nābighah al-Dhubyānī, *Dīwān*, 173.
132. The etymological hesitations concerning the relationship of Vesta and Hestia are traced in *Paulys Real-Encyclopädie der classischen Altertumswissenschaft*, ed. Georg

Wissowa and Wilhelm Kroll (Stuttgart: J. B. Metzlersche Buchhandlung, 1912), 15 (Semi-Volume): 1257–1303. A recent, more radical and comprehensive approach to Hestia/Vesta etymology is by Nagy, *Greek Mythology and Poetics*, 104–105, 143ff.

133. As Ginette Paris points out, "when the Persians laid siege to Athens and extinguished the sacred fire, the Athenians, after defeating them, sent for fire at the great temple of Hestia at Delphi to re-kindle the fire of their own city" (Ginette Paris, *Pagan Meditations: The Worlds of Aphrodite, Artemis, and Hestia*, trans. Gwendolyn Moore (Dallas: Spring Publications, Inc., 1986), 168.

134. Ibid, 168.

135. See above, p. 174.

136. Günter Lüling has already noted the actual leaning of the qur'ānic occurrences of the noun *al-khuld* toward a *negative Wertung*, as well as toward the more balanced positive-negative distribution of the participial pl. meaning. He also stressed the overall "negative intention" of the root *kh-l-d* in the Qur'ān. He failed, however, to draw the appropriate conclusion of the ultimate meaning of that which he calls "negative" as well as what he calls "positive," for both meanings are no more than aspects—one direct, the other indirect—of their original chthonic provenance. See Günter Lüling, *Über den Ur-Qur'ān: Aufsätze zur Rekonstruktion vorislamischer christlicher Strophenlieder im Qur'ān* (Erlangen: Verlagsbuchhandlung H. Lüling, 1974), 215.

137. Thus to the poet Ḍaḥḥāk Ibn ʿUmārah Ibn Mālik al-ʿAdawī, "avarice does not give survival to its practitioner," only the pursuit of glory in war secures it (*Der Dīwān des arabischen Dichters Ḥātim Ṭej, nebst Fragmenten*, ed. and trans. Friedrich Schulthess [Leipzig: J. C. Hinrichs'sche Buchhandlung, 1897], 33; or, similarly, in verse 54 of Ṭarafah's *Muʿallaqah* [Al-Anbārī, *Sharḥ al-Qaṣā'id al-Sabʿ*, 192]).

138. Notice further Qur'ān 3:107, where, if viewed purely stylistically, *jannah*, or *jannāt*, has with equal chthonic force been replaced by *raḥmah*: *"fa fī raḥmati Allāhi hum fīhā khālidūna."*

139. Al-Nābighah al-Dhubyānī, *Dīwān*, 14–16 (vv. 27–31). We find the term *yamāmah* used by the Umayyad poet ʿUrwah Ibn Ḥizām in a context of augury (*Al-Aghānī* [Beirut, 1961], 23:298). Here the "augurer" is termed *ʿarrāf*—thus cf. the discussion above of *ʿarīf* in the context of the motif of the *athāfī*. One should be able to make a further general observation concerning the two terms for "dove" (*ḥamāmah/yamāmah*) that *yamāmah*—even as it occurs in the name of the legendary Zarqā' al-Yamāmah in al-Nābighah al-Dhubyānī's ode—is a bird used in augury as well, although it is not part of the symbol of the tripod of the *athāfī*.

140. It could be, however, that in *ḥamāmāt/ḥumm* we may not have a false etymology after all, if we consider as analogical the etymology of the German word *Taube*, which, according to Jacob and Wilhelm Grimm, should be relatable to the old Irish *dub* ("black"), itself analogical to the Greek *pelios* ("*schwarzblau*") (*Deutsches Wörterbuch* [Leipzig: Verlag von S. Hirzel, 1935], Vol. 11, Section 1, Part 1 (*t - treftig*), 166.). Cf. the *Oxford English Dictionary*'s "suggested" derivation of "dove" from "to dive" (!). The latter appears to me as an altogether desperate attempt.

141. Robertson Smith, *The Religion of the Semites*, 377.

142. Alberto Ravinell and Whitney Green, *The Role of Human Sacrifice in the Ancient Near East* (Missoula, Mont.: Scholars Press for The American School of Oriental Research, 1975), 183–184n.356.

143. Al-Nābighah al-Dhubyānī, *Dīwān*, 2.

144. The text of the verses quoted is not according to the Shukrī Fayṣal edition of al-Nābighah's *Dīwān* (113). I have chosen to adhere to the more commonly referred-to version found in Luwīs Shaykhū, *Kitāb Shuʿarā' al-Naṣrānīyah—qabla al-Islām*, 2nd ed. (Beirut: Dār al-Mashriq, 1967), 699; and contained also in W. Ahlwardt, ed., *The Divans of the Six Ancient Arabic Poets: Ennābiga, ʿAntara, Tharafa, Zuhair, ʿAlqama and Imruulqais* (London: Tübner and Co., 1870), 23.

145. Al-Nābighah al-Dhubyānī, *Dīwān*, 196–197.
146. ʿAntarah Ibn Shaddād, *Dīwān* (Beirut: Dār Ṣādir/Dār Bayrūt, 1385/1966), 229.
147. Ibid., 56.
148. See this verse also discussed above.
149. Lyall, *Mufaḍḍalīyāt*, 1:837 (no. 124).
150. Ibid., 1:485 (no. 54), 1:827 (no. 122, esp. v. 6), 1:355 (no. 38, esp. v. 3), 1:743 (no. 114, v. 4).
151. Dhū al-Rummah, *Dīwān*, 402 (no. 41), 587 (no. 67).
152. *Shiʿr al-Walīd Ibn Yazīd*, ed. Ḥusayn ʿAṭwān (Oman: Maktabat al-Aqṣā, 1979), 130 (no. 104).
153. ʿUmar Ibn Abī Rabīʿah, *Dīwān*, 315.
154. Al-Buḥturī, *Dīwān*, 3:1788 (no. 686).
155. We know that of the two *al-simākayni* the intended one is Spica, not Arcturus, because only the former is associated with rainfall. See Lane, *Lexicon*, s.v. *s-m-k*.
156. Abū Tammām, *Dīwān*, 4 vols., recension of al-Khaṭīb al-Tibrīzī, ed. Muḥammad ʿAbduh ʿAzzām, 3rd ed. (Cairo: Dār al-Maʿārif bi Misr, 1970), 2:395 (no. 99).
157. Ibid., 3:222–223 (no. 144).
158. Such a fragmentary quotation of Abū Tammām's *nasīb* appears in Ḍiyā' al-Dīn Ibn al-Athīr, *Al-Istidrāk fī al-Radd ʿalā Risālat Ibn al-Dahhān al-Musammah bi al-Ma'ākhidh al-Kindīyah min al-Maʿānī al-Ṭā'īyah*, ed. Ḥifnī Muḥammad Sharaf (Cairo: Maktabat al-Anjlū al-Miṣrīyah, 1958), 33.
159. Mihyār al-Daylamī, *Dīwān*, 2:250.
160. Ibid., 4:24. The three cited verses correspond to verses 31, 32, and 33 of the *qaṣīdah*. This expanded *nasīb* stance is not unusual in Mihyār al-Daylamī's sense of *qaṣīdah* form. It is also to be noted that in v. 31 there is an enjambment across the hemistich division, and that, furthermore, because of this, there is also imbalance, or rather "license," in the last foot of the first hemistich and the first foot of the second.
161. Luwīs Shaykhū, *Shuʿarā' al-Naṣrānīyah*, 163.
162. Ibid., 164.
163. Luwīs ʿAwaḍ, *Usṭūrat Ūrīst wa al-Malāḥim al-ʿArabīyah* (Cairo: Dār al-Kātib al-ʿArabī li al-Ṭibāʿah wa al-Nashr, 1968), 94–95.
164. Muḥammad Ibn ʿĪsā, ed., *Kitāb Mukhtaṣar al-Imām al-Amjad wa al-ʿAlam al-Mufrad al-Khayr al-Shaykh Aḥmad al-Mahdī al-Ghazzāl fī Dhikr Nasab wa Sīrat Mashāyikh wa baʿḍ Manāqib Manbaʿ al-Asrār wa Maṭlaʿ al-Anwār*, 2nd ed. (Tunis, 1349 H.), 286.
165. ʿAbd al-Badīʿ Ṣaqr, ed., *Shāʿirāt al-ʿArab* (Al-Dawḥah: Manshūrāt al-Maktab al-Islāmī, 1387/1967), 407. The transmission is according to al-Aṣmaʿī.
166. Michelangelo Buonarroti, *Le Rime*, preface and notes by Aldo Foratti (Milan: Casa Editrice R. Caddeo, [1921]), 61. The quotation is from Michelangelo's postscript to his epitaph no. 36 for Cecchino Bracci.
167. William Gesenius, *A Hebrew and English Lexicon of the Old Testament—With an appendix containing the biblical Aramaic*, trans. Edward Robinson (Boston and New York: Houghton Mifflin Company, 1907), 982. Also see Alexander Heidel, *The Gilgamesh Epic and Old Testament Parallels* (Chicago: University of Chicago Press, 1963 [first pbl. 1946]), 173–188.
168. Ibid., 982, 1043.
169. It is quite notable that, in spite of the taciturnity of the lexicographers as regards *sheōl* and the aspect of its etymology which concerns us here most directly, Cyrus H. Gordon should yet state quite matter-of-factly, albeit only in a footnote, that "this Hebrew word means 'asking,' referring to the inquiring of the dead through witchcraft; cf. 1 Samuel 28:16 where the root of 'Sheol' expresses Saul's inquiring of Samuel's ghost. The Greek *puhthésthai* 'to inquire (of the dead)' is used in a similar context in Odyssey 11:50." See Cyrus H. Gordon, *The Common Background of Greek and Hebrew Civilizations* (New

York: W. W. Norton and Company, Inc., 1965 [1962]), 86n. Heidel's (*The Gilgamesh Epic and Old Testament Parallels*, 189–190) theologically conditioned dismissal of the story of I Samuel 28:6–25 as "a demonic delusion," its main protagonists, King Saul and the Sibyl of ʿEn Dōr, as "benighted" and "Godforsaken," and the story itself as "devoid of all argumentative value" is, in intellectual terms, laughable.

170. Paul Diel, *Symbolism in Greek Mythology: Human Desire and Its Transformation* (Boulder and London: Shambhala, 1980), 129ff.

171. Chrétien de Troyes, *The Story of the Grail (Li contes del graal), or Perceval*, ed. Rupert T. Pickens, trans. William W. Kibler (New York and London: Garland Publishing, Inc., 1990). See lines 1628–1636 (pp. 80/81): Perceval instructed by his mentor "not to be too talkative"; lines 3168–3175 (pp. 156/157): Perceval observes "the marvel" of the white lance with the drop of blood on its tip but refrains from asking how it came about, "for he recalled the admonishment given by the gentleman who had knighted him"; lines 3179–3180 (pp. 156/157): two squires come carrying in their hands candelabra; and lines 3186–3213 (pp. 156/157–158/159): a maiden carrying "a grail" in her two hands, maiden with the grail passing before the bed of the Fisher King into another chamber, the young knight watching the procession "but did not dare ask who was served from the grail, for in his heart he always kept the wise gentleman's advice."

172. Of hermeneutical relevance to us at this point should be the Akkadian story of Adapa, which, as an epic-mythical text, is very much a companion to the epic of Gilgamesh. In its segment (B) from the El-Amarna archives (fourteenth century B.C.) the hero Adapa is summoned to heaven to appear before Anu. At departure he is advised by Ea not to eat, when offered before Anu, of "the bread of death" nor to drink of "the water of death." Adapa follows the advice, only to hear Anu exclaim: "Come now, Adapa! Why didst thou neither eat nor drink? / Thou shalt not have (eternal) life! Ah, *per*[*ver*]*se* mankind!" / "Ea, my master, / Commanded me: 'Thou shalt not eat, thou shalt not drink'" / "Take him away and return him to his earth." For, indeed, Adapa had thus abstained from partaking of "the bread of life" and of "the water of life." See James B. Pritchard, ed., *The Ancient Near East*. Volume I: *An Anthology of Texts and Pictures* (Princeton: Princeton University Press, 1973 [1958]), 77–79. See also the reference in Gordon, *The Common Background of Greek and Hebrew Civilizations*, 86–87.

173. Roger Sherman Loomis, ed., *Arthurian Literature in the Middle Ages: A Collaborative History* (Oxford: Clarendon Press, 1961 [1st. ed. 1959]), 189–190; but see also the entire chap. 15 by Jean Frappier, "Chrétien de Troyes," in ibid., 157–191.

174. Northrop Frye, *Myth and Metaphor. Selected Essays, 1974–1988*, ed. Robert D. Denham (Charlottesville and London: University Press of Virginia, 1990), 346. See T. S. Eliot, *The Waste Land and Other Poems* (New York and London: Harcourt Brace Jovanovich, 1979), 3, 7, i.e., Prufrock's, "To lead you to an overwhelming question . . . / Oh, do not ask, 'What is it?'" and "To roll it toward some overwhelming question, / To say: 'I am Lazarus, come from the dead, / Come back to tell you all, I shall tell you all'—."

175. Also of interest here should be Eugene J. Weinraub's study which addresses itself centrally to Perceval's "question" before the grail (*Chrétien's Jewish Grail: A New Investigation of the Imagery and Significance of Chrétien de Troyes's Grail Episode Based upon Medieval Hebraic Sources* [Chapel Hill: North Carolina Studies in the Romance Languages and Literatures, U.N.C. Department of Romance Languages, 1976]). In it the author points out highly interesting similarities between the "grail" and the "question" passages in Chrétien's *Perceval* and the key ritual aspects of the Jewish *Seder/Haggadah*—particularly those of the obligatory ritual "questions" that must be asked as an introduction to the ceremonial retelling of the story of the Hebrews' Exodus from Egypt. The symbolic aspect of the "questioning" within its "salvation" context thus becomes paramount. Note esp. Plate 1: "The Simple Son and the Son Who Knows Not How to Ask"; and ch. 3 ("A New Judaic Interpretation"), 50–87. Above all, however, Eugene J. Weinraub produces a Jewish "reading" of Chrétien's Grail story (104ff.), which, in itself,

confirms the universality of the Grail and the symbolic dimension of the "question"; by broadening his perspective to that degree, even his idea of Perceval as the Errant Jew (111) becomes a legitimate "reading."

176. */der ūf Munsalvaesche reit,/ unt der den rehten kumber sach,/ unt der deheine vrāge sprach,/ daz bin ich unsaelec barn/.* Wolfram von Eschenbach, *Parzival und Titurel.* Part I: Text, ed. Ernst Martin (Halle: Verlag der Buchhandlung des Waisenhauses, 1920 [new printing]), 172 [488, 16–19]. See also Loomis, *Arthurian Literature in the Middle Ages,* 235–236.

A further confluence may be found here in the very choice of von Eschenbach's symbolic landscape, or "locale," for his Munsalvaesche—as the landscape of the Grail—is translatable literally, and as symbolic circumstance, into the Bedouin poet's *arḍ qifār*, the "wasteland" of his "campsite ruin." For the interpretation, or interpretations, of the meaning of Munsalvaesche, see Herbert Kolb, *Munsalvaesche: Studien zum Kyotproblem* (Munich: Eidos Verlag, 1963), esp. 130–135. Even Kolb's preference for the meaning/etymology of *salvagium*, which leads him to a "prefiguration" of a *locus amoenus*—"einen paradiesischen Ort" (140)—does not clash with the meaning of the Bedouin poet's "abandoned encampment," which, ultimately, is that poet's *locus amoenus* lost.

177. On the Orphic dimensions of the *qaṣīdah*, see also John Seybold's conclusions, below, ch. 5.

# III

# GUISES OF THE *GHŪL*

## DISSEMBLING SIMILE AND SEMANTIC OVERFLOW IN THE CLASSICAL ARABIC *NASĪB*

*Michael A. Sells*

The Early Arabic *qaṣīdah* presents us with an unusually dense texture of similes, a vivid imagistic surface, and an intricate rhetoric and diction of description. In this century, description has been the dominant paradigm through which the poetic language of the qaṣīdah has been interpreted. In an earlier essay, I suggested that the consensus view of the qaṣīdah as being primarily descriptive ultimately failed to allow critical access to the poetry, and that this failure was then projected onto the poetry through characterization of the qaṣīdah as merely descriptive, purely objective, lacking in imagination, an atomized series of images, and, most persistently, "stereotyped"—all of which were in fact attributes of the dominant Western critical discourse on the qaṣīdah.[1] The flaws and limitations of this paradigm have not gone unchallenged.[2] What is still needed is a study specifically devoted to offering an alternative interpretation of the poetic function of the simile in the early qaṣīdah.

In this chapter I will examine the simile within the first section of the qaṣīdah, the *nasīb*, or remembrance of the beloved, with special attention to that section of the nasīb conventionally called the description of the beloved.[3] Although the poetic language is descriptive in the purely conventional sense used by the classical Arabic commentators who discuss certain sections of the poems as *waṣf* (description) and *naᶜt* (characterization), the simile functions in a manner far too complex to be reduced to mere description of the beloved. The simile sets up an expectation that the beloved will be described. It then goes on to evoke the beloved. But what is presented in these similes is not in fact the beloved as an object of description, but the mythopoetic world of the lost garden or meadow.

At this point it may be helpful to adopt the common division in literary theory between two primary forms of poetic signification: the metaphorical, based on relations of similarity, and the metonymic, based upon relationships of contiguity.[4] In the nasīb, the metaphors and similes that are engendered by the mention of the beloved function at first on the metaphorical level, the level of similarity: the curl of the beloved's hair is like the curl of the grapevine, her mouth is like a draught of wine, her fragrance is like the fragrance of musk. In most cases the original metaphor or simile touches off a chain of additional similes. Because the original simile was directly linked to a feature of the beloved, the reasonable expectation results that the entire chain of similes will be descriptive of the beloved. In fact, the similes seem to extend, either through the elaboration of one simile or through a chain of simple similes, far beyond the original point of comparison.

Given the original expectation of a description of the beloved, the simile dissembles. The primary referent of these similes is not the beloved but a symbolic analogue of the beloved, the lost garden. Underneath the similes, related one to another by the most precise and vivid material correspondences, is created a set of elements that are related metonymically, especially through the process of synecdoche (substitution of a part for the whole) to the lost garden. At the intersection of the metaphorical and metonymic axes, there occurs a semantic overflow.

The relationship between the apparent object of description (the beloved) and the symbolic analogue (the lost garden) is further complicated by the erotic play within the passages. Time after time, in what from the descriptive perspective would be purely digressive wanderings, a dynamic polarity of sexual union and ablution or purification is introduced. At the most intensely erotic moments, the same water imagery, for example, will signify, at the same time, sexual water and ablutionary water.

The dissembling nature of the description of the beloved and the associative logic that governs it is best revealed when a number of examples of such descriptions are brought together. I have chosen for detailed analysis passages from several classical nasībs that are particularly well known within the tradition. In the course of the analysis, however, it becomes apparent that the description of the beloved is not self-contained as an isolated and stylized convention. Rather, its underlying symbolic associations are tied into the entire nasīb, and will lead, therefore, to a discussion of the nasīb proper.[5]

Our first example is taken from the *Mufaḍḍalīyah* ode of ʿAlqamah, *hal mā ʿalimta* (Is what you learned?). In this case, the description of the beloved is introduced as part of the *ẓaʿn* motif, the departure of the beloved and her tribe. The procession of departure is depicted at the moment the beloved is led away in her howdah, the elaborately brocaded camel litter that is a major element in the ẓaʿn episode. In this case the beloved is referred to as an *utrujjah* (etrog, citron). The original metaphor then generates a stream of similes:

6. They carried an utrujjah away.
A saffron-scented perfume trailed.
Before the senses even now
her fragrance lingers.

7. The folds of her hair
redolent as musk when the pod is opened.
Reaching out to touch it
even the stuff-nosed is overcome.

8. Liken my weeping eye to a water bag
dragged down the well slope
by a roan-mare camel, withers
bound to the saddle stay

9. For a full season unsaddled,
until her hump hardened,
firm as the rounded side
of a smith's bellows,

10. Cured of the mange
and covered
with a resinous balm,
clear and pure,

11. Spilling water into channels
as grain husks part
from the ripening fruit,
the flooded slopes flowing over.

12. To remember Salma! to recall
times spent with her
is folly, conjecture about the other side,
a casting of stones,

13. Breast sash crossed
and falling, gown folds
at the hip, clinging, soft
as a gazelle fawn reared within the yard.[6]

6. *yaḥmilna utrujjatan naḍkhu l-ʿabīri bihā*
*ka'anna taṭyābahā fī l-anfi mashmūmū*

7. *ka'anna fa'rata miskin fī mafāriqihā*
*li l-bāsiṭi l-mutaʿāṭī wahwa mazkūmū*

8. *fa l-ʿaynu minnī ka'an gharbun taḥuṭṭu bihī*
*dahmā'u ḥārikuhā bi l-qatbi maḥzūmū*

9. *qad ʿuriyat zamanan ḥattā staṭaffa lahā*
*kitrun ka ḥāfati kīri l-qayni malmūmū*

10. *qad adbara l-ʿarru ʿanhā wahya shāmiluhā*
*min nāṣiʿi l-qaṭirāni ṣ-ṣirfi tadsīmū*

11. *tasqī madhāniba qad zālat ʿaṣīfatuhā*
*ḥadūruhā min atiyyi l-mā'i maṭmūmū*

12. *min dhikri salmā wa mā dhikrī l-awāna bihā*
*illā s-safāhu wa ẓannu l-ghaybi tarjīmū*

13. *ṣifru l-wishāḥayni mil'u d-dirʿi kharʿabatun*
*ka'annahā rasha'un fī l-bayti malzūmū*

Here we have one of the most famous of all the classical descriptions of the beloved. Yet for all the apparatus of description, we are actually given very little precise description of the beloved herself. Instead, the poetic voice seems to get caught up in its very first metaphor, that of the beloved as *utrujjah*, the citron or etrog. The apparently non-Arabic etymology of this term suggests that it was not common in the Arabian peninsula. The etrog has important symbolic associations in the ancient Middle East, attested to in Talmudic literature as the "the goodly fruit," of Deuteronomy.[7] Its fragrance and texture are particularly sensuous. The image is one of several round images, such as the egg and the pearl, used in the classical qaṣīdah in symbolic association with the beloved.

The passage is made up of four major sections. The first consists of two verses governed by the opening metaphor of the beloved as *utrujjah*, and by two subsidiary similes involving fragrance beginning with *ka'anna* (as if), the first of which extends through the second hemistitch of verse 6, the second of which begins with verse 7 and extends throughout the verse. As is often the case, the antecedent is ambivalent: the fragrance could be that of the beloved, or it could also be the *utrujjah*. Where the original metaphor leaves off is never specified.

The second section shifts perspective from the beloved to the poet. It begins with a comparison of the poet's eye to a water bag (*ka'an gharbun* . . . ), a simile that takes up three hemistichs. That simile yields to a fourth simile comparing the hump of the camel to the rounded side of a smith's bellows (*ka ḥāfati kīri l-qayni*), which then turns into an extended depiction of the camel smeared with balm and recovering from mange, resolving finally into a tableau depicting the irrigation camel mare pouring water into channels.

The structured rhetoric of description reveals successively larger "waves" of semantic overflow set in motion by the original symbolic reference to the beloved. The buildup in wave length can be seen by following the intervals between simile markers: one hemistich, two hemistichs, three hemistichs, four and one-half hemistichs. The last wave is strong enough to pull away from the diction governed by similes and to establish an independent vignette, ending in the lush imagery of the watered garden (grain husks part from the ripening fruit / the flooded slopes flowing over).

The third section is confined to verse 12 and is a moment of what in other poems is called *ṣaḥw* (waking). In terms of poetic diction it is a "coming to" from the reverie of semantic overflow. The poetic voice tries to put the reverie and overflow in perspective. It is all "from memory of Salmā" (*min dhikri salmā*). Such memory is nothing but foolishness, conjecture about the hidden side (*ẓannu l-ghaybi*),[8] a casting of stones (*tarjīm*). Whatever the casting of stones refers to, be it some kind of divination, pre-Islamic stoning of evil, or the placing of stones on a grave, the perspective of *ṣaḥw* comes through strongly. (Note: because the interplay of memory, *dhikr*, and waking, *ṣaḥw*, will become a central critical category in this chapter, from here forward I will not be repeating the translation of these two key Arabic terms).

Yet the poem seems to protest too much. The strength of conviction, the abuse leveled at the previous reverie, are straightaway overcome by another wave of reverie: "Breast sash crossed / and falling, gown folds / at the hip clinging, soft / as a gazelle fawn reared within the yard." This final wave consists of one hemistich made up of epithets and the second consisting of a final simile. The epithets bring us back to the figure of the beloved. *Kharʿabatun* denotes a young, fresh twig, but takes on as well the meaning of a particularly attractive woman, echoing the human-plant analogy of the *utrujjah* metaphor that constituted the beginning of the entire movement. The first hemistich of the verse, with its string of epithets attached to the figure (in both senses of the term) of the beloved, brings the entire movement back from its peregrinations through the various senses and various stages of reverie to its starting point with the bodily allure of the beloved, presented with the strongest visual and tactile presence of the section.[9] The overt sexuality of this imagery is quickly covered over in the following hemistich, in which the beloved is compared to "a gazelle fawn reared within the yard." As this chapter progresses, the rapid movement from sexual suggestion to images of tenderness toward the young will be seen to be a common feature of the dissembling simile.

This final string of epithets is the closest we get to a description. Yet they tell us little about the beloved's appearance. If the beloved is indeed the object of description, the entire section is remarkably inefficient in terms of descriptive economy. Eight full verses yield a metaphor, a series of tangential similes, and a final run of stylized epithets. Either the poetry is poetically flawed—the conclusion to which the emphasis upon description so often has led—or its deeper poetic intent is something other than description. A first hint of an alternative poetic agenda can be found in what, from a descriptive point of view, would be an irrelevant aside: the double-modified depiction of the balm upon the healing camel as clean and pure (*nāṣiʿi l-qaṭirāni ṣ-ṣirfi*). As more examples of nasīb descriptions are given, purity will become an essential aspect within almost all of the dissembling similes and a compelling interior logic will be revealed in an image that has been considered a prime example of pure digression.

The next description of the beloved is taken from the *Muʿallaqah* of ʿAntarah:

13. She takes your heart
with the flash edge of her smile,
her mouth sweet to the kiss,
sweet to the taste,

14. As if a draft of musk
from a spiceman's pouch
announced the wet gleam
of her inner teeth,

15. Or an untouched meadow,
bloom and grass
sheltered in rain, untrodden,
dung free, hidden.

16. Over it the white,
first clouds of spring
pour down, leaving small pools
like silver dirhams,

17. Pouring and bursting,
evening on evening
gushing over it
in an endless stream.

18. The fly has it all to himself,
and is not about to leave,
droning softly,
like a wine drinker humming a tune,

19. Then buzzing, elbow on elbow,
like a one-armed man
kindling a fire,
bent down over the flint.

13. *idh tastabīka bi dhī ghurūbin wāḍiḥin*
*ʿadhbin muqabbaluhū ladhīdhi l-maṭʿamī*

14. *wa ka'anna fa'rata tājirin bi qasīmatin*
*sabaqat ʿawāriḍahā ilayka min al-famī*

15. *aw rawḍatan unufan taḍammana nabtahā*
*ghaythun qalīlu d-dimni laysa bi maʿlamī*

16. *jādat ʿalayhī kullu bikrin ḥurratin*
*fa tarakna kulla qarāratin ka d-dirhamī*

17. *saḥḥan wa taskāban fa kullu ʿashiyyatin*
*yajrī ʿalayhā l-māʾu lam yataṣarramī*

18. *wa khalā dh-dhubābu bihā fa laysa bi bāriḥin*
*gharidan ka fiʿli sh-shāribi l-mutarannimī*

19. *hazijan yaḥukku dhirāʿahū bi dhirāʿihī*
*qadḥa l-mukibbi ʿalā z-zinādi l-ajdhamī*

In this passage,[10] we have a similar set of images constructed around the elements of fragrance, water, and lush vegetation. Unlike the ʿAlqamah passage, however, where the water imagery relates back to the poet's tears, here it is introduced through a simile whose ostensible referent is the beloved rather than the poet. A reference to the wet mouth of the beloved (v. 13), yields to a simile pitting the visual against the olfactory (v. 14), which then in verse 15 returns to the visual. Verses 14–15 are two parts of a compound simile, "as if . . . or" (*ka'anna . . . aw)*, but the link holding the two parts together is tenuous. The first part of the simile, verse 14, is directly related to a specific image of the beloved, her inner teeth (*ʿawāriḍahā*), a word that brings forth sensual connotations of her open, wet mouth. The second part of the compound simile drifts on into an extended tableau that is not related to the beloved through any particular similarity at all. This language of depiction *evokes* the beloved, but what is *described* is the untouched meadow.

Both syntax and rhetoric of descriptive comparison strain under the wave of *dhikr*. The poetic voice outruns the logic of the "or" (*aw)*, and the syntactical governance of the simile is replaced by an associative governance. Once the poetic voice overflows the original context of description of the beloved, the passage turns to an independent vignette similar to that in ʿAlqamah—idyllic garden, flowing water, abundant growth. Unlike the ʿAlqamah passage, however, the ʿAntarah passage never turns back to the beloved. It ends with the final similes comparing the fly to a wine drinker and then, in an implied simile that is as disturbing as it is paradoxical, the comparison of the fly's rubbing its arms together to the rubbing of the arms of a one-armed man (*qadḥa l-mukibbi*)[11] bent over a flint, a simile that prefigures themes of mutilation that will occur throughout the latter part of ʿAntarah's qaṣīdah.

An apparent description of the beloved again has shown itself to be something quite other. The image of her wet mouth leads into a chain of similes that extend through various aspects of the sensorium and outrun any logic of descriptive comparison. Yet one finds an underlying associative logic in the language used for the garden scene. The beloved vignette begins, as most do, in an erotic mode, with reference here to the sweet taste of her wet mouth and to the scent of musk that announced the gleam of her inner teeth. We then move from the human to the environmental, as the simile runs over from evocation of musk to evocation of the garden, the garden now only loosely connected to the logic of the simile.

The garden takes on a life, independent from the original descriptive point. Here the language changes from eroticism to purification. As is often the case, ʿAntarah's poetic language is particularly revealing: the garden is untouched (*unuf*), and the clouds that water it are virgin (*bikr*). At this point we might recall Mary Douglas's discussion of orifices as the boundaries of the body and the analogy they can take on to the boundaries of society.[12] The nasīb is constructed around the joining of the tribes at the spring encampments and their subsequent separation. In ʿAntarah's *Muʿallaqah*, this phenomenon is depicted in the tragic mode, and the relationship of the personal and the societal is reflected in the analogy between the flash edge of the beloved's smile and the flash edge of the sword of the warrior who is fighting his beloved's tribe. The union of lover and beloved that is the point of departure for the nasīb is a microcosm of the union of the differing tribes. It will become increasingly clear that hidden behind the dissembling similes of the nasīb is a logic of union and purification that functions both on the individual and communal levels.

The erotic/purificatory polarity that governs the overrun simile in ʿAntarah reappears in Kaʿb Ibn Zuhayr:[13]

1. Suʿād is gone,
 my heart stunned,
 lost in her traces,
 shackled, unransomed.

2. What was Suʿād
 the morning they went away
 but a faint song,
 languor in the eyes, kohl,

3. Revealing as she smiled
 side teeth wet
 as a first draught of wine
 or a second,

4. Mixed with the hard cold
 of a winding, backsloped,
 gorge-bottom stream, pure,
 cooled in the morning by the north wind,

5. Filtered through the winds,
then flooded
with rains of a night traveler,
flowing white and over.

6. Misery she
who might have been a friend
had she kept her promise,
had a well-meant word been taken.

7. Some friend! In her blood
brew trouble and lies,
the withdrawal of vows,
the trade-in of lovers.

8. From form to form,
she turns and changes,
like a ghoul
slipping through her guises.

9. She makes a vow,
then holds it
like a linen sieve
holds water.

1. *bānat suʿādu fa qalbī l-yawma matbūlu*
*mutayyamun ithrahā lam yuzja makbūlū*

2. *wa mā suʿādu ghadāta l-bayni idh raḥalu*
*illā aghannu ghaḍīḍu ṭ-ṭarfi makḥūlū*

3. *tajlū ʿawāriḍa dhī ẓalmin idhā btasamat*
*ka'annahū munhalun bi r-rāḥi maʿlūlū*

4. *shujjat bi dhī shabamin min mā'i maḥniyyatin*
*ṣāfin bi abṭaḥa aḍḥā wa hwa mashmūlū*

5. *tajlū r-riyāḥu l-qadhā ʿanhū wa afraṭahu*
*min ṣawbi sāriyatin bīḍun yaʿālīlū*

6. *ya wayḥahā khullatan law annahā ṣadaqat*
*ma waʿadat aw law anna n-naṣḥa maqbūlū*

7. *lakinnahā khullatun qad sīṭa min damihā*
*fajʿun wa walʿun wa ikhlāfun wa tabdīlū*

8. *fa mā tadūmu ʿalā ḥālin takūnu bihā*
*fa mā talawwanu fī athwābihā l-ghūlū*

9. *wa mā tamassaku bi l-waṣli l-ladhī zaʿamat*
*illā kamā tumsiku l-mā'a l-gharābīlū*

The passage begins with a phrase that will turn out to be of particular interest: *wa mā suʿādu . . . illā* (what was Suʿād but). That phrase governs a two-verse series of image flashes that move quickly from sense to sense: sound (*aghannu*: "a faint sound"); sight (*ghaḍīḍu ṭ-ṭarfi*: "langour in the eyes"); sight again (*makḥūl*: "[covered with] kohl"); sight/taste (*dhī ẓalmin*: "side teeth wet"); taste (*ka'annahū munhalun*: "as a first draught of wine"). This movement from sense to sense then settles down into an extended simile (vv. 3–4) based upon the "as a first draught of wine" simile. The draught of wine is said to be mixed (*shujjat*) with stream water, and at this point the simile opens up into an independent vignette, the human imagery again yielding to the natural. Both beloved and poet recede completely into a precultural world of purified elements, the winds and rains refining one another to their separate, unmixed essences. Yet of course the original draught of wine to which the mouth of the beloved was compared was said to be mixed with such water. Verse 5 then marks the return to *ṣaḥw*, and as it always is and must be to be effective, the return to *ṣaḥw* is abrupt: *lakinnahā khullatun qad sīṭa min damihā* (Some friend! / in her blood brew . . . ) and the purity of verses 4–5 is put into direct contrast to the mixing and pollution of her blood.

The chain of elements that are mixed in the beloved's blood is placed in a paratactic order in verse 7: "trouble and lies, / the withdrawal of vows / the trade-in of lovers" (*fajʿun wa walʿun wa ikhlāfun wa tabdīlū*). The following verse transforms this synchronic catalogue into a dynamic process as it moves from the personal to the mythical, the beloved to a *ghūl* who changes color (*lawn*) or form as she transforms herself (*[ta]talawwanu*) through various guises. The synchronic mixture of various elements has now turned into a temporal transformation through various states, the two versions of the beloved still united by the indictment of mixture, but separated by the distinction between the human and personal (as represented by the blood of the beloved) and the mythic and pseudohuman (or semispirit), as represented by the bloodless ghūl transforming herself through her guises or gowns (*athwāb*).

At this point we encounter a moment of textual self-reference. By this I mean that the image evoked refers not only to a theme within the poem (the ghūl), or symbolically, the changing loyalty of the beloved, but to the poem's own process of signification, the dissembling simile. What it speaks *about* is momentarily identical with what it speaks *through*. A closer look at the attributes of the ghūl shows them as being identical to the attributes of the dissembling simile. In the qaṣīdah, the ghūl is a female subspecies of the *jinnī* that would bewilder the desert traveler or the would-be lover through constant change of form (*talawwun*), thus becoming known as *dhātu alwānin* or *dhū lawnayni*: "she-with-many-guises" or "the double-guised."[14] The nasīb simile can also be characterized by *talawwun*. It evokes the beloved, powerfully. And it presents a series of similes that give the impression that the beloved has been described. However, when we look again at that description, we find that the beloved has dissolved into a series of transformations. The simile is a poetic shifter. It channels the flow of energy and shifts it back and forth through a labyrinthine web of modes—sense to sense, personal to environmental, human to nonhuman, evocation of union to purification, *dhikr* to *ṣaḥw*, poet to beloved, subject to object—to name only a few—and in each case back again.

When we consider the mythology of the ghūl conjured by the poem in relationship to the first verse of our passage, "what was Suᶜād but . . ." (*wa mā suᶜādu . . . illā* ), we can sense how the poem's multiform and changing referential vectors turn suddenly upon themselves for a moment of transparence or self-reference. What is Suᶜād, the poem asks, but a song,[15] a lowered glance, kohl, gleaming wetness of her side teeth, wet as a first draught of wine or a second. When we turn the same language to the question of description, we can ask: what is she indeed, as it becomes clear that Suᶜād is really never described, despite the apparatus of description. The similes, like the ghūl, dissemble. They create the illusion of a fixed shape for the beloved, a form, and image, but in fact, by blending into one another or by outrunning their descriptive point, they offer none. The image world presented by the similes is not unrelated to the beloved; otherwise the beloved would not be evoked so compellingly. But the image world that is presented is not a description of the beloved.

In the rapid movement through the sensorium, based upon a series of simile transitions that function through the logic of synaesthesia, the beloved gradually becomes completely immanent to a world of sense fulfillment. In Kaᶜb this reverie consists of a movement through the senses of hearing, sight, and taste, and then a reverie on winds and stream. In ᶜAlqamah, the movement was from various experiences of scent (inspired by the *utrujjah* metaphor), through purity (in the camel salve) through the scene of the irrigated garden. In ᶜAntarah the movement is from taste (wet mouth of the beloved) and scent (musk) to the purification of rains and the hidden, untouched garden.

What occurs in the so-called description passages of the nasīb then is a four-part movement: from the sense image, through images of purification, of atmospheric ablutions, to a garden scene, to the *ṣaḥw* or awakening from the *dhikr*. The first part consists of a rapid, orgasmic movement through fulfillment of the various senses. That such a designation is proper and not merely a loose metaphor is shown by the consistent manner in which the most sensual passages are followed by reveries centering on purification. The continual association of the sense-fulfillment passages with a language of purification can be interpreted in the light of the common practice of ablutions after intercourse or ejaculation that are set down in classical Semitic legal traditions.[16] That a poetic language of ablutions would almost invariably go along with the sense-fulfillment passages serves as a confirmation of the intensity of the imagery's sexual suggestion.

From a critical view analogous to the poetic perspective of *ṣaḥw* we can ask: what then is the description of the beloved but a constant poetic transformation through the various image frames and her immanence within them, just as a ghūl is nothing but her transformation through her various guises (*athwāb*). These transformations are governed by the chains of similes. The similes are the means by which the guises are transformed, from sense to sense, from personal, to environmental, to mythic, to cultural, from reverie (in which the images are presented without ironic distance) to *ṣaḥw* (in which they are presented as deceptive).

Verses 6–7 together form the beginning of a larger *ṣaḥw* section. The *talawwun* simile in verse 8, "like a ghūl slipping through her guises" (*ka mā talawwana fī athwābihā l-ghūlū*), moves in verse 9 to another *ṣaḥw*-governed simile, one that shifts us back from the mythic to the everyday: "like a linen sieve / holds water" (*illā kamā tumsiku l-mā'a l-gharābīlū*), and returns us to the image of water, not the purified water of the *dhikr*-reverie, but the elusive water of the deceptive dream of stability.

The so-called description of the beloved is a movement of semantic, emotive, and erotic overflow that is channeled by the similes, "like," "as if," "just as," "what . . . but" (lit. "nothing . . . but") (*ka, ka'anna, kamā, mā illā*). The poetic flow is generated by *dhikr* and controlled (to the extent it can be controlled) by *ṣaḥw*. In the passage from Kaᶜb, we see that the first two similes channel and direct the overflow. They set up a descriptive point only to be overrun through the semantic overflow of the passage. The movement of the poem continually overflows the descriptive points the simile poses. The last two similes in Kaᶜb also direct and channel the semantic overflow, but this time they are controlled by *ṣaḥw*.

The combination of poetic necessity and freedom of movement from sense fulfillment to purification can be seen in the *Muᶜallaqah* of Ṭarafah. In this poem, the garden scene and description of the beloved are intertwined in a particularly strong fashion. The beloved is introduced through the beloved-as-gazelle metaphor. In some later Arabic poetry such a metaphor might be only formal, almost a synonym for the beloved. But here, the metaphorical relationship is both enhanced and made problematic, as both gazelle and beloved are described simultaneously. At some points the attributes given would be appropriate for either the beloved or the gazelle, but at other points it is not clear whether the attributes apply to the gazelle or to the beloved. Within this interaction, there is a movement from the mouth of the beloved, to the lost garden, to the language of purification.

After comparing the howdah of his beloved to a ship, the poet extends the simile:[17]

5. It cleaves the rippled waves,
bow-breast submerged
like the hand of a child at play
scooping through the soft soil.

6. Among the tribe is a gazelle,
a wine-dark yearling,
shaking down the Arak berries and draped
string on string, with chrysolite and pearl.

7. She lags. From a dune thicket
she watches the herd.
She pulls at the Arak branches
until they clothe her.

8. From a deep red mouth she smiles,
a camomile blossom,
dew-moistened,
breaking through a crest of pure sand,

9. Given a draught of the rays of the sun,
except for the gums,
darkened with antimony
that hasn't yet worn away.

10. As if the sun had loosed
its robe
upon her face, glowing,
washed in light, smooth.

5. *yashuqqu ḥabāba l-mā'i ḥayzūmuhā bihā*
*kamā qasama t-turba l-mufāyilu bi l-yadī*

6. *wa fī l-ḥayyi aḥwā yanfuḍu l-marda shādinun*
*muẓāhiru simṭay lu'lu'in wa zabarjadī*

7. *khadhūlun turāʿi rabraban bi khamīlatin*
*tanāwalu aṭrāfa l-barīri wa tartadī*

8. *wa tabsimu ʿan almā ka'anna munawwaran*
*takhallala ḥurra l-ramli diʿṣin l-lahū nadī*

9. *saqathū iyātu sh-shamsi illā lithātihī*
*usiffa wa lam takdim ʿalayhi bi-athmudī*[18]

10. *wa wajhun ka'anna sh-shamsa ḥallat ridā'ahā*
*ʿalayhī naqiyyu l-lawni lam yatakhaddadī*

The passage selected here begins with a sensual depiction of the ship's breast cleaving the bubbling waters, then yields to another simile "like the hand of a child at play / scooping through the soft soil."[19] The simile is apparently based upon a physical analogy involving the parting of a malleable element. As in the ode of ʿAlqamah, a simile with highly erotic suggestions is followed by one that changes the associative register from sexual to parental, and that changes the emotional register from desire to tenderness. At this point a new metaphor is introduced: the beloved as a gazelle; only in this case, as opposed to what we found in ʿAlqamah, the gazelle will be used to heighten rather than disguise the erotic mode. The extension of this metaphor over the next several verses reveals a poetics that is far removed from the simple substitution of gazelle for beloved. The gazelle imagery and that of the beloved are developed synchronically. It becomes difficult to tell whether the object of description is the beloved or the gazelle. In other terms, the tenor and the vehicle of the metaphor are developed simultaneously, momentarily collapsing into one another at key points.

The gazelle topos seems fairly clear in the first two verses (6–7). Though introduced apparently as a metaphor for the beloved (the apparent justification for the placing of the gazelle among the tribe, *fī l-ḥayyi*), the poet seems to forget the original motivation (descriptions of the beloved) and gets caught up in the depiction of a gazelle doe. The doe is shaking the Arak berries. She lags behind the rest of the herd, and in a moment of intense lyricism, she becomes so entangled within the Arak bushes that they are said to clothe her.

Yet there are moments even in this passage of pure description for description's sake that challenge the gazelle's independence from the beloved. "She" is said to be draped with chrysolite and pearl, and though such imagery can be interpreted as referring to the gazelle doe's markings, the jewelry topos is strongly associated with the beloved as well. The clothing of the doe within the Arak bush increases tension between nature and culture. Like the metaphor of jewelry, that of clothing brings up the human world, the world of adornment. Thus within the central metaphor, beloved as gazelle, we have a sustained depiction of the gazelle with interior metaphors that reverse the tenor-vehicle direction: gazelle as beloved.

The following verse, with its interior simile comparing her teeth to a camomile breaking through the dew-moistened sand, could apply equally to the gazelle and the beloved. The vehicle and tenor have fused momentarily. Yet the erotic quality of the imagery seems to indicate that it is the beloved that is foregrounded. The next two verses could also apply to either gazelle or beloved. The reference to the gums tainted with antimony brings up the human world and the topos of adornment, but the verb *takdim* (referring to wearing away of the antimony on the gums) is a term usually applied to the biting or grazing of animals. The passage ends with a depiction of the face as cloaked or veiled by the sun, a simile whose poetic power is partially due to the sense of oxymoron. Normally, we think of being veiled from the sun and cloaked in shade. The previous use of the more standard metaphor (the gazelle cloaked within the Arak bush) ensures that the reversal here will be poetically effective.

Ṭarafah has been criticized for forgetting the original intent of the gazelle as a metaphor for the beloved.[20] The interpretation here suggests that, far from being a poetic lapse, the overflowing of the original descriptive point here is a fundamental aspect of the poetics of the dissembling simile, an aspect Ṭarafah's nasīb shares with the other passages discussed above. In the mixed identity of beloved and gazelle, in the intricate interplay between tenor and vehicle that is sustained throughout the passage, in the parallel interplay between nature and culture, sense fulfillment and purification, Ṭarafah's nasīb achieves a singular intensity that allows it, despite its brevity, to motivate the long and powerful *Muʿallaqah* as a whole. Parallel to the complex interplay between tenor and vehicle, and nature and culture, is the interplay between sense fulfillment and purification. The sexual overtones of the first verse cited from Ṭarafah (cleaves the rippled waves, bow-breast submerged) are underscored when the poem turns to the beloved's mouth, one of the more explicitly erotic images within the qaṣīdah tradition. They are then further recalled and underscored by the later image of the camomile, "dew-moistened, breaking through a crest of pure sand." Yet, as in the nasībs discussed above, the sexual suggestions are balanced by the language of purification. The camomile is breaking through dew-soaked sand that is pure (*ḥurra r-ramlī*), and later the sun loosens its robe upon her face, a face that is "pure of color" (*naqiyyu l-lawnī*). The purification is again associated with water, though in this case the water is brought metaphorically in references to sunlight. Yet even in the purificatory language, there is embedded an extraordinarily intimate language of suggestion and union, the sun loosening its robe upon her face. That the most erotically intense passages will be also those that are purificatory in their explicit language is a phenomenon that we will find throughout a wide variety of nasībs.

At this point we can step back and look at the various nasībs discussed above with the intent to draw some larger conclusions concerning the dialectic of sense-fulfillment and purification. Below are two-part outlines of the passages discussed to this point. Presented in the first part is the chain of dissembling similes (*dhikr*) and, where relevant, the attempts to interrupt the chain through *ṣaḥw*. The chain of similes will allow a quick review of the various senses activated in each passage. In the second part, a comparison is made between (1) passages involving water and (2) those involving explicit vocabulary of purification. At this point the erotic suggestion within the scenes of gushing water and penetration of moist sand should stand out without need of explicit comment, especially given the invariable language of purification that surrounds those passages. In some cases the gushing water generates an erotic connotation which then generates the language of purification. In other cases the movement reverses, with the purificatory waters preceding the erotic connotations. At the points of highest erotic tension, the imagery is both sexual and purificatory at the same time.

1. ʿAlqamah

*dhikr*: *utrujjah*, perfume, musk, weeping eye, waterbag pulled by the camel, which is fattened and cured with pure balm, spilling water into channels, ripening fruit, flooded slopes flowing over
*ṣaḥw*: folly, conjecture, a casting of stones
*dhikr*: breast sash, gown folds
(1) spilling water into channels/as grain husks part/from the ripening fruit/the flooded slopes flowing over
(2) balm: clear and pure (*nāṣiʿi l-qaṭirāni ṣ-ṣirfi*)

2. ʿAntarah

*dhikr*: mouth of the beloved, wet side teeth, musk pod, untouched garden, watered by pure or full-breasted clouds, silver dirham, water bursting in a continuous flow, fly, humming like a wine drinker
*ṣaḥw*: arms like a one-armed man bent over a flint
(1) Over it the white/first [or virgin] clouds of spring/pour down . . . Pouring and bursting/evening on evening/gushing over it/in an endless stream
(2) Untouched, unknown meadows (*rawḍatan unufan, laysa bi maʿlamī*); pure, virgin clouds (*bikrin ḥurratin*) or full-breasted virgin clouds (*bikrin tharratin*)

3. Kaʿb

*dhikr*: Suʿād, lowered gaze, faint sound, kohl, wet side teeth, first or second draught of wine, gorge-bottom stream cooled by the north wind, filtering winds, night-traveling clouds
*ṣaḥw*: false friend, impure blood, ghūl's changing guises, water through sieve, lies of ʿUrkūb, etc.
(1) Then flooded/with rains of a night traveler/flowing white and over
(2) pure water (*ṣāfin*), filtered by the winds (*tajlū r-riyāḥu l-qadhā ʿanhu*): opposite of: impure of blood (*qad sīṭa min damihā*), colors or guises of the ghūl: (*talawwanu fī athwābihā*)—compare to *naqiyyu l-lawni*

4. Ṭarafah

*dhikr*: howdah, ship of an ʿAdawlīyan, bow-breast submerged, cleaving the waves, hand of a child, scooping the soft soil; beloved, gazelle fawn, lagging, clothes of Arak bushes, strings of chrysolite and pearls, teeth, camomile, cloak of sun
*ṣaḥw*: none
(1) It cleaves the rippled waves, bow-breast submerged . . . From a deep red mouth she smiles . . . a camomile blossom,/dew moistened,/breaking through a crest of pure sand . . . a draught of the rays of the sun.

(2) breaking through a crest of pure sand (*takhallala ḥurra r-ramli*); washed in light [literally, clean of color] (*naqiyyu l-lawni*)

Up until this point, I have discussed as isolated units those sections of the nasīb that are commonly called descriptions of the beloved. However, as the analysis above shows, there is in fact very little actual description of the beloved in these sections. Often what was actually described in these passages was one version or another of the lost garden, or hidden garden, or untouched garden. The depiction of an idyllic garden can also be an independent part of the nasīb and occur without explicit reference to the beloved. In fact, as we follow the deeper thematic and symbolic threads within the description of the beloved, we find them branching out into other parts of the nasīb. As a result, we cannot really do justice to the units conventionally called descriptions of the beloved without showing how they fit into the nasīb proper. The nasīb of the *Mufaḍḍalīyah* of Mukhabbal al-Saʿdī, *Dhakara r-Rabāba*, is representative of the more complex type of nasīb movement.[21] An examination of it will reveal some of the underlying associative logic within the description of the beloved and will enable us to relate the beloved section to the rest of the nasīb.

1. He remembered Rabāb.
        Her memory was sickness.
    He was young again.
        He didn't know.

2.          When her phantom came round
        my eye stung
            along the tear lines
        and began to water,

3. Pearls
        slipping
    from a necklace
        poorly strung.

4.          I make out a dwelling there,
        hers,
            amid the pools of Sidān,
        traces unfaded,

5. Ashes, cold,
        banked and sheltered
    from the winds
        by blackened hearthstones,

6. Ruins of a flood-break,
stone walls
around the base,
broken in,

7. As if what the side winds
and rains had left
there on the empty yards
were a tattoo.

8. Doe oryx pasture there,
following along toward water,
white-backs
and brown-backs mingling,

9. The fawns of oryx
and gazelle,
around her tracings,
like kids and lambs.

10. Rabāb might have alighted there,
with an advance guard,
well-armed,
to ward off enemies.

11. Graceful as a rush of papyrus,
beauty comes to her
before others,
and she grows into it early.

12. She reveals to you
a delicate face,
paper-smooth,
glowing

13. Like the pearl of pearls
distant Persians use
to light up the throne hall
of a sultan

14. Purchased at high price,
retrieved by a diver,
bone-thin,
like an arrow,

15. His chest smeared with oil,
bringing it out
from the billow-waved deep
of the swordfish.

16. Or an egg of the dunes,
set into the earth,
smooth to the touch,
and perfectly curved,

17. The first-laid of the nest,
warmed by a clump wing,
his matted feathers
like a heap of rags.

18. He draws it in
beneath his wings,
black forefeathers
encompassing it.

19. There the torrent beds
are uneffaced,
at Lost Place,
Bend of the Trail, and Zukhm.

20. Her maids lose their combs
in the thickness
of her curls,
thick as the curls of the grapevine.

21. Why not find consolation
for a yearning
for a bond of union
that's broken.

1. *Dhakara r-rabāba wa dhikruhā suqmū*
*fa ṣabā wa laysa li man ṣabā ḥilmū*

2. *wa idhā alamma khayāluhā ṭurifat*
*ʿaynī fa mā'u shu'ūnihā sajmū*

3. *ka l-lu'lu'i l-masjūri ughfila fī*
*silki n-niẓāmi wa khānahu n-naẓmū*

4. *wa arā lahā dāran bi aghdirati s-*
*sīdāni lam yadrus lahā rasmū*

5. *illā ramādan hāmidan dafaᶜat*
*ᶜanhu r-riyāḥa khawālidun suḥmū*

6. *wa baqiyyata n-nu'yi l-ladhī rufiᶜat*
*aᶜḍāduhū fa thawā lahū jidhmū*

7. *fa ka'anna mā abqā l-bawāriḥu wa l-*
*amṭāru min ᶜaraṣātihā l-washmū*

8. *taqrū bihā l-baqaru l-masāriba wa kh*
*talaṭat bihā l-ārāmu wa l-udmū*

9. *wa ka'anna aṭlā'a l-ja'ādhiri wa l-*
*ghizlāni ḥawla rusūmihā l-bahmū*

10. *wa laqad taḥullu bihā r-rabābu lahā*
*salafun yafullu ᶜaduwwahā fakhmū*

11. *bardiyyatun sabaqa n-naᶜīmu bihā*
*aqrānahā wa ghalā bihā ᶜaẓmū*

12. *wa turīka wajhan ka ṣ-ṣaḥīfati lā*
*ẓam'ānu mukhtalajun wa lā jahmū*

13. *ka ᶜaqīlati d-durri staḍā'a bihā*
*miḥrāba ᶜarshi ᶜazīzihā l-ᶜujmū*

14. *aghlā bihā thamanan wa jā'a bihā*
*shakhtu l-ᶜiẓāmi ka'annahū sahmū*

15. *bi labānihī zaytun wa akhrajahā*
*min dhī ghawāriba wasṭuhu l-lukhmū*

16. *aw bayḍati d-diᶜṣi l-latī wuḍiᶜat*
*fī l-arḍi laysa li massihā ḥajmū*

17. *sabaqat qarā'inahā wa adfa'ahā*
*qaridu l-janāḥi ka'annahū hidmū*

18. *wa yaḍummuhā dūna l-janāḥi bi daff [[ihi]]*
*wa taḥuffuhunna qawādimun qutmū*

19. *lam taʿtadhir minhā madāfiʿu dhī*
*ḍālin wa lā ʿuqabun wa lā z-zukhmū*

20. *wa tuḍillu midrāhā l-mawāshiṭu fī*
*jaʿdin aghamma ka'annahū karmū*

21. *hallā tusallī ḥājatan ʿaliqat*
*ʿalaqa l-qarīnati ḥabluhā jidhmū*

I would divide the section as follows:

1–3: Opening: *Ṭayf*, phantom of the beloved.
4–7: *Aṭlāl*
8–10: Idyl
11–20: Description of the Beloved
11–12: Papyrus Metaphor (Human—Plant)
13–15: Digressive Simile of the Pearl (Human—Animal—Mineral)
16–18: Digressive Simile of the Ostrich Egg (Human— Animal)
19: Stations or Manāzil of the Beloved
20: Grape Vine Simile (Human—Plant)
21: *Ṣaḥw*, transition verse to *Raḥīl*[22]

The analysis of this nasīb will begin with the section that is conventionally considered a description of the beloved (vv. 11–20) and will then move on to take in the other verses. The description of the beloved begins with two verses dependent upon the epithet *bardiyyah*, which indicates that the beloved is in some way like the papyrus rush (*bardī*). There is then an abrupt transition to a simile in which the beloved is likened to a pearl, the transition made through the simple introduction of *ka* (like). But the poem immediately overflows any descriptive point of likeness (rareness, beauty, preciousness) into an independent vignette of three verses in which the pearl diver is depicted retrieving the pearl from the billow-waved deep of the swordfish. The pearl is introduced in the second case ostensibly to indicate the rareness, beauty, preciousness of the beloved, and serves a similar function in this to the *utrujjah* in ʿAlqamah's ode, or to the comparison of her mouth to wine imported from distant lands in the *Mufaḍḍalīyah* of Muraqqish the Younger.[23]

Yet the poetic voice overflows this descriptive "point" into an independent scene involving the pearl diver's anointing himself with oil and then diving through the waves to retrieve the pearl from the billow-waved deep of the swordfish. At this point we ask whether the distinction between the sense fulfillment or sexual suggestion and the purification that follows can ultimately hold, or if the two sides are not resolved back into one another. Is this anointing, is this plunging of the bone-thin, anointed diver into the liquid deep a sexual allusion, a purificatory allusion, or both?

Then, as if in reaction to the erotic undertones in the episode of the diver and the pearl, a new simile is introduced in which the beloved is compared to the ostrich egg. While still highly sensuous, the language here is one of nesting and parental tenderness, with the male ostrich depicted enveloping and enfolding the egg—an interesting inversion of the male diver's retrieval of the pearl (egg) from the enfolding sea.[24] Finally the poem, after a brief reference to the stations of the beloved, returns to the human-plant analogy, this time in the form of a simile likening the hair of Rabāb to the curls of the grapevine.

The short idyl involving lush vegetation and desert animals birthing or caring for their young often appears in the nasīb, sometimes as in this case within the description of the beloved, at other times replacing the description of the beloved. At this point I would like to interrupt momentarily the discussion of Mukhabbal's poem to give an example of such a replacement. In the *Muʿallaqah* of Labīd, the depiction of the barrenness of the aṭlāl yields suddenly to the invocation of rains upon them:[25]

4. Replenished by the rain stars
of spring and struck
by thunderclap downpour, or steady,
fine-dropped, silken rains

5. From every kind of cloud
passing at night,
darkening the morning,
or rumbling in peals across the evening sky.

6. The white pond cress has shot upward,
and on the wadi slopes,
gazelles among their newborn,
and ostriches,

7. And the wide-of-eyes
silent above monthling fawns.
On the open terrain
yearlings cluster.

4. *ruziqat marābīʿa n-nujūmi wa ṣābahā*
*wadqu l-rawāʿidi jawduhā fa rihāmuhā*

5. *min kulli sāriyatin wa ghādin mudjinin*
*wa ʿashiyyatin mutajāwibin irzāmuhā*

6. *fa ʿalā furūʿu l-ayhuqāni wa aṭfalat*
*bi l-jalhatayni ẓibāʾuhā wa naʿāmuhā*

7. *wa l-ʿīnu sākinatun ʿalā aṭlā'ihā*
*ʿūdhan ta'ajjalu bi l-faḍā'i bihāmuhā*

These verses may well refer to the purificatory waters, or they may refer to the sexual, life-giving waters. Much depends upon the use of the end-rhyme syllable *hā* in Labīd's poem. In it, the syllable is for the most part used as the third-person pronominal suffix, a suffix that can refer to plural objects, grammatically feminine, singular, inanimate objects, or to feminine, animate beings. The referent is often vague and the pronominal force is reflexive, referring back in a general way to the context of the noun to which it is appended. However, the continual appearance of *hā* in the end rhyme sets up a quasi-personified sound symbol that, in the highly charged nasīb context, evokes the beloved even though she is not formally depicted. Thus, for example, the first word of verse 4, *ruziqat,* has an ambivalent referent: may it/she/they be blessed. The most immediate reference is to the aṭlāl: may they be blessed. But given the symbolic associations of the aṭlāl, and of the description that will follow, we cannot help hearing another reference echoing through the expression: may she, the beloved, be blessed. Again, as with Mukhabbal, we have an image involving water followed by an idyl depicting the growth and nurturing of young desert animals. Though not as immediate in sexual suggestion as the pearl diver episode of Mukhabbal, the evocation of the rains pouring down upon the traces of the lost beloved is carried out with an extraordinary sensuousness, suggesting a similar dialectic between images evoking sexual union and later images evoking the birth and care of the young.

That there is no explicit description of the beloved in Labīd is significant. In the first part of this essay, the "descriptions of the beloved" were revealed to be based upon a series of dissembling similes that promised, but never delivered, a description of the beloved. They were shown to have been grounded in an associative logic based upon tensions between the sexual and the purificatory, *dhikr* and *ṣaḥw*, and in the last case, water imagery and sexual allusion followed by the idyl. In other words, the description of the beloved is not only made up of guises, but also, as an apparently self-standing and independent feature of the nasīb, is itself a guise. It is the underlying tensions and dynamic polarities that become the motivating force for the poem. Thus a poem such as the *Muʿallaqah* of Labīd can do without an independent section devoted to the description of the beloved and still achieve the essential poetic effect of her evocation by harnessing the deeper polarities within the idyl motif.

Labīd's ode has no formal description of the beloved, but does contain an idyl with a sustained depiction of the well-watered garden or meadow and the animals at peace with their young. Mukhabbal's ode has no idyl as such, but manages to bring in idyllic themes through dissembling similes involving the papyrus rush, ostrich egg, and the curls of the grapevine. At the mythopoetic level, the evocation of the beloved and depiction of elements of the idyl (hidden garden, well-watered meadow, animals birthing or caring for their young) are two sides of the same coin—and are made up of the same essential elements.

As the conventional boundaries separating the description of the beloved from the rest of the nasīb begin to fall away, the symbolic connection between the beloved and the idyl emerges as central to the dissembling simile. Before examining that connection further, it will be useful to reconsider the popular "pure description" theory of the early qaṣīdah in the light of the discussion above. Gustav von Grunebaum, among others, propounded the purely descriptive nature of qaṣīdah language, a language aimed at detailed reproduction of the thing described (above, n. 1). Renate Jacobi has offered a more recent version of this theory in her *Studien zur Poetik der altarabischen Qaṣide*.[26] Jacobi divides the extended simile, what she calls the self-standing simile (*der selbständige Vergleich*), into two principle types (p. 157), the associative image (*das assoziativ erweiterte Bild*) and the episode (*die Episode*). She associates the former with the description of the beloved and the latter with depictions of desert animals in the journey section. Though for Jacobi the two types differ in some incidental ways, they are united in the way they employ the simile. As a primary example of the extended associative image, she gives the passage from ʿAlqamah discussed above.

As opposed to H. Ritter, who maintained the pure subjectivity of the qaṣīdah simile,[27] Jacobi maintains that the qaṣīdah simile is exclusively objective. The poet's vision "insists upon objectivity" (*dringt auf Objekivität*, p. 165). The result is a poetic image world that is missing a dimension in its relationship to reality. While the Homeric simile puts the two worlds brought together by the simile into close relationship with one another, the Arabic simile remains at the level of merely exterior analogy.[28] The qaṣīdah simile, in comparison with its analogue in Homer, reveals a "profound insufficiency" (*ein tiefes Ungenügen*). It falls short of the kernel of reality (*Wesenskern der Dinge*).[29]

As an example of a qaṣīdah simile that exceeds the poetic level of the early qaṣīdah and approaches that of the allegedly more developed Homeric model, Jacobi cites Shanfarā's comparison of the hunger-driven poet searching for food to a pack of starving jackals. This example makes clear that what is valued in the simile is a clear analogy between the subject and object of the simile. As Jacobi states, "the jackal becomes the symbol for the human outside of society, living a life of privation."[30] At the descriptive level, Jacobi's discussion of this simile is convincing. The simile in Shanfarā does offer a more accessible and more immediate interpretive payoff. It may even be the case that such qualities make it resemble later poetry more than the pre-Islamic.[31] Indeed, the charge that Shanfarā's *Lāmīyah* was a later forgery may in part reflect such a suspicion.

On the other hand, the similes discussed in this chapter present a very different face to the interpreter. In one sense, Jacobi is correct in saying that they are not easy to appreciate—if appreciation depends upon a straightforward relationship between image and aesthetic object. We cannot say of these similes, as Jacobi said of Shanfarā's comparison, that X is a symbol for Y. The range of meaning contained in "Y" and the complex and slippery mode of symbolism within the dissembling simile would make any such statement a betrayal of the simile's deeper structures and movement.

The crucial problem lies in the interpretation of the difference between the typical simile of the early qaṣīdah and the analogical simile favored by Jacobi. For Jacobi, the qaṣīdah similes remain at the level of reproduction (*Wiedergabe*). In those few cases where we can speak of a connection between image (*Bild*) and object (*Gegenstand*), the context is limited, if not mechanical. Thus, for example, the poetic motivation of the woman-gazelle is limited to "corporeal characteristics and typical behavior."[32] However, the beloved-gazelle simile in the *Muʿallaqah* of Ṭarafah has shown clearly that corporeal characteristics and typical behavior represent only the most superficial aspect of the simile. The same phenomenon showed itself in the other passages discussed above. In each case, the force or *dynamis* of the simile was found beneath and at odds with its apparent intent. Despite all that allegedly objective description, we know almost nothing about the actual appearance of these different beloveds. There is no clear image of how they look, talk, or act. If we met them, we could not tell them apart. Jacobi's position that the qaṣīdah simile aims at an unreflectively complete "reproduction" and "illustration" is based upon a misunderstanding of the nature of the early Arabic simile.[33]

Part of the effect of the poem is in its ability to offer us the appearance of a description of the beloved, and part of the aesthetic enjoyment of hearing the poem is to be entranced by such an appearance. The simile acts "as if" (*ka'anna mā*) it were going to present a description, reproduction, or illustration of the beloved. But it dissembles. It dissembles, not because it has remained in a pure subjectivity, beneath the objectivity found in Western poetry (as Ritter would have it), nor because it has remained in a pure objectivity, as Jacobi puts it, beneath any conceptual or truly poetic connection between image and object. When we look at the dissembling simile on its own terms, we find, not a stereotype (as Jacobi calls the similes involving the wet mouth of the beloved, p. 113), or superficiality (*flächenhaft*, Jacobi, p. 165, see n. 19 above), but the surface point of the most profound semantic channels. Shanfarā's jackal simile, admirable as it is, is easy to appreciate precisely because its register is contained. The similes discussed above, and the more characteristic similes in the pre-Islamic journey section, demand more. One cannot easily explicate the analogy they posit. As we are led through guise after guise back to the mythopoetic and archetypal underpinnings, we encounter meanings that, like the ghūl, elude our grasp.

At this point we return to Mukhabbal. His ode begins with *dhikr* and the appearance of the *ṭayf al-khayāl*, the phantom of the lost beloved that disturbs the poet. When the phantom appears, the poet states that "my eye stung / along the tear lines / and began to water, // pearls / slipping / from a necklace / poorly strung." The term translated as "tear lines," *shu'ūn*, is key here. The *shu'ūn* are the lines or passages behind the eye that the pre-Islamic Arabs believed governed the flow of tears. In the verses that immediately follow the *shu'ūn* reference, the poem moves on to a different kind of water channel: "I make out a dwelling there, / hers, / amid the pools of Sidān, / traces unfaded // Ashes, cold, / banked and sheltered / from the winds / by blackened hearthstones // Ruins of a flood-break, / stone walls / around the base, / broken in." Here we have the paradigmatic analogy between the channels within, the *shu'ūn* through which the tears well up, and the channel without, the combination of trench and embankment (*nu'y*) that breaks the flood and which has now become part of the central symbol of remembrance, the aṭlāl. The water channels within and the water channels without mirror one another, but that mirroring can be discovered only beneath expectations aroused by vivid material qualities of the similes that the comparison is based only upon corporeal characteristics. The subjective world and the objective world are implicated in one another in a manner too intimate for the kind of straightforward analogy that Jacobi is seeking.

The mirroring of the exterior world within the interior world that we found within the nasīb of Mukhabbal also occurs across various qaṣīdahs. If we trace our way back up through the chain of dissembling similes in ʿAlqamah's irrigated garden, we find in the poet's tears the poetic source for the water that irrigates the garden. By contrast, in the ode of Kaʿb we find the source, not with the poet, but with the wet mouth of the beloved. In the *Muʿallaqah* of Labīd, the aṭlāl include as a part of them the very torrent channels that help efface the traces of the beloved. The dissembling simile mediates the impersonal nature of the archetype and the personal quality of each remembrance. The beloved appears, or rather appears to appear. To quote Kaʿb, "what is Suʿād but . . ." (*mā Suʿādu illā*). Try to seize such a "description," so seemingly present in its sensuality and allure, and it slips through the hand "like water through a linen sieve." The images, so clear, so precise, so true in themselves, make up a picture that is ultimately not that of the beloved. To find the real Suʿād, remembrance progresses back to the mythopoetic associations simultaneously rediscovered and disguised within the dissembling simile. Within those associations, the subjective and objective perspectives are intersecting and interchanging, and at their most intense moments of discovery, interfused.

The analysis above allows us now to engage some suggestions concerning the nature of those mythopoetic associations rediscovered and disguised within the dissembling simile as well as concerning the process of simultaneous discovery and disguise. The metaphors and similes engendered by the mention of the beloved function on two intersecting planes. Their apparent function is similarity. The objects to which the beloved is compared are usually introduced with some implied similarity (her mouth is like wine, her fragrance like that of musk). But the initial likeness is then developed, beyond any logic of similarity, into chains of similes or extended simile. A brief review of the objects presented in these passages would include the following: animals giving birth or caring for their young in idyllic peacefulness; untouched gardens or meadows or specific elements (grapevine, camomile plant, pond cress) of the gardens; intoxicating fragrances and perfumes; lush vegetations, water that is gushing, overflowing, or pouring down. When viewed as a group, these elements can constitute the mythopoetic world of the lost garden. Though there is no theological definition of this lost garden or meadow, it comprises within the context of the qaṣīdah a world of the sacred as intense as early Islamic notions of paradise, which feature some of the same elements.[34] We might speak of this sacred world as transcendent in the sense that is it beyond the world of the poet and unattainable by him. While the Islamic garden can be regained in the future, the qaṣīdah garden is part of an unretrievable past, and can be reached only through memory. Yet it achieves a kind of immanence within the poetic language, inhabiting as it were the simile world introduced through the mention of the beloved.

An extended discussion of patterns of the sacred and the mythopoetic within the qaṣīdah would be beyond the boundaries of this chapter.[35] The point at issue here is the manner through which the simile links this world of the lost garden to the qaṣīdah. The link is one not of similarity, but of metonymy, in particular, the synecdoche variety of metonymic association, a part used to express the whole. The curl of the grapevine, introduced by Mukhabbal according to its similarity to the curl of the beloved's hair, functions beyond such similarity to evoke, through synecdoche, the lost garden. The mention of the curl of the grapevine, the camomile blossom, one of the animals of an idyllic animal world undisturbed by predators calls up through synecdochic association the other elements of the lost garden.

It is at the intersection of the logic of similarity and the logic of association that meaning overflows. The original similarity involving some corporeal characteristic of the beloved (her mouth, her fragrance, her skin, her eye, her gait) leads to an extended imagery that has elicited and continues to elicit admiration for its vivid, sensual, material nature. To hear the poem is to be lured by the imagery into the impression that the beloved has been described or presented, made present. But what gives these similes their effect is not only material association. It is the combination of a precision of poetic observation with an underlying mythopoetic world of the sacred that seldom reveals itself directly. The seemingly digressive nature of the simile, the apparent delight that the poet takes in randomly describing this and that are explicable in terms of the simile's less apparent synecdochic associations. Meaning "overflows" the original descriptive point, the original point of the similarity, as it taps into its deeper mythopoetic source.

Yet this intersection of metaphoric logic (based on similarity) and metonymic logic (based in this case on synechoche), although it can help explain the simile's apparently digressive nature, cannot fully account for its erotic quality in these passages. At this point we need to introduce a third axis of meaning, performative displacement. Not only do the description-of-the-beloved passages present elements that depict, through metonymic association, the lost garden, but they present a series of sense experiences as well. Not all five senses are actualized within each depiction of the beloved, but several of them usually are. Mention of the beloved generates a movement from sense to sense of excited rapidity.

When this sense excitement is taken into account, many of same elements that make up the lost garden can be viewed as part of a performative reenactment of sexual union. Sexual union with the beloved is seldom mentioned and never described directly; rather it is intimated by the rapid movement through the sensorium that occurs with mention of her. Key to this series of associations and sensual evocations is the depiction of water that appears at the center of so many of the more erotically charged passages, especially the dynamic polarity of water as sexual and ablutionary.

An analogue of this dynamic polarity is found in mythology of the ghūl. It was said that if you strike the ghūl with your sword once, you will kill it.[36] If you hit it a second time, it will spring back to life. This feature of dynamic polarity is bound up with its epithet *dhū lawnayni* (the double-guised), as opposed to the epithet *dhātu alwānin* that indicates the protean quality of *talawwun*, the perpetual transformation through forms. The principle of dynamic polarity, along with the various guises of dissemblance, makes up the primary motive force behind the similes. In the case of water we found that it could suggest sexual union and climax or purification; fertility and growth or erosion and effacement; the poet (through tears) or the beloved (through her wet mouth); the interior, subjective world (through the *shu'ūn* or tear channels behind the eyes) or the exterior world (through the torrent beds *madāfiʿ*) or the tent trench (*nu'y*); part of the aṭlāl or the element that effaces the aṭlāl. These are only the dynamic polarities of water within the nasīb. The symbolic matrix of dynamic polarities within the rahīl and *fakhr*, and that among the three major sections of the qaṣīdah are equally complex. Within the dynamic polarity lies the *coincidentia oppositorum* where both seem to exist simultaneously—as in those cases where it was impossible to tell whether the water depicted was sexual or ablutionary.[37]

As a postscript to this exploration of the beloved as lost garden, and of the play of similes that links the two, I can find no better verses than those of Dhū al-Rummah, *khātam al-shuʿarā'*, the seal of the early poets. Cited below is the description-of-the-beloved passage from his ode "O Two Abodes of Mayyah" (*a manzilatay mayyin*). What we find can be termed a description of the beloved only in the purely conventional sense. What actually occurs in the poem is a metamorphosis of the beloved into the idyllic garden, or in this case, the oasis:

16. After sleep she is languor.
The house exudes her fragrance.
She adorns it
when she appears in the morning,

17. Her anklets and ivory,
as if entwined around a calotrope
stopping the flow
in the bed of a wadi,

18. With buttocks like a soft dune
over which a rain shower falls
matting the sand
as it sprinkles down.

19. Her hair-fall
over the lower curve of her back,
soft as the moringa's gossamer flowers,
curled with pins and combed,

20. With long cheek hollows
where tears flow,
and a lengthened curve at the breast sash
where it crosses and falls.

21. You see her ear-pendant
along the exposed ridge of her neck,
swaying out,
dangling over the abyss.

22. With a red thornberry tooth-twig,
fragrant as musk and Indian ambergris
brought in in the morning,
she reveals

23. Petals of a camomile
cooled by the night
to which the dew has risen at evening
from Rāma oasis,

24. Wafting in from all sides
with the earth scent of the garden,
redolent as a musk pod
falling open.

25. The white gleam of her teeth,
her immoderate laugh,
almost to the unhearing
speak secrets.[38]

16. *anātun yaṭību l-baytu min ṭībi nashrihā*
*buʿayda l-karā zaynun lahū ḥīna tuṣbiḥū*

17. *ka'anna l-burā wa l-ʿāja ʿījat mutūnuhū*
*ʿalā ʿusharin nahhā bihi s-sayla abṭaḥū*

18. *lahā kafalun ka l-ʿāniki stanna fawqahū*
*ahāḍību labbadna l-hadhālīla nuḍḍaḥū*

19. *wa dhū ʿudharin fawqa dh-dhanūbayni musbalun*
*ʿalā l-bāni yuṭwā bi l-madārā wa yusraḥū*

20. *asīlatu mustanni d-dumūʿi wa mā jarā*
*ʿalayhi l-mijannu l-jā'ilu l-mutawashshaḥū*

21. *tarā qurṭahā fī wāḍiḥi l-līti mushrifan*
*ʿalā halakin fī nafnafin yatatawwaḥū*

22. *wa tajlū bi farʿin min arākin ka'annahū*
*min al-ʿanbari l-hindiyyi wa l-miski yuṣbaḥū*

23. *dhurā uqḥuwānin rāḥahu l-laylu wa rtaqā*
*ilayhi n-nadā min rāmata l-mutarawwiḥū*

24. *taḥuffu bi turbi l-rawḍi min kulli jānibin*
*nasīmun ka fa'ri l-miski ḥīna tufattiḥū*

25. *hijāna th-thanāyā mughriban law tabassamat*
*li akhrasa ʿanhū kāda bi l-qawli yufṣiḥū*

# Notes

1. M. Sells, "The *qaṣīdah* and the West: Self-Reflective Stereotype and Critical Encounter," *Al-ʿArabiyya* 20 (1987): 307–357. A representative formulation of the objective-description view of Arabic poetry is that of Gustav von Grunebaum, "The Response to Nature in Arabic Poetry, *Journal of Near Eastern Studies* 4 (1945): 139–140: "The poet is wholly dedicated to the task of adequately describing his theme down to its most intimate and, at the same time, most typical peculiarities. Whatever the subject, it is presented for its inherent interest, never for any emotion it may have touched off in the observer or listener. . . Whatever his subject, he will reproduce it as it is, or perhaps rather as tradition has taught him to see it . . . If we disregard the perfection of form and language, the beauty of his presentation derives entirely from the fidelity of his observation." A. S. Tritton offers another example: "The poet looks on the world through a microscope. Minute peculiarities of places and animals catch his attention and make his poetry

versified geology and anatomy; untranslatable and dull. Forceful speech is his aim and the result is—to Western minds—often grotesque or even repulsive." See A. S. Tritton, art. "Shiʿr," *The Encyclopaedia of Islam*, 1st ed., ed. M. Th. Houtsma et al. (Leiden: E. J. Brill, 1913–36).

For R. Jacobi's more recent and more detailed version of the objective description hypothesis, see below.

2. See Jaroslav Stetkevych, "Arabic Poetry and Assorted Poetics," in *Islamic Studies: A Tradition and Its Problems*, ed. Malcolm H. Kerr (Malibu, Calif.: Undena Publications, 1980), 114–115 and *passim*. See also the discussion of Labīd's *Muʿallaqah* in Kemal Abu Deeb, "Toward a Structural Analysis of Pre-Islamic Poetry (I): The Key Poem," *International Journal of Middle East Studies* 6:148–184.

3. In a complementary essay, I focus upon the question of description in the *nāqah* (camel mare) passages of the journey section of the qaṣīdah: "Bashāma's Dromedarian: Simile, Symbol, and Symbolic Displacement in the *Nāqa* Section of the Early Arabic Qasida," presented at the Middle East Studies Association (MESA), San Antonio, Texas, November 11, 1990, and published as "Like the Arms of a Drowning Man: Simile and Symbol Worlds in the Nāqa Section of Bashāma's *Hajarta Umāma*," in *A Festschrift in Honor of Ewald Wagner*, ed. W. Heinrichs and G. Schöler (Beiruter Texte und Studien, 1993).

4. This distinction has been given special attention since Roman Jakobson's essay, "Two Aspects of Language and Two Types of Aphasic Disturbances," written in 1954 and published first in Roman Jakobson and Morris Halle, *Fundamentals of Language* (The Hague: Mouton, 1956), and then in Ruth Nanda Anshen, ed., *Language: An Enquiry into Its Meaning and Function* (New York: Harper, 1957).

5. Before entering into the analysis of specific verses, I should mention a dilemma facing those who would embark on such a study. As will be seen below, the description of the beloved within the context of the nasīb is a complex and sophisticated poetic world of its own. To do justice to it requires that discussions of other sections of the qaṣīdah and of the relationship of those other sections to the description of the beloved within the context of the nasīb be put off for another occasion. A similar problem exists when, in the following analysis, particular passages from specific qaṣīdahs are cited and discussed. To discuss the entire qaṣīdah of which they are a part would be beyond the boundary of this chapter and would draw the discussion off in a number of conflicting directions. Yet if the viewpoint articulated here is to have validity, it must be faithful to the structure of the qaṣīdah as a whole and to the meaning and structure of each individual qaṣīdah it addresses. Thus, while this chapter is deliberately self-contained within the parameters set out here, it is also a part of a wider study. In each case where I have cited, discussed, and translated a passage from a particular qaṣīdah, I will refer to other works where I have translated and discussed the qaṣīdah as a whole, integrating the points argued here into the larger context of the poem.

6. Aḥmad Shākir and ʿAbd al-Salām Hārūn, eds., *Al-Mufaḍḍalīyāt* (Cairo: Maṭbaʿat al-Maʿārif, 1944) 2:197–98; Charles James Lyall, ed. and trans., *The Mufaḍḍalīyāt: An Anthology of Ancient Arabian Odes compiled by Al-Mufaḍḍal son of Muḥammad, according to the recension and with the Commentary of Abū Muḥammad al-Qāsim ibn Muḥammad al-Anbārī.* Vol I: *Arabic Text*; Vol. II: *Translation and Notes* (Oxford: Clarendon Press, 1918), 1:790–797; Abū Zakarīyā al-Tibrīzī, *Sharḥ Al-Mufaḍḍalīyāt*, ed. ʿAlī Muḥammad al-Bijāwī (Cairo: Dār Nahḍat Miṣr, 1977), 1326–1331. In the ode of ʿAlqamah, the first verse consists of the implied poet asking himself whether or not the lost beloved has kept faithful the secret (*sirr*). The poem then moves directly into the *ẓaʿn* tableau, a tableau introduced in this case by the poet's remembrance of his own weeping at the beloved's departure. Verses 3–5 refer to the beloved's accompaniment, the processional leading in of the camel stallions by the maidservants, and the rich trappings of the howdahs, their deep red dye streaks and tassels bewildering birds of prey into plucking at them as if they

were stained with blood. Verse 6 introduces what would traditionally be termed the description of the beloved. The *Dīwān* versions place within the nasīb, as verse 10, a verse (*ka'anna ghislata khatmīyyin bi mishfarihā* . . . ["dromedarian lips tinged by a wash of green mallow . . ."]) that is part of the raḥīl in the *Muᶜallaqāt* versions. See W. Ahlwardt, *The Divans of the Six Ancient Arabic Poets* (Osnabrück: Biblio Verlag, 1972), 111; and Al-Aᶜlam al-Shantamarī, *Ashᶜār al-Shuᶜarā' al-Sittah al-Jāhilīyīn*, vol. 1 (Beirut: Dār al-Afāq al-Jadīdah, 1983), 150. For an introduction to and translation of the full poem, see M. Sells, *Desert Tracings: Six Classic Arabian Odes* (Middletown: Wesleyan University Press, 1989), 11–20.

7. To be found in the *Sukkôt* treatise of the Babylonian Talmud.

8. An expression that resonates in an interesting manner with the qur'anic use of *ẓann*.

9. There is another matrix of meaning within this verse that cannot be discussed at this point. A hint of it can be found in the variant reading of *bahkanatun* for *kharᶜabatun*: Tibrīzī, *Mufaḍḍalīyāt*, 1331. Both are quadrilateral epithets for a particularly desirable woman. Both bring in the idea of foreignness, rareness, the exotic. I have translated *bahkanatun* as "belle" in order to bring across this idea. Tibrīzī's alternate reading brings the verse even closer than it already is to the verse in the famous ode of al-Aᶜshā, *waddiᶜ hurayrata* (bid Hurayrah farewell): *ṣifr ul-wishāḥi mil'u d-dir'i bahkanatun // idhā ta'attā yakādu l-khaṣru yankhazilū* ("Full at the bodice, / at the waist sash nil, / a belle, seeming as she comes near / to divide in two"). For an introduction to and discussion of this poem, see Sells, *Desert Tracings*, 57–66. What we have here is an example of the distinctive intertexuality of the oral tradition of the qaṣīdah. A certain set of terms coalesced around a particular point in the description of the beloved. It was not so much that one poet borrowed the terms from another, but that these terms were rediscovered out of the poetic heritage as a new context revealed a new way of using them. Al-Aᶜshā's verse, for example, is satirical, as is the entire passage in which it is found, the poet playfully exaggerating the effect to the point of self-parody.

10. The Muᶜallaqah of ᶜAntarah, al-Zawzanī, *Sharḥ al-Muᶜallaqāt al-Sabᶜ*, ed. Muḥammad al-Dimashqī (1352 H.), 176–179. See also Abū Zakarīyā' al-Tibrīzī, *Kitāb Sharḥ al-Qaṣā'id al-ᶜAshr*, ed. Sir Charles Lyall (Calcutta: Dār al-Imārah, 1894), 93–94, vv. 13–19; and Abū Bakr Muḥammad ibn al-Qāsim al-Anbārī, *Sharḥ al-Qaṣā'id al-Sabᶜ al-Ṭiwāl al-Jāhilīyāt*, ed. ᶜAbd al-Salām Hārūn (Cairo: Dār al-Maᶜārif, 1980), 307–315. See Sells, *Desert Tracings*, 45–56. For verse 16, Ahlwardt's version of Shantamarī's *Dīwān*, as well as Anbārī (312), chooses the interesting variant *tharratin* for *ḥurratin*, which is chosen by Zawzanī (178) and Tibrīzī (94). In the area of erotic undertones, *tharratin* (pierced) brings up sexual connotations of penetration, functioning as an opposite on the formal level to *ḥurratin*, or focusing upon another stage, postcoital as opposed to precoital.

11. For a careful discussion of the grammatical forms the simile can take, see Renate Jacobi, *Studien zur Poetik der altarabischen Qaṣide* (Wiesbadan: Franz Steiner, 1971), 115–129.

12. Mary Douglas, *Purity and Danger: An Analysis of the Concepts of Pollution and Taboo* (London: Routledge and Kegan Paul, 1966, 1980).

13. With the exception of some single-word variants, I have based my translation upon the Dīwān version and have for the most part followed the verse order given in Tadeusz Kowalski, *Le Diwan de Kaᶜb ibn Zuhair: Edition Critique* (Kraków: Nakładem Polskiej Akademii Umiejetności, 1950). Elsewhere I have integrated the points made here concerning the nasīb of Kaᶜb's poem into a translation and commentary upon the poem as a whole: M. Sells, "*Bānat Suᶜād*: Translation and Interpretive Introduction," *Journal of Arabic Literature* 21, no. 2 (1990): 140–154. This article also contains citations of the wide number of translations, commentaries, and editions of Bānat Suᶜād.

14. The ghūl of classical Arabic poetry should be distinguished from the ghūl of later Arabic folklore, the latter of which is usually portrayed as male and easier to please than the poetic ghūl, and becomes identified with spirit inhabiting and feeding on graves. This

creature is similar to the European ogre and becomes the referent for the loan-word from Arabic, "ghoul." To avoid the misleading connotations now carried by the English word *ghoul*, I will use the transliterated form *ghūl*. For the ghūl in folktale, see *Arab Folktales*, trans. and ed. Inea Bushnaq (New York: Pantheon Books, 1986).

15. The commentators give various explanations for the word *aghannu* here, many suggesting that it refers explicitly to the gazelle. While the gazelle metaphor is a definite possibility here, it is not a certainty, and I have chosen not to use it in the translation.

16. A good discussion of purity in Islamic law can be found in Kevin Reinhart, "Impurity/No Danger," *History of Religions* 30, no. 1 (August 1990): 1–24.

17. See Tibrīzī, 31–32; Anbārī, 137–149; Zawzanī, 55–57; *The Dīwān de Ṭarafa ibn al-ʿAbd al-Bakrī accompagné du commentaire de Yousouf al-Aʿlam de Santa-Maria*, ed. Max Seligsohn (Paris: Librairie Émile Bouillon, 1901); and M. Sells, "The Muʿallaqa of Ṭarafa," *Journal of Arabic Literature* 17 (1986): 21–33.

18. *Ithmid, uthmud*: antimony used as collyrium. See Hava (*thamada*, i, to dig up [a hole for water]), *al-Farā'id al-Durrīyah* (Beirut: Dār al-Mashriq, 1986), 72.

19. In my translation I follow the interpretation of *mufāyil* given by Anbārī, 138, al-Shantamarī, and the *Lisān al-ʿArab*. The nature of the game is paraphrased from the latter two sources by Seligsohn, 91: "Les enfants divisaient un tas de sable en deux et cachaient un objet quelconque dans un des deux tas; puis ils disaient à l'enfant qui pariait avec eux: 'Devine où se trouve l'objet.' S'il devinait, il avait gagné; si non, il avait perdu. Ce jeu s'appelle *fiyāl* et celui qui y joue *mufāyil*." Tibrīzī, 31, mentions the game as if it were already understood and does not explain it. Zawzanī's attribution of the game to a man (*rajul*) seems problematic (Zawzanī, 55).

20. Mary Catherine Bateson, *Structural Continuity in Poetry: A Linguistic Study of Five Pre-Islamic Odes* (Paris: Mouton, 1970), 45.

21. See Shākir and Hārūn, *Mufaḍḍalīyāt*, 1:111–116 (poem no. 21); Lyall, *Mufaḍḍalīyāt*, 1:207–224; Al-Tibrīzī, *Sharḥ al-Mufaḍḍalīyāt*, 398–409. Verses 1, 2, 4, 5, combined with four verses from the *fakhr* of Mukhabbal's poem and two final verses that do not occur in it, make up a poem attributed to Ṭarafah. See Seligsohn, *Dīwān Ṭarafah*, poem no. 33, pp. 87, 163–4, and 159 (of Arabic text). For a translation and analysis of the full poem, see M. Sells, "Along the Edge of Mirage: The *Mufaḍḍalīyah* of Mukhabbal as-Saʿdī," in Mustansir Mir, ed., *Literary Heritage of Classical Islam: Arabic and Islamic Studies in Honor of James A. Bellamy* (Princeton: Darwin Press, 1993), 119–136.

22. Lyall, *Mufaḍḍalīyāt*, 2:74, divides the section into the following subunits: 1–3 (unnamed); 4–10, description of the deserted dwellings; 11–20, the charms of his mistress. Shākir and Hārūn, 111, give the following categories (without numbering the verses contained in them): Remembrance (*dhikrā*) and Phantom (ṭayf); description of the abodes of the beloved and their habitation by desert animals (*waṣafa dāra ṣāḥibatihi . . .*); description of the beloved (*thumma naʿata ṣāḥibatahu*); comparison of the beloved to a pearl, description of the pearl and its retrieval, and (comparison) of the beloved to the ostrich egg protected by the male ostrich. For further discussion of the pearldiver in this poem and others, see the fine article by Charles Lyall, "The Pictorial Aspects of Ancient Arabian Poetry," *Journal of the Royal Asiatic Society* (1912): 131–152, 499–502.

23. Lyall, *Mufaḍḍalīyāt*, 1:495–496. See the translation by John Seybold (below, ch. 5) of *Mufaḍḍalīyah* 55, verses 8–11.

24. The ostrich episode itself has a series of important resonances with other sections of the classical qaṣīdah particularly those involving the appearance of the clump-winged bird within the raḥīl. Though important for a full understanding of the ostrich passage here, a discussion of these resonances would lead us far from our principle investigation. I discuss at greater length this particular ostrich scene in Sells, "Along the Edge of Mirage." Cf. the raḥīl ostrich scenes in ʿAlqamah's *hal ma ʿalimta* and the *Muʿallaqah* of ʿAntarah (Sells, *Desert Tracings*, 11, 15–16, 45, 50).

25. See Tibrīzī, 68–69. Sells, *Desert Tracings*, 32–44.

26. Renate Jacobi, *Studien zur Poetik der altarabischen Qaṣide* (Wiesbaden: Franz Steiner, 1971), esp. 157–167.

27. H. Ritter, *Über die Bildersprache Niẓāmīs* (Berlin and Leipzig, 1927). See Jacobi, 110ff, 157–165.

28. Jacobi, 165: "Aber das 'Wesen' der Dinge is für den arabischen Menschen jener Epoche noch flächenhaft. Es fehlt eine Dimension, die den Gleichnissen Homers zusätzlich Bedeutung verleiht . . . finden wir in der altarabischen Dichtung nur die Analogie der äußeren Erscheinung." See also ibid., 110: "Die Beziehung von Bild und Sache bleibt die einer nur von äußeren Merkmalen bestimmten Analogie."

29. Jacobi, 167: "Die altarabische Bilderwelt steht auf einer Stufe der poetischen Entwicklung, die man mit aller gebotenen Einschränkung als "vorhomerisch" bezeichnen könnte. Für sich betrachtet erregen die Vergleiche Bewunderung, aber sieht man die Gleichnisse Homers daneben, so wird man ein tiefes Ungenügen empfinden. Denn ein Bild ist letztlich nicht ohne seinen Gegenstand, seine ästhetische Beziehung zu ihm, zu würdigen, und in dieser Hinsicht bleibt die Leistung der arabischen Vergleiche mit seltenen Ausnahmen (s.o.) hinter der poetischen Wirkung der homerischen Gleichnisse zurück. Es entsteht der Eindruck, als sei ein schöpferischer Prozeß bis zu einem bestimmten Punkt gelangt, ohne die in ihm angelegte Endphase zu erreichen. Der letze Schritt, der von der äußeren Erscheinung zum Wesenskern der Dinge führen müßte, ist den arabischen Dichtern nicht gelungen." Jacobi bases her views of Homer on the work of W. Schadewaldt, "Die homerische Gleichniswelt und die kretisch-mykenische Kunst," in *Von Homers Welt und Werk*, 3rd ed. (Stuttgart, 1959), 130–154. For an excellent recent discussion of the digressive simile in Homer, see Norman Austin, "The Function of Digression in the Iliad," in *Essays of the Iliad: Selected Modern Criticism*, ed. John Wright (Bloomington: Indiana University Press, 1978), 70–85. Wright points out the long history of criticism and disparagement of the Homeric digression (a fact Jacobi ignores) and reevaluates its poetic function by interpreting it as a index of a poetic intensity too great to allow the narrative to continue uninterrupted. What would seem essential in any comparison between the simile in the qaṣīdah and that in Homer would be a discussion of the different genres involved. Because of the primarily narrative nature of the Homeric epic, the simile might well be used to fulfill a fundamentally different, though in some ways analogous, purpose from its counterpart in the quite different lyric-heroic genre of the qaṣīdah.

30. Jacobi, 165–166: "Seine ausführliche Schilderung des hungrigen Schakals auf Nahrungssuche trägt die Züge eines echten Gleichnisses; bezeichnenderweise ist es durch *ka-mā* eingeleitet (Verse 26). Dem Vergleich liegt ein Vorgang zugrunde, das morgendliche Ausziehen des Dichters nach Beute. Aber die Beziehung zwischen Bild und Gegenstand geht tiefer. Der Schakal wird zum Sinnbild des Menschen außerhalb der Gesellschaft, der ein Leben voller Entbehrungen führt, zugleich aber Mut und Kraft besitzt, es zu ertragen. Dem Dichter Shanfarā ist mit diesen Versen etwas gelungen, was in der gedanklichen Konzeption, wenn auch vielleicht nicht in der Straffheit der poetischen Form, über die Dichtung seiner Zeit hinausführt."

31. In the language of Schiller, the simile that expresses sentiment directly, with a more straightforward narrative and analogical rationale, might be characterized as sentimental as opposed to the more "naive" simile typical of the early qaṣīdah. For Schiller, the sentimental mode is often a later development, one that grows out of the tradition established by the original naive poetry. Schiller views the sentimental as lacking the depth of its earlier, naive forerunner. F. Schiller, *Naive and Sentimental Poetry*, trans. from the German (*Über Naive und Sentimentalische Dichtung*) J. Elias (New York: F. Unger, 1967).

32. Jacobi, 165: "Wo bei Homer, zumal in den Tierbildern, Verglichenes und Vergleichsgegenstand in engste Beziehung zueinander treten und sich gegenseitig erhellen . . . , da finden wir in der altarabischen Dichtung nur die Analogie der äußeren Erscheinung. Auch hier bestehen fest Zuordnungen von Bild und Gegenstand, aber die Bezugspunkte

sind nach Art der Verbindung Frau-Gazelle fast immer auf körperliche Eigenarten oder besondere Verhaltensweisen beschränkt."

33. Jacobi, 111–112: "Die Bildgestaltung dieser Stufe ist in ihrer Unreflektiertheit oft äesthetisch unbefriedigend. Ihr Vorzug, die Genauigkeit der Wiedergabe und die dadurch erreichte Anschaulichkeit, erscheint am vollkommensten dort, wo der Dichter Bewegungsvorgänge ins Bild umsetzt." As an example of such unreflective descriptive reproduction, Jacobi cites (112) Ṭarafah's comparison of the ship's bow-breast cleaving the waves to the hand of someone at play." As was mentioned above, this simile, far from being the result of an unreflective reproduction of exterior reality, is motivated by a complex set of poetic factors, including the disguising of the erotic quality of the original image.

34. See, for example, the traditions concerning the perfumes Adam took with him after he was expelled from paradise in *The History of al-Ṭabarī = Ta'rīkh al-rusul wal-mulūk*, vol. 1, *General Introduction and From the Creation to the Flood*, trans. Franz Rosenthal (Albany: State University of New York Press, 1989), 296–298.

35. An examination of the larger world of mythopoetic elements of the sacred in the qaṣīdah has been reserved for a separate occasion. At this point it might be helpful to list some of those elements: the sacred enclosure of which the aṭlāl are a particularly charged example; the manāzil of the departing beloved as resonant with pre-Islamic pilgrimage stops (manāzil); the relationship among the aṭlāl, the ṭayf or phantom, the poet standing over the traces, and the process of incubation whereby the visit to a shrine often resulted in a visitation of the saint or goddess of that shrine—indicated by Seybold (below, ch. 5); and, of course, a topic touched upon here, the beloved as lost garden—to cite only a few major examples.

36. See the discussion and citations in Maḥmūd al-Ālūsī al-Baghdādī, *Bulūgh al-Arab fī Maʿrifat Aḥwāl al-ʿArab* (Cairo: Al-Maṭbaʿah al-Raḥmānīyah), 1924: 431–432.

37. For another approach to the symbolism of water in the classical qaṣīdah, see Adnan Haydar, "The *Muʿallaqah* of Imru' al-Qays," *Edebiyât* II (1977): 227–261, III (1978): 51–82.

38. Sells, *Desert Tracings,* 67–76. For the Arabic text of the passage cited here, see *Dhū al-Rumma, the Dīwān of Ghaylān ibn ʿUqba*, ed. Carlile Henry Hayes Macartney (Cambridge: The University Press, 1919), 80–83.

# IV

# "NO SOLACE FOR THE HEART"

## THE MOTIF OF THE DEPARTING WOMEN IN THE PRE-ISLAMIC BATTLE ODE

*Hassan El-Banna Ezz El-Din*

This chapter examines a particular motif within pre-Islamic Arabic poetry, that of the "departing women" (*ẓaʿāʾin*), which, along with the ruined encampment (*aṭlāl*) and the dream phantom (*ṭayf al-khayāl*), constitutes one of the dominant motifs of the opening section (*nasīb*) of the ode.* My aim is to demonstrate that the appearance of the ẓaʿāʾin motif does not constitute the mere arbitrary repetition of a literary convention, but functions as part of a larger poetic paradigm, and that, in so doing, it may signal what may be designated in structural terms as a "battle ode."

My point of departure, here as in my earlier work on the dream phantom and the ruined abode,[1] is the fact that Arabic poetry still requires creative exploration, not mere statistical description with charts of rhetorical themes and structures. What is required, rather, is a framework for dealing with the poetic texts and a method derived from a close reading of these texts with an eye to their internal logic. Within this framework, I have concentrated on the history of individual items of poetic diction, their etymological derivation, their cumulative, implicit meanings, and their incorporation into a meaningful poetic context.

Critical to all studies of pre-Islamic Arabic poetry is the recognition that it is originally oral in nature and, as such, serves as an instrument by which cultural traditions are established and maintained.[2] Furthermore, as M. V. McDonald has established, warfare is characteristically a central theme of oral poetry.[3] Therefore, the search for a structural typology of a "battle ode" within this poetry *qua* oral poetry ought to be a fruitful critical endeavor. The goal here is to demonstrate that such a typology indeed exists and, further, that it does not consist of the mere appearance of explicitly martial themes in the final section (*fakhr*) of the poem, but is structurally imbedded in the total poetic structure and, in certain structurally defined situations, is signaled by the ẓaʿāʾin motif.

Previous scholarship on the subject of war in pre-Islamic poetry may be divided into two categories. The first is composed of recent studies limited to the discussion of verses that explicitly mention war, its implements, stages, and so forth. Not surprisingly, critics pursuing this line of inquiry have reached a dead end in their search for a formally recognizable "battle ode"; for they have focused exclusively on the literal descriptions of war, without any regard to the poetic structures in which such descriptions occur.[4]

The second approach is based primarily on an observable quantitative extratextual phenomenon. Thus the medieval critic Ibn Sallām al-Jumaḥī (d. ca. 230/845) observes that poetry proliferated as wars occurred among the tribes, such as those between al-Aws and al-Khazraj, or between raiding and raided tribes. He then states that the paucity of poetry among the Quraysh was due to the fact that there was no enmity among its clans and, so, they did not wage war.[5]

Extrapolating from Ibn Sallām's remarks, we can suggest that war was a sociocultural institution inculcated in the collective consciousness of society via poetry, in such a way that there came to be an intimate link between war and poetry. Pursuing a similar line of thought, Muṣṭafā Nāṣif noted in the early 1970s that "regardless of the specific subject it deals with, pre-Islamic poetry cannot be separated from the idea of war."[6] In fact, Nāṣif tends to see war as underlying several important motifs, such as the ruined abode.[7] He has observed further that "the curious thing that strikes the reader in all pre-Islamic poetry is that war seems to be more important than peace or, at least, the only means to achieve [peace]."[8]

Although the latter approach is consonant with the method I have proposed for analyzing pre-Islamic Arabic poetry, its proponents have yet to go beyond these initial observations to explain in structural terms the relation of the apparently nonmartial elements of the ode to the explicitly martial ones. This, then, is my aim here.

The ẓaʿā'in, "departing women," is one of the dominant motifs of the nasīb. It consists primarily of the poet's description of the women departing in their camel litters. The moment of description generally occurs after the poet has stopped at the ruined campsite, as we find in the *Muʿallaqah*s of Zuhayr, Ṭarafah, and many others. In other poems, the poet may begin with a reference to the departure of a neighboring tribe (*khalīṭ*), from which he proceeds to a description of the departing women themselves. My analysis of the connection of the ẓaʿā'in motif to the theme of war will be conducted on three levels: (1) diction, (2) imagery, and (3) structure.

*(1) Diction:* The pre-Islamic poets used the verb *ẓaʿana* only in the nasīb and in the fakhr, or boast, section that concludes the ode and consists primarily of threats of violence against the enemy. This verb, then, semantically binds the two sections, a link that is further strengthened by the absence of this term from the *raḥīl*, or middle section of the poem. This, in spite of the fact that the Arabic

root *ẓ-ʿ-n* in purely lexical terms appears to be synonymous with *r-ḥ-l*, meaning "to depart."

After examining a large corpus of pre-Islamic odes, we find that the verb *ẓaʿana* (to depart) in the nasīb creates a sense of sorrow and longing in the poet, since the subject of the verb is the departing beloved and her tribe. As Bishr says:[9]

*Alā ẓaʿanat li-niyyatihā idāmu*
*wa-kullu wiṣāli ghāniyatin rimāmu.*

Ah, gone on her way is Idām,
but every tie to a fair one
must one day wear out and snap.
[trans. Charles Lyall]

Or again:[10]

*Wa ādhana ahlu salmā bi -rtiḥālin*
*famā li l-qalbi idh ẓaʿanū ʿazāʾu.*

Salmah's folk announced their departure,
and now they're gone—
no solace for my heart.

Still on the level of diction, an additional example deserves mention here. In a line by Al-Muraqqash the Elder, the poet expresses in the first hemistich his physical separation from the departing tribe of his beloved and, in the second, his continued emotional attachment:[11]

*Idhā ẓaʿana l-ḥayyu l-jamīʿu -jtanabtuhum*
*makāna n-nadīmi li n-najiyyi l-musāʿifi.*

When the tribe in a body started on their way,
I kept apart from them as far as a boon companion
keeps from his comrade and helper.
[trans. Charles Lyall]

Likewise in the fakhr, or boast, this verb has a negative connotation, but not of sorrow and longing as in the nasīb. Rather, it is used in a deprecating sense as the poet reproaches a neighboring tribe for leaving its residence in search of a more fertile place in time of drought or, significantly, for seeking a refuge in time of war. In either case, the poet regards the neighboring tribe's departure as disgraceful, although at the same time, its disgrace serves as a counter to the heroic perseverance of his own people. Thus, reproaching his departing neighbors, Ṭufayl says:[12]

*Wa dārin yaẓʿanu l-ʿāhūna ʿanhā*
*li niyyatihim wa yansawna z-zimāmā.*

Many a home from which
the evil-doers travel to their destination—
and forget their obligations.
[trans. F. Krenkow]

In another poem Ṭufayl boasts of his own tribe:[13]

*Lā yaẓʿanūna ʿalā ʿamyā'a in ẓaʿanū*
*wa lā yuṭīlūna ikhmādan ʿani s-surabi.*

They do not travel aimlessly if they go,
nor do they keep the campfire out for long
for fear of sneak attacks.
[trans. F. Krenkow]

Here, the conditional clause "if they go . . ." suggests that the poet's tribe departs only when it resolves to do so, and only on its own terms.

So rooted, however, did the negative connotation of the verb *ẓaʿana* become that another poet, al-Ḥādirah, could say:[14]

*Wa nuqīmu fī dāri l-ḥifāẓi buyūtanā*
*zamanan wa yaẓʿanu ghayrunā li l-amraʿi*

*Wa maḥalli majdin lā yusarriḥu ahluhu*
*yawma l-iqāmati wa l-ḥulūli li martaʿi.*

And we pitch our tents
in the place where honor calls
and stay there, steadfast,
while other men travel to richer pastures.

Those who hold the place of glory
do not drive their camels to feed abroad
on the day they must pitch their tents there
and hold it!
[based on Charles Lyall]

Salāmah Ibn Jandal ends a famous ode of his with a line that serves further to explicate al-Ḥādirah's words about steadfastness and the preservation of one's honor:[15]

*Ḥattā turiknā wa mā tuthnā ẓaʿāʾinunā*
*yaʾkhudhna bayna sawādi l-khaṭṭi fa l-lūbi.*

So stand we, great in men's eyes:
Our ladies are never turned aside
When they travel between al-Khaṭṭ
and the upland lava plains.
[trans. Charles Lyall]

Thus, whereas the despicable tribe, unable to endure hardship and afraid of its enemies, departs, the noble tribe remains, enduring the fear and hardship and thereby making for itself a name that terrifies its enemies, repelling them from its territory, and, hence, guaranteeing its ladies, the ẓaʿāʾin, freedom and safety of journey from place to place.

Three further examples confirm the predominantly negative connotation—i.e., that of flight—of the verb *ẓaʿana* in the fakhr section of the ode. The first is by Ṭufayl, who praises a man from another tribe who came to prevent war:[16]

*Wa anta bnu ukhti ṣ-ṣidqi yawma buyūtunā*
*bi Kutlata idh sārat ilaynā l-qabāʾilu*

*Bi ḥayyin idhā qīla -ẓʿanū qad utītumu*
*aqāmū falam turdad ʿalayhim ḥamāʾilu.*

You acted like a true kinsman
the day when our tents were pitched at Kutlah,
when the tribes came against us.

Your tribe is one that, whenever the cry goes up,
"Depart! The enemy is upon you!"
stays and needs not gird the sword.
[trans. F. Krenkow]

From the poem's larger context, it is worth noting that the tribe that stands its ground despite the threat of war is the one that has the authority to prevent war between other conflicting tribes.

The second is from the fakhr section of the poem that we began with, that is, by Bishr:[17]

*Wa qālū lan tuqīmū in ẓaʿannā*
*fa kāna lanā wa qad ẓaʿanū maqāmu.*

They said to us, "You cannot remain if we depart."
Yet after they departed, we remained.

In this verse Bishr plays, as did al-Ḥādirah above, on the moral polarity of remaining and departing, here through a double antithesis of *aqāma* (to remain or abide) and *ẓaʿana* (to depart).

Finally, in a line similar to Bishr's, Ibn Muqbil first presents the same antithesis between *iqāmah* (remaining, abiding) and *ẓaʿn* (departing), now introducing the element of gender. For it is a sign of strength that the men of the tribe are never forced to send their women away to safety. A further addition is the antithesis between seeking and granting protection: the powerful tribe need never depart to seek protection, but rather, is the granter of protection to any refugee that comes to it:[18]

*Naḥnu l-muqīmūna lam tabraḥ ẓaʿā'inunā*
*lā nastajīru wa man yaḥlul binā yujari.*

It is we who stay,
our women (ẓaʿā'in) do not leave.
We do not seek protection,
we grant it.

This examination of pre-Islamic poetic usage reveals a structurally determined differentiation in the significance of *ẓaʿana*. That is, the poet employs this verb and its derivative terms in both the nasīb and the fakhr sections of the ode, but with quite distinct connotations. In the nasīb, these terms refer to the departing beloved and her tribe and therefore evoke a sense of sorrow, longing, and reverie on the part of the poet-lover. By contrast, in the fakhr or boast section, these terms convey rather the disgrace and degradation of the women of weak tribes—normally the enemy—whose men cannot defend them. (Or even, in dire circumstances, for the poet's own womenfolk.) Here we find the poet boasting of his tribe's ability to protect its women while forcing the women of the enemy to desert their homeland.

What is clear is that diction is not really separable from imagery and structure. In other words, our reading of the word *ẓaʿana* will depend on its context in terms of imagery and structure. This is confirmed by the confusion, or fusion, of the two connotations—the nasīb one and the fakhr one—in a decontexualized line attributed to Labīd in his dīwān:[19]

*Bakatnā arḍunā lammā ẓaʿannā*
*wa ḥayyatnā safīratu wa l-ghayāmu.*

Our land wept over us when we departed,
while the ruins of Safīrah and Ghayām greeted us.

In the pre-Islamic nasīb one rarely encounters the verb *ẓaʿana* referring to the poet's own tribe or references to the land weeping, or ruins greeting the poet. Rather, one finds the tribe of the poet's beloved departing and the poet himself greeting and weeping over the deserted dwelling place. The inversion here seems to express bitter self-mockery and grief. In addition, Labīd's use of the plural pronoun confirms that the weeping in the nasīb does not express a purely personal concern but, rather, a communal one. But it is precisely at this point that we begin to ask ourselves whether this line is purely nasīb, or does it partake, too, of the connotations of the fakhr section? For it is also an inversion of the tribal boast of our previous example. Then too, the first-person plural is characteristic of fakhr. The verb *ẓaʿana*, here applied to the poet's own tribe, thus acquires the deprecating tone of its fakhr connotation, now turned into self-deprecation. It is lines such as this that reveal the underlying relationship of the ẓaʿn in the nasīb (sorrow at the departure of the beloved's tribe) and of the fakhr (satisfaction for being able to protect the women of one's own tribe from having to depart).

*(2) Imagery:* Turning to the image of the departing women itself, it appears that even in the nasīb, it is the threat of war that compels the tribe to desert its dwelling and depart. In other words, it is ultimately war—or the threat of war—that motivates the ẓaʿā'in image of the nasīb. It should be noted that this result of my research disproves the conventionally accepted interpretation of the ẓaʿn motif of the nasīb as referring merely to seasonal migration in search of water and pasturage.[20] Although such an interpretation is true of the poetry of the Islamic period, our examination of the pre-Islamic corpus shows otherwise: that the ẓaʿn is provoked predominantly by the threat of tribal warfare. For example, the poet Bishr says:[21]

*Alā ẓaʿana l-khalīṭu ghadāta rīʿū*
*bi shabwata fa l-maṭiyyu binā khuḍūʿu*

*Ajadda l-baynu fa -ḥtamalū sirāʿan*
*famā bi d-dāri idh ẓaʿanū katīʿu.*

Alas the neighbors have departed on a morning
when they were alarmed at Shabwah,
so our mounts now stand, necks bowed.

Separation became inevitable;
so in haste they packed up, and once they departed,
not one of them remained.

Indeed, we sometimes come across lines in the nasīb that explicitly relate the ẓaʿā'in to the theme of war; Ṭufayl says:[22]

*Ẓaʿāʾinu abraqna l-kharīfa wa shimnahu*
*wa khifna l-humāma an tuqāda qanābiluh.*

Litter-borne women [ẓaʿāʾin] who watch
for the lightning of autumn,
gazing toward it,
And fear that the armies of the king
may be led forth.
[based on F. Krenkow]

Also accompanying the ẓaʿāʾin motif are specific images relating the departing women to war and death, such as that of the birds of prey which swoop down on the coverings of the litters, mistaking them because of their blood-red color for carrion. Thus we read in a nasīb by ʿAlqamah:[23]

*ʿAqlan wa raqman taẓallu ṭ-ṭayru takhṭafuhu*
*ka'annahu min dami l-ajwāfi madmūmu.*

. . . [B]irds hung in the air
plucking at the dye streaks and tassels
as if they'd been stained
heartsblood crimson.
[trans. Michael A. Sells]

Finally, in one of his ẓaʿāʾin poems, Bishr introduces the motif of the departing women, using the term *khalīṭ* (the departing tribe) at the end of the nasīb, then in the fakhr section returns to dwell on the description of the departing women as ẓaʿāʾin. His lines recall ʿAlqamah's nasīb image—now in the fakhr section and in the context of war. Here Bishr refers to the enemy's women who are present at the scene of the battle:[24]

*Lahum ẓuʿunātun yahtadīna bi rāyatin*
*kamā yastaqillu ṭ-ṭāʾiru l-mutaqallibu.*

They have women in their howdahs [ẓuʿunāt]
guided by a banner,
like a flighty bird rising
in the air.

Thus we see that the ẓaʿāʾin images in the nasīb and fakhr sections are not unrelated, but rather resonate in such a way as to reinforce the theme of war.

*(3) Structure:* On the structural level of the qaṣīdah, the motif of the departing women, in its diction and imagery, creates an explicit and implicit tension

within the poem. This tension is manifested in the departing-women qaṣīdah in accordance with defined structural principles. Thus we find that in the tripartite qaṣīdah, that which exhibits the raḥīl (journey) section, when the ẓaʿāʾin is the sole motif in the nasīb, the pre-Islamic poet does not refer to the theme of war in the fakhr section.[25] When, however, the poet omits the raḥīl section to form a bipartite pattern of the qaṣīdah, he appears to connect the ẓaʿāʾin motif and the theme of war by the extensive development of the latter in the fakhr section.[26] The following illustrates this poetic principle:

(a) *The tripartite qaṣīdah*:
1. nasīb: ẓaʿāʾin as sole motif.
2. raḥīl: wild animals, portraying the she-camel (*nāqah*), struggling with their enemies.
3. fakhr: no mention of war theme.

(b) *The bipartite qaṣīdah*:
1. nasīb: ẓaʿāʾin as the sole motif.
(no raḥīl)
2. fakhr: war theme appears.

That is, it appears that in the bipartite ẓaʿāʾin qaṣīdah, the raḥīl (which is based on the description of wild animals to which the nāqah [she-camel] is likened, such as the wild bull and the wild ass, in their struggle with the human hunter and his dogs) is replaced by the theme of war in the fakhr section. For the poet tests or proves himself either through the ordeal of the solitary journey or of the tribal battle; one makes the other redundant. This poetic "law," as it were, leads to an important result, namely, that the predominance of the ẓaʿāʾin motif within the nasīb of the bipartite qaṣīdah constitutes a paradigmatic battle qaṣīdah.

On the other hand, we find that in tripartite qaṣīdahs in which the ẓaʿāʾin occurs as only one of several motifs, the theme of war may appear in the fakhr. The appearance of the war theme in the fakhr occurs in two types of tripartite qaṣīdah pattern: the first is when the ẓaʿāʾin motif is not the predominant one in the nasīb, and, hence, does not determine the poetic structure. The second is when the ẓaʿāʾin motif is the governing but not the sole motif in the nasīb, in which case we find that the raḥīl unit is abbreviated. Significantly, the raḥīl in such cases does not contain the comparison of the she-camel (nāqah) to the struggle or hunt of wild animals that characterizes type (a) described above.[27] Otherwise we find that the raḥīl is omitted altogether, thereby producing the same bipartite pattern as that established above for the monomotival ẓaʿāʾin nasīb.

The *Muʿallaqah* of ʿAmr ibn Kulthūm[28] demonstrates this bipartite pattern: it consists of a polymotival nasīb in which the ẓaʿāʾin is the governing motif and moves, without a raḥīl, to an extensive fakhr section dominated by the theme of war.

Following his opening praise of wine and call for the cup (vv. 1–7), the poet beseeches the departing women to wait so that he may tell them of battles and impending death, and of their uncertain future due to the warring tribes:

8. *Wa innā sawfa tudrikunā l-manāyā*
*muqaddaratan lanā wa muqaddarīnā*

9. *Qifī qabla t-tafarruqi yā ẓaᶜīnā*
*nukhabbirki l-yaqīna wa tukhbirīnā*

10. *Qifī nas'alki hal aḥdathti ṣurman*
*li washki l-bayni am khunti l-amīnā*

11. *Bi yawmi karīhatin ḍarban wa ṭaᶜnan*
*aqarra bihi mawālīki l-ᶜuyūnā*

12. *Wa inna ghadan wa inna l-yawma rahnun*
*wa baᶜda ghadin bimā lā taᶜlamīnā.*

8. And surely death will seize us;
it is fated to us; we to it.

9. So halt, departing woman, before the separation,
that we may tell you the truth
and you may do the same.

10. Halt, that we may ask you:
"Have you cut us off to hasten the separation,
or have you deceived a trusted one?

11. On a day of war, of striking and thrusting,
pleasing to your cousins.

12. For truly today, tomorrow, and the day after
are a pledge to what you know not."
[trans. A. J. Arberry]

In these verses, ᶜAmr addresses the departing woman in an explicit context of war and death, which calls into question any future relationship between him and his beloved; war causes rupture between cousins and the forced flight of the womenfolk. In the verses that follow (13–20) the poet describes his beloved, intensifying the sense of separation and loss. She resembles a pure-white virgin she-camel, while the grief-stricken poet is like a she-camel that has lost her foal, like a grey-haired woman who has buried her nine sons, yet another reference to the devastations of war.

In a manner consistent with the typology established above, ʿAmr ibn Kulthūm's *Muʿallaqah* does not have a raḥīl, the section in which the poet traditionally crosses the harsh desert on his noble and sturdy she-camel symbolic of the poet's own lineage and fortitude. Instead, ʿAmr heightens the elegiac tension with the image of the grieving she-camel in the nasīb (vv. 14–19), while adding a second ẓaʿā'in description that exhibits explicit references to war and battle:

21. *Tadhakkartu ṣ-ṣibā wa -shtaqtu lammā*
*ra'aytu ḥumūlahā uṣulan ḥudīnā*

22. *Fa aʿraḍati l-yamāmatu wa -shmakharrat*
*ka-asyāfin bi aydī muṣlitīnā*

23. *Abā hindin falā taʿjal ʿalaynā*
*wa anẓirnā nukhabbirka l-yaqīnā*

24. *Bi annā nūridu r-rāyāti bīḍan*
*wa nuṣdiruhunna ḥumran qad ruwīnā.*

21. And I remembered youth and yearned
when I saw her camels urged on in the evening.

22. Then Yamāmah arose and towered above us
like swords in the hands of the unsheathers.

23. Father of Hind, don't be hasty with us;
give us a moment to tell you the truth,

24. Of how we take to battle white banners
and bring them back saturated crimson!
[trans. A. J. Arberry]

With this transition, ʿAmr enters the fakhr section, containing more than sixty verses on battle and war, where he claims that he and his fellow kinsmen have waged war on behalf of their womenfolk who stand behind them on the battlefield:

84. *ʿAlā āthārinā bīḍun ḥisānun*
*nuḥādhiru an tuqassama aw tahūnā*

. . .

90. *Ẓaʿā'inu min banī jushami bni bakrin*
*khalaṭna bi mīsamin ḥasaban wa dīnā*

91. *Wamā manaᶜa ẓ-ẓaᶜā'ina mithlu ḍarbin*
*turā minhu s-sawāᶜidu ka l-qulīnā*

92. *Ka'annā wa s-suyūfu musallalātun*
*waladnā n-nāsa ṭurran ajmaᶜīnā.*

84. Upon our tracks follow fair, noble ladies
that we take care shall not be left behind,
nor be insulted.

. . .

90. Litter-borne ladies [ẓaᶜā'in] of the
Banū Jusham ibn Bakr
who combine good looks with good
lineage and obedience.

91. Nothing protects the litter-borne ladies like a smiting
when the forearms fly like play chucks.

92. As if we, swords drawn,
gave birth to all people, the lot of them!
[based on A. J. Arberry]

It should be noted that the women referred to by the term ẓaᶜā'in in verses 90–91 are not the women of a neighboring tribe who, in the nasīb, depart at the threat of war. Instead, the litters contain the wives of the warriors of the poet's own tribe who urge their husbands on to protect them by defeating the enemy. Thus, in the nasīb of ᶜAmr's "battle qaṣīdah," the death and destruction of war are prefigured in the description of the departing women of the beloved's tribe. The nasīb ẓaᶜā'in are then mirrored in the fakhr, as litter-borne ladies of the poet's own tribe who wait in the background as the battle rages. In the end only war can reestablish for the tribe the power and authority that alone guarantee the honor and the safety of the ẓaᶜā'in. This, then, is the source of the final image of the life-generating power of war.

In conclusion, we can see from the analysis of the ẓaᶜā'in motif in terms of diction, imagery, and qaṣīdah structure, that the repeated use of this motif in the pre-Islamic ode was by no means a random repetition of a conventional motif. Rather, the analysis presented here reveals that there is in operation in the pre-Islamic ode a complex and highly organized poetic structuring of motifs and themes. Thus the appearance of the ẓaᶜā'in motif in the nasīb signals precise possibilities for thematic and structural development. Its appearance in the fakhr section is likewise not arbitrary, but resonates its nasīb appearance and is poetically predetermined by it. In a highly form-determined tradition, such as that of the pre-Islamic Arabic ode, it is only through learning to read the formal structure of the poem that we can really read the poem.

# Notes

* I would like to thank Nancy N. Roberts for her translation work on the early draft of this paper.

1. Ḥasan al-Bannā ʿIzz al-Dīn, *al-Ṭayf wa al-khayāl fī al-shiʿr al-ʿarabī al-qadīm* (Cairo: Dār al-Nadīm lil-Nashr wa al-Tawzīʿ wa al-Ṣaḥāfah, 1988); *al-Kalimāt wa al-ashyā': al-taḥlīl al-binyawī li qaṣīdat al-aṭlāl fī al-shiʿr al-jāhilī: dirāsah naqdiyyah* (Beirut: Dār al-Manāhil, 1989).

2. Eric A. Havelock, *The Muse Learns to Write: Reflections on Orality and Literacy from Antiquity to the Present* (New Haven and London: Yale University Press, 1986), 71. To apply this principle to pre-Islamic Arabic poetry, see A. J. Arberry, *The Seven Odes: The First Chapter in Arabic Literature* (London: George Allen and Unwin Ltd/New York: The Macmillan Company, 1957), 14, where he quotes Ibn Rashīq al-Qayrawānī (d. 1064) in his passage on the social importance of pre-Islamic poets. See also Andras Hamori, *On the Art of Medieval Arabic Literature* (Princeton: Princeton University Press, 1974), 21–22, where he comments and elaborates on H. A. R. Gibb's remark on the hieratic quality of the qaṣīdah in the Islamic period.

3. M. V. McDonald, "Orally Transmitted Poetry in Pre-Islamic Arabia and Other Pre-Literate Societies," *Journal of Arabic Literature* 9 (1978): 29–31. About "war" as a holy function, and the "camp" as a holy place, among the Semites, see W. Robertson Smith, *Lectures on the Religion of the Semites* (London: A. and C. Black Ltd, 1923), 455. About sacrifice by victorious warriors, especially among the Arabs, see ibid., 491–492. See also Hamori, *On the Art,* 23: "we must recall the verses in which war is all important, but which lack all historical particulars because war taken generically is the medium in which the heroic taken generically manifests itself."

4. See, for example, Muḥammad al-ʿĪd al-Khaṭrāwī, *Shiʿr al-ḥarb fī al-Jāhilīyah ʿinda al-Aws wa al-Khazraj* (Damascus and Beirut: Dār al-Qalam, Mu'assasat ʿUlūm al-Qur'ān, 1980); Nūrī Ḥammūdī al-Qaysī, *Shiʿr al-ḥarb ḥattā al-qarn al-awwal al-hijrī* (Beirut: ʿĀlam al-Kutub, Maktabat al-Nahdah al-ʿArabāyah, 1986) esp. 12–13; and Muḥammad Saʿīd Mawlawī, ed., *Dīwān ʿAnṭarah* (Beirut: al-Maktab al-Islāmī, 1970), 100, where he refers to ʿAnṭarah's care in describing the women's caravan and the war machine, i.e., horses. He does not, however, go beyond the consideration of the she-camel as the mount which brings the poet to his beloved and the horses as a means of transportation in peace and war.

5. Muḥammad Ibn Sallām al-Jumaḥī, *Ṭabaqāt fuḥūl al-shuʿarā'*, ed. Maḥmūd Muḥammad Shākir, 2 vols. (Cairo: Maṭbaʿat al-Madanī, 1974), 1:259. Poets do sometimes praise their tribes for being able to move from one place to another, but this does not happen in the context of ẓaʿā'in motif; see Charles James Lyall, ed. and trans., *The Mufaḍḍalīyāt: An Anthology of Ancient Arabian Odes compiled by Al-Mufaḍḍal son of Muḥammad, according to the Recension and with the Commentary of Abū Muḥammad al-Qāsim ibn Muḥammad al-Anbārī.* Vol. I: *Arabic Text*; Vol. II: *Translation and Notes* (Oxford: Clarendon Press, 1918), 2:149–154.

6. Muṣṭafā Nāṣif, *Qirā'ah thāniyah li shiʿrinā al-qadīm* (Beirut: Dār Lubnān lil-Ṭibāʿah wa al-Nashr, n.d.), 112.

7. Ibid., 112–114.
8. Ibid., 108.
9. Bishr Ibn Abī Khāzim al-Asadī, *Dīwān*, ed. ʿIzzat Ḥasan (Damascus: Maṭbaʿat Mudīrīyat Iḥyā' al-Turāth al-Qadīm, 1960), 201. All translations from the Arabic are mine unless otherwise noted.
10. Ibid., 1.
11. ʿAbd al-Salām Hārūn and Aḥmad Shākir, eds., *Al-Mufaḍḍalīyāt* (Cairo: Dār al-Maʿārif, 1964), 176.
12. Ṭufayl al-Ghanawī. *Shiʿr, riwāyat Abī Ḥātim al-Sijistānī ʿan al-Aṣmaʿī*, ed. and trans. F. Krenkow (Leiden: E. J. Brill, 1928), 29, 64.
13. Ṭufayl, *Shiʿr*, 22, 56. See also Ibn Muqbil, *Dīwān*, ed. ʿIzzat Ḥasan (Damascus: Wizārat al-Thaqāfah, 1962), 34, where the poet wishes that he and his tribe were as before, i.e.:

*Bi ḥayyin idhā qīla -ẓʿanū qad utītumū*
*aqāmū ʿalā athqālihim wa talaḥlaḥū.*

Among a tribe who, if they are told:
"Depart! You are attacked!"
stay steadfast and don't leave.

14. Lyall, *Mufaḍḍalīyat*, 2:17. See also al-Ḥādirah, *Dīwān*, ed. Nāṣir al-Dīn al-Asad, 2nd ed. (Beirut: Dār Ṣādir, 1980), 53–55, and 53n.3, 55n.2.
15. Lyall, *Mufaḍḍalīyat*, 2:81. See also Salāmah Ibn Jandal, *Dīwān, riwāyat al-Aṣmaʿī wa Abī ʿAmr al-Shaybānī*, ed. Fakhr al-Dīn Qibāwah (Aleppo: Al-Maktabah al-ʿArabīyah bi Ḥalab, 1968), 130–133.
16. Ṭufayl, *Shiʿr*, 27, 61–62.
17. Bishr, *Dīwān*, 206.
18. Ibn Muqbil, *Dīwān*, 88.
19. Labīd ibn Rabīʿah, *Dīwān*, ed. Iḥsān ʿAbbās (Kuwait: Wizārat al-Irshād, 1964), 293.
20. Ibn Qutaybah (d. 276/889) in his renowned description of or prescription for the thematic order of the qaṣīdah refers to the *ẓāʿinūn* (departing people) as those who left their campsites in search of water and pasturage. No connection is made between the ẓaʿn motif and the theme of war. This is, however, not surprising inasmuch as Ibn Qutaybah's remarks, although framed as descriptive of the pre-Islamic qaṣīdah, are primarily prescriptive of the neoclassical panegyric qaṣīdah (madḥ). See Ibn Qutaybah, *al-Shiʿr wa al-shuʿarā'*, ed. Aḥmad Muḥammad Shākir (Cairo: Dār al-Maʿārif, 1982), 75. For a translation, see R. A. Nicholson, *A Literary History of the Arabs* (Cambridge: Cambridge University Press, 1969), 77–78.
21. Bishr, *Dīwān*, 129. Other poets use the same verb, *rīʿa* (be alarmed, terrified), in the ẓaʿā'in image. See, for example, ʿAmr Ibn Qamī'ah, *Dīwān*, ed. Khalīl Ibrāhīm al-ʿAṭīyah (Baghdad: Dār al-Ḥurrīyah lil-Ṭibāʿah, 1972), 55; ʿAntarah in al-Zawzanī, *Sharḥ al-Muʿallaqāt al-sabʿ* (Beirut, n.p., n.d.), 193; and Ṭufayl, *Shiʿr,* 16, 42. On the other hand, see also, ʿAnṭarah, *Dīwān*, 272–273 and Maymūn Ibn Qays al-Aʿshā, *Dīwān* (Beirut: Dār Ṣādir, 1966), 143, where both of them refer to their alarm at the sudden nighttime departure of the beloved and her tribe. Even when the poet expects their departure he refers to his pessimism; see ʿAnṭarah, *Dīwān*, 262–266. In all of these examples the poet expresses not only his sorrow but also his anxiety over what may happen as a consequence of the others' departure, i.e., war.
22. Ṭufayl, *Shiʿr*, 19, 48.
23. Hārūn and Shākir, *Mufaḍḍalīyāt*, 397; and Michael A. Sells, *Desert Tracings: Six*

*Classic Arabian Odes* (Middletown: Wesleyan University Press, 1989), 14. See also Ṭufayl, *Shiʿr*, 17, 43. Related to this image are others in which poets mention that groups of birds caw (*tanʿab*) on the roads the women's caravan takes. See al-Aʿshā, *Dīwān*, 10–12. See also Jirān al-ʿAwd al-Numayrī, *Dīwān* (Cairo: Dār al-Kutub al-Miṣriyyah, 1931), 34–42, where he mentions that the women come to a valley in which the voices of pigeons sound like the mourning voices of *Anbāṭ mathākīl*, i.e., Nabateans bereaved of children. Furthermore, pre-Islamic poets repeatedly mention a blood-red color in the description of the women's litters. See, for example, Bishr, *Dīwān*, 192–200 (line 6); Zuhayr in Zawzanī, *Sharḥ al-Muʿallaqāt*, 100–107 (line 7); ʿAbīd Ibn al-Abraṣ, *Dīwān*, ed. Ḥusayn Naṣṣār (Cairo: Muṣṭafā al-Bābī al-Ḥalabī, 1957), 127–129 (line 3); and al-Ḥuṭay'ah, *Dīwān*, ed. Nuʿmān Amīn Ṭāhā (Cairo: Muṣṭafā al-Bābī al-Ḥalabī, 1958), 77, where he mentions *dam al-jawf*, i.e., heart's blood, as in the example of ʿAlqamah cited above.

24. Bishr, *Dīwān*, 11. This image, which relates the birds to war, became very much identified with war scenes in some famous lines of Islamic panegyric poets such as Abū Tammām. Its origins lie, however, in the pre-Islamic poets in a context of tribal fakhr. For two examples of this image in the context of war (fakhr), see Ṭufayl, *Shiʿr*, 5, 13, and 8, 22. For a discussion of such lines, see Suzanne Pinckney Stetkevych, *Abū Tammām and the Poetics of the ʿAbbāsid Age* (Leiden: E. J. Brill, 1991), 54–58, and the Arabic text, 362–363.

25. See, for example, Bishr, *Dīwān*, 54–58; and Imru' al-Qays, *Dīwān*, 56–71.

26. See, for example, Bishr ibn Abī Khāzim in Lyall, *Mufaḍḍalīyāt*, 1:278–83; al-Ḥādirah, *Dīwān*, 69–78; Muraqqish the Elder, in Lyall, *Mufaḍḍalīyāt*, 1:173–74; and Salāmah ibn Jandal, *Dīwān*, 188–195.

27. See, for example, ʿAmr ibn Qamī'ah, *Dīwān*, 69–73; and Bishr, *Dīwān*, 54–58.

28. Al-Zawzanī, *Sharḥ al-Muʿallaqāt*, 168–190; trans. in Arberry, *The Seven Odes*, 204–209. (I have followed the order of verses in al-Zawzanī's recension.)

# V

# THE EARLIEST DEMON LOVER

## THE *ṬAYF AL-KHAYĀL* IN *AL-MUFAḌḌALĪYĀT*

*John Seybold*

The *ṭayf al-khayāl*—or "night visit by the phantom of the beloved"—was a topic consistently neglected and even scorned by Arabists of former generations.* The dream-vision was easily classified as a "conventional motif" of classical Arabic poetry and hence dismissed almost without analysis.[1] Yet, for example, the ṭayf al-khayāl appears in no less than nine poems by eight different authors in the *Mufaḍḍalīyāt,* the famous anthology of pre- and early Islamic verse by al-Mufaḍḍal al-Ḍabbī (d. 786 C.E.).[2]

Four of the poems are less than twenty lines long and none exceeds forty lines. All but one (*No. 46*, a pure *nasīb*) may be called composite, that is to say, juxtapositions of different genres. Probably only two, *Nos. 1* and *10*, would be considered full qaṣīdahs.

The phantom as it appears in the *Mufaḍḍalīyāt* is distinguished as a dramatic type by its being nonhuman. Of course, we must remember that the qaṣīdah contains a long list of animal characters, other than the camel and the horse, and that these animals are archetypes, serving a metaphorically iconic function far removed from natural science.[3] But even outside the sphere of human or animal life, the phantom is only one of a long list of supernatural spirits inhabiting the qaṣīdah. Another bizarre poetic creature is the *ghūl*, who appears in the *raḥīl* or journey section, personifying the dangers of the road, the terrors of night travel. In a note to the introduction of his translation of *The 1001 Nights*, Edward Lane describes the ghūl:

> One of these is the Ghool, which is commonly regarded as a kind of Sheytan, or evil Jinnee, that eats men. . . . The Ghool is any Jinnee that is opposed to travel . . . it is said to appear in the forms of various animals, and of human beings, and in many monstrous shapes; to haunt burial-grounds and other sequestered spots; to feed upon dead human bodies . . . it appears to a person travelling alone in the night and in solitary places, and, being supposed by him to be itself a traveller, lures him

> out of his way . . . the female Ghool, it is added, appears to men in the deserts, in various forms, converses with them, and sometimes prostitutes herself to them. . . .[4]

We find an echo of the ghūl in the last line of *Mufaḍḍalīyah No. 57*:

> The young man has a destroyer [*ghā'ilun*]
> to snatch him away [*yaghūluhu*],
> Oh, Bint ʿAjlān, from the fall of fate.[5]

*Ghāla/yaghūlu* means "to take a thing away unexpectedly; to cause anyone to perish; to intoxicate." The ghūl is also suggested in the closing lines of *Mufaḍḍalīyah No. 6*, where the poet describes his horse:

> To avoid disease, she is hung with amulets,
> Amulets knotted in her necklaces.
>
> She brings within our grasp, when we hunt,
> The wild ass bewitched by luxuriant grass,
>
> As she swoops like an eagle on Mt. ʿArdah made keen
> By a night-roving hare in Dhū al-Ḍamrāni.[6]

*Asʿalahu al-jamīmu*: "bewitched by luxuriant grass," or, in Charles James Lyall's translation, "whom the lush herbage has made as strong as a demon."[7] The fourth form here, *asʿala*, derives from *siʿlāh*, "an ogress, witch, termigant," according to Lyall, "the most dangerous of the female demons called ghūl, or an enchantress of the jinn."[8] This ending, in which amulets protect the horse from evil spirits of disease and the *siʿlāh* intoxicates the carnal ass with grass, is especially interesting since the poet is afflicted at the poem's outset by the ṭayf al-khayāl and by the end has gained the sober clarity of a hungry bird of prey.

Yet the ṭayf al-khayāl seems inescapably different from the ghūl. A closer look at the words *ṭayf al-khayāl* may help us in determining the phantom's ontological status in the hierarchy of supernatural poetic creatures. Ṭayf is a verbal noun (*maṣdar*) deriving from *ṭāfa/yaṭīfu*, "to appear [in sleep, phantom]." The second form, *ṭayyafa*, means "to circuit, go around." The word is also related to *ṭāfa/yaṭūfu*, "to circumambulate; to ramble; to appear [in sleep, phantom]." Thus the verb also connotes circular travel. The verb most frequently used to describe the phantom's night visit, however, is *ṭaraqa*, "to come to anyone by night, to knock at a door, ring [bell], play [musical instrument]." This verb's aural connotations are interesting, as is its connection with *ṭarīq*, or "road." *Khayāl* derives from the well-known *khāla/yakhālu*—"to think, suppose, fancy, imagine." It should be mentioned that the expression "ṭayf al-khayāl" occurs nowhere in our collection. The phantom is always referred to simply as "al-khayāl." The verb *ṭāfa* occurs only once (*No. 112*, line 2) to describe the khayāl's night visit. Also, the khayāl, while obviously a dream-vision of the beloved, is always referred to in the masculine, resulting occasionally in some pronominal gender confusion. (The pronoun "it" is used here in translation.) The point behind this brief analysis is that the ṭayf al-khayāl seems a creature far more purely imaginary than the malignant ghūl. The very word khayāl connotes, not an evil supernatural spirit, but an imaginative projection in a dream or dreamlike state. Whereas a ghūl might devour its victim, the worst consequence of frequent visits from the phantom would be madness.

In eight of the nine poems, the phantom appears at the opening. In six of the eight poems, the phantom appears in the very first line or *maṭlaᶜ*. The single exception, *No. 57*, where the phantom occurs in the middle of the poem, will, for this very reason, be one of our specimens to be quoted in full. In poems opening with the khayāl, the figure occurs nowhere else.

Ibn Qutaybah's famous description of the structure of the qaṣīdah begins thus:

> I have heard from a man of learning that the composer of odes began by mentioning the deserted dwelling-places and the relics and traces of habitation. Then he wept and complained and addressed the desolate encampment, and begged his companion to make a halt, in order that he might have occasion to speak of those who had once lived there and afterwards departed. . . . Then to this he linked the erotic prelude (nasīb). . . .[9]

Ibn Qutaybah makes clear that the qaṣīdah's entire first section is not properly called the nasīb. Rather, the nasīb follows an elegiac beginning that we will call the motif of the *aṭlāl*, or abandoned campsite. Obviously, the ṭayf al-khayāl takes the place of the abandoned campsite. The switch need not surprise us. The nasīb, like the qaṣīdah itself, has almost infinite polythematic elasticity. Frequently the early ode does not use the aṭlāl subtheme for its elegiac section; rather, the poet's emotion is aroused by the departure of the lady's caravan, by a crow or an owl crying out or a dove cooing, by a dream-visit from the lady's phantom. Thus the ṭayf al-khayāl is one possible subtheme, cognate to the aṭlāl, for the elegiac theme of the nasīb. Can we glean more from the equation of these two opening conventions? Put as a riddle—how is a phantom like an abandoned campsite?

### *Muffaḍḍalīyah No. 55* by Muraqqish the Younger[10]

Is it because of an abode's trace that your eyes shed tears,
 A place whose people came in the morning and left
  in the evening,

Whose lambs are urged by pug-nosed gazelles,
    Whose calves are the very reddest rose in al-Jaww?

Is it from Bint ʿAjlān that this far-flung phantom
    Came when my saddle had fallen and been set aside?

When I became conscious of the phantom, it startled me:
    Ah! it was only my saddle and the countryside empty!

Still it is a visitor that wakes a sleeper
    And wounds his heart.

In every shelter it comes to us, and in every camp.
    If only she would stay till morning when she
        comes at night!

Then she left, having spread the frustrated desires that you see,
    And my love for her, when she let tears fall, was
        most ill-fated.

No red wine, redolent of musk,
    Raised over the strainer once and ladled out,

Having dwelt for twenty pilgrimages in the captivity of a jar
        Plastered with mud and cooled,

Imported by distant Jews
    From Jīlān, brought to market by a profiteer

Was sweeter than her mouth when I came visiting
    From out of the night—no, her mouth was more
        pleasant, purer.

I went out hunting in the morning on an even-colored mount,
        like a leafless palm branch under a horse cloth.
    I trained him till he was lean and slender,

A sleek, noble steed without defect,
    A bay like unmixed wine, three white legs and a blaze.

On such a one, I come to the tribal council proudly,
    Pondering inwardly: which course is more profitable?

Hunted, he outstrips; hunting, he overtakes
And gets out of a tight spot and wounds.

You can see him fully armed, collecting his energy,
After the attackers are cut down.

On him, I raided in a long line
And in the morning met many spears.

Like a gazelle kid, when you ask for speed,
He jumps up and bolts, head held high.

He gushes like subterranean waters bubbling up in a spring
Where gravel and roots are stripped from underneath.

This poem opens with the aṭlāl and the ṭayf al-khayāl side by side, a unique case in the *Mufaḍḍalīyāt,* but one that proves that the two motifs are not mutually exclusive. The phantom appears to the poet while he stops for the night at the abandoned campsite. It is usually not so clearly stated that the phantom appears directly in the ruins, although such an assumption would be natural. For, just as the aṭlāl, despite their intriguing place names, are not true places, but rather figments of places, mere scratches in the sand, so too the ṭayf al-khayāl is only the shadow of a person. Both are constructed in the imagination by desire out of past experience. Particularly relevant here is line 4:

When I became conscious of the phantom, it startled me.
Ah! it was only my saddle and the countryside empty!

We should be aware that the ṭayf al-khayāl is no dream-image or dream-vision, however convenient these designations may be. The poet is not sleeping; he is always wide awake and suffering acute anxiety. Sleeplessness is a keyword, a prerequisite for the appearance of the phantom. It is always the others who are sleeping; the poet is alone in his wakefulness. Often the poet's attention is concentrated on watching the stars or flashes of lightning; he is divorced from people, alone with himself, both anxious and entranced by the transcendental displays of nature.

Rarely is hallucination so clearly indicated as in this verse. We are given not only the phantom but also the actual object upon which the phantom is hallucinated, its "objective correlative," as it were, as though a single reality were viewed two ways, one objective and the other subjective. And how strange that the phantom's objective correlative would be a saddle—an icon of the poet's mounted wandering. Yet, we often find the phantom connected with the idea of travel from afar, as in the opening of *Mufaḍḍalīyah No. 46* by Muraqqish the Elder:[11]

At night, a phantom came from Sulaymā
And kept me awake while my companions slept.

I spent the night revolving the matter in my mind every
which way,
Awaiting her people though they were far away—

For my gaze had been raised to a fire
Whose fuel was gathered in Dhū al-Arṭā . . .

*Ba*ʿ*īd*, "far away," is another keyword in the context of the phantom. But distance here is paradoxical: the lady is far away while her phantom is near. Distance is nearly always spatial, and the phantom's triumph is finding the right way over endless rough terrain. But distance also has a temporal dimension: the lady exists in the past as a memory while the phantom appears in the present as a desire. Simultaneously far and near, past and present—again, two views of a single reality. Thus in the opening of *Mufaḍḍalīyah No. 62* by al-Ḥārith ibn Ḥillizah al-Yashkurī:[12]

The phantom made a night visit—never was such a night!—
Clinging to our saddles, but it didn't stay.

Oh, you came the right way, but not on foot,
After the tribe had crossed the rough ground of Sajsaj

And grown tired and their mounts weak,
Except for a swift one in a howdah frame.

Particularly fascinating in these verses is the phrase *sadikan bi arḥulinā*, "clinging to our saddles," literally, "addicted to our saddles." Again the phantom is strangely dependent on the poet's saddle; again the tribe has departed. As often happens, the poet addresses the phantom and naively wonders how she (or it) could have made such a grueling journey. The phantom, like the aṭlāl, never responds.

Whether the phantom travels by foot is debated. Here is the opening of *Mufaḍḍalīyah No. 1*, a well-known ode by Ta'abbaṭa Sharran:[13]

O return of remembrance! how with thee come longing
and wakefulness
and the passing of a phantom darkling, spite of
terrors by the way!

Barefooted by night it comes, making nought of fatigue
and snakes—
my soul be thy sacrifice—what a traveller by night afoot!
[trans. Lyall]

Whether or not the phantom is barefooted *(muḥtafiyan)*, clearly the journey is treacherous, filled with terrors that earlier we found personified in the ghūl. Also of interest in these lines is the use of the key verb *sarā/yasrī*, "to travel by night." This verb occurs nearly as frequently as *ṭaraqa* to describe the phantom's night visit. Further, *sarā* is a key verb in the middle section of the traditional qaṣīdah, the raḥīl (desert journey) of the poet.

We began with the line by Muraqqish the Younger:

> When I became conscious of the phantom, it startled me.
> Ah! It was only my saddle and the countryside empty!

We have already made some progress by understanding that the nasīb itself embodies a night journey. There are many parallels between the poet's journey and the phantom's. The dangers of the road and the exhausting distance are the same: however, whereas the poet and his mount must suffer, the phantom never complains. The phantom is drawn to the poet or his restless saddle as to a magnet. Out of nowhere, accidentally, the poet comes to the aṭlāl, but he recognizes the spot. The desolation of the ruins reflects the insomnia and anxiety necessary for the appearance of the phantom. The effects of time are, on the one hand, physical and, on the other, psychological. The ruins bespeak decay and disintegration. But whose? We think of Hopkins's lines:

> Margaret, are you grieving
> Over Goldengrove unleaving?

The poet is weeping for himself. In addressing the ruins and their former inhabitants, he confronts his own death and is inspired to a vision of rebirth, the nasīb proper, the paradise of his past, now lost. The phantom too is a lost person—out of space, out of time.

We have begun to answer our riddle—how is a phantom like an abandoned campsite?

### *Mufaḍḍalīyah No. 57* by Muraqqish the Younger[14]

> There are traces of Bint ʿAjlān in al-Jaww
> Uneffaced, though the time has been long,
>
> Of Bint ʿAjlān, when we were together—
> But say, because of time, what state ever lasts?
>
> Is it because of abodes whose trace has been effaced
> That your eye overflows—because of their trace?

They reveal bare desert where once,
    In former generations, many-herded lords lived.

They died, and I came after them,
    Thinking myself eternal, never to depart.

Oh, Bint ʿAjlān, the things I endure
    Like sculpture under an ax!

In her mouth is a shudderingly good wine
    Bubbling out of the jar so that the cup overflows,

Mixed with cold water
    From an old skin hung from soaked straps.

In every night-shelter she has a censer
    Full of prepared frankincense and hot bath water.

She needn't tend the fire at night or
    Be awakened to prepare food—she's a great silly sleeper!

Troublesome lightning kept me awake tonight
    With no friend to help.

Who is there to help against a phantom that arises at midnight
    And overwhelms me with worry and sickens my heart?

Many a sleepless night I've spent
    That anxiety made repeat on my eyes.

Through them I didn't shut my eyes till the end,
    Watching the stars after the peaceful had fallen asleep.

You cry over Time, but Time is the one
    That made you cry, your tears gushing like a
        worn-out water skin.

By God! Do you know, whenever
    You criticize my love for her, what you're criticizing?

You hurt a friend and show suspicion,
    guarding one arrow and quivering another.

How many rich men have I seen
    On whose wealth tyrannical Time has fallen,

And how many strong defenders, unapproachable,
    Marked with wounds!

One is prosperous, then lo! it is gone
    While for another bad luck changes to good.

One departs on a long journey,
    Then lo! undoes his saddle, while another,
        settled, hurries away.

The young man has a destroyer to snatch him away,
    Oh, Bint ʿAjlān, from the fall of Fate.

In this poem the phantom appears not at the beginning but in the middle. It nevertheless remains in the nasīb. The poet makes no desert journey, and the final section is not self-praise, but a sort of proverbial, wisdom genre. The poem and its nasīb still seem to work, even with such an oddly positioned phantom. The aṭlāl opening sparks the memory of an idyllic past, the poet's own paradise lost: "In her mouth is a shudderingly good wine. . . ." This idyllic memory lies at the heart of the nasīb, the last stop in its journey back through time. Yet, on the basis of the poems quoted, we might feel that the phantom opening could have sparked such memory just as well. What common factor makes the motifs of the abandoned campsite and the phantom function correctly only as the opening of the nasīb?

The Umayyad poet Dhū al-Rummah was once asked, "What would you do if your genius did not help you to compose poems?" Dhū al-Rummah answered that that could not happen since he knew an ever-effective means to stir his genius up. "It is," he said, "just to remember your beloved while you are alone."[15] Dhū al-Rummah seems less interested in either attracting an audience or thinking of his beloved than in acquiring the poetic utterance, its inspired knowledge and eloquence. Here, then, is one last, undeveloped answer to our riddle, a last connection between the aṭlāl and the ṭayf al-khayāl. The two motifs together describe nicely the practice of incubation—"sleeping in a temple or sacred place for oracular purposes." Is it too much to see the abandoned campsite as a mythic, unremembered (or purposefully forgotten) figure for a temple or holy place or even, as Lane suggests, a burial ground, and the phantom as the prophetic priestess or a visionary token signaling the onset of oracle? The pre-Islamic poet is often presented as a sort of magician, in league with the spirits and demons or with his own familiar spirit, his genius. And who knows from what ancient ritual this hackneyed concept of the poet as seer itself derives? Did the poet have a tribal religious function—to contact the spirit world of dead ancestors? In any case, mythically, the poet's first task is clear—to conjure up the angel of death.

# Notes

* This paper was first presented at the 17th annual meeting of the Middle East Studies Association of North America (MESA), Chicago, Illinois, November 4, 1983.

1. For example, when the khayāl appears in the first line of the first poem of Lyall's edition and translation of the *Mufaḍḍalīyāt*, he comments in a footnote merely, "'Phantom,' i.e., of the beloved. This is a constantly mentioned convention of these amatory preludes." There is nothing further, and at all later occurrences of the khayāl, which by his own admission are frequent, Lyall refers the reader back to this note. Charles James Lyall, ed.and trans., *The Mufaḍḍalīyāt: An Anthology of Ancient Arabian Odes Compiled by al-Mufaḍḍal son of Muḥammad According to the Recension and With the Commentary of Abū Muḥammad al-Qāsim ibn Muḥammad al-Anbārī.* Vol. I: *Arabic Text*; Vol. II: *Translation and Notes* (Oxford: Clarendon Press, 1918), 2:5. A monograph on this motif as it occurs in early Arabic poetry generally has appeared since the writing of this study; see Ḥasan al-Bannā ʿIzz al-Dīn, *al-Ṭayf wa-al-khayāl fī al-shiʿr al-ʿArabī al-qadīm* (Cairo: Dār al-Nadīm lil-Nashr wa-al-Tawzīʿ wa al-Ṣaḥāfah, 1988).

2. Ilse Lichtenstädter, art. "al-Mufaḍḍal," *The Encyclopaedia of Islam*, 1st. ed., ed. M. Th. Houtsma et al. (Leiden: E. J. Brill, 1913–36).

3. See Jaroslav Stetkevych, "Name and Epithet: The Philology and Semiotics of Animal Nomenclature in Early Arabic Poetry," *Journal of Near Eastern Studies* 45 (1986): 89–124.

4. Edward Lane, trans., *The Thousand and One Nights, Commonly Called, in England, The Arabian Nights' Entertainments* (London: Charles Knight and Co., 1841), 36.

5. Lyall, *Mufaḍḍalīyāt*, 1:507.

6. Ibid., 1:44.

7. Ibid., 2:13.

8. Ibid., 2:14.

9. Reynold A. Nicholson, *A Literary History of the Arabs* (Cambridge: Cambridge University Press, 1956), 77.

10. Lyall, *Mufaḍḍalīyāt*, 1:493–499.

11. Ibid., 1:460.

12. Ibid., 1:515–516.

13. Ibid., 1:2, 2:3. See also the discussion and translation of this qaṣīdah in Suzanne Pinckney Stetkevych, *The Mute Immortals Speak: Pre-Islamic Poetry and the Poetics of Ritual* (Ithaca: Cornell University Press, 1993), ch. 3.

14. Lyall, *Mufaḍḍalīyāt*, 1:503–507.

15. Ibn Rashīq al-Qayrawānī, as cited in A. Kh. Kinany, *The Development of Ghazal in Arabic Literature* (Damascus: The Syrian University Printing House, 1950), 60.

# VI

# "TANGLED WORDS"

## TOWARD A STYLISTICS OF ARABIC MYSTICAL VERSE

*Th. Emil Homerin*

The relationship between mysticism and poetry is necessarily enigmatic.* Because the mystical experience is ineffable, mystical doctrine is approximate, mystical language allusive. And, so, mystics have often turned to poetry with its phonemic patterning and symbolic richness to speak of their experiences and beliefs. But how are we to interpret this verse? There is no doubting the poet's personal involvement in his poem, but intricate and abstract mystical verse cannot be reduced to autobiographical anecdote. Similarly, while many mystical poems reflect religious dogma or theological positions, the emotive effects of this verse lead us beyond solemn creeds and scholastic arguments. Clearly, the secret of mystical poetry is more than a poet's life and belief, and if we are to read and interpret this verse insightfully, we must return to his poetic language.

This is a particular necessity in the case of early Islamic mystical verse, whose appearance was a significant literary and religious development of the early Abbasid period (8th-9th c. C.E.). This poetry was often simple and ascetic, but Ṣūfīs soon appropriated the Arabic poetic tradition and, in time, composed longer and more abstract poems. However, this close affinity to nonmystical verse, together with Ṣūfī poetry's spiritual substance, led to confusion, which some Ṣūfī writers tried to dispel:

> This [Ṣūfī] poetry has in it that which is obscure and that which is clear, and in it for [the Ṣūfīs] are subtle allusions and refined meanings. So one who reads it should treat it with circumspection so that he may grasp [the Ṣūfīs'] intentions and symbols and, thereby, not connect its speaker to what is not befitting him. And when [the reader] doubts and does not understand, let him ask someone who does. . . .[1]

But such warnings hardly resolve the problem and, in fact, raise the nagging but pivotal question: what makes a poem mystical? Is a poem spiritually transformed by context, by the listener's position, or the author's aim? And does the poet point the way with words or with syntax, themes and allusions?

*lī nushwatāni wa-lin-nudmāni wāḥidatun*
*shay'un khuṣiṣtu bihī baynahumū waḥdī*

To me two inebriations,
to my companions, one—
by this I am marked
among them alone![2]

A single alteration made two centuries after this verse was composed by the great court wine poet Abū Nuwās (d. ca. 198/813) yields dramatic results:

*lī sakratāni wa-lin-nudmāni wāḥidatun*
*shay'un khuṣiṣtu bihī baynahumū waḥdī*

To me two intoxications,
to my companions, one—
by this I am marked
among them alone!

The Ṣūfī anthologist al-Qushayrī (d. 465/1073) quotes this second version by his spiritual guide and father-in-law Abū ʿAlī al-Daqqāq (d. 405/1015), in a chapter on mystical sobriety (*ṣaḥw*) and intoxication (*sukr*).[3] This context, together with al-Daqqāq's substitution of the Ṣūfī technical term *sakrah* ("intoxication") for *nushwah* ("inebriation"), gives a mystical hue to this verse in which the verb *khuṣṣa* ("to be distinguished") could also be read in its specialized meaning of "to be marked for God's favor."[4] A simple revision has rarefied Abū Nuwās' very palatable wine.

Similiar to such Ṣūfī wine poetry, the majority of early Islamic verse on mystical love is so reliant on conventional Arabic poetry as to be often indistinguishable from it:

*wa-lammā-ddaʿaytu-l-ḥubba qālat kadhabtanī*
*fa-mā lī arā-l-aʿḍā'a minka kawāsiyā*

*fa-mā-l-ḥubbu ḥattā yalṣaqa-l-jildu bil-ḥashā*
*wa-tadhbula ḥattā lā tujība-l-munādiyā*

*wa-tanḥala ḥattā lā yubaqqī laka-l-hawā*
*siwā muqlatin tabkī bihā aw tunājiyā*

And when I claimed love, she countered:
"You lied to me!
Why are your limbs
still clothed in flesh?

"There's no love
until skin clings to bone
and you, so parched,
can't answer the caller,

"And you dry up,
shrivelled by passion,
left with an eye
to weep and confide!"[5]

This poem by the noted mystic Sarī al-Saqaṭī (d. 253/867) and similar verses ascribed to other Ṣūfīs could have been attributed as easily to poets of secular love. How then are we to decide whether a poem intimates the secret longings of a heart or details the passions of lust? Commonly, such ambiguous situations have been resolved by contexts, as much of the Arabic verse recognized as mystical is found in Ṣūfī manuals and biographies.[6] The authors of these mystical tracts generally cite verse to illustrate their subjects and to summarize doctrines,[7] such as Dhū al-Nūn al-Miṣrī's (d. 245/859) teaching that the sincere Ṣūfī must abandon worldly life and society to achieve total devotion to God:

*man dhāqa ṭaᶜma-l-wadādi*
*ḥamiya jamīᶜa-l-ᶜibādi*

*man dhāqa ṭaᶜma-l-wadādi*
*qaliya jamīᶜa-l-ᶜibādi*

*man dhāqa ṭaᶜma-l-wadādi*
*saliya ṭarīqa-l-ᶜibādi*

*man dhāqa ṭaᶜma-l-wadādi*
*anisa bi-rabbi-l-ᶜibādi*

He who tastes the taste of love
scorns all mankind!

He who tastes the taste of love
hates all mankind!

He who tastes the taste of love
shuns mankind's road!

He who tastes the taste of love
nears mankind's Lord![8]

Based on our extant sources, we may conclude that the modest Arabic corpus of early mystical poetry represents verse which was occasionally quoted by Ṣūfīs, perhaps during teaching sessions. Like other educated members of the religious establishment, these scholars with their mystical proclivities would have enjoyed composing and reciting verse. But this hardly made them serious mystical poets, with the known exception of al-Ḥallāj (d. 309/922), who appears to have composed more poetry than any other early Ṣūfī.[9] In contrast to didactic and moralizing poems, much of al-Ḥallāj's verse revolves around ineffable states and abstruse theosophical doctrines. These concerns are mirrored in his intricate and sophisticated Arabic style, a style characterized by antithesis (*ṭibāq*), paronomasia (*jinās*), and the repetition of verbs and an abundance of prepositions in contrast and opposition within a single verse. The result is paradox which ruptures the psychological barriers of space, time, and rationality:

*al-ʿishqu fī azali-l-āzāli min qidamin*
*fīhi bihī minhu yabdū fīhi ibdā'u*

*al-ʿishqu lā ḥadathun idh kāna huwa ṣifatan*
*min aṣ-ṣifāti li-man qatlāhu aḥyā'u*

*ṣifātuhu minhū fīhi ghayru muḥdathatin*
*wa-muḥdathu-sh-shay'i mā mabdāhu ashyā'u*

*lammā badā-l-bad'u abdā ʿishqahū ṣifatan*
*fīmā badā fa-tala'la'a fīhi la'lā'u*

Eros in the eternity of eternities
from the primordial—
in it, by it, from it
appearance appears in it.

Eros before time
is an attribute
among the attributes
of him whose victims live.

His attributes are
from him, within him,
without time,
while the temporal
depends on creation.

When creation appeared
he invoked Eros,
an attribute in creation,
and so a gleam glimmered in it.[10]

The message and intent of these verses are not grasped easily. The opening line suggests the timelessness of a Neoplatonic pre-eternity where divine love has a favored place among God's eternal attributes. This love martyrs the spiritual warriors that they may live forever with their Lord (v. 2; cf. Qur'ān 3:169-170). Since God creates by means of his attributes, they must exist before time and creation, which cannot be originated by another temporal thing (vv. 2-3). So at the dawn of creation, Eros sparks the inner flame enlivening and illuminating every created thing (v. 4).[11]

Whatever its precise allusions and meanings, this and similar verse plays on formal literary devices to induce a shift in perspective, to transcend rational abstractions to speak about nonrational concerns.[12] Yet as is evident from the example cited, this type of poetry, because of its themes and sheer syntactical complexity, is often esoteric to the point of being unintelligible. This fact, together with the sparsity of poetic compositions by early Ṣūfīs, may account for the lack of serious attention paid to mystical verse by medieval litterateurs who, otherwise, might have distinguished characteristics particular to Ṣūfī poets and their verse. In fact, the two references on the subject that I have found in literary works are the exceptions that prove the rule, as both comments involve not the poetry of a Ṣūfī but verses by al-Mutanabbī (d. 354/965), the greatest Arab court poet.[13]

One of al-Mutanabbī's most critical commentators, al-Thaᶜālibī (d. 429/1038), censured the poet for "imitating the expressions of the Ṣūfīs and using their tangled words and abstruse meanings" (*imtithālu alfāẓi-l-mutaṣawwifah wa-istiᶜmālu kalimātihim al-muᶜaqqadah wa-maᶜānīhim al-mughlaqah*).[14] It is apparent from the verses cited by al-Thaᶜālibī as examples of this fault that he was referring specifically to the use of multiple and contrasting prepositions, the repetition in a single hemistich of a verb with two different subjects, and, above all, the creation of paradox within a verse. It should be noted that al-Thaᶜālibī was critical of these elements on poetic grounds, not religious ones, since some of his examples do not lend themselves readily to mystical interpretations. For instance, he cites al-Mutanabbī's description of a war-horse whose fine qualities are self-evident:

*sabūḥun lahā minhā ᶜalayhā shawāhidu*

A hard charger,
to it, from it, for it—
pedigrees![15]

Al-Thaᶜālibī cites another example of al-Mutanabbī's paradoxical use of contrasting prepositions and phrasing:

*wa-lākinnaka-d-dunyā ilayya ḥabībatun*
*fa-mā ᶜanka lī illā ilayka dhahābu*

Beloved,
you are the world to me,
so my leaving you
is but my return![16]

In this verse, al-Mutanabbī extravagantly declares his patron to be the entire world such that, no matter where the poet goes, he will always encounter his beloved master. Al-Thaᶜālibī was not impressed by the poet's wit and so judged this verse and another on the beloved to be quite repugnant:

*naḥnu man ḍāyaqa-z-zamānu lahū fī-*
*ka wa-khānathu qurbaka-l-ayyāmu*

For your sake
time crushed us—
the days made off
with your nearness![17]

Al-Thaᶜālibī declared that had this verse been recited in "the statements of al-Junayd or al-Shiblī, the Ṣūfīs would have argued endlessly over it!"[18] Perhaps al-Thaᶜālibī took exception to al-Mutanabbī's choice of the word *qurb* ("nearness"), which, in the Ṣūfī lexicon, refers to the mystic's spiritual proximity to God.[19] Further, al-Thaᶜālibī probably compared al-Mutanabbī's verse to statements made by the celebrated Ṣūfīs al-Shiblī (d. 334/945) and al-Junayd (d. 298/911) because of the latters' frequent use of paradox as we see, for instance, in al-Junayd's characterization of spiritual proximity and union as ". . . the worshipper's last returns to his first, that he is as he was when he was before he was" *(rajaᶜa ākhiru-l-ᶜabdi ilā awwalihi an yakūna kamā kāna idh kāna qabla an yakūna)*.[20]

Two of al-Thaᶜālibī's remaining examples of al-Mutanabbī's reliance on Ṣūfī diction deal with wine and its effect. In the following verse, the poet repeats the same verb to allude to the amazing power of wine:

*nāla-l-ladhī niltu minhu minnī*
*lillāhi mā taṣnaᶜu-l-khumūru*

That which I took from, took from me—
By God, what wines can do![21]

And al-Mutanabbī ends a second verse with a phrase composed of two identical prepositions, *baynī wa-baynī*, literally "between me and me." This phrase has been interpreted to mean "between me and my reason," that is to say, "I won't get senselessly drunk":

*idhā mā-l-ka'su arʿashati-l-yadayni*
*ṣaḥawtu fa-lam taḥul baynī wa-baynī*

When the cup startles my hands
I sober up—
it won't part
me from myself![22]

Another commentator, Abū al-Fatḥ ʿUthmān Ibn Jinnī (d. 392/1002), also noted the similarity of this last line to Ṣūfī verse, saying that al-Mutanabbī "took this from the style [*ṭarz*] of Ṣūfī speech, like the statement of one of them:

*ʿajibtu minka minnī*
*afnaytanī bika ʿannī*

*aqamtanī bi-maqāmin*
*ẓanantu annaka anī*

I am amazed by you and me—
you annihilated me
in you from me!

You stood me in a station
where I supposed
that you were me!"[23]

Ibn Jinnī's example of Ṣūfī verse shows that he, too, considered the use of multiple prepositions, antithesis, and paradox to be characteristic of mystical language and verse. His observations along with al-Thaʿālibī's, as brief as they are, indicate that some types of poetry or, more specifically, certain linguistic and stylistic elements of verse, were associated with early Islamic mystics. An awareness of these formal characteristics can enhance and expand our contextual readings, giving internal evidence of a poem's mystical intent. Yet creative ambiguities remain, for, as we have seen, al-Mutanabbī employed these same forms and expressions to nuance his refined courtly verse. And, so, we may never be certain whether the spirit of a given poem is courtly or mystical, or both:

*ana man ahwā wa-man ahwā anā*
*naḥnu rūḥāni ḥalalnā badanā*

*fa-idhā abṣartanī abṣartahu*
*wa-idhā abṣartahū abṣartanā*

I am he whom I love,
and he whom I love is me—
we are two spirits in one body!

When you see me,
you see him,
and when you see him,
you see us both![24]

# Notes

* I thank Ruth Tonner, Temple University, and Michael Sells, Haverford College, for reading and commenting on my paper. An earlier draft was read at the 198th meeting of the American Oriental Society, Chicago, Illinois, March, 1988.

1. Abū Naṣr al-Sarrāj, *Kitāb al-Lumaʿ fī al-taṣawwuf*, ed. R. A. Nicholson (London: Luzac and Co., 1914), 257.
2. Abū Nuwās, *Dīwān* (Beirut: Dār Ṣādir, 1961), 180, v. 5.
3. Abū al-Qāsim al-Qushayrī, *al-Risālah al-Qushayrīyah*, ed. ʿAbd al-Ḥalīm Maḥmūd and Maḥmūd ibn al-Sharīf (Cairo: Dār al-Kutub al-Ḥadīthah, 1972), 2:621, 1:237. For al-Qushayrī, see H. Halm, art. "al-Ḳushayrī," in *The Encyclopaedia of Islam*, 2nd ed., ed. H. A. R. Gibb et al. (Leiden, E. J. Brill, 1960-) (hereafter *EI2*); and al-Subkī, *Ṭabaqāt al-Shāfiʿīyah al-kubrā*, ed. Maḥmūd Muḥammad al-Tanāḥī and ʿAbd al-Fattāḥ Muḥammad al-Ḥilw (Cairo: ʿĪsā al-Bābī al-Ḥalabī, 1964), 4:329-331.
4. E.g., al-Sarrāj, *al-Lumaʿ*, 337.
5. Ibid., 251. Concerning Sarī al-Saqaṭī, see A. J. Arberry, *Muslim Saints and Mystics* (London: Routledge and Kegan Paul, 1966), 166-172.
6. E.g., Annemarie Schimmel, *As Through a Veil: Mystical Poetry in Islam* (New York: Columbia University Press, 1982); and ʿAlī Ṣafā Ḥusayn, *al-Adab al-Ṣūfī fī Miṣr* (Cairo: Dār al-Maʿārif, 1964).
7. The exception is al-Sarrāj, who quotes a number of verses in a separate chapter on poems by Ṣūfīs; *al-Lumaʿ*, 246-257. I am preparing a translation and analysis of this anthology of early Ṣūfī verse.
8. Abū Nuʿaym al-Iṣfahānī, *Ḥilyat al-awliyā'* (Cairo: 1932; reprint ed., Beirut: Dār al-Kutub al-ʿArabī, 1980), 9:377. Concerning Dhū al-Nūn al-Miṣrī, see al-Iṣfahānī's biography of him, ibid., 9:331-384; and Arberry, *Saints*, 87-99.
9. The collected verse of al-Ḥallāj adds up to about five hundred verses of which two hundred are of questionable authenticity. See Louis Massignon, *Le Dīwān d'al-Hallāj* (Paris: Librairie orientaliste Paul Ceuthner, 1955); Louis Massignon, *Dīwān Hoceïn Mansūr Hallāj* (Paris: Éditions des cahiers du sud, 1955); and *Sharḥ Dīwān al-Ḥallāj*, ed. Kāmil Muṣṭafā al-Shaybī (Beirut: Maktabat al-Nahḍah, 1974). For more on al-Ḥallāj, see L. Massignon and L. Gardet, art. "al-Ḥallādj" in *EI2*.

10. Al-Ḥallāj quoted by Abū al-Ḥasan al-Daylamī, *ʿAṭf al-alif al-maʾlūf*, ed. J.-C. Vadet (Cairo: Maktabat al-Maʿhad al-ʿIlmī al-Faransī lil-Āthār al-Sharqīyah, 1962), 44. See also Massignon, *Dīwān Hoceïn*, 20-22; and *Sharḥ Dīwān*, 142-145. See also Schimmel, *Veil*, 21-23, 30-34.

11. I am preparing a translation and analysis of the complete poem by al-Ḥallāj.

12. Concerning earlier nonmystical Arabic poetry using literary devices (*badīʿ/badāʾiʿ*) as a method of abstraction, see Suzanne P. Stetkevych, *Abū Tammām and the Poetics of the ʿAbbāsid Age* (Leiden: E. J. Brill, 1991), Parts 1 and 2. See also Schimmel, *Veil*, 21-23, 30-34. Regarding similar dynamics in later Ṣūfī discourse see Michael Sells, "Ibn Arabī's Polished Mirror: Perspective Shift and Meaning Event," *Studia Islamica* 67 (1987): 121-149.

13. See R. Blachère, art. "al-Mutanabbī," in *The Encyclopaedia of Islam*, 1st ed., ed. M. Houtsma et al. (Leiden: E. J. Brill, 1913-1936) (hereafter *EI1*).

14. Al-Thaʿālibī, *Yatīmat al-dahr fī shuʿarāʾ al-ʿaṣr* (Cairo: Maktabat al-Ḥusayn al-Tijārīyah, 1947), 1:171. Concerning al-Thaʿālibī, see R. A. Nicholson, *A Literary History of the Arabs* (Cambridge: Cambridge University Press, 1907), 308-313.

15. Al-Thaʿālibī, *Yatīmat*, 1:171, and al-Mutanabbī, *Dīwān*, ed. Muṣṭafa al-Sayqā et al. (Cairo: Dār al-Maʿārif, 1936), 1:270, v. 10.

16. Al-Thaʿālibī, *Yatīmat*, 1:171, and al-Mutanabbī, *Dīwān*, 1:201, v. 43.

17. Al-Thaʿālibī, *Yatīmat*, 1:171, and al-Mutanabbī, *Dīwān*, 3:343, v. 2.

18. Al-Thaʿālibī, *Yatīmat*, 1:171.

19. See, for example, al-Sarrāj, *al-Lumaʿ*, 146, and al-Qushayrī, *al-Risālah*, 1:257-260.

20. Abū al-Qāsim al-Junayd quoted in Ali Hassan Abdel-Kader, *The Life, Personality and Writings of al-Junayd* (London: Luzac and Co., 1976), 56-57 (Arabic text), my translation. Concerning al-Junayd, see A. J. Arberry, art. "al-Djunayd," in *EI2*; and Arberry, *Saints*, 199-213. For for al-Shiblī, see L. Massignon, art. "al-Shiblī," in *EI1*; and Arberry, *Saints*, 277-286.

21. Al-Thaʿālibī, *Yatīmat*, 1:171; al-Mutanabbī, *Dīwān*, 2:138, v. 1, and note the commentary given in the *Dīwān*.

22. Al-Thaʿālibī, *Yatīmat*, 1:171; al-Mutanabbī, *Dīwān*, 4:193, v. 1, and note the commentary given in the *Dīwān*.

23. See the commentary to al-Mutanabbī, *Dīwān*, 4:193, v. 1. A version of this poem has been ascribed to al-Ḥallāj; see *Sharḥ Dīwān*, 143. For Ibn Jinnī, see J. Pedersen, art. "Ibn Djinnī," in *EI2*.

24. Al-Ḥallāj, *Sharḥ Dīwān*, 279-285.

# VII

# THE RISE AND FALL OF A PERSIAN REFRAIN

## THE *RADĪF "ĀTASH U ĀB"*

*Franklin D. Lewis*

The recognition that poets suffer influence-anxiety is much older than we may suppose; Samuel Johnson had already identified it when he said:

> It is, indeed, always dangerous to be placed in a state of unavoidable comparison with excellence, and the danger is still greater when that excellence is consecrated by death . . . . He that succeeds a celebrated writer, has the same difficulties.[1]

In an even more distant time and tradition, the Persian literary historian al-Rāvandī, writing in 599 A.H./1202–03 C.E., had already illustrated this point in specific terms by means of an anecdote: Sayyid Ashraf Ḥasan-i Ghaznavī, a Ghaznavid poet who flourished in the middle of the sixth/twelfth century, advised a promising young poet that he should select and memorize two hundred lines of verse that pleased him from each of the modern poets, along with the proverbs and poetry of the Arabs and the moralistic verses of the *Shāh Nāmah*. Reading the *Shāh Nāmah* is a must to write excellent poetry, our poet-tyro was told, but the poems of Sanā'ī, Muʿizzī, ʿUnṣurī, and Rūdakī should be avoided. That is to say that the hopeful poet should not hear the poetry of these masters recited and must not read them, because the towering poetic genius of these masters could only stifle the talent of an aspiring poet and hinder him from achieving his purpose.[2]

The *Qābūs Nāmah* (w. 475/1082) also has some advice for the apprentice poet: If a given phrase or image strikes your fancy and you wish to appropriate it as your own, you should use it in a different context—a line of panegyric can be copied, for example, in a satire, and a line of love poetry in an elegy, etc.[3]

Of course, if plagiarism was done openly and decorously, in the form of *istiqbāl* (honoring or vying with an earlier poem and its creator by imitating, alluding to, or pastiching it) or *tazmīn* (quotation), it was permissible and even desirable, so long as the later poet proved himself a worthy imitator. Niẓāmī ʿArūẓī, in fact, in his *Chahār Maqālah* (w. 551–52/1156–57), urges the would-be poet to memorize thousands of lines of the poetry of his predecessors, and gives no hint that all this influence might be bad for a hopeful bard:

> To ensure that his reputation endures, a poet's work must be written down in books [whether in anthologies or individual collected works is not specified] and it must be read by the right people [*bar alsinah-yi aḥrār maqrū'*] and recited in the cities [*va dar madā'in bikhvānand*]. To attain this degree a poet should, in the early prime of his youth, memorize 20,000 lines from the poets of old [*mutaqaddimān*] and 10,000 words/lines [*kalimah*] from the recent poets [*muta'akhkhirān*]. He should be constantly perusing and learning the dīvāns of the masters to see how they handled the difficulties and subtleties of language [*sukhan*], until the methods and genres of poetry are etched in his brain and his nature. Then, when his ability to versify has become firmly grounded and his language fluid, he should study the science of poetics and prosody . . . criticism [*naqd-i maʿānī*], aesthetics [*naqd-i alfāẓ*], plagiarism [*sariqāt*], and biography [*tarājim*]. He should read these matters with a capable master so that he will become worthy of the title "maestro," and his name appear in the annals of the day just like the names of the other master-poets whom we have mentioned, so that he will be able to befittingly repay with lasting fame what he has received from his patron and employer.[4]

Thus we have two opposing models proposed by literary historians: one in which the influence of certain strong talents can nip the talent of an aspiring poet in the bud, and the other in which it is absolutely necessary to study and memorize in great quantity the poetry of both recent and past masters. This chapter aims to discover, by tracing the rise and fall of the refrain "fire and water" in Persian literature, which of these psychologies of influence more accurately describes the normative modus operandi of the Persian poet during the classical period.

## The Radīf

Rashīd al-Dīn Vaṭvāṭ in his treatise on poetics, *Ḥadāyiq al-siḥr fī daqāyiq al-shiʿr* (Gardens of Magic in the Minutiae of Poetry), written in the sixth/twelfth century, explained that peculiar feature of Persian verse, the *radīf*, or refrain, in the following terms:

> The radīf is a word, or more than one word, in Persian poetry which recurs [in each line] after the rhyming word. Such poetry is called by practi-

> tioners of the craft *muraddaf*—poetry with a refrain. The Arabs do not use refrains, except in the case of recent innovators attempting to display their virtuosity. . . . Most Persian poems have a refrain, for the expertise and versatility of the poet is made obvious in composing poems with a refrain.[5]

Although the radīf appears as a formal feature of modern Persian verse from a very early period,[6] and was perhaps derived from a similar feature that seems to have existed in Middle Persian verse,[7] it became increasingly longer and more complex as the tradition progressed. At first, a radīf typically consisted of a rhyming noun followed by a recurrent verb at the end of each line, usually a simple verb in the third person, such as *būd* or *ast* or *āmād*, but by the fifth/eleventh century nouns had become more and more prevalent in refrains, the length of which were gradually increasing to encompass as many as four or even five syllables after the rhyming vowel. By the time of Farīd al-Dīn ʿAṭṭār (d. 618/1221?), refrains were, indeed, as prevalent as Rashīd al-Dīn claims in the passage above—over half the poems in ʿAṭṭār's *Dīvān* have a chorus after the rhyme.

Certain words or phrases appeared as the radīf in so many poems that it became virtually *de rigueur* for all poets to compose their own variations on these themes.[8] As an example, the radīf *āftāb* (sun) or *imshab* (tonight) recurs in perhaps the majority of collections of Persian poetry from the sixth/twelfth century through the early part of the present century, to the extent that poems with such refrains can almost be thought of as minor genres of their own. Other, less time-honored refrains, because they seem to find favor for a time and then gradually go out of vogue, can reveal to us quite a bit about changes in style and taste through the ages. Furthermore, because it is generally easier to unearth the evolution of radīfs consisting of nouns as opposed to those consisting of common verbs, the historical development of such telltale refrains may provide us with more precise information about which poets were influenced by whom, as well as the ways in which this influence, clearly different from the hand-wringing, anxiety-producing influence of Harold Bloom, reverberated through the classical Persian poetic tradition.

## The Refrain "Fire and Water"

The refrain *ātash u āb* (fire and water), usually set in a qaṣīdah with a *mujtas̲s̲* meter (typically ^ – ^ – ^^ – – ^ – ^ – ^^ – ), became quite fashionable at the end of the fifth/eleventh century and remained so up until the last quarter of the sixth/twelfth century. After this, though the theme continued to ring in the ears of later poets, its use as the tonic chord or the *idée fixe* of a given poem fell out of favor, as poets, for the most part, seem to have determined either that it was a worn-out motif, best avoided, or a theme which could be coyly and cleverly deconstructed and put to other uses, with the charming advantage of vague familiarity.

It is hardly surprising that Persian poets developed the theme "fire and water" into a refrain. Empedocles's ideas about the nature of the physical world were widely accepted throughout the Hellenistic, and later the Islamic, world, so that allusions to the four essential elements are repeatedly found in Persian poetry.[9] Fire and water made not only a phonetically pleasant pair—*ātash u āb*, *āb u ātash*—but also a magnificent structural opposition with inexhaustible opportunities for oxymorons and other rhetorical artifices, many of which flow naturally from some basic motifs of Persian poetry—the burning flames of passion and the tears of unrequited love.[10]

Once four- and five-syllable radīfs became fashionable, it was virtually inevitable that the fire-and-water motif would become a refrain. Already at the court of Maḥmūd the Ghaznavid, the mention of fire within a line of verse often summoned forth water within the same line or in the line immediately following.[11] Farrukhī (d. 429/1037–38), for example, composed a qaṣīdah in the meter *ramal* (basic foot – ^ – –) for Muḥammad, the son of Sultan Maḥmud, where the opening line describes the drowning and burning sensations simultaneously experienced by the yearning lover:

*Tā biburdī az dil u az chashm-i man ārām u khvāb*
*Gah zi dil dar ātash-i tīzam gah az chashm andar āb*

You stole from my heart and from my eyes, the one's peace
and the other's sleep, and ever since
I've wallowed, now in the hot fire of my heart, now in
the water of my eyes.[12]

Manūchihrī (d. 432/1040–41) develops the same theme in these two lines from a slightly later qaṣīdah for Khvājah Aḥmad, one of Sultan Masʿūd I's ministers:

*Var hamī ātash furūzad dar dil-i man, gū furūz*
*Shamʿ rā chun bar furūzī rawshanī paydā kunad*

*Var zih dīdah āb bārad bar rukh-i man gū bibār*
*Naw bahārān āb-i bārān bāgh rā zībā kunad*

And if the beloved sets my heart ablaze, let it burn!
The candle shines brightly when you set it afire;

And if my eyes spill tears upon my cheeks, let it rain!
Fresh spring raindrops set the bowers abloom.[13]

The monorhyme . . .*āb* appears frequently in the dīvāns of poets writing in the fifth/eleventh century, often set in the *mujtaṣṣ* meter. ʿUnṣurī uses this rhyme in other meters, but Farrukhī, Qaṭrān-i Tabrīzī, ʿAmʿaq-i Bukhārā'ī, and Azraqī-yi Haravī all have at least one *mujtaṣṣ* poem rhyming in . . .*āb*, bringing us one step closer to the "discovery" of the qaṣīdah in *mujtaṣṣ* with the refrain of *ātash u āb*.[14] Nāṣir Khusraw (d. 481/1088), in fact, in a didactic poem on the ephemeral nature of the world, puts the four elements all into one *miṣra*ʿ (hemistich), making the phrase *ātash u āb* fall in the rhyming position, perhaps for the first time,[15] though this particular poem is in the meter *khafīf* (basic feet ^ ^ – – and ^ – ^ –), rather than in the favored *mujtaṣṣ* of the later radīf:

*Gar nadīdī tanāb'hāsh bi-bīn*
*Jumlagī khāk u bād u ātash u āb*

If you have not seen [the four ropes which hold up the
tent of the material world], look close:
It's all earth and air and fire and water.[16]

Writing in the west of Iran, Qaṭrān-i Tabrīzī (d. after 465/1073) mixes both elements into one line of a *mujtaṣṣ* meter in praise of a certain Abū al-Muẓaffar Surkhāb:[17]

*Magar kih sūkhtan ātash zih tīgh-i ū āmūkht*
*Chunānkih rādī āmūkht az du kaffash āb*

Could it be that fire learned to burn from his sword
Just as [sea]water learned munificence from the
example of his open hands?[18]

Even more significantly, Qaṭrān uses the following as the tie-line of a *tarjī*ʿ*-band* (a stanzaic poem where each stanza is followed by a refrain that ties the verses together) in the meter *hazaj* (basic foot ^ – – –) praising the arrival of spring and the rule of Amīr Abū al-Faẓl ʿAlī:[19]

*Bi shāhī dar jahān tā hast āb u ātash u bādā*
*Amīr u sayyid u Manṣūr Bu'l-Faẓl ʿAlī bādā*

So long as water and fire and wind endure on earth
So long let live and rule the victorious Amīr and
Sayyid Bū al-Faẓl ʿAlī.[20]

This epistrophe is repeated after each of the poem's eleven stanzas, perhaps suggesting to poets of the next generation that earth, wind, fire, and water could be made the elements of a radīf.[21] It was not to catch on immediately in the east, however, for Azraqī-yi Haravī, who flourished in Herat during the last three or four decades of the fifth/eleventh century,[22] frequently made use of the fire-and-water theme and, indeed, has one *mujtas̲s̲* qaṣīdah rhyming in . . .*āb* that utilizes the phrase *ātash u āb* in the rhyming position:

*Bahārī abr-i siyah fām-i tund u pīchandah*
*Bi mār afʿī mānad dahān pur ātash u āb*

In spring, the swift, jet-black, twisting cloud
Resembles a poisonous viper, its mouth full of spit and fire.[23]

The first poet for whom the use of the phrase *ātash u āb* as a radīf can be concretely attested is Masʿūd-i Saʿd Salmān (b. ca. 440/1049, d. 515/1121), who begins his rondo-qaṣīdah with this line:

*Nishastah-am zi qadam tā sar andar ātash u āb*
*Tavān nishastan sākin chunīn dar ātash u āb*

I sit here covered from head to toe in fire and water;
Do you imagine it's possible to sit calmly, thus, in fire and water?[24]

He is aware that the audience might find a sixty-one-line qaṣīdah with each line ending in . . .*ar ātash u āb* somewhat repetitious, the more so since it contains, not only the phrase *ātash u āb* sixty-two times, but also the inverse phrase *āb u ātash* in five additional places. Perhaps the audience is unaccustomed to such relentless development and recurrence of a single phrase and theme; hence Masʿūd Saʿd dedicates the last three lines of the poem to an explanation of the form:

> I have composed an innovative [*badīʿ*] panegyric in the form you see here, filling the page with the expression *ātash u āb*. I heard Kamālī recite a poem like this built upon the radīf *ātash u āb*. I am not fond of repetitious phrases in poetry, but this is a radīf, and that's why it's repeated, *ātash u āb*.[25]

Although Masʿūd Saʿd was not, as he freely admits, the first to use this radīf, it was apparently he who popularized the *āb u ātash* phrase as a formal theme in the meter *mujtas̲s̲*, at least among the poets at the Ghaznavid court. He himself liked the phrase so much that he composed two other qaṣīdahs with the same meter and refrain, one in seventy lines, expanding the radīf to *az ātash u āb* (from fire and water), and a shorter one in thirty-three lines, concluding with . . .*ar ātash u āb*. The first of the three poems, as well as the seventy-line recapitulation, was dedicated to the Ghaznavid Sultan Masʿūd III (r. 492/1099–508/1115), who, we can therefore surmise, must have rather enjoyed this topos, while the shorter version was dedicated to a Ghaznavid minister, Abū Naṣr-i Fārsī, himself a poet, who had fallen afoul of Sultan Masʿūd. The fire-and-water poems addressed to Sultan Masʿūd, though not without humor, are for a martial occasion, evidently when Masʿūd Saʿd, the poet, was in attendance at court and not in prison. It is therefore possible to ascribe the *ātash-u-āb* poem to the year of the Sultan's accession, 492/1099, immediately prior to Masʿūd Saʿd's second term of imprisonment or, perhaps, to the years between 500/1106 and 508/1114, after the poet had been released again from jail. The fire-and-water ode addressed to Abū Naṣr, with whom Masʿūd Saʿd served time for suspicion of treason, appears to have been written when Abū Naṣr was still languishing in jail, which would likewise fix the poem in Sultan Masʿūd's reign.[26]

The existence of several *mujtas̲s̲* panegyrics rhyming in . . .*āb*, but with no refrain, indicate that Masʿūd Saʿd utilized the fire-and-water motif in his poetry before hitting upon the idea of *ātash u āb* as a radīf; in one ode (*Dīvān*, pp. 29–30) for Sultan Ibrāhīm (r. 451/1059–492/1099), and in four others for Sayf al-Dawlah Maḥmūd (pp. 32–33, 33–35, 35–37, 39–40), there are several references to fire and water. In fact, fire and water are mixed in the first hemistich of two qaṣīdahs rhyming in . . .*āb* for Prince Maḥmūd; one in *mujtas̲s̲* where the phrase *ātash u āb* occurs, though the poem has no radīf (p. 33), and one in *khafīf* (p. 37).[27] Maḥmūd was appointed governor of India in 469/1076–77 and seems to have died by the time of his brother's accession in 492/1099; it is thus likely that Masʿūd Saʿd was toying with the fire-and-water theme for some time prior to taking Kamālī's hint and opting, rather late in his poetic career (he would have been between fifty and seventy years of age), to introduce the innovative refrain at the court of the Sultan.

The Kamālī to whom Masʿūd Saʿd credits the invention of this radīf is probably Kamālī of Bukhārā, a prince and panegyrist, whose dīvān is no longer extant, associated with the court of the Seljuk Sultan Sanjar.[28] Writing in his *Lubāb al-albāb* a century later, Muḥammad ʿAwfī spoke highly of Kamālī, attributing to him a qaṣīdah in *ramal* with the radīf *bād u khāk* (wind and earth), which frequently brings the wet and hot elements into the equation as well, as in the following:

*Bād u khāk ar ḥilm u inṣāf-i tu rā munkir shavand*
*Bīnad az āb u zi ātash ranj, munkar bād u khāk*

Were the wind and the earth to deny your justice and restraint,
They would see suffering, wicked wind and earth, at
the hands of water and fire.[29]

The inclusion of the fire-and-water phrase four times in this seventeen-line poem, as well as the plodding and more complex sonority of the radīf *khāk u bād*, would suggest that this poem postdates the *ātash u āb* radīfs of Masʿūd Saʿd, as in fact is borne out by ʿAwfī's statement that the poem was dedicated to Sanjar, who ruled from 511/1118 to 552/1157. Here, then, is an example of one poet making a stylistic innovation, which is then picked up and popularized by an older and (in retrospect) more famous poet, and is then, in turn, borrowed back and nearly parodied by its creator.

Thus, the fire-and-water radīf is now established in both the Ghaznavid and the Seljuk courts. Abū al-Faraj Rūnī, who died sometime between 492/1099 and 508/1114, was a friend and contemporary of Masʿūd Saʿd. Like Masʿūd Saʿd, Abū al-Faraj sent a poem of sympathy and greetings in *mujtas̱s̱* with the radīf *ātash u āb* to Abū Naṣr-i Fārsī, while the latter was apparently in jail. He also composed a similar qaṣīdah in honor of and sympathy for S̱iqat al-Mulk Ṭāhir bin ʿAlī, an important Ghaznavid official and patron of the arts in the reigns of Ibrāhīm and Masʿūd, whose intercession was responsible for Masʿūd Saʿd's release from prison.[30] Both these poems are self-referentially aware of the literary popularity which the fire-and-water radīf was then enjoying, as the opening line of the latter poem shows:

*Girift mashriq u maghrib savār-i ātash u āb*
*Rubūd ḥirṣ-i imārat qarār-i ātash u āb*

The horseman "fire and water" has conquered both the east and the west;
An object of envy throughout the realm, that successful combination of water and fire.[31]

Sanā'ī (d. 535/1140?), too, climbed on the bandwagon, devoting a sixty-two-line qaṣīdah in this radīf to another Ghaznavid poet, Muḥammad bin Nāṣir al-ʿAlavī.[32] According to the *Lubāb al-albāb*, Muḥammad bin Nāṣir did not compose enough poetry to collect into a dīvān, but he did compose a *mujtas̱s̱* qaṣīdah in the radīf *ātash u āb* for Sultan ʿAlā' al-Dawlah (i.e., Masʿūd III), who, therefore, received at least three such dedications.[33]

Not every Ghaznavid poet, however, took a fancy to this theme. ʿUs̱mān-i Mukhtārī, an older contemporary of Sanā'ī, did not use this refrain at all and, in fact, addressed almost all of his qaṣīdahs rhyming in . . .*āb* to rulers other than the Ghaznavids and their officials, as if to avoid having to speak the faddish fire-and-water words. This, no doubt, is attributable in part to his lengthy absence from the court at Ghazna while in Kirmān, where, no doubt, the fire-and-water refrain was unknown or had not won favor. On occasion, however, ʿUs̱mān diffidently acknowledges his awareness of the motif's popularity. In a qaṣīdah containing several short descriptive tableaux, ʿUs̱mān describes a sword in terms of the fire-and-water motif, a favorite source of metaphors for earlier poets. This qaṣīdah is dedicated to Abū al-Fatḥ Yūsuf bin Yaʿqūb, the minister of the Ghaznavid Sultan Malik Arslān (r. 509/1115–511/1117), and thus echos a trope occurring frequently in the fire-and-water refrains for Masʿūd III. Another allusion can be found in a rubāʿī addressed to Ṡiqat al-Mulk, the same official who had earlier received a fire-and-water poem from Abū al-Faraj.[34]

Subsequent Ghaznavid poets were still quite clearly conscious of the erstwhile popularity of the radīf *ātash u āb*, as is evident from the frequent occurrence of this topos in the examples given by ʿAwfī, though fire-and-water no longer appears as a radīf in the examples that have been preserved, nor even as a poem's leitmotif, except in the case of Sayyid Ashraf. Of course, since only scattered examples of the work of Ghaznavid poets after Bahrām Shāh (r. 512/1118–547/1152) have been preserved, it is impossible to say with certainty that no further *ātash-u-āb* radīfs were composed at the Ghaznavid court. However, from various samples preserved in anthologies which either contain the phrase *ātash u āb* or play upon this motif, it seems that the fashion for this refrain began to lose steam in Ghazna during the latter part of the reign of Bahrām Shāh. The *Dīvān* of Sayyid Ashraf (who, it will be remembered, discouraged young poets from following the example of the great masters like Sanā'ī and Muʿizzī) does contain a poem with the radīf *ātash* dedicated to Bahrām Shāh. The direct inspiration for this, however, is not the fire-and-water odes of Sayyid Ashraf's predecessors at the Ghaznavid court, but rather a poem by Rashīd al-Dīn Vaṭvāṭ at the court of Atsiz (see below), where the fire-and-water motif had found new life.[35] Sayyid Ashraf left the service of Bahrām Shāh in 544/1149–50,[36] and it would seem that after his departure, the poets who did remain at Ghazna no longer felt enough attraction to the symbols of fire and water to make them the central theme of an entire poem. Indeed, it may be that the theme had become burdensome, that its possibilities had been well-nigh exhausted. Furthermore, the passage of time had extinguished the social circumstances and the audience which earlier fueled the fashion for this refrain, leaving neither the poets nor the patrons who had once delighted in fire-and-water's elixir. Later poets allude to the motif and its popularity in one line, or sometimes in several consecutive lines, often separating the two elements one from the other, but these images are then allowed to sputter out before the poem reaches its end.[37]

The torch was passed on, however, to poets outside the Ghaznavid court. Amīr Muʿizzī, a contemporary of Masʿūd Saʿd and Abū al-Faraj Rūnī, who attended the courts of the Seljuk rulers Malik Shāh (465/1072–485/1092) and Sanjar (r. 511/1118–552/1157) in Khorasan, addressed a panegyric with the fire-and-water refrain to an unnamed government official, apparently paying his respects to Masʿūd Saʿd's poem for Sultan Masʿūd.[38] It is evident that this theme was hit upon late in his career, and that the idea was borrowed, because his earlier poems in *mujtaṣṣ* rhyming in . . .*āb* make scant reference to the fire-and-water motif.[39] Anvarī, on the other hand, well aware of this radīf, but feeling it has become somewhat stale, refrains from using it as such. Instead, he turns the chorus into a repetend, placing fire and water in the first hemistich of each line, with wind and earth in the second hemistich of each line of this twenty-three-line tour de force in the *ramal* meter for Sultan Sanjar:

*Āb-i chashmam gasht pur khūn z-ātash-i hijrān-i yār*
*hast bād-i sard-i man bar khāk az ān kāfūr-bar*

The fire of separation from the beloved has turned the
water of my eyes to blood,
The cold wind of my [sighs] brings down a snow of
camphor on the earth.[40]

Adīb-i Ṣābir, the poet-spy of Sanjar killed by the Khvārazm-Shāh Atsiz about 540/1145, likewise seems to have felt a growing taboo against the repetition of the fire-and-water radīf. He alters the motif in a qaṣīdah for Sanjar, using many of the same images and ideas with the less constraining radīf of *ātash* unmitigated by *āb*.[41]

Further north, at the court of the Khvārazm-Shāh Atsiz (r. 521/1127–551/1156), where the fire-and-water chorus has not yet been heard, Rashīd al-Dīn Vaṭvāṭ (d. 573/1177 or 578/1182) tried several variations on this theme, dedicating two *mujtas̱s̱* meter panegyrics in the radīf *ātash u āb* to Atsiz, another *mujtas̱s̱* for Atsiz with the radīf *ātash*, and a *muẕāriʿ* (typically – – ^ – ^ – ^ ^ – – ^ – ^ –) for him with the radīf *āb*.[42] Jamāl al-Dīn Iṣfahānī (d. 588/1192), writing toward the end of the century far to the west of the courts where the fire-and-water theme had been brought to a boil, uses the *ātash-u-āb* radīf with some rather fresh imagery and expressions in a twenty-nine-line qaṣīdah praising an unnamed ruler, toward the end of which he boasts:

*Ravā buvad zi pas-i īn qaṣīdah gar zīn pas*
*Bar ū nibishtah shavad dāstān-i ātash u āb*

It is only fitting and proper from now on, after this qaṣīdah,
That the story of fire and water be told on the basis
of this, my account.[43]

From that point in both time and space, however, there were few poets interested in telling the whole story of fire and water. The *ātash-u-āb* refrain was now played decrescendo, in slightly disguised forms, such as the spin-off versions of Anvarī and Rashīd al-Dīn mentioned above, and, in later centuries, in ever more attenuated derivations. Sūzanī of Samarqand (d. 569/1174 or 575/1179), a poet associated with the Qarakhanid court and noted for his satire and invective, has several serious poems built on this theme, but none of them utilize the refrain per se: a *mujtas̱s̱* with the radīf *ātash*; an entire poem in *ramal* where, though neither fire nor water are in a rhyming position, they are opposed to one another in every line; and a ghazal in *ramal* describing the winter landscape.[44] Sayf al-Dīn Isfarangī, who flourished around the turn of the seventh/thirteenth century, contributed a *mujtas̱s̱* meter qaṣīdah with the radīf *āb*.[45] We have seen how Sayyid Ashraf modeled a qaṣīdah for Bahrām Shāh with the radīf *ātash* on the model of a poem by Rashīd al-Dīn in faraway Khvārazm. Other poets of the sixth/twelfth century, including some who flourished at the time the fire-and-water refrain was in vogue and some whose acknowledged mentors had earlier employed the refrain, were apparently not greatly interested in the *ātash/āb* leitmotif or its sequels.[46]

The splitting of fire from water to create the simpler refrains began prior to 557/1162, when Sayyid Ashraf died,[47] and we may conclude that the rage for this radīf began to fizzle out after fifty years or so of common practice. After a further fifty years, the refrain, and indeed the theme, had lost much of its original glow and luster. No doubt this was in part a result of the decline of the qaṣīdah, although, if it had still been perceived as a vital and vibrant motif, this radīf could surely have been transferred to the ghazal, as were other qaṣīdah refrains (such as *āftāb* and *imshab*). In fact, fire-and-water does appear as a refrain in at least one ghazal (set, of course, in a *mujtas̱s̱* meter) by a much later poet active in Azerbaijan, Badr-i Shīrvānī (789/1387–854/1450).[48] The ghazal genre also appropriated the later fractured variations of the theme; the dīvān of the Sufi Sayf al-Dīn Muḥammad Farghānī (fl. ca. 1300 C.E.), for example, has a ghazal in *mujtas̱s̱* with the radīf *az ātash* and two *rajaz* meter (basic meter – – ^ –) ghazals in the radīf *ātasham* with water flowing abundantly throughout the poem;[49] Kamāl al-Dīn Iṣfahānī (ca. 568/1172–635/1237), son of the aforementioned Jamāl al-Dīn, though stepping over the gauntlet laid down by his father to compose an *ātash-u-āb* radīf after his style, does offer a ghazal in the radīf *bar ātash* rhyming in . . .*āb* and, like Rashīd al-Dīn, a qaṣīdah with the radīf *khāk*.[50]

In the seventh/thirteenth and eighth/fourteenth centuries, echoes of the fire-and-water theme can be faintly heard from time to time,[51] but the major poets—such as ʿAṭṭār, Saʿdī, Rūmī, Ḥāfiẓ[52]—for the most part ignore the formula, the phrase, and often even the very idea of water mixed with fire. Saʿdī, in fact, seems to ring the death knell of the motif in the following line from a qaṣīdah written circa 663/1265:

*Digar khalāf nabāshad miyān-i ātash u āb*
*Digar nizāʿ nayuftad miyān-i gurg u ghanam*

There is no longer opposition between fire and water,
No longer a struggle between wolf and lamb.[53]

Allusions to the theme can, nevertheless, be detected in the following centuries, though they are comparatively few and far between. Clearly, the prevailing literary taste either forgot this radīf or deliberately set it aside, and one can infer from the relative infrequency of the mention of fire in connection with water where it might naturally have occurred that poets were stylistically inhibited from reference to this theme. After the passage of time, however, the old flame was rekindled by several poets of the tenth/sixteenth, eleventh/seventeenth, and twelfth/eighteenth centuries, usually in ghazals with a refrain containing some variation on either the word *ātash* or the word *āb*, but not both together.[54] Finally, in the neoclassical *bāz gasht* period, the consciously archaizing Qā'ānī (1223/1808–1270/1854) revived the full fire-and-water refrain for the benefit of a Qajar official, posing this question in the opening line:

*Chih jawhar ast kih hast iᶜtibār-i ātash u āb*
*Chih gawhar ast kih zībad nigār-i ātash u āb*

What elements are there as respected as fire and water?
What jewel is there that can adorn the beloved whose
name is "fire and water"?[55]

A number of other poets of the Qajar period also played with variations on the theme, but none was as confident as Qā'ānī to use the *āb-u-ātash* theme as a radīf: Yaghmā (c. 1196/1782–1276/1859) composed two refrains in *dar āb* (in water) on this theme; Mīrzā Jaᶜfar Riyāẕ-i Hamadānī (d. 1269/1852–53), has one *mujtas̱s̱* qaṣīdah in the radīf *ātash* where every line is filled with water; Ṣuḥbat-i Lārī (d.1251/1835) added a ghazal with the radīf *dar āb*; the aptly pen-named Sharar (Sparky), Ḥusayn ᶜAlī Bayk (b. prior to 1195/1780 and d. 1254/1838 or later) composed ghazals with the refrains of *dar āb* in *mujtas̱s̱* and *bih zīr-i āb* (under the water) in *muẕāriᶜ*; Āshuftah-yi Shīrāzī (d. 1288/1871) contributed a *ramal*-meter ghazal in *dar āb* with two flashes of fire.[56] Despite these and other examples, the poets of the nineteenth century C.E. and the traditional poets of the twentieth century avoided (with the exception of Qā'ānī) the full-blown fire-and-water refrain, whether because they were unaware of it, found it unattractive, could discover no new ways to make the theme their own, or perhaps felt that a long and blatantly oxymoronic motif such as "fire and water" would be seen as evidence, not of the poet's virtuosity, but of his fondness for euphuism and purple patching.

## Conclusions

Very few studies have as yet set about the task of documenting systematically and in detail the changes of style in classical Persian literature and the concomitant question of poetic influence—borrowing, imitation, pastiche, and originality.[57] Further studies of this nature will make it possible to speak more precisely and convincingly about trends, styles, fashions, and innovations in Persian poetry, though it must be admitted that the genesis and subsequent development of the fire-and-water refrain does not cry out for an immediate and radical reinterpretation of the conventional classification of the major styles and periods of Persian literary history—Khorasani, ᶜIrāqī, Indian, neoclassical, and modern.[58] It is obvious, however, that these categories and the criteria which allow us to describe and define them can be greatly refined if close and careful attention is paid to specific incidences and case histories of emulation, imitation, and pastiche (all of which are subsumed under the Persian term *istiqbāl*).

It is neither possible nor necessary to isolate every pairing of the words *ātash* and *āb* that has ever occurred throughout the length and breadth of Persian literature, but the history of the *ātash-u-āb* radīf outlined above does give us sufficient evidence to comment upon the dilemma posed at the beginning of this chapter by the contrary testimonials on the creative psychology of the Persian poet and the diffusion of poetic influence within the Persian literary tradition.[59]

It seems clear that Persian poets of the fifth/eleventh and sixth/twelfth centuries were highly conscious of the poetry being written by their contemporaries and immediate predecessors. Different poets often composed for the same patrons, whether at the court of the ruler or in the lesser banquets of state officials and nobles. This sociopolitical nexus encouraged repetition and allusion to the works of other poets, whether such comparison was done by way of self-aggrandizement, paying homage, or simply catering to the audience's taste.

Mas'ūd Sa'd, Abū al-Faraj, and Sanā'ī all attended the same court and composed for many of the same patrons. They addressed versions of the *ātash u āb* poem as tributes to personal friends, who happened to be poets or state officials. Mu'izzī also dedicated a version to a Seljuk state official. But the poem was popularized by Mas'ūd Sa'd as a royal panegyric, and the epigonic treatments by Anvarī, Adīb-i Ṣābir, Rashīd al-Dīn Vaṭvāṭ, and Sayyid Ashraf were all dedicated to monarchs. Jamāl al-Dīn Iṣfahānī, too, dedicates his rendition to a ruler. The deployment of this radīf, then, has an extraliterary component as an act of ritual homage to the ruler.[60] A given potentate could compete with other rulers in the literary realm as well as on the battlefield, and having a poem in a certain radīf dedicated to him allowed him to appropriate the symbols of power of his royal rivals. Thus, Sanjar and Atsiz can compete with Mas'ūd and the Ghaznavid dynasty, with its fabled array of poets—as it were, match the literary weapons in the Ghaznavid arsenal—by having their own fire-and-water poems.

Courtly poetry, in addition to providing the ruler with the sacraments of kingship, was meant to be entertaining, and in this aim rather closely resembles the popular arts of the twentieth century.[61] Difficulty was not a fault in and of itself, but neither was originality, in the way that we mean the word today, a desideratum. Indeed, in popular literature, the demands of the marketplace and the expectations of the audience must be met. Publishers of contemporary mystery novels or gothic romances would surely admit that they look for artistic products that fit the mold, that will be profitable, that will receive the approval of the audience. For the same reason that film producers churn out several sequels of financially successful movies, Persian court poets took turns doing renditions of forms and themes that were, though originated by one poet at a specific time, considered to be in the public domain. Once a formula proves that it can strike a responsive chord in the audience, it would be foolish not to manipulate the formula, play with it, alter it, exploit it. After a time, when the audience tires of the formula, or when a new audience with different expectations takes its place, the formula will most likely fall into desuetude, as was the case with the fire-and-water framework once the political and social network that made it fashionable passed from the scene. In these circumstances, the anxiety the court poet feels is commercial, as well as artistic. The audience must approve, the sultan must pay the poet.[62]

In such circumstances the aesthetic goal of the poet is typically conservative and Harold Bloom's theories of misprision would hardly seem to apply;[63] the poets who followed Masʿūd Saʿd in deploying the radīf *ātash u āb* did not "misread" the poems of their predecessors and, more importantly, the audience for their poems did not demand that they do so. Imitation, emulation, variation, even pastiche were expected, indeed desired, by the audience and cultivated by the poet. The fact that a poet rewrites or "reprises" the poem of a predecessor or a contemporary is no indication that a titanic struggle of poetic egos is taking place. Though there is obviously a hint of challenge implicit in a latecomer's rendition of a familiar topos, poets appear to have been motivated to repetition and variation by a sense of decorum and courtly fashion, rather than by an oedipal urge. In this sense, the latecomers to the fire-and-water radīf, though there are many "strong poets" among them, did not so much try to overthrow their predecessors as they worked to fill in the interstices of the literary space opened up by the motif, much the way that a Persian miniature or a Persian carpet concentrates on fine detail and craftsmanship, vividness of imagery, and boldness of color rather than originality of theme, pattern, or design.

The repetition of themes, motifs, and entire phrases (e.g., the radīf *ātash u āb*) in classical Persian poetry has a parallel in the musical tradition of the West, as suggested here throughout.[64] Giambattista Vico's speculation on the cultural phenomenon of repetition, as amplified in a musical example by Edward Said, has particular pertinence to the radīf structure in Persian poetry and the concept of *istiqbāl* in general. Speaking of Bach's *Goldberg Variations*, Said says:

> By these devices [of repetition] a ground motif anchors the ornamental variations taking place above it. Despite the proliferation of changing rhythms, patterns, and harmonies, the ground motif recurs throughout, as if to demonstrate its staying power and its capacity for endless elaboration. As Vico saw the phenomenon in human history, there is in these musical forms a tension between the contrariety or eccentricity of the variation and the constancy and asserted rationality of the cantus firmus. Nothing Vico could have said about mind's triumph over irrationality can equal the quiet triumph that occurs at the end of the Goldberg Variations, as the theme returns in its exact first form to close off the aberrant variations it has generated. These uses of repetition conserve the field of activity; they give it its shape and identity, as Vico saw repetition confirming the essential facts of what he called gentile human history.[65]

The virtues of repetition hold true, not only for the individual poem, but also from poem to poem within a tradition. The expectation that well-loved themes will reappear in later poems, forms will remain constant, and motifs be reused constitutes a kind of basso continuo within the ensemble of tradition. The basic ground notes are given and the poet is expected to fill in the harmonies, to provide the elegant variation and ornamentation around the formulaic foundation.

Within a tradition such as this, to speak of intertextuality is stating the obvious.[66] To be a poet is, as Niẓāmī ʿArūẕī tells us, to memorize the lines of your predecessors in great quantity (he takes it for granted that the poet shows some promise of talent). If you are a capable actor, and have learned your lines, you may then take up the mantle of a predecessor and try it on for size. If the mantle can be worn convincingly—either in earnest or in jest[67]—the later poet has established a place for himself in the pantheon; if not, it is obvious to everyone that he has stolen his master's coat. But the suggestion of Sayyid Ashraf that an aspiring poet memorize two hundred favorite lines from each of the contemporary poets is equally instructive. A poet need not, and it appears should not, engage in an exhaustive reading of the poems of one of his older contemporaries or immediate predecessors. Rather than reading in depth, he is to read broadly; presumably he can learn the techniques of his craft in this manner without scarring his psyche. The burden of the past is not so heavy when it is borne in common; influence is not incapacitating when it is diffuse.

However, even in the sixth/twelfth century, the head-on encounter with a towering genius, Sayyid Ashraf warns us, can consume the poet's imagination and cripple his poetic soul. When a tradition reaches the point where the borders and margins have all been filled in, the style, and often the forms, must change.[68]

Indeed, within a generation or two after Sayyid Ashraf begins to falter under the weight of the past, the reigning style begins to give way. By the end of the sixth/twelfth century, the ghazal begins to replace the qaṣīdah as the form of choice, the influence of the Ghaznavid and Seljuk poets begins to wane, the language of mysticism begins to permeate courtly poetry. In the specific terms of the fire-and-water poem, though Jamāl al-Dīn Iṣfahānī would seem to have opened up space for further poetic discourse on the theme by treating of it in a markedly different way, his challenge to perpetuate this topos had the opposite effect. Perhaps the very fact that, by daring all newcomers to take their inspiration from his rendition of this refrain, he inadvertently draws their attention to the cumulative weight of literary history impinging upon this refrain, thereby discouraging further singing of this chorus.[69]

According to Bloom, in the Edenic days before the post-Enlightenment, when art was craftsmanship and poets had no fear of influenza, the poet did not demand of himself originality and was not, therefore, anguished about his relationship to his predecessors.[70] And yet, at least some Persian poets were worrying about the harmful effects of influence in the sixth/twelfth century. In the eighth/fourteenth century, we encounter Ḥāfiẓ, a bellicose and highly original poet who engages in battle with one forefather after another by appropriating their lines and building far greater monuments on their foundations, deftly managing thereby to run his rivals to the dust in nearly every encounter. After Ḥāfiẓ, poets are once more concerned about influence, and styles again begin to change. Once the styles have changed, however, poets at a safe remove of time can return to an earlier style to salvage it, either by resurrecting it as a period piece (as Qā'ānī has done with the *ātash u āb* refrain), transcribing the piece to the contemporary idiom (as in the case of Badr-i Shirvānī, who appropriates the qaṣīdah radīf *ātash u āb* for the ghazal), or cannibalizing it for parts, as in the case of the later poets who use variations of *ātash* or *āb* as refrains.

In spite of the conservative reliance upon previous poetic authority and the dictates of literary conventions which we have determined to be the norms for classical Persian poetry, poets do get tired of the tradition and begin to worry about influence. If this were not so, fashions and styles would never change.

# Notes

1. Cited by W. Jackson Bate in *The Burden of the Past and the English Poet* (New York: W. W. Norton, 1970), 3.

2. Najm al-Dīn Abū Bakr Muḥammad al-Rāvandī, *Rāḥat al-ṣudūr va āyat al-surūr*, ed. Muḥammad Iqbāl (Leiden: E. J. Brill; London: Luzac, Gibb Memorial New Series, no. 2, 1921), 57–58.

3. ʿUnṣur al-Maʿālī Kaykā'ūs bin Vushmgīr, *Qābūs Nāmah*, ed. Saʿīd Nafīsī, 6th ed. (Tehran: Ufsit-i Marvī, 1366 Sh./1987 C.E.), 139–140.

4. Aḥmad bin ʿUmar bin ʿAlī Niẓāmī-yi ʿArūẓī-yi Samarqandī, *Chahār Maqālah*, ed. Muḥammad Muʿīn, 3rd ed. (Tehran: Kitābfurushī-yi Zavvār, 1333/1954), 47–48. (All translations are those of the present writer.)

5. Rashīd al-Dīn Vaṭvāṭ, *Ḥadāyiq al-siḥr fī daqāyiq al-shiʿr*, ed. ʿAbbās Iqbāl (Tehran: Kitābkhānah-yi Kāvah, 1308/1930), 79–80. Despite Rashīd al-Dīn's enthusiasm, it is not clear that the typical Persian refrain necessarily requires any greater verbal dexterity than a poem with lines ending in a simple rhyme, but it can create, in the hands of a competent composer of verse, a rather captivating mood, serious or trifling, as the circumstances require (think of the mesmerizing sublimity of the refrain in Psalm 136—"For his mercy endureth for ever"—and the contrastingly ridiculous effect produced by the trisyllabic rhymes in the lines of certain limericks). Like the choral refrain in a musical piece, a radīf can involve the listener or reader in a poem by intensifying expectations, allowing him to anticipate how the variable elements of each line will be dovetailed with the refrain, and how the refrain will acquire subtle new shades of meaning through that process. (For an example of how the convention of the radīf might feel in English verse, see John Hollander's poem "Ghazals," *Nation*, July 10, 1989, p. 68.) The words "refrain" and "chorus" will be used interchangeably with radīf in this discussion.

6. See Gilbert Lazard, ed., *Les premiers poètes persans (IX$^{e}$-X$^{e}$ siècles): Fragments rassemblés, édités et traduits, v. 2, Textes persans* (Tehran: Département d'Iranologie de l'Institut Franco-Iranien, 1964) (Persian title page: *Ashʿār-i parākandah-yi qadīmtarīn shuʿarā-yi fārsī-zabān* [1341/1962]), where radīf poems by the following poets appear:

Maḥmūd-i Varrāq with the radīf *-t nadaham*; Shahīd-i Balkhī with the radīf *ast*; Abū Shukūr with the radīf *ast*; Maʿrūfī with the radīf *shud*; and Daqīqī with the radīf *-i taw mānad.* See also Rūdakī's famous poem on old age with the radīf *būd* and his famous radīf-ode urging the Amir toward Bukhara (*bū-yi jū-yi mūliyān āyad hamī*). All these poems date from the tenth century C.E. or before and include some of the earliest surviving examples of modern Persian (neo-Persian) verse.

7. Seven lines of the Middle Persian poem "*Draxt-e Āsūrīg*" contain the phrase ". . . *azh man karend* . . . " and seem to display certain characteristics, including rhyme, which can be taken as a not yet rigidly formulaic type of radīf (similar to what some Persian theoreticians later called "*radīf-i maḥjūb*" [see Rashīd al-Dīn, *Ḥadāyiq al-siḥr*, 80], where the refrain precedes the rhyme word). See *Manẓūmah-yi "Drakht-i āsūrīg": Matn-i pahlavī, ādā nivisht, tarjumah-yi fārsī, fihrist-i vāzhah'hā va yāddāsht'hā*, ed. Māhyār Navvābī ([Tehran]: Intishārāt-i Bunyād-i Farhang-i Īrān, 1346/1967). Cf. also W. B. Henning, "A Pahlavi Poem," *Bulletin of the School of Oriental and African Studies* 13, no. 3 (1950): 642–648.

8. A similar phenomenon can be observed in Western classical music, where several composers will try their hand at a given form in the same key as a famous predecessor, e.g., the Violin Concerto in D major, a form and key which Vivaldi repeatedly essayed and which was then taken up in the classical period by pseudo-Boccherini (G486, formerly ascribed to Boccherini, and thought to be the model for Mozart's renditions of this form, is now believed to be a forgery) and by Haydn, whose concerto for violin, 2 oboes, 2 horns, and strings, composed before 1765, is unfortunately lost. In 1775 Mozart canonized this key signature with his two violin concertos in D (K.211 and K.218; two further violin concertos on D are attributed to Mozart, but appear to be the work of other composers). Two years later Carl Stamitz added his own D major rendition of the violin concerto form. Beethoven followed suit with his only concerto for violin (op. 61, 1806; it should be noted, however, that Beethoven had earlier toyed with the composition of a violin concerto in C, which he never completed). Beethoven's concerto was initially unsuccessful, perhaps convincing Schubert not to devote a full concerto to the violin; instead, he produced a shorter form, a Concertstück for violin and orchestra (D.345) in 1816. On the other hand, Paganini's Concerto No. 1 for violin and orchestra (op. 6, circa 1817) is usually transcribed from its original key of E-flat major to D major, the key in which it has entered the concert repertoire. Later composers also picked up the D major violin concerto gauntlet: Brahms (op. 77) and Tchaikovsky (op. 35), both in 1878, and, in 1917, Prokofiev (Violin Concerto No. 1 in D), who perhaps had the same models in mind once again in 1946 when he composed his String Concerto in D. See the *New Grove Dictionary of Music and Musicians*, under the relevant composers and the art. "concerto."

9. An early example of this pairing of the elements in poetry is to be found in Firdawsī:

*az āghāz bāyad kih dānī durust*
*sar-i māyah-yi gawharān az nukhust*
*kih yazdān zi nāchīz chīz āfarīd*
*bidān tā tavānā'ī āmad padīd*
*vu-zū māyah-yi gawhar āmad chahār*
*bar āvardah bī ranj u bī rūzigār*
*yakī ātash-i bar shudah tābnāk*
*miyān bād u āb az bar-i tīrah khāk*
*nukhustīn kih ātash zi junbish damīd*
*zi garmīsh pas khushkī āmad padīd*
*vu-zān pas az ārām sardī numūd*
*zi sardī hamān bāz tarrī fuzūd*

In the beginning you must rightly know
the primal source and origin of the elements:
God created existence out of nothingness
as a manifestation of His might;
and from it came four elemental substances,
brought forth with no expense of toil or time.
One was fire, emerging red-hot
from amongst the wind and water over the dark earth.
As the flames first broke through the roil
their heat took hold and dryness then prevailed;
but after that, all simmered down and then grew cold,
and from the chill, moisture again arose.

*Shāh Nāmah*, ed. Djalal Khaleghi-Motlagh (New York: Bibliotheca Persica, 1988/1366), 6–5. For pairing of the words *āb*, *bād*, *gard*, and *dūd*, see ibid., p. 74, line 50.

10. The *Shāh Nāmah* supplies us as well with a lyrical usage of the fire-and-water motif. Sarv, the Shah of Yemen, when pressured to give the hands of his daughters away in marriage to the sons of Farīdūn, says:

*va gar ārizū rā rasānam bidūy*
*shavad dil pur ātash pur az āb rūy*

If I grant him his desire
my heart will be filled with fire
and my face drenched with water.

Ibid., 96, line 111.

11. Fire also frequently appears in conjunction with kabob in Persian poetry (which the followers of Claude Lévi-Strauss will doubtless appreciate), as in the following line by ʿUnṣurī:

*Guftam ātash bar ān rukhat kih furūkht*
*Guft ān kū dil-i tu kard kabāb*

I asked, "Who lit the fire that burns in your cheeks?"
"The one who grilled your heart like kabob," she replied.

12. *Dīvān-i Ḥakīm Farrukhī-yi Sīstānī*, ed. ʿAlī ʿAbd al-Rasūlī ([Tehran]: Majlis, 1311/1932), 8. Prince Abū Aḥmad Muḥammad was Sultan Maḥmūd's final choice for his successor, though Masʿūd was obviously the stronger candidate. Muḥammad was made governor (Amīr) of Gawzgān in 401/1010–11, and in 421/1030 became the Sultan of the Ghaznavid empire, a post which he held only for a matter of months, though he did ascend to the throne again, briefly, in 432/1041, after Masʿūd's death. Because the supporters of Muḥammad were punished when Masʿūd gained control, it is unlikely that Farrukhī's poem could have been composed after 421/1030. It can thus be dated between the years 401/1010–1011, when Muḥammad functioned as Amīr of Gawzgān, and Rabīʿ II 421/April 1030, when Maḥmūd died.

13. *Dīvān-i Manūchihrī-yi Dāmghānī*, ed. Muḥammad Dabīr-Siyāqī, 5th ed. ([Tehran]:

Kitābfurūshī-yi Zavvār, 1326/1947), 25. This poem must date between the ascension of Masʿūd in 421/1030 and 432/1041, when both Sultan Masʿūd and Manūchihrī died.

14. *Dīvān-i Farrukhī*, 11–13; *Dīvān-i Ḥakīm Qaṭrān-i Tabrīzī*, ed. Muḥammad Nakhjavānī (Tehran: Chāpkhānah-yi Fardīn, 1362), 34–36, 36–38; *Dīvān-i ʿAmʿaq-i Bukhārā'ī*, ed. Saʿīd Nafīsī (Tehran: Kitābfurūshī-yi Furūghī, 1339/1960–61), 128–133. (Though ʿAmʿaq lived well into the reign of the Seljuks, the poem in question is dedicated to the Qarakhanid Shams al-Mulk Naṣr, who reigned from 460/1068–472/1080, thus dating the poem to the eleventh century.) ʿUnṣurī uses this rhyme in three poems, one for Sultan Maḥmūd, one for Amīr Naṣr (Maḥmūd's brother), and one for Sultan Masʿūd, though none of these is in *mujtas̤s̤*; see *Dīvān-i Ustād ʿUnṣurī-yi Balkhī*, ed. Sayyid Muḥammad Dabīr-Siyāqī, 2nd ed. ([Tehran]: Kitābkhānah-yi Sanā'ī, 1342/1963–64), 7–14. Nāṣir Khusraw also uses the same rhyme, though not in the *mujtas̤s̤* meter (see the following note).

15. *Dīvān-i ashʿār-i Ḥakīm Abū Muʿīn Ḥamīd al-Dīn Nāṣir bin Khusraw-i Qubādiyānī*, ed. Ḥājī Naṣr Allāh Taqavī and Mihdī Suhaylī ([Tehran]: Amīr Kabīr/Chāpkhānah-yi Gīlān, 1339/1960), 33. See also *Dīvān-i Nāṣir-i Khusraw*, vol. 1, ed. Mujtabā Mīnuvī and Mihdī Muḥaqqiq (Tehran: Intishārāt-i Dānishgāh-i Tihrān, 1353/1974), 27. Nāṣir Khusraw uses the rhyme . . .*āb* in five poems, none of them in *mujtas̤s̤*.

16. Nāṣir Khusraw is fond of mentioning the four elements, and does so on several occasions (*Dīvān*, ed. Taqavī and Suhaylī, 82, 153, 185), once with water and fire in the rhyming position, where the word for fire is *āẕar*, not *ātash* (see the *hazaj* meter poem beginning on p. 153). In a *mujtas̤s̤* meter rhyming in . . .*ar* (p. 185), he mentions the natural opposition between the four essential elements (line 2).

17. Surkhāb is the name of an area near Tabriz; therefore, the addressee of this panegyric is probably not the Shaddadid ruler Abū al-Muẓaffar Faẕlūn b. Abī al-Savār, also a patron of Qaṭrān, who ruled in Ganja (now Kirovabad) until the Seljuks took over in 468/1075. Abū al-Muẓaffar, judging by the toponym Surkhāb (which, for our purposes, ironically means "crimson water"), was more likely associated with the Rawwadid court at Tabriz. This poem probably dates, therefore, to the period between 438/1046 and 455/1063, when, it seems, Qaṭrān was at the Rawwadid court. Qaṭrān had met with Nāṣir Khusraw during the latter's journey through Tabrīz in 438/1046 and asked him the meaning of some obscure words in the Persian (Fārsī) poetry of Khorasan. It is possible that Qaṭrān acquired a taste for the four elements directly from Nāṣir Khusraw, who had a distinct predilection for philosophical and scientific motifs in his poems. See line 2 of the qaṣīdah in *hazaj* for Abū al-Muẓaffar Faẕlūn (*Dīvān-i Qaṭrān*, 3), which perhaps has as its model the poem in *hazaj-i akhrab-i makhfūf* with the same rhyme by Nāṣir Khusraw (*Dīvān*, ed. Taqavī and Suhaylī, 2).

18. *Dīvān-i Qatrān*, 35.

19. It is clear from the context of another poem addressed to the same patron that he and his brother, Abū al-Ḥasan, were princes, though it is not clear which ruler was their father.

20. *Dīvān-i Qaṭrān*, 420–424.

21. *Qaṭrān* also has a *rubāʿī* (quatrain) rhyming in . . .*āb* that utilizes the fire-and-water motif (along with kabob) in one of its four lines (*Dīvān*, 524). The fire-and-water phrase will appear in many subsequent rubāʿīs; one such rubāʿī is attributed to ʿUmar Khayyām (d. 525–6/1131–2?):

*Mā'īm u may u muṭrib u īn kunj-i kharāb*
*Jān u dil u jām u jāmah pur durd-i sharāb*
*Fārigh zi umīd-i raḥmat u bīm-i ʿazāb*
*Āzād zi khāk u bād v-az ātash u āb*

Here we are in this abandoned ruin, you and I,
wine and song;
Our heart and soul, chalice and clothes drenched
in the dregs of wine;
Free of any hope for mercy, as well as any fear
of hell's torment;
Released from the hold of earth, wind, water and fire.

(See *Rubāʿiyyāt-i Ḥakīm Khayyām-i Nayshābūrī*, ed. Muḥammad ʿAlī Furūghī and Qāsim Ghanī [Tehran, 1321; Reprint, Berkeley, Calif.: Iranzamin, n.d.]), 3. Mahsatī also has several rubāʿīs which play upon the four elements motif, including a great number where water and fire figure prominently, as in, for example, quatrains 6, 7, 8, 11, 12, 21, 39, 52, 60, 64, 78, 84, 97, 110, 129, 131, 132, etc., in Fritz Meier, *Die schöne Mahsatī: ein Beitrag zur Geschichte des persischen Vierzeilers* (Wiesbaden: Franz Steiner Verlag, 1963).

22. Probably between 440/1048 and 475/1083. The traditional date of his death is given as ca. 526 or 527/1133 (which the editor of his dīvān, Saʿīd Nafīsī, accepted), but Ẕabīḥ Allāh Ṣafā (*Tārīkh-i adabiyyāt dar Īrān*, 7th ed. [Tehran: Intishārāt-i Firdaws, 1366 Sh./1987], 2:435–436) thinks Azraqī died ca. 475, because there are no poems in his dīvān praising any of the Seljuks after Amīrān Shāh Qāvurd (d. 466) and Tughān Shāh (d. ca. 475). George Morrison (*History of Persian Literature from the Beginning of the Islamic Period to the Present Day, Handbuch der Orientalistik* [Leiden and Cologne: E. J. Brill, 1981], 40) also sides with an earlier date (before 466/1073), this date being based upon the argument in Muḥammad Qazvīnī's notes to *Chahār Maqālah* (ed. Muḥammad Muʿīn, 218n.). However, Djalal Khaleghi-Motlagh (art. "Azraqi Heravi" in *Encyclopaedia Iranica*) says "the truth probably lies somewhere in between" the estimates of Nafīsī and Qazvīnī: "Azraqi certainly lived till late in the 5th/11th century, but does not appear to have seen any events of the 6th/12th C." We can give the *terminus ad quem* of this poem, therefore, as ca. 492/1100, though it likely was written a few decades prior to this.

23. *Dīvān-i Azraqī-yi Haravī*, ed. Saʿīd Nafīsī (Tehran: Kitābfurūshi-yi Zavvār, 1336/1957), 3. It should be pointed out that the loss of albums of poetry dedicated to later rulers could account for the fact that we know of no poems by Azraqī dedicated to rulers subsequent to Tughān Shāh; the 2,600 or so lines of his that have been collected are a small number for a man who made his career as a court poet. Azraqī plays on the opposition between fire and water frequently, as in lines 306 (p. 13), 433 (p. 17), and 1533 (p. 60); qaṣīdah 12, in *mujtaṣṣ*, which has three lines pairing fire and water (pp. 16–18); qaṣīdah 13 (pp. 18–21); qaṣīdah 16, where all four elements occur repeatedly throughout the poem (pp. 23–25); qaṣīdahs 24 (pp. 48–51), 46 (pp. 65–68), 51 (pp. 74–76); qaṣīdah 52, which is a *mujtaṣṣ* (pp. 76–78); and qaṣīdah 64 (pp. 90–92). There are also two rubāʿīs with fire and water paired in the same *miṣraʿ* (pp. 96–97).

24. *Dīvān-i Masʿūd-i Saʿd Salmān*, ed. Rashīd Yāsimī, 2nd ed. (Tehran: Amīr Kabīr, 1362/1983–4), 23.

25. Ibid., 25.

26. It is possible that Masʿūd Saʿd composed this qaṣīdah for Abū Naṣr at the same time he composed the fire-and-water poem for Sultan Masʿūd as an indication that, though he had affected a rapprochement with the monarch, he still sympathized with the injustice that had been done to his old friend and benefactor, Abū Naṣr.

27. There is also a qaṣīdah in *muẕāriʿ* for ʿAbd al-Ḥamīd Aḥmad bin ʿAbd al-Ṣamad, who served as vizier for Ibrāhīm and Masʿūd from ca. 470/1077 to 512/1118 but was apparently executed by Bahrām Shāh after the latter ascended the throne in 512/1118; see C. E. Bosworth, *The Later Ghaznavids* (New York: Columbia University Press, 1977), 71–72. This poem (*Dīvān*, 40–41) does make one reference to the theme. A later ode in *ramal* for Bahrām Shāh (written between 512/1118 and 515/1121) has water mixed with

another word for fire, *āẕar* (74). A *ḥabsiyyah* (prison lament) in *mujtaṡṡ* rhyming . . .*āb kunad* from the period of Masʿūd Saʿd's imprisonment mentions both fire and water, but not in relation to each other (95–97). Like Qaṭrān and Khayyām, Masʿūd Saʿd also uses the phrase *āb u ātash* in a rubāʿī (683).

28. There was also a poet by the name of Kamāl al-Dīn Ḥusayn Ḥasanī Ḥājib-i Ghaznavī active at the court of the Khvārazm-Shāhs in the sixth century A.H. Another poet, Muḥammad-i Nāṣir al-ʿAlavī, is given the title "Akmal al-Shuʿarā'" by Muḥammad ʿAwfī, but is referred to as "Sayyid al-Shuʿarā'" by Sanā'ī (see below, note 31); in any case, it does not seem that either of these poets used the pen name "Kamālī."

29. Muḥammad ʿAwfī, *Lubāb al-albāb*, ed. E. G. Browne and Muhammad Qazvini (Leiden: E. J. Brill, 1906), 1:88. See also Ṣafā, *Tārīkh-i adabiyyāt*, 2:681–685.

30. *Dīvān-i Abū al-Faraj Rūnī*, ed. Maḥmūd Mahdavī Dāmghānī (Mashhad: Kitābfurūshī-yi Bāstān, 1347/1968–69), 18–20, 21–23.

31. Ibid., 18.

32. *Dīvān-i Ḥakīm Abū al-Majd Majdūd bin Ādam Sanā'ī-yi Ghaznavī*, ed. Muḥammad Taqī Mudarris-i Raẕavī, 3rd ed. ([Tehran]: Kitābkhānah-yi Sanā'ī, 1362/1983–84), 62–66. Sanā'ī also has the now seemingly obligatory use of the phrase in a rubāʿī (*Dīvān*, 1110), and makes use of the fire-and-water trope in one line of a number of ghazals (e.g., *Dīvān*, 806, 827, 982, 994, etc.) and qaṣīdahs (e.g., 230, 238, 483, etc.). A reference to the motif likewise occurs in the lines praising ʿUṡmān-i Mukhtārī (see below) in the *Kār Nāmah-yi Balkh*, for which see *Maṡnavī'hā-yi Ḥakīm-i Sanā'ī*, ed. Muḥammad Taqī Mudarris-i Raẕavī (Tehran: Intishārāt-i Dānishgāh-i Tihrān, 1348/1969), 168; and in a prose passage from a letter to his friend Khvājah Aḥmad Masʿūd in *Makātīb-i Sanā'ī*, ed. Naẕīr Aḥmad (Aligarh, India: Aligarh Muslim University, 1962), 33. Sanā'ī was also very fond of combining all four elements in one line (*Dīvān*, 255, 393, 412, 799, 974), which in one case, at the beginning of his *Ḥadīqat al-Ḥaqīqah* (ed. Mudarris-i Raẕavī, 2nd ed. [Tehran: Intishārāt-i Dānishgāh-i Tihrān, 1359/1981], 60), seems to be modeled directly on the genesis passage from the *Shāh Nāmah* quoted above, note 9.

33. Part of Sayyid Jamāl al-Dīn Muḥammad-i Nāṣir al-ʿAlavī's *ātash u āb* poem for Sultan ʿAlā' al-Dawlah Masʿūd III is quoted by ʿAwfī, *Lubāb al-albāb*, 2:267–269. ʿAwfī indicates that Muḥammad-i Nāṣir won great esteem at the court of Bahrām Shāh (r. 512/1118–547/1152), but it is clear that Muḥammad-i Nāṣir, who is warmly praised by Sanā'ī in his *Kār Nāmah-yi Balkh* (where he is referred to as Sayyid al-Shuʿarā'), must have already won a place in the poetry circles which Sanā'ī frequented in Ghazna during the reign of Masʿūd. Sanā'ī composed his *Kār Nāmah* in Balkh in or prior to the year 508/1115 (see J. T. P. de Bruijn, *Of Piety and Poetry: The Interaction of Religion and Literature in the Life and Works of Hakim Sana'i of Ghazna* [Leiden: E. J. Brill, 1983], 56), the same year in which Sultan Masʿūd died. This, then, is the *terminus ad quem* for Muḥammad-i Nāṣir's ode. It is strange, though, that Muḥammad-i Nāṣir had too little poetry to make a *dīvān*, as ʿAwfī asserts, if he was active at the court of Sultan Masʿūd as well as at the court of Bahrām Shāh. His prominence at the court of Bahrām Shāh could well be an indication that he lived longer than Sanā'ī, though the list of Ghaznavid poets given by Niẓāmī ʿArūẓī (*Chahār Maqālah*, 44), which is roughly chronological, places Muḥammad-i Nāṣir closer to Masʿūd Saʿd and Abū al-Faraj than to Sanā'ī. The fact that Sanā'ī has composed an ode for Muḥammad-i Nāṣir also tends to suggest that the latter was either older or more established than Sanā'ī (Sanā'ī also wrote deferential *qāsīdahs* for Masʿūd Saʿd and ʿUṡmān-i Mukhtārī, who were older), or at least that Sanā'ī perceived Muḥammad to be his peer. It should be noted that Muḥammad-i Nāṣir's younger brother, Sayyid Ashraf al-Dīn Abū al-Ḥasan bin Nāṣir al-ʿAlavī (the family evidently claimed descent from the Prophet), is not the famous Sayyid Ashraf whose *dīvān* has survived to our time. See Muḥammad Taqī Mudarris-i Raẕavī, intro. to *Dīvān-i Sayyid Ḥasan-i Ghaznavī mulaqqab bih Ashraf* (Tehran: Intishārāt-i Dānishgāh-i Tihrān, 1328/1949), i-vi.

34. *Dīvān-i ʿUs̲mān-i Mukhtārī*, ed. Jalāl al-Dīn Humāʾī (Tehran: Bungāh-i Tarjumah va Nashr-i Kitāb, 1341/1962), 176–177, 608. See also ibid., 22, 31, 128, 163, 167, 188, 245, 259, 330, 371, 398–401, 428, 445, 557.

35. *Dīvān-i Sayyid-i Ḥasan-i Ghaznavī*, 100–103. For other instances of the fire-and-water motif without the refrain, see Ashraf's poems for Bahrām Shāh (pp. 16, 18–19 [this poem is also attributed to Sanāʾī as a panegyric for Sultan Sanjar and appears as such in Sanāʾī's *Dīvān*, but is more likely a poem by Sayyid Ashraf for Bahrām Shāh], 60, 64, 86–90 [this poem dates from 544/1149–50, after Ashraf had left Ghazna]); the ode for Sanjar, in which fire and water are the leitmotif (pp. 28–31); and the poem for Qavām al-Dīn (95–98). See also his rubāʿīs (e.g., nos. 2, 4, 13, 18, 24, 26, 29, 33, 80, 111, 112, 138, 188, 190), which frequently make use of the topos.

36. Bosworth, *The Later Ghaznavids*, 108.

37. See ʿAwfī, *Lubāb al-albāb*, vol. 2, ch. 10, for poems illustrating this phenomenon. Among the poets at the court of Bahrām Shāh are Abū Bakr bin Muḥammad bin al-Rūḥānī (see pp. 282–283, 286) and Muḥammad bin ʿUs̲mān al-ʿUtbī al-Kātib (p. 291); at the court of Khusraw Malik (r. 555/1160–582/1186) are ʿAlī bin ʿUmar al-Ghaznavī (p. 406) and Abū Bakr bin al-Musāʿid al-Khusravī (pp. 408 and 410); and also Shaykh Aḥmad bin Muḥammad "al-Mīm . . . ?" (p. 412).

38. *Dīvān-i Amīr al-Shuʿarāʾ Muḥammad bin ʿAbd al-Mulk-i Nayshābūrī mutakhalliṣ bih Muʿizzī*, ed. ʿAbbās Iqbāl ([Tehran]: Kitābfurūshi-yi Islāmiyyah, 1318/1940), 72–74. See also his rubāʿī on this theme (p. 800).

39. There are several poems in this rhyme in Muʿizzī's *Dīvān*: a *mujtas̲s̲*, for Niẓām al-Mulk (k. 485/1092), which has no reference to our topos (*Dīvān*, 60–62); another *mujtas̲s̲*, this for a government official during the reign of Malik Shāh (r. 465/1072–485/1092), Sharaf al-Mulk Abū Saʿd Muḥammad, which treats of the fire/water opposition in one line (57–60); two for Malik Shāh himself, one of which is a wine ode in *mujtas̲s̲* describing the juice of the vine over the course of three lines as firewater and insisting that, though fire and water are diametrically opposed, they reach an accord in the hand of the Shah (827–828; this is an interesting extended use of the fire/water topos before it came to be a radīf); a *ramal* for the same Shah, which brings all four elements together in one line (828–829); three odes for Muʾayyid al-Mulk bin Niẓām al-Mulk (k. 494/1101), one in the meter *mujtas̲s̲* in which fire appears four times, once with water (53–56); a *muẓāriʿ* meter (56–57), which pairs the two elements in one line; and a *ramal* which pits water against fire in three lines (62–65); one poem which has no allusion to the topos for an unnamed Padishah, perhaps, judging from the reference to the ruler's unerring arrow, Sanjar (65–66); one for the Ghaznavid Bahrām Shāh in *ramal*, which pairs water with the summer heat and with the stars, fire with kabob (66–68); one reference in a poem for Fakhr al-Maʿālī (74–76); near allusions in the *abr u āftāb* (clouds and sun) radīf for Mujīr al-Dawlah (70–72); and one reference in a *ramal* qaṣīdah for Sanjar's vizier (between 518/1124 and 521/1127) Muʿīn al-Dīn Mukhtaṣṣ al-Mulk. Fire and water are the leitmotif of one rubāʿī (800) and also figure in a quatrain which helped Muʿizzī to win Malik Shāh's favor (811; see also *Chahār Maqālah*, 68).

40. *Dīvān-i Anvarī*, ed. Muḥammad Taqī Mudarris-i Raẓavī, 2 vols. (Tehran: Bungāh-i Tarjumah va Nashr-i Kitāb, 1337/1959 and 1340/1961), 1:190–191. For other uses of this motif in Anvarī's *Dīvān*, see 1:77, 300, 396, 452; 2:519, 593; and the three rubāʿīs on p. 947.

41. *Dīvān-i Adīb-i Ṣābir-i Tirmiẕī*, ed. ʿAlī Qavīm (Qavīm al-Dawlah) (Tehran: Kitābfurūshi-yi Khāvar, 1331/1952), 144–146. There is also the obligatory rubāʿī (309) and scattered other uses of the theme, such as on pp. 69, 72, and 258 (the last, a poem composed for Ibrāhīm the Ghaznavid prior to Masʿūd Saʿd's popularization of the radīf).

42. *Dīvān-i Rashīd al-Dīn Vaṭvāṭ*, ed. Saʿīd Nafīsī (Tehran: Kitābkhānah-yi Bārānī, 1339/1960), 64–66, 66–68, 283–287, and 61–64, respectively. The two fire-and-water poems are rather repetitive, relying on basically the same images and metaphors; the water

radīf is somewhat more original in its treatment and lingers for a moment longer on the *nasīb* before moving onto the panegyric. Surprisingly, Rashīd does not focus on the fire-and-water theme in his rubāʿīs, though he does make passing allusions to it in at least two quatrains (pp. 616 and 617). Nor does Rashīd ignore the earthier elements of the topos, but composes a 30-line qaṣīdah in the radīf *khāk* (earth or dust) for Atsiz which brings in the other elements as well (pp. 302–303).

43. *Dīvān-i Kāmil-i Ustād Jamāl al-Dīn Muḥammad bin ʿAbd al-Razzāq-i Iṣfahānī*, ed. Vaḥīd Dastgirdī (Kitābfurūshī-yi Ibn-i Sīnā, 1320/1941), 49. Besides his 59-line qaṣīdah in the radīf *ātash* (*Dīvān*, 201–205) for the Ṣāʿidiyān ruler in Iṣfahān, Rukn al-Dīn Masʿūd, fire and water appear as important themes in his poem on the bathhouse (190–192) and in another qaṣīdah for Shihāb al-Dīn Khāliṣ (194–195) and in many scattered lines throughout the *Dīvān*. Rubāʿīs 9 and 25 also contain references to the motif, but are merely echoes of the earlier thematic quatrains woven around it. It should be noted that Jamāl al-Dīn has shown his admiration for Anvarī, Rashīd al-Dīn, and Sayyid Ashraf (e.g., *Dīvān*, 265), all of whom have poems which incorporate the *ātash-u-āb* radīf or a variation thereof. He also speaks highly of Khāqānī and Ẕahīr-i Fāryābī.

44. *Dīvān-i Ḥakīm Sūzanī-yi Samarqandī*, ed. Nāṣir al-Dīn Shāh Ḥusaynī ([Tehran]: Amīr Kabīr, 1338/1959). The 33-line *ātash* radīf (pp. 226–227) is for ʿAlī bin Aḥmad (?r. 551/1156–556/1161). The 26-line fire-and-water leitmotif (pp. 307–308) rhyming in . . .*ān* is for Tāj al-Dīn Maḥmūd (?r. 526/1132–536/1141) and appears to be modeled on Anvarī's previously mentioned poem on the subject of fire and water. The 8-line *ramal* (p. 380) on the earth in winter is the first time (insofar as I am aware) this theme appears as a central feature of a ghazal. See also the rubāʿī that pairs fire and water (p. 493).

45. *Dīvān-i Sayf al-Dīn Isfarangī*, ed. Zabīdah Ṣadīqī (Multan, Pakistan: Qawmi Ṣaqāfatī Markaz-i Bihbūd, 1979), 130–132. Sayf al-Dīn was traditionally believed to have been born in 571/1176 or 581/1185–86 and died in 666/1267–68, but he may have died as early as the turn of the century (ca. 600/1203).

46. ʿAbd al-Vāsiʿ Jabalī (d. 555/1160), an itinerant panegyrist in the east of the Iranian world, has many lines throughout his dīvān playing upon the opposition of water and fire (e.g., pp. 39, 43, 47, 89, 104, 503) and two rubāʿīs based on this theme (p. 662), but no refrains based on either *ātash* or *āb*; see *Dīvān-i ʿAbd al-Vāsiʿ Jabalī*, ed. Ẕabīḥ Allāh Ṣafā, 2 vols. (Tehran: Intishārāt-i Dānishgāh-i Tihrān, 1339/1960 and 1341/1962). Qavāmī of Rayy, (fl. ca. 512/1118 to 550/1155), a Shiite poet, concerned himself with religious themes and cannot, therefore, be expected to ape the ways of the court poets. Nevertheless, there are scattered pairings of the hot and wet elements in his poems, though his long *mujtaṣṣ* qaṣīdah rhyming in . . .*āb* only makes use of it once; see *Dīvān-i Sharaf al-Shuʿarā' Badr al-Dīn Qavāmī-yi Rāzī*, ed. Mīr Jalāl al-Dīn Ḥusaynī Urmavī Muḥaddiṣ (n.p.: Chāpkhānah-yi Sipihr, 1334/1955), 89–91, 161. Aṡīr-i Akhsīkatī (d. 570/1174–75 or 577/1181–82), born in Transoxiana and familiar with the poets in the eastern Iranian realms, though most of his poetry is dedicated to rulers in western Iran—especially the Ildegizid dynasty in Azerbaijan—makes use of the topos in scattered lines of various poems, but never as a dominant theme; see *Dīvān-i Aṡīr al-Dīn Akhsīkatī*, ed. Rukn al-Dīn Humāyūn-Farrukh (Tehran: Kitābfurūshī-yi Rūdakī, 1337/1958), 33, 329, 416, 473, etc. Also in the northwest of Iran, Falakī of Shirvān (d. 577/1181 or 587/1191?) has a few scattered lines pairing fire and water; see *Dīvān-i Ḥakīm Najm al-Dīn Muḥammad Falakī-yi Shirvānī*, ed. Ṭāhirī Shihāb (Tehran: Kitābkhānah-yi Ibn-i Sīnā, 1345/1966), 25, 38, 42, 97, 108, etc. (It should be noted that Falakī is reputed to have composed between five and seven times the number of lines of verse that have been preserved in the printed edition of his dīvān). More widely traveled, but also based in Shirvān, Khāqānī (d. 595/1199) has one rubāʿī on this theme (p. 702); a ghazal in the radīf *zīr-i āb* (under water), which has fire in one line (p. 554); an elegy in the radīf *khāk*, which makes very little reference to fire or water (237–239); another ghazal which carries the fire-and-water theme in the first two lines (p. 568); and an elegy that refers to it in three lines (p. 793). For these examples,

see *Dīvān-i Afẕal al-Dīn Badīl bin ᶜAlī Najjār-i Khāqānī-yi Shirvānī*, ed. Ẕiyā' al-Dīn Sajjādī (Tehran: Kitābfurūshī-yi Zavvār, 1338/1959). Ẕahīr-i Fāryābī (d. 598/1201–02) who composed for patrons in both the east and the west of Iran, has, again, scattered lines pairing fire and water, and one rubāᶜī on the theme (p. 448, though this is of uncertain authorship); *Dīvān-i Ẕahīr-i Fāryābī*, ed. Taqī Bīnish (Mashhad: Kitābfurūshī-yi Bāstān, 1337/1959).

47. *Dīvān-i Sayyid-i Ḥasan-i Ghaznavī*, 100–103. Water appears in four to five lines of this poem.

48. *Badr-i Shīrvānī: Dīvān*, ed. Abū al-Faẕl Hāshim Ūghulī Raḥīmuf (Moscow: Dānish, Shuᶜbah-yi Adabiyyāt-i Khāvar, 1985), 570–571.

49. *Dīvān-i Sayf al-Dīn Muḥammad-i Farghānī*, ed. Ẕabīḥ Allāh Ṣafā, 2 vols. (Tehran: Chāpkhānah-yi Dānishgāh-i Tihrān, 1341/1962), 2:32–33, 296–299. Sayf al-Dīn was active in the last half of the seventh and first half of the eighth century H.

50. *Dīvān-i Khallāq al-Maᶜānī Abū al-Faẕl Kamāl al-Dīn Ismāᶜīl-i Iṣfahānī*, ed. Ḥusayn Baḥr al-ᶜUlūmī (Tehran: Intishārāt-i Kitābfurūshī-yi Dihkhudā, 1348/1970), 775, 444–445. Kamāl al-Dīn's poetry has frequent one-line references to the fire-and-water motif throughout the *Dīvān*, though no radīf as such. Aside from the two radīfs mentioned in the text, Kamāl al-Dīn has one poem based on water as the leitmotif (629–630) and one ghazal based on the ideas of water and burning (p. 710).

51. Imāmī of Herat (d. 686/1287), for example, has a *ramal*-meter qaṣīdah rhyming in . . .*āb* for Fakhr al-Mulk in which the fire/water opposition is a central theme; see *Dīvān-i kāmil-i Raẕī al-Dīn ᶜAbd Allāh bin Muḥammad bin Abī Bakr ᶜUs̱mān Imāmī-yi Haravī*, ed. Humāyūn Shahīdī, ([Tehran]: Mu'assisah-yi Maṭbūᶜātī-yi ᶜIlmī, 1344/1965), 73–78. Muḥammad bin Badr al-Jājarmī includes in his anthology (dating from 741/1340) *Mūnis al-aḥrār fī daqā'iq al-ashᶜār* (ed. Mīr Ṣāliḥ Ṭabībī, vol. 1 [Tehran: Chāpkhānah-yi Ittiḥād, 1337/1959], and vol. 2 [Tehran: Intishārāt-i Anjuman-i Millī, 1350/1971]) a number of poems which indicate that the motif has certainly not been forgotten, including the description by Khvājū-yi Kirmānī (d. 753/1352?) of a bathhouse (1:83–85; see also the bathhouse poem by Jamāl al-Dīn Iṣfahānī, mentioned earlier), several poems by Farīd al-Dīn Aḥval al-Asfarā'inī (d. after 663/1265) (1:75–77; 2:426–429), a poem in the radīf *ātash* by As̱īr al-Dīn Awmānī (d. 665/1267) in which water features prominently (2:707–709), a *mujtas̱s̱* qaṣīdah rhyming in . . .*āb* with the radīf *andākht* by Shams al-Dīn Ṭabasī (d. 626/1229) which mentions water only twice and fire only once, not in the same line (2:736–738).

52. Ḥāfiẓ is, of course, a master at reworking the lines of previous poets and dropping allusions to specific poems. It comes as no suprise, therefore, that he makes reference to the *ātash u āb* tradition. However, though it is true that Ḥāfiẓ pairs the words *ātash* and *āb* in 15 lines (e.g., ghazals 17, 18, 31, 125, 135, 252, 259, 260, 289 [where the pair appears three times in a poem with the radīf *chu shamᶜ*—like a candle], 369, 419, 425, 457), more often than not, Ḥāfiẓ employs one member of this dynamic duo without the other (see, for example, ghazals 10, 18, 27, 57, 71, 76, 87 [line 3], 90, 102, 134, 148, 155, 156, 173, 179, 205, 214, 237, 267, 399, 410, 417, 438, where *ātash* occurs without *āb* in the same or nearby lines, and the even greater number of lines where water occurs without fire, as in ghazals 3, 11, 12, 17, 30, 31, 40, 66, 74, 87 [line 11], 92, 93, 97, 120, 121, 128, 153, 163, 175, 178, 190, 210, 215, 247, 350, 402, 414, 424, 467, 478: this list, though long, is by no means exhaustive). There are many lines, however, in which the hint of opposition between liquid and flame is not far distant, even though the words "water" and "fire" are not both physically present, e.g., in ghazals 13, 18 [line 4], 26, 87 [line 6], 122, 145, 172, 213, 245, 277, 326, 332, 346, 359, 375, 392, 397, 405, 406, 415, 428). In a new twist on the elements, water and dust (*khāk*, *ghubār*, *turāb*) are often paired (as in ghazals 9, 74, 167, 233, 234, 242, 252, 265, 325, 335, 354, 408, 414, 452). Though Ḥāfiẓ is particularly fond of water imagery, he has several *mujtas̱s̱*-meter poems rhyming in . . . *āb* which make no use of the fire/water opposition (e.g., ghazals 2, 216, 257, 299, 413) and several poems in other meters rhyming in . . . *āb* (or with this syllable as part of the rhyme) which likewise ignore the

*ātash* and *āb* pair (13, 14, 16, 387, 388, 414, 424, 425 [two of three lines with the word *āb* lack *ātash*]. *Dīvān-i Ḥāfiẓ*, ed. Parvīz Nātil Khānlarī, 2 vols., 2nd ed. (Tehran: Sahāmī, 1362/1983–84).

53. *Kulliyāt-i Saʿdī*, ed. ʿAbbās Iqbāl, 4 vols., ([Tehran]: Iqbāl, 1363/1984), 4 (*Qaṣāyid-i Saʿdī*): 38. This is from a qaṣīdah for the Salghurid Atabeg, Muẓaffar al-Dīn Saljuqshāh.

54. ʿUrfī of Shiraz (963/1555–999/1591) has a ghazal in *mujtas̱s̱* rhyming in . . .*āb* with the refrain *mīsūzad* ([it's] burning), stressing the fiery nature of the juice of the vine; see *Kulliyāt-i ʿUrfī-yi Shīrāzī*, ed. Ghulām-Ḥusayn Javāhirī (n.p.: Chāpkhānah-yi Muḥammad ʿAlī ʿIlmī, n.d.), 358. The Indian-born poetess Zīb al-Nisā' Makhfī (1048/1638–1113/1701) has two ghazals in *ramal* with the radīf *ātash ast*, two in *hazaj* with radīf *ātash* and a *muẓāriʿ* in . . .*āb kū*, all of which allude to the theme; *Dīvān-i Zīb al-Nisā' Makhfī*, ed. Aḥmad Karamī ([Tehran?]: Silsilah-yi Nashrīyāt-i "Mā", 1362/1983–84), 49, 62, 184–185, 239. Qaṣṣāb-i Kāshānī (d. before 1165/1751–52) has poems in the following radīfs: *dar āb* (in the water) (30: *ramal*), *mī-uftad dar āb* ([it, he, she] falls in the water) (34: *ramal*), *kunad dar āb* (does or puts in the water) (36: *muẓāriʿ*), and *mīshavad ātash* (catches fire) (179: *hazaj*); see *Dīvān-i Qaṣṣāb-i Kashānī*, ed. Ḥusayn Partuv-i Bayẓā'ī (Tehran: Ibn-i Sīnā, 1338/1959), 20, 21–22, 22–23, 102.

55. *Dīvān-i Mīrzā Ḥabīb Allāh Qā'ānī-yi Shīrāzī*, ed. Sayyid Jaʿfar Maḥjūb (Tehran: Amīr Kabīr, 1336/1957), 80–81.

56. *Majmūʿah-yi as̱ār-i Yaghmā-yi Jandaqī*, vol. 1, ed. Sayyid ʿAlī Āl Dāvūd (Mashhad: Intishārāt-i Ṭūs, 1357/1978), 101–103; *Dīvān-i Mīrzā Jaʿfar Riyāẓ-i Hamadānī* (n.p.: Intishārāt-i Furūghī, Chāpkhānah-yi ʿIlmī, 1356/1977), 104–107; *Dīvān-i Ṣuḥbat-i Lārī*, ed. Ḥusayn Maʿrifat (Shiraz: Kitābfurūshī-yi Maʿrifat-i Shīrāz, 1333/1954), 25; *Faghān-i dil: majmūʿah-yi ashʿār-i Ḥusayn-i ʿAlī Bayg Baygdilī Shāmlū Sharar-i Qummī*, ed. Shams al-Dīn Muḥammad ʿAlī Mujāhidī (Qum: Mu'assisah-yi Maṭbūʿātī Dār al-ʿIlm, 1349/1970), 17–19; *Dīvān-i Āshuftah*, ed. ʿAlī Dād-Ā'īn (Shiraz: Intishārāt-i Kānūn-i Tarbiyat, n.d.), 42.

57. See Paul Losenky's study of the Indian Style in Persian poetry (below, ch. 8). While it is true that the editors of the dīvāns of classical Persian poets frequently mention several poems which the poet in question imitated and cite examples of later poets emulating various poems of the dīvān at hand, such discussions do not trace the development of the emulated poem (whether it be a simple rhyme or a radīf) over the course of a long period of time, nor do they provide much stylistic analysis. At least two earlier studies do treat the question of *istiqbāl* and *taẓmīn* with reference to specific poems throughout Persian literary history: Muḥammad Jaʿfar Maḥjūb, *Sabk-i khurāsānī dar shiʿr-i fārsī* (Tehran: Sāzimān-i Tarbiyat-i Muʿallim va Taḥqīqāt-i Tarbiyatī, 1345/1966–67), esp. 108ff, 521ff, 624ff; and Ẓiyā al-Dīn Sajjādī, "Sayr-i yik qaṣīdah dar nuh qarn," in *Nāmah-yi Mīnuvī: majmūʿah-yi sī u hasht guftār dar adab va farhang-i īrānī*, ed. Ḥabīb Yaghmā'ī, Īraj Afshār, and Muḥammad Rawshan (Tehran: Chāpkhānah-yi Kāviyān, 1350/1971), 563–588. Cf. the important work of Muḥammad-Riẓā Shafīʿī-Kadkanī on the development of imagery and metaphor, *Ṣuvar-i khayāl dar shiʿr-i fārsī*, 3rd ed. ([Tehran]: Mu'assisah-yi Intishārāt-i Āgāh, 1366/1987). There are, of course, many broader surveys of the development of the styles and genres of Persian poetry, which, though not dealing with the question of *istiqbāl* in specific terms, nevertheless cover sanguine ground. See Alessandro Bausani, *La letteratura persiana* (Florence: G. C. Sansoni and Milan: Edizioni Accademia, 1968); Ehsan Yarshater, ed., *Persian Literature* (New York: Bibliotheca Persica, 1988); Jerome W. Clinton, *The Divan of Manūchihrī Dāmghānī: A Critical Study* (Minneapolis: Bibliotheca Islamica, 1972); Julie Scott Meisami, *Medieval Persian Court Poetry* (Princeton: Princeton University Press, 1987); and, of course, the monumental multivolume work of Ẕ. Ṣafā, *Tārīkh-i adabiyyāt dar Īrān* (cited above, n. 22). An article by Mattitiahu Peled entitled "On the Concept of Literary Influence in Classical Arabic Criticism" came to my attention after the present chapter was already written. See Sasson Somekh, ed., *Studies in Medieval Arabic and Hebrew Poetics* (Leiden: E. J. Brill, 1991).

58. See the introduction to Maḥjūb, *Sabk-i khurāsānī*, esp. 37–43. For prose styles and trends, see Muḥammad Taqī Bahār (Malik al-Shuʿarā'), *Sabk shināsī*, 3 vols. (Tehran: Chāpkhānah-yi Khvudkār, 1321/1942).

59. Although this chapter has focused on the formulaic deployment of the fire-and-water theme as a refrain in Persian poetry, it would be most illuminating to examine and catalogue the development of the metaphors and imagery based upon the structural opposition of these two elements—the burning heart and teary eyes, the flaming body dripping wax like a candle, the flaming sword of the ruler's justice and the boundless ocean of his liberality—in the epic and romantic *maṣnavīs* (narrative poems in rhymed couplets) as well as in panegyric, occasional, and lyric poetry.

60. Sabine G. MacCormack explains the ceremonial role of art and poetry in the rituals of adventus, consecratio and accession of the ruler in the Roman and Byzantine context. See *Art and Ceremony in Late Antiquity* (Berkeley: University of California Press, 1981). The ritual function of Arabic poetry has been described by Suzanne Pinckney Stetkevych above, ch. 1, and in her previous articles, especially "The Rithā' of Ta'abbaṭa Sharran: A Study of Blood-Vengeance in Early Arabic Poetry," *Journal of Semitic Studies* 31, no. 1 (1986): 27–45 and "al-Qaṣīdah al-ʿarabīyah wa ṭuqūs al-ʿubūr: dirāsah fī al-bunyah al-namūdhajīyah," *Majallat Majmaʿ al-Lughah al-ʿArabīyah bi-Dimashq* 60, no. 1 (1985): 55–85. See further Suzanne Pinckney Stetkevych, *The Mute Immortals Speak: Pre-Islamic Poetry and the Poetics of Ritual* (Ithaca: Cornell University Press, 1993).

61. See Glending Olson, *Literature as Recreation in the Later Middle Ages* (Ithaca: Cornell University Press, 1982); and Glending Olson, "Toward a Poetics of the Late Medieval Court Lyric," in *Vernacular Poetics in the Middle Ages*, ed. Lois Ebin (Kalamazoo: Medieval Institute Publications, 1984), 227–248). The latter article points out that "late medieval lyrics are more a manifestation of manners, broadly taken, than of literary inspiration" (238) and draws a parallel to the formulaic popular songs of the twentieth century (242–43).

62. It was Trotsky who pointed out: "Artistic creation is always a complicated turning inside out of old forms, under the influence of new stimuli which originate outside of art. In this larger sense of the word, art is a handmaiden. It is not a disembodied element feeding on itself, but a function of social man indissolubly tied to his life and environment" (*Literature and Revolution* [Ann Arbor: University of Michigan Press, 1960], 179). However, in fairness, I feel obliged to point out that Marx, already in 1852, had proposed in *The Eighteenth Brumaire of Louis Bonaparte* that the accumulation of political history is oppressive to the activist in a way that neatly presages the arguments of Bate and Bloom with regard to literary history and the poet: "Men make their own history, but they do not make it just as they please; they do not make it under circumtances chosen by themselves, but under circumstances directly found, given and transmitted from the past. The tradition of all the dead generations weighs like a nightmare on the brain of the living. And just when they seem engaged in revolutionising themselves and things, in creating something entirely new, precisely in such epochs of revolutionary crisis they anxiously conjure up the spirits of the past to their service and borrow from them names, battle slogans and costumes in order to present the new scene of world history in this time-honored disguise and this borrowed language" (quoted in *The Marx-Engels Reader*, ed. Robert C. Tucker [New York: W. W. Norton, 1972], 437).

63. Admittedly, Bloom does allow that, in an earlier period of literary history, poets may not have operated on the same principles he describes. Thus, in Harold Bloom, *The Anxiety of Influence: A Theory of Poetry* (London and New York: Oxford University Press, 1973) he states: "So Ben Jonson has no anxiety as to imitation, for to him (refreshingly) art is hard work. But the shadow fell, and with the post-Enlightenment passion for Genius and the Sublime, there came anxiety too, for art was beyond hard work" (27). Yet his theory of poetry (note the subtitle does not stipulate "a theory of post-Enlightenment English poetry") is predicated on the universal "truths" of Freudian psychology and, if

this is so, should presumably describe the creative, poetic process of the pre- just as well as the post-Enlightenment. Bloom seems to make subconsciously just such a claim in *A Map of Misreading* (Oxford: Oxford University Press, 1975): "To the poet-in-a-poet, a poem is always the other man, the precursor, and so a poem is always a person, always the father of one's Second Birth. To live, the poet must misinterpret the father, by the crucial act of misprision, which is the re-writing of the father" (19). And, indeed, he postulates that modern English poets can be mired down by the ancient but no less invidious influence of classical Greek poetry, when he speaks of the "belated realization that the modern crisis-ode descends, however remotely, from Pindar's epinician or victory odes, so that Hart Crane spoke truly when he saw himself as the Pindar of the Machine Age . . ." (*Agon: Towards a Theory of Revisionism* [Oxford: Oxford University Press, 1982], 239). Bloom, it is true, does caution us against equating influence with style: "Poets need not look like their fathers, and the anxiety of influence more frequently than not is quite distinct from the anxiety of style. Since poetic influence is necessarily misprision [!], a taking or doing amiss of one's burden, it is to be expected that such a process of malformation and misinterpretation will, at the very least, produce deviations in style between strong poets" (*Map of Misreading*, 20). Yet Bloom is able to speak of influence and poetic repression in terms of the echoes of specific phrases, or in other words the repetition of patterns of thought or speech, which are usually closely associated with questions of style: "Poetic crisis—the occasion of strong Post-Enlightenment poems—is always a crisis in which a quotation or quotations from another poem or poems are being repressed. The overcoming of crisis—in a poem—is never a true overcoming but is always an out-talking of a rival poem. This hyperbolical out- or over-talking achieves what Longinus called elevation or the Sublime . . ."(*Agon*, 239–240).

Though it is clear that I am not in complete accord with Bloom, his theory of influence, along with the sober explanations of W. Jackson Bate (*The Burden of the Past*), has the advantage of taking into account the personality of the poet, the relative degree of genius he possesses, and his formative influences in a way that deconstructionist theories of literary discourse do not. I am sure, therefore, that Professor Bloom will not object if I misprise his theories to my own ends.

64. The analogy between the classical sonata structure of Western music and the tripartite structure of the Arabic qaṣīdah has already been made by Jaroslav Stetkevych, whose thinking on this subject has influenced me greatly. See specifically his article "The Arabic Qaṣīdah: From Form and Content to Mood and Meaning," *Harvard Ukrainian Studies*, 3/4 (1979–1980):774–85, esp. 779–81. See further Jaroslav Stetkevych, *The Zephyrs of Najd: The Poetics of Nostagia in the Classical Arabic Nasīb* (Chicago: University of Chicago Press, 1993), ch. 1, pt. 2.

65. Edward W. Said, *The World, the Text, and the Critic* (Cambridge: Harvard University Press, 1983), 114.

66. The conservative reliance upon authority within medieval literature has already been explained in detail by Ernst Robert Curtius, *European Literature and the Latin Middle Ages*, trans. Willard R. Trask (New York: Harper and Row, 1963); C. S. Lewis, *The Discarded Image* (Cambridge: Cambridge University Press, 1964); and A. J. Minnis, *Medieval Theory of Authorship*, 2nd ed. (Philadelphia: University of Pennsylvania Press, 1988). As Bloom puts it for all poetry: "Poems . . . are neither about 'subjects' nor about 'themselves.' They are necessarily about other poems . . . " (*Map of Misreading*, 18). Thomas Greene tests Bloom's theory against European poetry of the Renaissance in Thomas M. Greene, *The Light in Troy: Imitation and Discovery in Renaissance Poetry* (New Haven: Yale University Press, 1982), 30–32, 41.

67. Indeed, satire and ridicule can be weapons of last resort in the struggle with a poetic predecessor. This is, of course, but another excuse for covering the same ground as a predecessor, and, though it is in itself great fun, it is often the only way that epigones can wrest any ground at all from preceeding geniuses who have brought a particular style or

form to its apogee. Consider, for example, Sūzanī's taunting manner of doing battle with his predecessors by ridicule and curses, or Abū Isḥāq Shaykh-i Aṭʿimah's culinary spoofs on the poems of Ḥāfiẓ.

68. As Northrop Frye has worded it in Northrop Frye, *The Secular Scripture: A Study of the Structure of Romance* (Cambridge: Harvard University Press, 1976): "The history of literature seems to break down into a series of cultural periods of varying length, each dominated by certain conventions. During these periods, what one distinguished scholar of this university has called the burden of the past increases rapidly in weight and oppressiveness. Writers improve and refine on their predecessors until it seems that no further improvement is possible. Then the conventions wear out, and literature enters a transitional phase where some of the burden of the past is thrown off . . ."(28–29).

69. The paralyzing anxiety that Kamāl al-Dīn Iṣfahānī must have suffered as both the biological and the poetic son of Jamāl al-Dīn is painful to contemplate.

70. As Rene Wellek and Austin Warren phrased it prior to Bloom in Rene Wellek and Austin Warren, *Theory of Literature*, 3rd ed. (New York: Harcourt Brace, 1956): "Originality is usually misconceived in our time as meaning a mere violation of tradition or it is sought for at the wrong place, in the mere material of the work of art, or in its mere scaffolding—the traditional plot, the conventional framework. In earlier periods, there was a sounder understanding of the nature of literary creation, a recognition that the artistic value of a merely original plot or subject-matter was small. The Renaissance and Neo-Classicism rightly ascribed great importance to translating, especially the translating of poetry, and to 'imitation' in the sense in which Pope imitated Horace's satires or Dr. Johnson, Juvenal's" (258–259).

# VIII

# "THE ALLUSIVE FIELD OF DRUNKENNESS"

## THREE SAFAVID-MOGHUL RESPONSES TO A LYRIC BY BĀBĀ FIGHĀNĪ

*Paul E. Losensky*

"If speech were not repeatable, it would have been exhausted":[1] This statement is attributed to the Imam ʿAlī and, like all good epigrams, it says more than its few words would seem to allow. On the linguistic level, it is a commonsense way of expressing the economy of the linguistic system, a principle that forms the cornerstone of modern structuralist and generative linguistics. From a limited number of sounds and a fixed system of rules, speakers of a language are able to form an infinite number of meaningful statements.[2] Language can serve as a means of communication in a constantly changing environment precisely because of systemic patterns of repetition. By placing this citation at the beginning of his discussion of "plagiarisms" or "borrowings" (*al-sariqāt*), the critic Abū Hilāl al-ʿAskarī (d. 1005) implies that something similar is true of literature. On the literary level, this aphorism indicates the central importance of repetitions between literary texts (what is now known as "intertextuality") in medieval Arabic and Persian poetry. Writing in a given genre, drawing on a set stock of images and tropes, alluding to or imitating a previous work, the poet constantly repeats what has been spoken before. These repetitions result from the poet's knowledge of the established standards and models that define literature as a system of signification and give meaning to each individual utterance. To create literature is always in part to repeat the literary past. The critic Ibn Rashīq (d. between 1064 and 1070 C.E.) begins his chapter on literary borrowing with a less aphoristic, but equally pointed statement of the same principle: "Not one of the poets can claim to be free of it."[3]

The repetitions between literary texts are not all of a kind. As a first step, we can broadly distinguish between formulaic or conventional usage and conscious allusion. Faced with a similarity between two texts, we must first decide whether it is an intentional allusion to a specific subtext or "a topos that conventional repetition has removed from the purview of any one author or work."[4] Formulaic or conventional repetitions are most like linguistic utterances: they must be referred to the rules and "vocabulary" of the shared system of literary conventions. A conscious allusion, on the other hand, refers to a specific previous utterance, as when we knowingly quote or paraphrase someone else's words in everyday speech. It is a particular, not a systemic, repetition.

In the evanescent give and take of daily conversation, there is little need to draw this distinction too closely. Although native speakers may be able to produce an unending stream of new sentences, they are under no particular obligation to do so. But the poet is. High value is placed on originality in literary discourse.[5] To some extent, the poet's performance is judged by his ability to give new and unique expression to the literary code and past performances. To create literature is always in part to invent anew. There is no need to expound on the virtue of originality for the modern reader. The Romantic aesthetics of the last two or three centuries have made originality the ultimate literary value. The "illusion of radical originality"[6] devalues all forms of repetition. The very word "imitation" comes to indicate mimicry or a slavish, unimaginative copying. Influences necessarily have a negative normative value and become anxieties, subject to repression.[7] The authority of an earlier work or writer is authoritarian and domineering.[8] Originality is antagonistically opposed to influence and repetition.

In the Arabic and Persian tradition, however, such extreme opposition is only one possibility in a more dynamic dialectical relationship between originality and imitation.[9] The distinction between systemic repetition and conscious allusion is fundamental to medieval Arabic discussions of *sariqāt*, but it is not an easy one to draw. Ibn Rashīq limits the question of plagiarism to the theft (*sarq*) of what is original (*badīʿ*) or out of the ordinary. Most themes, images, and metaphors (*al-maʿānī*) belong equally to all poets, and only a particular turn of phrase or conceit can be an object of intentional borrowing. Ibn Rashīq takes a middle ground between those critics who restrict plagiarism to matters of form and wording and those who extend it to include all later uses of any image or metaphor with an ascertainable source. He also gives ample latitude to *tawārud*, "unintentional coincidences" between two texts resulting from similarity of topic, demands of meter and rhyme, and plain forgetfulness.[10] Distinctions between open and hidden plagiarism and degrees of plagiaristic culpability further compound the difficulty of ascertaining an allusive intent. "Felony plagiarism" of a choice conceit in both wording and content is rare and seldom goes uncaught. If an improvement is made on the model in brevity or elaboration, the theft is not only "justifiable" but also positively laudable. In the most praiseworthy plagiarisms, however, the "thief" leaves no clues behind. If a poet borrows successfully and hides his theft (*ikhfāʾ al-sarq*), all traces of his intention and his original source vanish, and we cross over into a realm "of real and independent *ibtidāʿ*, original invention."[11] As Franklin D. Lewis shows (above, ch. 7), even as distinctive a usage as *ātash u āb* (fire and water) in the *radīf* passes into and out of general usage over the course of a generation or two, and it becomes a tricky matter to separate borrowing from independent creation out of similar materials. In Arabic and Persian poetics and poetry, we must recognize many degrees and kinds of originality and imitation. The line between the two is elusive and shifting, and they are frequently indistinguishable.

These issues can perhaps be better studied outside the tenebrous regions of *sariqāt*, after we have identified an intentional borrowing or allusion (when the source is a well-known sacred or classical text, for example). In these cases, the poet consciously refers to an earlier text and expects his audience to recognize the reference. We must then distinguish broadly "between echoes so brief or peripheral as to be insignificant and a *determinate* subtext that plays a constitutive role in a poem's meaning."[12] The imitating poet decides how thoroughly the subtext will prevade his own poem. Strictly speaking, allusion is restricted to a single topos or line, and whether ornamental or essential to the meaning, it will not affect the overall development of the poem in which it is embedded. Allusions to several subtexts may often be packed into relatively brief passages: these allusive utterances refer, not to the rules of the language as a whole, but simultaneously to a number of previous utterances. In imitation narrowly defined (the *imitatio* of Renaissance literary theory), the entire subtext, or a significant portion of it, serves as a model for the surface text. This form of repetition refers, not to a scattering of previous utterances, but to a previous organized discourse.

Because classical Arabo-Persian literary theory focuses on the individual line, it has few resources to discuss imitation across a long passage or entire work. *Taḍmīn*, the quotation of an entire verse of an earlier poet, is necessarily judged by its placement in the context of the later work and often recalls the overall context of the original.[13] But according to Gustave von Grunebaum, only al-Jurjānī (d. 1078) discusses *imitatio* proper: "By *muʿāraḍah*, al-Jurjānī means the imitation of a passage in point of style with a view to outdoing the predecessor."[14] If later critics did not discuss *muʿāraḍah* in this sense, however, poets regularly practiced *muʿāraḍah* in its more technical meaning: writing a poem in response to an earlier poem in the same meter and rhyme.[15] Examples of this form of *imitatio* can be found throughout the history of Arabic and Persian poetry.[16] By the Safavid-Moghul period, this technique was better known as *istiqbāl* or *tatabbuʿ*, *javāb* or *naẓīrah-gūʾī*.[17] Adopting the rhyme and meter of an earlier poem largely solves the question of allusive intent—*istiqbāl* reveals its intentionality in its formal structure and demands to be read in dialogue with its source. Because the model and response can be compared at a number of points over a long stretch of text, the conscious remaking of the literary past and tradition, revealed fleetingly and elusively in the formula and allusion, emerges in its full complexity in *istiqbāl*. Publicly acknowledging the voice of the other, the poet interprets and evaluates the subtext and its world of meaning in their relationship to his communicative act and the semiotic matrix of his time.[18] Through the practice of *imitatio*, poets and poetry may tell us things about the interaction of originality and imitation that medieval criticism could not.

## A Vocabulary of *Imitatio*

Arabic and Persian contain many words for imitation and *imitatio*. This richly metaphorical vocabulary reflects the complexity of imitation and a diversity of attitudes toward it and helps make up for the lack of an explicit critical terminology. *Taqlīd* is the term that comes closest to conveying the negative connotations of the modern English word "imitation" as mimicry or copying. In its broadest sense, the second-form verbal noun *taqlīd* means to put something around the neck of something or someone else. It is used for putting a rope around an animal's neck, girding someone with a sword belt, or adorning someone with a necklace.[19] Despite this variety of usage, each action indicates the submission and obedience of the receiver to the giver. Much as a slave is adorned with an earring, someone adorned with a collar, necklace, or sword belt is bound and obligated. Physically or figuratively, they are led along on a leash. From this, the meaning of *taqlīd* developed to indicate a blind, unthinking obedience to a dogmatic authority. This term thus metaphorically portrays imitation as an unreflective, undeviating, and even involuntary submission to an authoritarian master. We might speak of the chains, if not the burden, of the past.

*Taqlīd* is used for imitation in its most general sense. *Tatabbuᶜ* is the basic term in Persian for imitation in the technical sense of writing a poem using the same rhyme and meter as an earlier one. We thus find the Safavid poet Ṣā'ib of Tabriz (d. 1670–71) closing one of his imitations of Bābā Fighānī of Shiraz (d. 1519) with this metapoetic advice to himself:

> Ṣā'ib, if you are going to imitate *[tatabbuᶜ]*
> someone's collected works,
> Emulate [*iqtidā*] Fighānī from among
> the firebreathing poets.[20]

Like the first form of this Arabic verb (*tabiᶜa*), the basic sense of the fifth form *tatabbuᶜ* is to follow behind or succeed. However, the fifth form adds two important shades of meaning. First is a reflexive element: in *tatabbuᶜ*, one makes oneself a follower, adding an element of volition and choice to the act of imitation. Further, there is an intensive element added to the root sense; in *tatabbuᶜ*, one follows step by step or with diligence and effort. When applied figuratively to political or doctrinal following, *tatabbuᶜ* has few of the negative connotations of *taqlīd* and rather suggests a loyal, but voluntary, attachment to a particular leader or party. As we say in English, "So-and-so was a follower of such-and-such a school."[21] Thus, Ṣā'ib's decision to imitate Fighānī is dependent on his decision to imitate anyone at all, and he selects Fighānī from among a particular group of poets. Another somewhat more sinister metaphor is tucked away in this word: *tatabbuᶜ* is also used to describe the action of a hunter or pursuer tracking down his prey. Not only is the following in *tatabbu*ᶜ voluntary, it can even be adversarial and predatory.

*Iqtidā* does not have the technical, rhetorical sense of *tatabbu*ᶜ, but it too conveys a sense of active, voluntary following and positive emulation.[22] The eighth verbal form seems to add a connotation of personal volition to a root sense of "to be near": "to be near for one's own advantage." In modern Arabic, one adopts a certain pattern or model of behavior (*iqtadā bihi*).[23] In Persian, *iqtidā* means more generally "to follow" or "to imitate," but something of the Arabic sense remains. As Ṣā'ib's usage shows, one usually follows a certain individual in *iqtidā*, setting him up as a standard—thus the sense of "following" (*iqtidā kardan*) an imam in prayer.[24] In this version of imitation, conscious admiration leads to voluntary emulation.

Even in *iqtidā*, the imitator remains inferior to or dependent on the original. Three other terms commonly associated with imitation, however, put the two poets on an equal footing. *Mushā*ᶜ*arah*, *musābaqah*, and *mu*ᶜ*āraḍah* are all Arabic third-form verbal nouns and implicitly contain the idea of competition and rivalry. *Mushā*ᶜ*arah* etymologically means "to address poetry to a rival," and in practice, it indicates two poets facing off in a poetic duel.[25] Such contests frequently took the form of competing poems written in the same meter and rhyme (*mu*ᶜ*āraḍah* or *tattabu*ᶜ). This sense of rivalry and opposition is also present in the Persian expression *musābaqah-'i adabī*, "literary competition or match." In Safavid-Moghul times, competing poets usually composed rival imitations of a single model poem.[26] Both these terms show the importance of the practice of *imitatio* in establishing the poet's talent, reputation, and identity.

Von Grunebaum translates *mu*ᶜ*āraḍah* as "matching," but this is a rather remote sense. The basic meaning of *mu*ᶜ*āraḍah* is "to face another." Like *mushā*ᶜ*arah* and *musābaqah*, *mu*ᶜ*āraḍah* (*bi'l-khilāf*, "in disagreement") conveys a sense of rivalry and antagonism, without superiority or priority belonging inherently to one party or the other. Two rival poets "face each other down." But there is an inherent ambiguity to this word. *Mu*ᶜ*āraḍah bi'l-withāq* ("facing in agreement") has a meaning more like *iqtidā*: one contends or vies with others in order to emulate or be more like them.[27] One strives to "face up" to the expectations or standards of an admired authority or model. In this ambivalence, *mu*ᶜ*āraḍah* conveys the attitude of a "generous rivalry"[28] that characterized *imitatio* in the Classical and Renaissance West: "To imitate in the true sense is to assimilate and remake in a spirit of admiration that inevitably shades over into active emulation and rivalry."[29]

*Naẓīrah-gū'ī* is compounded of the Arabic adjective *naẓīr* ("similar, like") and the present stem of the Persian verb *guftan* ("to say"). "Speaking the similar" is the most abstract and neutral term in this vocabulary. There are no indications of how or to what extent the two poems resemble one another, and *guftan* simply indicates that the resemblance is verbal. *Javāb-gū'ī*, another Arabic-Persian compound, introduces ideas of debate and inquiry to our concept of imitation. In "speaking in reply," the model poem becomes a question that calls for an answer or a problem that demands solution. The model does not lead to a battle for dominance and priority, but rather challenges understanding. The imitation is the considered reply and interpretative response to the problem presented by the original. Instead of an antagonistic opposition, we now have the image of a careful and reasoned debate across time. Moreover, *javāb* implies that if the model has the advantage of priority, the reply at least has the advantage of contemporaneity. The respondent has the latest, if not the last, word.

Perhaps the most frequent Persian word for *imitatio* in its technical sense is *istiqbāl*, and it offers yet another kind of interpersonal contact as a model for the relationship between the original and its imitation.[30] Etymologically, this Arabic tenth-form verbal noun means something like "seeking or demanding a friendly reception or greeting." It denotes a complex social ritual—as esteemed visitors approach a city, their host goes out to greet them on neutral ground outside the city and then ushers them in with all due pomp and respect. In going forth, the host implicitly acknowledges the status of his visitor and takes on the duties of hospitality, but at the same time, obtains the host's prerogatives and places his visitor under obligation to him. *Istiqbāl* presents the act of imitation as a form of social exchange. The imitator takes the initiative, but acknowledges the power of the original in receiving it. Bringing it back to his own poetic world, the host takes charge. Ultimately, the original is made to feel "at home" in its new surroundings, and the host legitimately acquires some of the dignity and honor that belongs to his visitor. *Istiqbāl* suggests a dialectical give and take between reception and revision, between the demands of the literary tradition and individual poetic intention.

The metaphors implied in *taqlīd* and *istiqbāl* could hardly be more dissimilar. As this wide range of figurative vocabulary indicates, *imitatio* is a multifaceted, complex act that requires careful and unprejudiced study. Only *taqlīd* presents the past as a coercive authority and burden; the past is otherwise regarded as a guide or a mentor, a friendly rival or guest. All these interpretative attitudes are found among Persian poets of the Safavid-Moghul period. Although these poets of the sixteenth and seventeenth centuries ascribed great value to the originality of their work, they were all vigorous practitioners of *istiqbāl*. The means and desire for innovation were found in imitation.

## Originality and Imitation in Ṣā'ib's Signature Verses

The demand for the new is often considered the defining feature of Safavid-Moghul poetics. In their quest for innovation, poets of this period introduced new vocabulary and imagery and invented unprecedented metaphors and intricate conceits, creating the distinctive style commonly known as the Indian.[31] The most famous lyric poet of the seventeenth century, Ṣā'ib of Tabriz, often boasts of his *shīvah-'i tāzah*, his "fresh style":

Writers consider me the master, for
from meanings and words
I have brought out the fresh style, not
the ancient manner.[32]

Other poets jealously guard the salient subtlety (*nuktah-'i bar jastah*) of their verse or take pride in their new tropes and images (*maʿnī-i jadīd*).[33] Even among those who invent fresh conceits and metaphors, however, Ṣā'ib considers the power of his imagination to be unique:

Among all those with fresh imaginations, Ṣā'ib's
imagination
with its delicate images stands out
like a lock of hair across a cheek.[34]

The key adjective *tāzah*, "fresh" or "new," often appears elsewhere in the concluding signature line (*takhalluṣ*) of Ṣā'ib's lyric poems (ghazals), when Ṣā'ib steps back to appraise his poetry. The fresh is not something that can be added as an afterthought. It is the constant, informing quality of Ṣā'ib's entire poetic output, as his perceptive listener observes:

Ṣā'ib, all your poetry is unmixed and fresh [*tāzah*].
One cannot create this kind of verses bit by bit.[35]

Infused with freshness, Ṣā'ib's poems shine with an effluent, effulgent creativity that rivals the sun:

From the effluence [*fayẓ*] of this fresh-faced
[*tāzah-rū*] poem, Ṣā'ib,
once again our luminous genius laughs at the sun.[36]

Ṣā'ib's creative light is refracted through his ghazals and fills the artistic heavens with a primal brilliance. In *tāzah-gū'ī*, "speaking the new," Ṣā'ib confronts the very source of creative light.

In this aesthetics of the new, there would seem to be little place for the confrontation with an earlier work that we find in *muʿāraḍah* or *istiqbāl*. Repetition is the domain of novices and neophytes:

He has given repetition over to the parrot who has just
learned to speak—
Ṣā'ib has gone beyond repeated speech.[37]

Compared to Ibn Rashīq, Ṣā'ib has a strict interpretation of plagiarism. He will not allow himself to borrow either words or tropes:

Friends strive after newness in wording.
Ṣā'ib strives after unfamiliar [*bīgānah*] meaning.[38]

In lines such as these, Ṣā'ib's emphasis on originality is almost modernist in its insistence. *Bīgānah* ("unfamiliar, strange") suggests the Russian formalist concept of "making it strange" (*ostranenie*), according to which the power of poetry resides in its ability to disrupt our normal perceptions of literature, language, and reality.[39] Similar notions have often served to justify the experiments of the literary avant-garde, from the *badīʿ* ("original, unprecedented") style of Arabic *belles lettres* in the ninth to tenth centuries to William Carlos Williams' injunction to "make it new" in the twentieth.[40] The power of poetry resides in its ability to disrupt our normal perceptions of literature, language, and reality. As the strange becomes the ordinary with the passage of time, as the exception becomes the rule, poetry must undergo constant innovation to remain vital and fresh:

Poetry has a liking for being difficult to please, Ṣā'ib,
for although the terrain is difficult, it is new [*tāzah*].[41]

In their search for the original, Ṣā'ib and other Safavid-Moghul poets often made use of the difficult, strange, and unexpected. The subtle manipulation of conceits, the delicate play of wit, and the often involuted language for which the Indian style is known all result from this quest for the new.

But for the Persian poet of the sixteenth and seventeenth centuries, the path to the new went by way of the old. Ṣā'ib, the proponent and master of *tāzah-gū'ī* ("speaking the new"), was also an active praticioner of *naẓīrah-gū'ī* ("speaking the similar"). His collected works contain literally hundreds of ghazals that respond in the same meter and rhyme to poems by dozens of his contemporaries and predecessors. These references span the history of the ghazal, from Sanā'ī and ʿAṭṭār before the Mongol invasions, through Saʿdī, Mawlānā Rūmī, Ḥāfiẓ, and Fighānī in the Mongol and Timurid periods, to his immediate predecessors Naẓīrī, Shāpūr, ʿUrfī, and Ṭālib.[42] Ṣā'ib often identifies his specific model using the compound verb *javāb guftan*—"Ṣā'ib, this is a response to that ghazal of so-and-so"—followed by a quotation (*taẓmīn*) of the first hemistich of the model. Ṣā'ib intends for his response to be read in dialogue with its model and expects the reader or listener to evaluate it in these terms. He invites his audience to behold the transformation of old into new before its very eyes.

Ṣā'ib is representative of Safavid-Moghul poets generally. Narrative poets looked back to the *khamsah* of Niẓāmī for their models. Fayẓī (d. 1595–96) and Zulālī (d. 1614–15) are only the most notable of the *tāzah-gūyān* who attempted to write responses to all five of Niẓāmī's romances.[43] Qaṣīdah writers replied to the works of Anvarī and Khāqānī. In the ghazal, later lyric poets looked back to Ḥāfiẓ to sanction their cultivation of *istiqbāl*—his works contain some 40 replies to Saʿdī, as well as numerous responses to other poets such as Amīr Khusraw, Awḥadī, and Khvājū of Kirman.[44] By the end of the Timurid period,

Ḥāfiẓ had replaced Saʿdī as the most popular model. The lyrics composed in the Timurid period, between the death of Ḥāfiẓ in 1390 and that of Bābā Fighānī in 1519, in turn, became among the favorite models of Safavid-Moghul poets. To take only Fighānī as an example: Ṣā'ib's works contain well over 125 replies to poems by Fighānī, and the same is true of the works of Shāpūr of Tehran (d. ca. 1616). Naẓīrī of Nishapur (d. 1612–13) and ʿUrfī of Shiraz (d. 1590–91) composed about half this number. Fighānī was a particular favorite at the court of the Safavid Shāh ʿAbbās. His poet laureate Shānī Takallū (d. 1614) wrote well over 200 responses to Fighānī, and when the biographer Fakhr al-Zamān Qazvīnī met the young poet Rukn al-Dīn Masīḥ (one of Ṣā'ib's teachers, d. 1655–56), he was busy composing a poem-by-poem reply to the works of Bābā Fighānī at the request of Shāh ʿAbbās.[45]

In the previous section, we heard Ṣā'ib call upon himself to emulate Fighānī and imitate his works. Ṣā'ib looks not simply to Fighānī's technical skills, but to his creation of a distinctive tone and voice. He judges Fighānī the best of the "firebreathers" and chooses him as a worthy master in the language and portrayal of intense passion. On another occasion, Ṣā'ib turns to Ḥāfiẓ as his master in eloquence:

> From among the melodious nightingales of this meadow, Ṣā'ib,
> be the disciple of the song of the melodious Ḥāfiẓ.[46]

Ṣā'ib's emulation of Mawlānā Rūmī goes beyond literary concerns and becomes a spiritual discipleship:

> Since he emulated [*iqtidā*] Mawlavī,
> Ṣā'ib's poetry is entirely gnosis.[47]

Each of these poets has his particular value as an object of emulation and imitation. Ṣā'ib selects and evaluates his models carefully and conscientiously, according to his needs in the present. He culls elements from a variety of sources to create his poetic voice and vision. Ṣā'ib in effect writes his own version of the history of Persian lyric poetry (with Sanā'ī and Rūmī as its great masters) and situates himself in that tradition.

As Ṣā'ib defined himself in relation to his predecessors, he also defined himself in relation to his contemporaries. In the social practice of poetry in the Safavid-Moghul period, *istiqbāl* was a frequent focus of the literary salon or *majlis* and an important way for the poet to establish his literary credentials among his peers.[48] "Imitation on demand" no doubt required tasks the scrupulous imitator would rather avoid:

> Ṣā'ib, what can one do about the impositions
> of dear friends?
> Otherwise, to confront Khvājah Ḥāfiẓ would
> have been blindness.[49]

In another signature line, Ṣā'ib allows the person who chose the model to defend him:

> If he was weak in answering the ghazal of Khvājah Ḥafiz,
> the fault's not Ṣa'ib's; the problem is mine.[50]

Success in imitation depended on a discriminating selection, not only among masters, but also among their works. A few masterworks gave little scope to the imitator—there was no possibility of improvement, no room for debate. An imitation could only be derivative or detract from the original. The imitation of such poems is indeed a matter for parrots who have just learned to speak.

Ṣā'ib, however, sometimes has no one to blame but himself for a failed imitation:

> Listen to this poem from Ḥakīm-i Ghaznavī [Sanā'ī]
> —it's enough
> for you to know that Ṣā'ib's speech is stuttering
> compared to his.[51]

Ṣā'ib attempted to meet the challenge of Sanā'ī's original, but was reduced to nervous stammering. He defers to his master and honestly refers the reader to the original. On other occasions, the voice of the past flows out of the poet unconsciously and automatically. Absorbed in the other poet's creation, Ṣā'ib imitates whether he wants to or not:

> From the effluence of Mawlānā Rūmī, Ṣā'ib, this poem
> arose from the tip of my sugar scattering pen
> without being sought.[52]

As a speaker of the new, Ṣā'ib's creative effulgence shines as brightly as the sun itself, but as a reader of the past, Ṣā'ib is overshadowed by the light of Rūmī's work. His poetic voice falls silent as Rūmī takes control of his pen. As a result of long and arduous study, Rūmī lives within Ṣā'ib and speaks through him.

The later poet takes much from his predecessors in terms of form, language, imagery, and ideas. For many poets, this was no doubt enough. Ṣā'ib, however, is after something else. In surrendering to Rūmī, Ṣā'ib soaks in the creative energy of Rūmī's poetry, its inner light. Ṣā'ib elsewhere likens the creative force of the past to the effects of wine:

> He has gotten drunk from the goblet of Ḥāfiẓ of Shiraz.
> Ṣā'ib's words are therefore the wine of Shiraz.[53]

By drinking down the heady wine of Ḥāfiẓ, Ṣā'ib is able to absorb its intoxicating essence and transform it into his poetry. Similarly, Ṣā'ib appeals to Fighānī, not as a past literary master, but as a guiding spirit that helps the poet reach the pinnacle of his art:

> Whoever sought aid, Ṣā'ib, from the spirit of Fighānī
> became a leader of the lords of poetry in a short time.[54]

Ṣā'ib is attempting to recover from the past work, not simply a style or manner, but the creative spirit that inspired it. The first step in imitation is an immersion in the work of the predecessor, a reading that captures its vital and informing principles.

The exchange of *istiqbāl*, however, demands that the poet give something back. What Ṣā'ib returns to the tradition is precisely the freshness and newness in which he and his colleagues take such pride. The formative originality of past works is slowly lost from view as they become part of the classical canon; their creative urgency is dampened by successive rereadings and interpretations. Persian poets of the sixteenth and seventeenth centuries could not be content simply to parrot the past or repeat it wholesale. This was to push tradition into cliché. In order to preserve the creative power of the tradition, they had to evaluate, revise, and re-create it. Ṣā'ib shows proper respect by lighting candles in Fighānī's memory from the candle of his own heart:

> With this poem, Ṣā'ib, which is the candle of my heart,
> I have lit candles on the grave of Fighānī.[55]

Only by answering the challenge of the past to fresh creation and innovation can Ṣā'ib succeed in reviving the spirits of the dead and revitalizing poetry:

> Ṣā'ib sought aid from Khvājah [Ḥāfiẓ] in this fresh poem,
> who did the work of Christ in bringing poetry
> back to life.[56]

On occasion, the phantoms of the past come to visit Ṣā'ib, and past and present masters pay tribute to one another:

> In this ghazal you've caught the eye of the Khvājah, Ṣā'ib.
> Pour wine in the goblet to the spirit of Ḥāfiẓ of Shiraz.[57]

As Ḥāfiẓ's shade flits through the assembly, Ṣā'ib offers him a drink of a wine that recalls the finest vintages of Shiraz, but that Ṣā'ib has pressed from the new and fresh:

> Ṣā'ib, whoever linked resplendent meaning with fresh words
> poured the wine of Shiraz in the bottles of Shiraz.[58]

New wine in new bottles—the image points first of all to a perfect matching of innovative meanings and original words. This newly bottled wine is nevertheless instilled with the intoxicating spirit that Ṣā'ib tasted at Ḥāfiẓ's goblet and that distinguished all the poetic wines of Shiraz.

This fermentation of old and new is the work of imitation. In adopting the formal rhyme and meter of an earlier poem, the poet acknowledges his debt and pays his respects to his model and its creator. To capture the creative spirit of the poem, however, the poet must speak in his own voice to his own times. The departures from the classical tradition that scholars have so often noted in the Indian style are not a sign of disregard or negligence of the poetic past, but rather a testimony to its continued creative vigor. In the ritual of *istiqbāl*, the honored guest of the past is shown respect by being made at home in the present.

By combining "speaking the new" and "speaking the similar," Ṣā'ib's poetics call into question the commonplace opposition between modern and classical approaches to originality and imitation. Speaking for the moderns, F. W. Galan writes:

> Although there are periods—for instance, classicism—in which artists are pledged to convention, more often—as during periods of romanticism and modernism—the heritage of earlier art, rather than being honored, is exposed, refigured, extended, or violated.[59]

Like their modern counterparts, Persian poets of the sixteenth and seventeenth centuries placed great value in the new and unprecedented and went to great lengths to achieve it, but they differed considerably in their attitude toward the literary past. In the spirit of generous rivalry, we might rewrite Galan's last two clauses: "the heritage of earlier art, in being honored, is interpreted, refigured, extended, or renewed."

## Three Replies to Bābā Fighānī

Contrary to the examples cited above, most of Ṣā'ib's imitations and those of other poets do not end with any overt mention of the model or its author. This was usually unnecessary. The rhyme and meter of a well-known poem would quickly be recognized by the informed Safavid-Moghul audience. It is easy to imagine the host reading the original before a number of imitations were presented in a literary salon. Be that as it may, *istiqbāl* implicitly involves a comparison of two complete poems. Unlike formulaic usage or allusion, *imitatio* intentionally recalls the entire subtext. Whatever we might learn about the variety and motivation of imitation from the vocabulary of *imitatio* and Ṣā'ib's metapoetical comments, we must examine a sequence of response poems to understand how the attitude of generous rivalry and the spirit of reviving the past worked in practice. One sequence of three response poems, however, can only represent certain possibilities across the spectrum of imitation.

As we saw earlier, the works of Bābā Fighānī of Shiraz were especially popular models among Persian poets of the sixteenth and seventeenth centuries. There are several reasons for this. He was accorded all the respect due an old master, but was regarded as the earliest of the moderns, or speakers of the new. Ṣā'ib and other poets and critics prized Fighānī's often intensely passionate lyrics, and the biographers' portrayal of Fighānī as an outcast tavern servant seemed to match this tone perfectly. Fighānī combined simple diction tending toward the colloquial with a subtle play of imagery and conceit, two stylistic features which the Indian style would develop and refine.[60] Finally, whereas the works of Ḥāfiẓ had been objects of imitation for several generations, Fighānī's ghazals were largely untouched and contained many new rhythmic and metrical patterns. Fighānī's distinctive style and voice were a new poetic challenge, and after the 1570s we often find as many as four or five replies to a single ghazal. Among these models is the following poem:

Awaken sleepy eyes, Saqi!
Drink wine
and make sweetmeats
from hearts, purified by blood!

The tulip takes its drunkenness too far,
and the rose is utterly defiled.
Arise and on the chalice of wine
cast the powdered musk!

If there's no sin in drunkenness,
there's no reward either.
There's no such recompense
for an action that's not been commanded.

The wine vessel carries me
beyond reason's whirlpool.
How else could I move easily
over this untraveled course?

What's not in the treasury of both worlds
is in the tavern.
Don't look with contempt
on this worn-out, mud-brick hut!

Zephyr, blow through the dust
of those embittered with separation
and sprinkle this salt
on the hearts of men who lead tranquil lives!

There's no writing
Fighānī's book of pain.
Don't squander lamp soot
on this mean workhouse.[61]

The meter of this poem (*ramal-i muṣamman-i maḥẕūf*) is a common ghazal meter, but Fighānī has combined it with an unusual rhyme scheme, *-ūdah-rā*. The suffix *-rā* is an oblique case marker (typically indicating either the objective or genitive case) and is not infrequently used as the final element in the refrain-like radīf. As a case marker, this suffix can be added only to nouns or noun phrases, but the sound sequence *-ūdah* appears in Persian almost exclusively as the past participial ending of about ten verbs, such as *ālūdan* ("to stain"), *pālūdan* ("to refine"), *farmūdan* ("to command"), and others of this pattern.[62] In order to receive the suffix *-rā*, these past participles must generally be used as adjectival modifiers of a preceding head noun. As a result, the poet's word choice and syntactical options are severely restricted. In spite of its relatively brief length of three syllables, this rhyme scheme is easily recognizable.[63] The mandatory repetition of the rhyme in the opening verse (or *maṭlaʿ*) of the ghazal serves to fix this unusual rhyme scheme in the listener's ear, much as the opening tonic chords and melodic motif of a piece of music establish its key. For a practiced, well-read listener, the use of this rhyme in this meter by a later poet would call to mind Fighānī's original and set up certain expectations in terms of vocabulary, imagery, and theme. The later poet is nevertheless free to fulfill, alter, or thwart these expectations as he chooses in his response.

Besides providing the time and key signatures of the ghazal, Fighānī's opening verse announces the poem's dramatic setting and theme. The speaker summons the *sāqī*, or cupbearer, to awaken his companions for the morning wine, or *ṣabūḥ*. This early morning drinking party is a traditional feature of the Arabo-Persian wine poem: in addition to alleviating the hangover from the previous evening's revelries, the morning draught symbolizes the drinkers' devotion to wine and their freedom from normal, quotidian routine. And this is no ordinary morning draught. The drinkers here are an elect with "hearts, purified by blood," and in an almost sacrificial ritual, these hearts are transformed into the "sweetmeats" (*nuql*) or hors d'oeuvres that accompany the wine. In the second verse (the second stanza in my translation), the natural world of the garden serves as a model for this sacrament of excessive drinking. In their lush, explosive blossoming, the tulip and rose appear to be staggering drinkers with a ruddy bloom on their faces, unfurling a beauty that is both intoxicated and intoxicating. Under the impact of this natural splendor, Fighānī asks the *sāqī* to sprinkle fragrant musk on the wine, so that it will share the flowers' exhilarating combination of color and odor. The correspondence with the tulip is particularly close: the dark-colored musk, as it settles in the red wine, resembles the dark coloring found at the bottom of the tulip's blossom. The rare, rich perfume of the musk also adds to the ritualistic atmosphere of this inebriating assembly. In these opening lines,

Fighānī and his companions, the cupbearer, and the flowers all celebrate a wine ceremony outside normal social restrictions and inhibitions.

In the next three verses (3–5), however, Fighānī considers the meaning of his drinking in terms of the larger realm of social mores and values. He begins with a neutral tone of legalistic, theological ratiocination. His drinking belongs to a value-neutral realm—it is neither a sin nor a virtue. By calling wine drinking "an action that's not been commanded" (*kār-i nā-farmūdah*), Fighānī implies that it belongs to the category of indifferent actions that God has neither ordained nor prohibited. But as Fighānī was well aware, he is fudging the issue considerably. For most Muslims most of the time, wine drinking is a sin pure and simple. Fortunately, wine itself allows Fighānī to sail past "reason's whirlpool" and these shoals of rationalization. Prohibited or not, wine has a unique existential value as a means of making one's way easily along life's unpredictable path. This leads to Fighānī's lofty claim in the first hemistich of verse 5: "What's not in the treasury of both worlds is in the tavern." The benefits of the intoxication of wine can be properly expressed only in negative terms. Its joys surpass the promised rewards of the next world and all the other pleasures of this one, while reducing threats of eternal punishment and social alienation to insignificance. Fighānī here comes close to the mystical intoxication of the Sufis, for whom wine symbolized the complete loss of ego and egotism in the transcendent experience of unity with God. Filled with a sense of his own righteousness, Fighānī turns to those men of the world and orthodox religion who know nothing of this experience and tells them not to be deceived by external appearances. The dilapidated, mud-brick tavern is a locus of spiritual insight that surpasses the ken of reason or doctrine.

However, Fighānī's outspoken defense of the tavern and wine drinking ill fits the ideal transcendence of everyday social and religious norms. The true spiritual adept would hardly care whether he and his tavern were regarded with contempt or not. The tone of the poem changes dramatically in verse 6, as Fighānī's deep-seated bitterness and alienation come to the fore. It is now the speaker who turns away in contempt, no longer speaking to his doubters directly, but instead addressing the Zephyr (*ṣabā*) in an apostrophe. Typically, the Persian poet calls on the east wind as a messenger of tidings of love and affection to a distant beloved. Here, however, Fighānī summons it as an agent of vengeance, transforming the Zephyr to a dusty, plague-ridden wind to strike at the hearts of his complacent, self-satisfied opponents. The joyous drinkers of the opening verses become "those embittered with separation," as the "powdered musk" is transformed first into the dust of the tavern and then into an irritating astringent.

In a final transformation of this particulate imagery, the dark musk becomes the soot (*dūdah*) clinging to the inside of the poet's lamp in the ghazal's final signature verse. Instead of urging the generous expenditure of a precious perfume, Fighānī now counsels against squandering either lamp oil or the ink made from its soot and withdraws sullenly.[64] What began as the description of a joyous, transcendent celebration finally becomes "Fighānī's book of pain" and hardly worth the trouble of recording. The humble tavern and its indescribable riches are seen in a harsher light as a dingy, squalid workhouse (*bayt al-ʿamal*). The intimations of transcendence go flat, as the poem follows the progression of a real-life drinking binge from ecstasy to belligerent defensiveness and finally to a bitter hopelessness and depression.

Safavid-Moghul critics also recognized this tension in Fighānī's poetry between the symbolic potential of wine and the social reality of drinking. In the biographical dictionary *Khulāṣat al-ashʿār va zubdat al-afkār* (completed in 1607–08), Taqī al-Dīn Kāshī expresses this theme in the form of a mock dialogue between Fighānī and "a learned man" (*yak fāẓil*). When questioned about his drinking, Fighānī launches into a quasi-philosophical disquisition, adorned with poetic quotations, on the correspondences between the physical qualities of wine and the spiritual qualities of love. Just as wine is hidden in the depths of the jugs, waiting to be released, so love is concealed in the lover's breast, waiting for an appropriate object of affection; just as love has no definite shape or form, so too wine takes on the shape of its container; and love and wine both flow through every limb and organ of the lover and drinker. Furthermore, wine makes the stingy generous, the base noble, and the cowardly brave and leads to an escape from ego and egotism. Fighānī's learned opponent, however, is not convinced by the poet's self-defense:

> What you said is true, but the utmost generosity of the drinker is spending dinars and the fruit of his nobility is pouring out dirhams and regret, instead of loss of self: the one drunk with love scatters the coin of his life before the beloved in every respect. . . . Also the bravery of drunkards is audacity and recklessness and being devoid of the qualities of fear of God and renunciation, while the courage of lovers is disregarding one's life and risking it in the path of the true beloved [*maʿshūq-i ḥaqīqī*].[65]

Taqī al-Dīn Kāshī leaves no doubt concerning the winner of this debate: "Bābā Fighānī derived no profit from the words of this learned man and asked to be excused from his assembly."[66] In Taqī Kāshī's opinion, Fighānī remained tied to the material world of wine and taverns, in spite of his nobler spiritual aspirations. The ghazal above lends support to Taqī Kāshī's moralizing interpretation of Fighānī's life. Since his passion lacks moral depth, it can only lead to debauchery and despair.

Aside from this ethical exegesis, however, Taqī Kāshī's story illustrates another important point: medieval readers of lyric poetry were aware of a disjunction between the literal and the figurative meanings of the ghazal's standard topoi and were able to distinguish between them. Not all wine was a symbol of mystical ecstasy, and not all the ghazal's lovely young boys and girls were embodiments of divine beauty. Several features of Fighānī's poem make it an inviting and challenging object of imitation—its distinctive rhyme scheme, its modulations in tone, and its exemplary position in Fighānī's *oeuvre*—but it is the gap between the reality and the promise of the ghazal's stock images that sets the theme for the responses to this poem by Shāpūr, Naẓīrī, and Ṣā'ib.[67]

Writing at approximately the same time as Taqī al-Dīn Kāshī, the wealthy and well-connected gentleman-poet Shāpūr of Tehran responded to Fighānī's ghazal with this short poem:

With wailing and lamentation,
I shorten my life, worn with grief,
that I might waken
my sleepy fortune.

Yearning for union is good
for the agitation of the heart,
but it gives no comfort
to my life, worn with grief.

I am tossed to and fro
in a lock of hair,
each strand of which
dishevels a hundred tranquil minds.

I came into being from nothingness
on the shoulders of Fate;
without feet I have traveled
this untraveled path.

The adviser has ordered me
to repent of my love of idols,
but, Shāpūr, there's no relying
on a repentance that's been commanded.[68]

The principle difference between Fighānī's poem and Shāpūr's reply is immediately apparent: Shāpūr has dropped all reference to wine, the dominant topic of Fighānī's poem. Shāpūr seems to have struck out on an entirely independent course, giving little regard to his model except as a formal framework. At first glance, there appears to be little ground for speaking of any meaningful dialogue between subtext and imitation.

From the opening verse, however, Shāpūr establishes his distinctive voice and tonality by selectively repeating and revising elements of Fighānī's ghazal. Thematically, Shāpūr's poem picks up where Fighānī's leaves off. Fighānī ends by dismissing the very act of writing poetry as a senseless waste of time and effort. With the initial phrase *az fighān u nālah*, "with wailing and lamentation," Shāpūr puns on his predecessor's name, as he acknowledges the debilitating effects of his acts of self-expression: his poetry "shortens" or "diminishes" his very life.

He nevertheless holds out the hope that these expressions of despair may have a purgative effect and somehow change his luck for the better. Shāpūr takes both rhyme words in his first verse from Fighānī's ghazal, but gives them a figurative turn. Fighānī's verse 5 uses *farsūdah* in its concrete meaning of "worn away, abraded" to describe the physical appearance of the mud-brick tavern. Shāpūr, however, combines this word with *gham*, "grief, sorrow," and figuratively employs the resulting adjectival compound *gham farsūdah* to describe his life or soul (*jān*). In the second hemistich, Shāpūr clearly refers to his model by repeating Fighānī's opening compound rhyme *khvāb ālūdah* ("sleepy" or, more literally, "stained with sleep"). However, whereas Fighānī uses this adjective literally to describe the eyes of his companions, Shāpūr applies it metaphorically to his fortune or fate (*bakht*). Fighānī's poem begins with a sense of immediacy by setting up a dramatic scene and depicting a speech act within that context. Shāpūr's opening verse, on the other hand, is more reflective and detached. We imagine him talking to himself or directly to his listener and self-consciously meditating on the value and purpose of his utterance.

In verse 2, Shāpūr names the transcendent goal that Fighānī hints at in his fifth verse: union (*vaṣl*) with the divine or true beloved. This "yearning for union" takes Fighānī to the taverns, where he ends up bitter and dejected. Shāpūr describes his disillusionment more abstractly: yearning for union is a hollow comfort—while it can temporarily calm "the agitation of the heart" with its promise of a permanent stasis and fulfillment, it ultimately does nothing to alleviate the poet's more profound dissatisfaction and sorrow. With an economy of means typical of all his work, Shāpūr drives home this feeling of gnawing, exhausting grief by repeating the entire rhyming noun phrase from the first hemistich: "my life [or "soul"], worn with grief" (*jān-i gham farsūdah-rā*). Compared with Fighānī's urgent, imperative tone and active imagery, Shāpūr's quiet lamentation is eloquently understated and relies on a simple and dignified language for its poetic effect.

Trying to fulfill his yearning for union, Shāpūr substitutes worldly love for Fighānī's wine. "A lock of hair" in verse 3 stands metonymically for the "idols" of the poem's final verse, the beautiful young men and women that arouse an agonized longing in the poet's soul in the here and now. This is the grief that wears away at the core of his being. In other contexts, this lock of hair might well symbolize the mystic's eternal beloved, but verse 4 makes clear that we are here dealing with a concrete, physical object that has symbolic value primarily in this world. The dishevelment of the beloved's hair represents not only the dishevelment of the poet's mind but also the directionless course of his life. As in Omar Khayyam's quatrains, life is here portrayed as an absurd, purposeless voyage out of nothingness and ultimately into nothingness. Shāpūr is subject to the dictates of a capricious, unknowable Fate. The ideal of a teleological goal of union is a comforting, but deceptive, illusion. Although Shāpūr travels "without feet," there is no feeling that he does so "easily," as Fighānī does (v. 4). There is no stable, final goal beyond the ever shifting forms of the beloved's tresses.

In the final verse, Shāpūr picks up the rhyme of Fighānī's verse 3 (*farmūdah*, without the negative prefix) to introduce the teachings of orthodox, conventional reason. Shāpūr knows that the desires that eat away at his soul are no more than a "love of idols," but he is nevertheless unable to give them up. While the enlightened mystic lover might be able to see the face of the true beloved in these multifarious manifestations, Shāpūr is not convinced that any ultimate reality informs the alluring idols of this world, and a forced conversion would be both unreliable and invalid. In the end, Fighānī was betrayed by the transcendental symbolism of wine, and this betrayal led to an angry and bitter despair. For his part, Shāpūr is more conscious of the distance and tension between the beauties of this world and their potential as mystical symbols. This awareness allows Shāpūr to view his grief more objectively and with less bitterness, although he is deprived of even the temporary ecstasy and joy that Fighānī enjoyed. Selectively repeating and revising his model, Shāpūr creates a very different poetic world—courtly love affairs take the place of wine parties—and refigures the underlying tension of Fighānī's poem for a new place and time.

Shāpūr's contemporary Naẓīrī of Nishapur, who made his living at the Moghul courts of India, offers the following reply to Fighānī's poem:

How long will I cloak this body,
worn with grief,
and release to the storm
this handful of powdery dust?

My clustered tears, like grapes,
are knotted within me,
so often have I swallowed
into my heart unpurified blood.

Ears have gone deaf. My "O Lord!
O Lord!"s have done me no good.
There's no opening, it seems,
in this roof smeared with tar.

Khiẕr came up to me at a hundred way stations,
and I didn't know who he was.
Yet again I must set off anew
down this well-traveled path.

Alas, there's no messenger
who's privy to this secret.
How long will I write down my story
on paper and then wash away the soot?

An ill fortune made me
abstain from useful wine.
When I was drinking wine,
I never suffered futile grief.

For my tears of pearl
and straw-yellow pallor,
in a crystal jewel box
the rose keeps powdered amber.

How can I keep those lips from
the allusive field of drunkenness?
Sweetness drips willy-nilly
from candy soaked in water.

When you're sitting with Naẓīrī,
don't listen to his words.
Don't disturb
your tranquil mind.[69]

Naẓīrī begins with the same rhyming compound *gham farsūdah* ("worn with grief") that is found in the first two verses of Shāpūr's poem. But it is Naẓīrī's physical body (*jism*) that is worn away, not his life or soul (*jān*) as in Shāpūr's poem. Naẓīrī's usage is thus much closer to the concrete sense of *farsūdah* found in Fighānī's verse 5. Like Fighānī's adobe tavern, Naẓīrī's body is visibly weathered and worn. The image of the storm in the second hemistich recalls Fighānī's seagoing metaphor of life (v. 4). Unlike Fighānī, Naẓīrī has no ship to carry him on this voyage besides a fleshy container already reduced by sorrow to a handful of dust. Although it is impossible to determine with final certainty exactly when Shāpūr's and Naẓīrī's poems were written or which was written first, Naẓīrī speaks from the perspective of an older, even aged person. The contrast between *jism* and *jān* appears intentional, as Naẓīrī extends the contrast between the literal and the symbolic meaning of the ghazal's imagery to the conflict between body and soul. Unlike Fighānī or Shāpūr, Naẓīrī is initially antagonistic to the physical and material world. His body, the tired manifestation of his immortal soul, is a wearying burden. His soul is doubly obscured, first in the cloak (*khirqah*) that wraps his body and second in the tattered body that envelopes his spirit, and Naẓīrī's anguished rhetorical question asks only for the release of death.

"Grapes" obliquely introduces the wine topos. As indicated by the change in rhyme from *pālūdah* to *nā-pālūdah*, from "purified" to "unpurified," Naẓīrī's second verse stands in direct contrast with Fighānī's opening, sacramental image. The unpurified blood that Naẓīrī swallows is most immediately his bloody tears, which he sheds from his bloodshot eyes only to recycle them back into his body. Traditional metaphors equate bloody tears with wine and wine with the spiritual essence of the grape. This complex metaphor unfolds like this: The soul expresses its anguish in a flood of blood stained tears; these tears become a contaminated wine, which the poet drinks. On their return to the body, the spiritual wine is reembodied in the form of grapes that cluster and press against his heart and further weigh down his soul in its physical prison. Every futile effort of the soul to express its sorrow only compounds this vicious circle of incarnation. In the ceremony of the wine party, Fighānī's cupbearer is called upon to free the pure heart's blood of the drinkers from its bodily substance. Left to his own devices, Naẓīrī's efforts to duplicate this transmutation only add another layer to the scars knotted around his heart. Naẓīrī holds out no hope that he can waken his fortune with his lament.

Just as the tears of Naẓīrī's soul fail to escape the containment of his body, so too his prayers remain trapped and go unheard in the next verse. On the surface, the image is simple enough: by a long-established poetic convention, the sky is called the roof of the world. Here Naẓīrī looks up at a night sky unilluminated by moon or stars—the roof is consequently "smeared with tar" or pitch dark. His prayers are unable to penetrate this unbroken field of darkness to reach God in his heaven. Naẓīrī's use of this conventional image, however, takes on a fuller meaning when we recall that the rhyme word *farsūdah* in the opening hemistich linked Naẓīrī's decrepit body with Fighānī's battered, mud-brick tavern. The memory of Fighānī's tavern and workhouse draws attention to the concrete image of a roof. Homes in the dry and arid climate of southern Iran commonly have a hatchway in the ceiling, which both serves as a chimney and allows the occupants to climb to the roof to catch the cool evening breezes. Lacking this convenient architectural feature, the solid ceiling of Naẓīrī's home conspires with the night sky to prevent his prayers from ascending to God. Sighs and prayers are often likened to smoke, rising from the burning heart. As a result of his appeals to God, Naẓīrī finds himself in a dingy room, filled with choking smoke. This constricted, claustrophobic feeling is consistent with the image of knotted tears in the previous verse. The soul's every effort to vent its emotions, to make its cry heard, only makes its physical prison darker and more oppressive. By carefully echoing the work of his predecessor, Naẓīrī gives a new richness of meaning to the old metaphor of "the world's roof."

Verses 4 and 5 also present images of repeated, futile effort. In contrast to the untraveled course (*rāh-i nā-paymūdah*) of Fighānī's life, Naẓīrī's spiritual journey covers the same ground again and again over a well-traveled path (*rah-i paymūdah*). The legendary guide of lost travelers, Khiẓr has repeatedly stood ready to lead Naẓīrī, but the poet's blindness is such that he failed to recognize him wherever they met. Just as Naẓīrī rides the gale wind in verse 1, so now he wanders in a circle, lost and without direction. In verse 5, Naẓīrī continues to write his story (*ḥāl*), wasting paper, lamp oil, and ink, even though there is no messenger who can be trusted to deliver it. Like his appeals to God, Naẓīrī's poetry is an unanswered call for help, a fruitless effort to be delivered from his self-consuming sorrow. This verse follows its rhyming counterpart in Fighānī's poem (v. 7) more closely in theme and imagery than does any other verse in Naẓīrī's response. This close echo of Fighānī's concluding signature line signals the end of the first half of Naẓīrī's ghazal, a structural division further marked by a repetition of the syntax of the rhetorical question from verse 1.

The sixth verse shows the overall structural strategy of Naẓīrī's response. The theme of wine from the first part of Fighānī's poem becomes the theme of the second movement of Naẓīrī's poem. Naẓīrī looks back wistfully to a time in his life when he, like Fighānī in his opening verses, could escape futile, enervating sorrow in a goblet of wine. Although he was well known among his contemporaries as a teetotaler (no small claim to fame among the poets of the Moghul court), Naẓīrī here blames his abstinence on an ill fortune or plain bad luck (*bakht-i bad*). With its complete lack of figurative language and its straightforward syntax and vocabulary, this line has a tone of simple nostalgia in sharp contrast to the first half of the poem. The repetition of the word *gham* ("grief") from verse 1 just before the final rhyme (*bīhūdah*, "futile, useless") highlights the disparity between a sorrowful present and a joyous past.

The simplicity of verse 6 also serves to set off the exquisite intricacy of the following verse. At first, the sparkling, jewel-encrusted images of verse 7 seem to stand apart from the rest of the poem in a world of their own, completely at odds with the earlier dark images of dust, tar, and soot. The sense of entering another world is enhanced by the initially uncertain referents of Naẓīrī's allusions. "My tears of pearl and straw-yellow pallor" are clear enough as descriptions of the face of the weeping poet, but the precious pearls and light colors utterly transform our impression of the Naẓīrī's suffering. We emerge from the dirty, confining enclosures of the poem's first movement into the dazzling, brightly lit open air. The repetition of the rhyme word from verse 1 reinforces the opposition between the contemptible powdery dust (*khāk-i sūdah*) of Naẓīrī's body and the precious powdered amber (*kahrubā-yi sūdah*). Together with the image of the rose, however, the rhyme word *sūdah* ("powdery") also takes us out of Naẓīrī's ghazal and back to Fighānī's verse 2 and supplies the key to the meaning of Naẓīrī's other images. Naẓīrī is describing Fighānī's chalice of wine (*jām-i sharāb*). The "rose" stands for the palm of the cupbearer's hand. The "crystal jewel box" is the goblet, and the "powdered amber" is the light-colored, white wine. Although images of white wine are not unusual in Arabic poetry, they are rather rare in the Persian tradition, which prefers ruddier vintages. Naẓīrī's choice here, however, is well motivated and effective. The word for amber in Persian, *kahrubā*, literally means "straw robber" because amber's static electrical charge attracts straw. The amber wine thus attracts the poet's "straw-yellow pallor," just as the crystal jewel box is an appropriate container for his pearl-like tears. The white wine and the suffering poet's face are made for one another. The image of the goblet of white wine with bubbles on its surface seems to meld with the image of Naẓīrī's yellow face covered with sparkling tears. This exquisite, composite image continues Naẓīrī's recollection of his happier, wine-drinking days in verse 6. In his nostalgic reverie, Naẓīrī imagines wine as an alluring elixir, ideally suited as a cure for his melancholia.

In the penultimate verse, Naẓīrī steps back and reflects metapoetically on the image he has just created. "The allusive field of drunkenness" (*kināyat-gāh-i mastī*) appeals to Naẓīrī, almost in spite of himself; only by alluding to wine and intoxication can he represent the possibility of transcending the pain and sorrows of the material world. He refers to "those lips" (*ān lab*) as though they were not fully subject to his rational control. After the bleak portrayal of the spirit caught in its fleshy coil with which the poem opened, this sweet vision of wine seems to appear from out of the beyond—*bīkhvud* ("willy-nilly") means literally "without self." The poem ends with this contradiction between the spirit's dark captivity and the glittering vision of escape unresolved. In the closing signature verse, Naẓīrī's listener advises others who might be tempted to listen to Naẓīrī's poetry not to bother. Such verses as his can only upset those who are at ease with themselves and their lives. Naẓīrī does not launch a bitter attack against those with "tranquil minds," as Fighānī does. The self-deprecating irony of this line instead suggests that Naẓīrī is a bit envious of those who are not tormented by the contradictions that he labors over between body and spirit, between reality and transcendental vision.

Naẓīrī reverses the development of Fighānī's poem, beginning with a tone of dark despair and bitterness and ending with a luminous image of wine tinged with transcendence. Naẓīrī first transforms the tension between the symbolic potential of wine and the reality of drinking in Fighānī's ghazal into the more fundamental dilemma of humanity's spiritual exile in the material world. From this new perspective, with the detachment of age and abstinence, Naẓīrī is able to extract the symbolic essence of Fighānī's wine in nostalgic recollection. Remembering Fighānī's wine and the wine of his youth, Naẓīrī catches a glimpse of light in the spirit's dark home. This glimpse is fleeting and perhaps illusory, but it breaks in on Naẓīrī's black mood and suggests to him in the final line that most people have better things to do than wrestle with such vexing questions. Like Shāpūr, Naẓīrī interprets and reimagines the model poem from a new vantage point and responds in his distinctive style and voice. What Shāpūr achieves with brevity and implication, Naẓīrī accomplishes with a dense weave of metaphor and allusion and a careful overall structuring of his response. Both Shāpūr and Naẓīrī demonstrate their generous respect for Fighānī's poem by creating it afresh and extending its language, imagery, and theme to encompass new situations and perspectives.

For the final poem in this sequence, we return to Ṣā'ib of Tabriz. Writing some fifty years after Shāpūr and Naẓīrī, Ṣā'ib was familiar with their work as well as Fighānī's, and he replies simultaneously to all three poems. He does not have the same attitude toward each of his subtexts however. As we saw above, Ṣā'ib was generally a confident and generous imitator of the "ancients" (including Fighānī) and sure of his ability to honor and revive the spirit of past masters in fresh, new creation. Ṣā'ib's feelings are more ambivalent toward his immediate predecessors—the first of the "speakers of the new," ʿUrfī, Naẓīrī, and Ṭālib. These poets had already done much of the work of reviving the past, and Ṣā'ib feels like a "late-comer" when compared with them:

> In poetry, he does not fall short of ʿUrfī and Ṭālib—
> Ṣā'ib's fault is this: that he does not belong to the
> ranks of the predecessors.[70]

This sense of belatedness in turn creates a deep sense of artistic inadequacy:

> Ṣā'ib become like Naẓīrī!? What fancy is this?
> ʿUrfī did not bring poetry to Naẓīrī's level.[71]

When reduced to stammering by a poem by the long-dead Sanā'ī, Ṣā'ib can turn the reader over to the original and move on. Naẓīrī, however, is a more pressing threat—if he has truly succeeded in reviving poetry, in authenticating the tradition in the present, then Ṣā'ib has nothing left to accomplish. Ṣā'ib's reply is thus characterized by a more urgent rivalry than either Shāpūr's or Naẓīrī's, but it is Naẓīrī, not Fighānī, that Ṣā'ib chooses to debate:

> The body tramples underfoot,
> at last, the tranquil heart.
> The robe becomes a shroud
> over the foot that's fallen asleep.
>
> Long hope has no yield but regret.
> How long will you travel,
> again and again,
> this well-traveled path?
>
> Would that he who yearns
> for love's endless path
> could see the heart and hand
> and foot of this worn-out man!
>
> At the least opportunity,
> heaven boxes the ears
> that won't listen and makes
> them hear and obey.
>
> The full moon begs black days
> from the heart of the night,
> now that it's seen
> that musk-smeared face.

When the heart neglects Truth,
it comes to serve the body:
the horse takes the sleepy rider
wherever it wants.

Ṣā'ib, how can I compare
the moon and the sun
with a face ground
into the threshold of humility?[72]

Ṣā'ib begins by making explicit the conflict between the spirit and the physical body that underlies the first half of Naẓīrī's poem. In contrast to the desperation of Naẓīrī's rhetorical question, Ṣā'ib's opening line is austerely objective and didactic. Complacent contentment and spiritual languor result in the final victory of man's earthly and fleeting material substance, a point driven home by the striking image of a man who sits so long that not only does his foot fall asleep, but he becomes one of the living dead. Naẓīrī was willing to let the man with a tranquil mind (*khāṭir-i āsūdah*) off the hook in his final verse, but Ṣā'ib is not so sympathetic and he launches a frontal attack on the false self-satisfaction of the tranquil heart (*dil-i āsūdah*). The rhyme word *āsūdah* ("tranquil") leads through Naẓīrī back to Fighānī. Ṣā'ib revives the aggression and righteousness of Fighānī's sixth verse and directs it against Naẓīrī and, less directly, Shāpūr. *Khvāb ālūdah* ("sleepy, fallen asleep") in Ṣā'ib's second hemistich similarly recalls Fighānī's initial request to the cupbearer to awaken his sleepy companions. Ṣā'ib's poem is a call to wakefulness—it is in effect the astringent salt that Fighānī calls on the Zephyr to deliver. *Gham farsūdah*, the first rhyme in both Shāpūr's and Naẓīrī's poems, gives prominence to the sense of isolation in Fighānī's verse 5 and the grief and weariness of Fighānī's verse 7. Ṣā'ib counters with an interpretation of Fighānī's poem that emphasizes the strong imperatives of Fighānī's verses 1 and 6.

Ṣā'ib's second verse again responds most immediately to Naẓīrī, in particular verse 4. Ṣā'ib critically questions the end and purpose of Naẓīrī's futile, repeated efforts to complete his spiritual journey. "Regret" (*pashīmānī*) indeed accurately characterizes the mood of the entire first half of Naẓīrī's poem. As he accuses Naẓīrī, however, Ṣā'ib also hints at a way that Naẓīrī might have stopped going in circles. *Ṭūl-i amal*, "long hope," punningly suggests its opposite, *ṭūl-i ʿamal*, "long labor" or "effort" (note Fighānī's *bayt al-ʿamal*, v. 7). Ṣā'ib thus dismisses Naẓīrī's vain expectation of a legendary guide such as Khiẕr in favor of a more active, self-initiated spiritual quest. These implications are spelled out explicitly in verse 3. Ṣā'ib displays the scars and callouses that have been inflicted on him by "love's endless path," as though they were badges of honor or signs that distinguish the true spiritual voyager. Love's way is not only endless; it is also filled with genuine physical and mental hardships and dangers. This verse extends Ṣā'ib's critique to include Shāpūr and Fighānī, as well as Naẓīrī. *Ārzū* ("yearning") echoes Shāpūr's second line: From Ṣā'ib's perspective, Shāpūr is naive to think that a yearning for union with the true beloved is "good for the agitation of the heart" and that it will give some consolation to his grief-ridden soul. Exactly the opposite is the case. At the same time, Ṣā'ib rejects the notion in Fighānī's verse 4 that one can "easily" traverse the uncharted course of love. Against all three of his predecessors, Ṣā'ib condemns surrendering the direction of one's life, whether it be to Khiẕr, Fate, or wine.

Ṣā'ib continues his critique of Naẓīrī in verse 4. Naẓīrī's third verse laments the fact that "ears have gone deaf" and that his prayers go unheeded. Ṣā'ib's retort is blunt—it is Naẓīrī's ears that have gone deaf, that refuse to hear heaven's hard lessons, and like a harsh schoolmaster, heaven slaps its recalcitrant student to bring him back to his senses. Up to this point, Ṣā'ib's critique and revision of his models is clear and consistent, in spite of the complexity with which he intertwines echoes of all three. Ṣā'ib carries out Fighānī's commands to the *sāqī* and the Zephyr, stirring all of his predecessors from their lethargy.

A loose associative link connects the personified heaven in verse 4 with "the full moon" in verse 5, but there is little else in the first four verses to prepare for the sudden change of tone and style. The small drama of the moon, the night sky, and the "musk-smeared face" is presented as an independent tableau, without any explicit didactic or explanatory comment. Ṣā'ib's sermonizing voice is temporarily silenced, and both speaker and reader seem to watch this drama unfold from a detached, objectivizing perspective. On catching sight of that "musk-smeared face," so like its own, the full moon is so humbled and disgraced that it calls on darkest "heart of the night" to eclipse it completely and hide its shame from all onlookers. "Black days" (*rūz-i siyāh*) not only paradoxically describes a pitch dark night (reminiscent of Naẓīrī's verse 3) but also implies the moon's humiliation and evil fate. Ṣā'ib leaves the precise referent of "that musk-smeared face" unidentified, allowing the image to unfold its full meaning in dialogue with all three subtexts. The combination of a full moon and a face in a single line indicates the most obvious meaning—"that musk-smeared face" is the archetypal "moon faced" beauty of the ghazal, with strands of dark hair falling across his or her face. Within this sequence of poems, this image calls to mind the lock of hair and the idols of Shāpūr's verses 3 and 5. The rhyme *mushk andūdah* ("smeared with musk") also resonantly echoes the rhyme of Fighānī's verse 2, *mushk-i sūdah* ("powdered musk"). "That musk-smeared face" thus becomes a metaphor for Fighānī's transcendent wine. The wine goblet, too, is often compared to a "two-week-old" or full moon.[73] Whether it is the beloved's face or a goblet of wine (and we will see yet another possibility shortly), an earthly object becomes the envy of the heavens and suggests the lofty spiritual possibilites of the physical world.

Although the goblet of wine is the secondary sense of the image of the "musk-smeared face," it most clearly indicates the significance of the placement of this image in Ṣā'ib's poem as a whole. This goblet recalls, not only Fighānī's musky wine, but also Naẓīrī's image of wine as "powdered amber" (*kahrubā-yi sūdah*). More importantly, Ṣā'ib's verse 5 occupies a structurally analogous position to Naẓīrī's verse 7: in both cases, highly wrought, detached images stand out from their immediate context. The first half of both ghazals is marked by the distinctive voice of a consistent speaker, Ṣā'ib's openly didactic exhortations countering Naẓīrī's self-absorbed meditations. In both poems, their speeches are interrupted by a sudden change in tone and perspective through complex metaphors whose referents (or "tenors") are not explicitly spelled out. Through these structural parallels, Ṣā'ib demonstrates that he, like Naẓīrī, is unable to keep his lips from "the allusive field of drunkenness." Both poets are distracted from their spiritual concerns by physical images of great power and beauty, which in spite of their attachment to this world, suggest a world beyond the here and now. Ṣā'ib's image is primarily one of human beauty, not of wine, but as Shāpūr's poem showed, the beloved's beauty and wine are alike in this series of poems in their uneasy combination of physical and spiritual attractiveness.

In verse 6, Ṣā'ib apparently returns to the moralizing tone of the first four verses. To support his abstract claim about the relationship between heart and body, Ṣā'ib employs the technique of *irsāl-i ma̱sal*, "adducing the example,"[74] citing the adage "the horse carries the sleepy rider wherever it wants." After the high moral tone of verses 1 to 4, Ṣā'ib concludes his sermonette on moral negligence with a homey, understated touch. His criticism here seems especially directed at Shāpūr and his undirected, footloose voyage through life. Ṣā'ib, however, is himself implicated in this charge of sleepy carelessness. In the preceding verse, Ṣā'ib was seduced by an image of physical, material beauty; however briefly, his heart neglected truth, and his line of poetic thought was led astray. Ṣā'ib's morally secure tone is disrupted, as he himself fails to live up to his own severe and perhaps impossible standards. The rhyming compound *khvāb ālūdah* ("sleepy") recalls Ṣā'ib's opening verse. He has softened his attack, no longer condemning the sloth of the living dead, but remonstrating the weary traveler for his drowsiness. The contrast is intentional—what the poem loses in didactic surety, it gains back by revealing a critical self-consciousness and the preacher's all-too-human failings.

This self-questioning is explicit in the final signature verse. Ṣā'ib undermines the basis of the metaphor in line 5. *Khāksārī* ("humility") etymologically means "earthiness," and the elaborate adjectival phrase "ground into the threshold of humility" (*bar āstān-i khāksārī sūdah*) recalls the rhyme in the first verse of Naẓīrī's poem, *khāk-i sūdah* ("powdery dust"). No matter how alluring, human beauty is compounded of mortal clay and is inherently incomparable to the heavenly bodies of the sun and the moon, not to mention higher spiritual entities. The poet too is bound to the earth: however aware he may be of his moral and spiritual duties on a conscious level, the least lapse of attention will draw him back into the transitory, physical realm in search of metaphors and comparisons. Ṣā'ib's final rhetorical question (*kay*, "how") also echoes Naẓīrī's first verse (*tā bi-kay*, "how long"), and this final note of doubt suggests that Ṣā'ib is more sympathetic to Naẓīrī's dilemma than the opening verses would indicate. Ṣā'ib's debate with Naẓīrī, like a good dialectical argument, begins with antithesis and ends with synthesis. On a more general level, Ṣā'ib ends by questioning the whole project of mystical poetry: If the physical and spiritual realms are essentially incomparable, what means does the poet have at his disposal to describe and discuss the ineffable beauties of the true beloved? Perhaps he can only do as Ṣā'ib does in his first four verses—describe the rigors of the spiritual path and admonish its traveler, but leave the final goal unspoken.

Ṣā'ib's final verse also introduces another possible referent for "that musk-smeared face," one that calls into question Ṣā'ib's suitability for carrying out even this limited admonitory function. "A face ground into the threshold of humility" represents the ideal posture of the self-effacing mystic before the majesty and beauty of God. In this context the "musk-smeared face" then becomes the face of the devout spiritual suppliant, of the "worn out man" who speaks in the first half of the poem. The suppliant's devotion transforms the earth on his face into a precious musk, making him the envy of the moon. Pride in pious self-abasement, however, is an obvious contradiction in terms. True humility permits no such self-aggrandizement, and the high moral tone in the opening verses seems tainted by an unjustifiable self-confidence and superiority. In falling victim to both sensuality and vanity, Ṣā'ib is no more than another sleepy rider, in spite of his lofty ideals.

Ṣā'ib's sweeping critique of his predecessors in the first four verses is thus turned by the self-directed irony of the last three verses into an unresolved meditation on the same problem that confronted them: What is the relationship between the substantial joys and beauties of the physical world and their potential significance in the spiritual realm? Ṣā'ib opens a sharp and acrimonious debate with Naẓīrī, obeying Fighānī's injunction to sprinkle salt "on the hearts of those who lead tranquil lives." Ṣā'ib rejects Naẓīrī's passive resignation and nostalgia, together with Fighānī's and Shāpūr's attachment to the material world. By this active engagement of his models, Ṣā'ib prepares the ground for the rich ambiguities and implications of the final three verses, where he integrates the troubled spirit of his models into his sterner moral vision. Escaping the allurements of the physical world requires a constant effort and vigilance that is perhaps beyond human capacity and that presents its own snares of vanity and pride.

Each poem in this sequence has a distinct style and poetic effect. The repetition of rhyme and meter makes this distinctiveness all the more conspicuous, as Shāpūr, Naẓīrī, and Ṣā'ib all make Fighānī's work their own, and imitation crosses over into original invention. A full understanding and appreciation of each of these replies depends on our knowledge of Fighānī's poem, but these replies in turn add to our understanding of that poem. Imitation begins with an interpretation of the model from a particular perspective. The model serves as an enabling inspiration, leading the poet to articulate a distinctive voice and vision. The form, imagery, and theme of Fighānī's powerful lyric inspired each of the later poets, without restricting their freedom to refigure, extend, and create their model afresh. Read as a sequence, each poem serves to refine and deepen our appreciation of the others, as the implications and exact shade meaning of each is made clear through contrast and comparison. The themes, imagery, and language of the ghazal were fixed in their essentials by the fifteenth century, and later poets had at their command a rich and precise means of artistic expression and communication. Few things demonstrate the ability of Safavid-Moghul poets to manipulate and revivify the poetic language bequeathed to them more convincingly than the study of *istiqbāl.*

# Notes

1. *Law lā anna al-kalāma yuʿādu la-nafid.* Abū Hilāl al-Ḥasan al-ʿAskarī, *Kitāb al-ṣināʿatayn*, ed. ʿAlī Muḥammad Bijāwī and Muḥammad Abū al-Faḍl Ibrāhīm, 2nd ed. (Cairo: ʿĪsā al-Bābī al-Ḥalabī, 1971), 202.

2. See John Lyons, *Introduction to Theoretical Linguistics* (Cambridge: Cambridge University Press, 1968), 53–54, 139–57.

3. *Lā yaqdiru aḥadun min al-shuʿarā'i an yaddaʿiya al-salāmata min-hu.* Ḥasan Ibn Rashīq al-Qayrawānī, *al-ʿUmdah fī maḥāsin al-shiʿr*, ed. Muḥyī al-Dīn ʿAbd al-Ḥamīd, 5th ed. (Beirut: Dār al-Jīl, 1981), 2:280.

4. Thomas M. Greene, *The Light in Troy: Imitation and Discovery in Renaissance Poetry* (New Haven: Yale University Press, 1982), 50. G. W. Pigman III poses the question somewhat differently: "Does a similarity between text and model result from conscious intention—the application of intellect—or an unconscious process?" ("Version of Imitation in the Renaissance," *Renaissance Quarterly* 30 [1980]: 12).

5. "Only art, exhibiting a low tolerance for repetition, for *derivative* imitation, generates a need for constant reform": F. W. Galan, *Historic Structures: the Prague School Project, 1928–1946* (Austin: University of Texas Press, 1985), 166 (emphasis mine). This "low tolerance for repetition" is characteristic of literary *parole* or performance; the literary *langue*, on the other hand, values repetition much more than everyday speech does: meter, rhyme, formal genres, etc. Literary *parole*, moreover, has a potentially greater effect on the *langue* than the *parole* of ordinary language: a single masterwork can change generic standards more drastically than any utterance can change the rules of language. The unusually dynamic interaction of *langue* and *parole*, a particular quality of the "aesthetic norm," offers a linguistic account of the tension between imitation and originality. See Jan Mukařovský, *Aesthetic Function, Norm and Value as Social Facts*, trans. M. E. Suino, Michigan Slavic Contributions, no. 3 (Ann Arbor: University of Michigan, 1979), 23–59.

6. Louis A. Renza, "Influence," in *Critical Terms for Literary Study*, ed. Frank Lentricchia and Thomas McLaughlin (Chicago: University of Chicago Press, 1990), 192. See also George C. Fiske's classical characterization of "the Romantic Tradition, according to which, like Minerva, the work of art springs fully armed from the head of each creative Jove" (George C. Fiske, *Lucilius and Horace: A Study in the Classical Theory of Imitation*, University of Wisconsin Studies in Language and Literature, no. 7 (Madison: University of Wisconsin, 1920), 28.

7. Göran Hermerén, *Influence in Art and Literature* (Princeton: Princeton University Press, 1975), 126–155. In his analysis of the concept of influence in contemporary criticism, Hermerén finds what he calls "the assumption of inferiority" (149), i.e., the influ-

enced work is assumed to be inferior to the one influencing. At the same time, he takes pains to point out that this is an historical and not a logical assumption. He suggests that an examination of borrowing in pre-Romantic literature would show that "... one should have a less moralistic view of influence: it need not be a fault or a sign of weakness to be influenced by others; and this, in turn, would be to challenge the basically Romantic conception of originality as the supreme value in art" (130–131).

In the writings of Harold Bloom, the assumption of inferiority translates into an Oedipal fear of the father's priority, generating a series of anxious displacements and repressions; see, for example, *The Anxiety of Influence: A Theory of Poetry* (London and New York: Oxford University Press, 1973) and *A Map of Misreading* (New York: Oxford University Press, 1975). Arabic and Persian poetry are not without examples of "anxious influence," but Bloom's underlying premises are generally unsuitable for the study of influence and imitation in this tradition. For more thoroughgoing critiques of Bloom's theory, see Elizabeth W. Bruss, *Beautiful Theories: The Spectacle of Discourse in Contemporary Criticism* (Baltimore: The Johns Hopkins University Press, 1982), 283–362; and Frank Lentricchia, *After the New Criticism* (Chicago: University of Chicago Press, 1980), 319–346.

8. On the pejorative connotations of "authority" in Bloom, see Renza, "Influence," 197.

9. Gustave E. von Grunebaum, "The Concept of Plagiarism in Arabic Theory," *Journal of Near Eastern Studies* 3 (1944): 234: "From all indications it is evident that originality played a very considerable part in the formation of the Arabs' literary judgment. It is no less evident, however, that the Arabic concept of originality, and hence the concept of plagiarism as well, do not coincide with those that have been current in the West for the last three or four centuries." Von Grunebaum, however, does not pursue this issue, and his article ends with a comment that assumes something very like the view "current in the West": "Little wonder that in this atmosphere originality never could displace imitation" (253). This suggests a modern, all-or-nothing idea of originality.

10. Ibid., 238; Ibn Rashīq, *al-ʿUmdah*, 280–294; Ibn Rashīq, *Qurāḍat al-dhahab fī naqd ashʿār al-ʿArab*, ed. al-Shādhilī Būyaḥyā (Tunis: al-Sharikah al-Tūnisīyah lil-Tawzīʿ, 1972), 12–20, 76–101.

11. Von Grunebaum, "Plagiarism," 245.

12. Greene, *Troy*, 50.

13. See Abū Ḥayyān's quotation of Labīd in Th. E. Homerin, "A Bird Ascends the Night: Elegy and Immortality in Islam," *Journal of the American Academy of Religions* 59 (1991): 247–279. *Taḍmīn* (*tażmīn* in Persian pronunciation) highlights not only Abū Ḥayyān's unique bereavement but also the contrast between two social orders. *Taḍmīn* and *muʿāraḍah* (*muʿārażah* in Persian) often overlap, since the quotation of an entire verse requires both poems to have the same meter and rhyme scheme. Ṣā'ib often concludes his imitations with a quotation from the model; see below. Abū Nūwās's use of *taḍmīn* often shades into a broader imitation of the quoted poem and bespeaks his extremely ambivalent attitude toward his literary past. Contrast his quotation of Dhū al-Rummah to his quotation of Jarīr: Abū Nūwās, *Dīwān Abī Nūwās*, ed. Aḥmad ʿAbd al-Majīd al-Ghazālī (Beirut: Dār al-Kitāb al-ʿArabī, 1984), 186, 169.

14. Von Grunebaum, "Plagiarism," 242. The other terms von Grunebaum mentions in this connection are *iḥtidhā'* and *ḥikāyah*.

15. Jabbūr ʿAbd al-Nūr, *al-Muʿjam al-adabī* (Beirut: Dār al-ʿIlm lil-Malāyīn, 1979), s. v. *muʿāraḍah* (254–255).

16. In addition to the examples below, see Stefan Sperl, *Mannerism in Arabic Poetry: A Structural Analysis of Selected Texts* (Cambridge: Cambridge University Press, 1989), 167–171 (al-Buḥturī and Muslim ibn al-Walīd); Thomas Emil Homerin, "Filled with a Burning Desire: Ibn al-Fāriḍ—Poet, Mystic, and Saint (Ph.D. dissertation, University of Chicago, 1987), 149–176 (al-Mutanabbī and Ibn al-Fāriḍ); Margaret Larkin, "Two Ex-

amples of *Rithā'*: A Comparison between Aḥmad Shawqī and al-Mutanabbī," *Journal of Arabic Literature* 16 (1985): 18–39; and Paul Sprachman, "The Comic Works of ʿUbayd-i Zākānī: A Study of Medieval Persian Bawdy, Verbal Aggression, and Satire" (Ph.D. dissertation, University of Chicago, 1981), 87–96 (*istiqbāl* as a form of literary lampoon in Sūzanī and ʿUbayd).

17. Ẕabīḥ Allāh Ṣafā, *Tārīkh-i adabīyāt dar Īrān*, 5 vols. (Tehran: Intishārāt-i Firdaws, 1366/1987–88), 5:549.

18. Greene, *Troy*, 20.

19. Ibn Manẓūr, *Lisān al-ʿArab*, 6 vols. (Cairo: Dār al-Maʿārif, n.d.), s.v. *q-l-d* (5:3717–3718); ʿAlī Akbar Dihkhudā, *Lughat'nāmah*, s.v. *taqlīd*.

20. Mīrzā Muḥammad ʿAlī Ṣā'ib Tabrīzī, *Kullīyāt-i Ṣā'ib-i Tabrīzī*, ed. with intro. Muḥammad ʿAbbāsī, 3rd ed. (Tehran: Nashr-i Tulūʿ, 1364/1985–86), 885. This ghazal replies to Bābā Fighānī, *Dīvān-i ashʿār-i Bābā Fighānī-i Shīrāzī*, ed. Aḥmad Suhaylī Khvānsārī, 2nd ed. (Tehran: Iqbāl, 1353/1964–65), 406–407.

21. Muḥammad Pādshāh Shād in his *Farhang-i Ānand Rāj* gives a more value laden definition of *tatabbuʿ*: it is used when the reply poem is inferior to the original, whereas *tanbīh*, "reproof," is used when the reply is superior, and *javāb* when the reply and the original are equal in quality. This appears to be a lexicographer's rationalization of a shifting and unstable critical vocabulary—as Ṣā'ib's verse suggests, *tatabbuʿ* in its regular usage does not carry any such negative connotation. See Maria Eva Subtelny, "A Taste for the Intricate: The Persian Poetry of the Late Timurid Period," *Zeitschrift der Deutschen Morgenländischen Gesellschaft* 136 (1986): 62n.33.

22. For the sake of consistency, I use the normal Persian pronunciation and spelling of *iqtidā*, which drops the final *hamzah* found in the Arabic verbal noun (*iqtidā'*).

23. *Al-Muʿjam al-wasīṭ*, 2nd ed. (Beirut: Dār al-Amwāj, 1987), s.v. *q-d-w*. This verb is used in Ibn Rashīq, *Qurāḍat*, 63, 88.

24. Dihkhudā, *Lughat'nāmah*, s.v. *iqtidā*. One of the verses Dihkhudā quotes gives a nice twist to this notion of imitation:

> And when we emulated [*iqtidā*] love,
> we became the leader [*muqtadā*] in the world of love.

ʿAṭṭār's pun on the root *q-d-w* suggests how imitation of the right models diligently pursued can turn the imitator into the one imitated.

25. Dihkhudā defines *mushāʿarah kardan* as "to do battle in poetry" (*Lughat'nāmah*). Perhaps the most famous poetic duel in Arabo-Persian literature is the *naqā'iḍ* of the Umayyad poets Jarīr and al-Farazdaq.

26. Zayn al-ʿĀbidīn Mu'taman, *Taḥavvul-i shiʿr-i Fārsī* (Tehran: Kitābfurūshī-yi Muṣṭafavī, 1339/1960), 76–77. *Mushāʿarah* in modern Persian usually indicates a contest of poetic memory: someone quotes a line of verse, and his opponent must quote a verse that begins with the same letter with which the previous verse ended. In Urdu, on the other hand, *mushāʿarah* has retained its original sense and is the name of any collective, public poetry reading.

27. Edward William Lane, *An Arabic English Lexicon* (London: Williams and Norgate, 1865) (photo offset ed., New York: Frederick Unger Publishing Co., 1955), s.v. *ʿ-r-ḍ*; and Dihkhudā, *Lughat'nāmah*, s.v. *muʿāraẓah*.

28. Fiske, *Lucilius and Horace*, 39, 42: "As a result of such aesthetic conceptions it followed that the existence of a great masterpiece which might serve as a model in any given genre, so far from deterring literary aspirants acted as a direct challenge to their powers."

29. Richard S. Peterson, *Imitation and Praise in the Poems of Ben Jonson* (New Haven: Yale University Press, 1981), 6.

30. Dihkhudā, *Lughat'nāmah*, s.v. *istiqbāl*.

31. See Ṣafā, *Tārīkh-i adabīyāt*, 5:543–549; Mu'taman, *Taḥavvul*, 360–363; Ehsan Yar-Shater, "Safavid Literature: Progress or Decline," *Studies on Isfahan, Part I, Iranian Studies* 7 (1974): 229–231.

32. Quoted in Ṣafā, *Tārīkh-i adabīyāt*, 5:547. Ṣā'ib's critical stature as *the* representative poet of the Safavid-Moghul period has perhaps been exaggerated, leading to the neglect of the great variety of poetic styles practiced during the period, but it has resulted in a large number of critical studies of his poetry (although his *dīvān* has only recently been published in its entirety). I here cite only those works that deal at some length with Ṣā'ib's biography: Ṣafā, *Tārīkh-i adabīyāt*, 5:1271–1284; Muḥammad Shiblī Nuʿmānī, *Shiʿr al-ʿAjam*, trans. into Persian M. Taqī Fakhr-i Dāʿī Gīlānī, 5 vols., 2nd ed. (Tehran: Ibn Sīnā, 1335–1339/1956–1960), 3:159–171; Aḥmad Gulchīn-i Maʿānī, *Farhang-i ashʿār-i Ṣā'ib*, 2 vols. (Tehran: Mu'assasah-'i Muṭālaʿāt va Taḥqīqāt-i Farhangī, 1364–1365/1985–1986), 1: *hifdah-chihil va chahār*.

33. Abū al-Fayẕ Fayẕī ibn Mubārak, *Dīvān-i Fayẕī*, ed. I. D. Arshad (Tehran: Intishārāt-i Furūghī 1362/1983), 459; and Ṭālib-i Āmulī, *Kullīyāt-i ashʿār-i Malik al-Shuʿarā Ṭālib-i Āmulī*, ed. Ṭāhirī Shahāb (Tehran: Sanā'ī, [1967?]), 310.

34. Mīrzā Muḥammad ʿAlī Ṣā'ib-i Tabrīzī, *Dīvān-i Ṣā'ib-i Tabrīzī*, ed. Muḥammad Qahramān, 6 vols. (Tehran: ʿIlmī va Farhangī, 1364/1985–1370/1991), 2:845.

35. Ibid., 2:1032.

36. Ibid., 1:320. As suggested by his pen name, Fayẕī develops this Neoplatonic notion of creative effluence (*fayẕ*) from a primal source extensively in his poetry.

37. Ibid., 2:965.

38. Ibid., 4:2022. See also Fayẕī's condemnation of *tavārud* and *taẕmīn*: Ṣafā, *Tarīkh-i adabīyāt*, 5:545.

39. Victor Erlich, *Russian Formalism: History–Doctrine*, 3rd ed. (New Haven: Yale University Press, 1981), 171–180. Safavid-Moghul poetry has attracted the attention of several modern Iranian poets, among them Amīrī Fīrūzkūhī and Shafīʿī Kadkanī.

40. On the *badīʿ*, see Suzanne Pinckney Stetkevych, *Abū Tammām and the Poetics of the ʿAbbasid Age* (Leiden: E. J. Brill, 1991).

41. Ṣā'ib, *Dīvān*, 3:1398. Ṣā'ib seems to pun on a remote meaning of *mushkil-pasandī*, such as "approving of difficulties," in addition to the normal sense of "fastidious, hard to please."

42. For poets not mentioned in a signature verse below, see Ṣā'ib, *Dīvān*, 2:725 (Saʿdī), 4:1601 (Shāpūr), 6:3183 (ʿAṭṭār).

43. Ṣafā, *Tārīkh-i adabīyāt*, 5:838–857, 965–976. Niẓāmī Ganjavī probably died in 1209.

44. The most extensive recent discussions of Ḥāfiẓ's imitations of earlier poets are found in the writings of Bahā' al-Dīn Khurramshāhī; see "Ḥaqq-i Saʿdī bih gardan-i Ḥāfiẓ," *Ẕikr-i jamīl-i Saʿdī*, 3 vols. (Tehran: Idārah-'i Kull-i Intishārāt va Tablīghāt, Vizārat-i Irshād-i Islāmī, 1364/1986), 1:305–334, and *Ḥāfiẓ-nāmah: sharḥ-i alfāẓ, aʿlām, mafāhīm-i kalīdī va abyāt-i dushvār-i Ḥāfiẓ*, 2 vols. (Tehran: Intishārāt-i ʿIlmī va Farhangī, 1367/1988), 1:40–90.

45. ʿAbd al-Nabī Fakhr al-Zamān-i Qazvīnī, *Taẕkirah-'i Maykhānah*, ed. Aḥmad Gulchīn-i Maʿānī (Tehran: Iqbāl, 1340/1961), 496. I will discuss the imitations of Fighānī in greater detail in a forthcoming study of Fighānī's legacy in the Safavid-Moghul period.

46. Ṣā'ib, *Dīvān*, 5:2411.

47. Ibid., 2:1082.

48. See, for example, the account given by Awḥadī-i Balyānī (the author of the *ʿArafāt al-ʿāshiqīn*) of his entrance into the literary circle of Ṭarḥī of Shiraz (Ṣafā, *Tārīkh-i adabīyāt*, 5:515–516) or of his contest with Shānī in Shāh ʿAbbās's presence (*Maktab-i vuqūʿ dar shiʿr-i Fārsī*, ed. Aḥmad Gulchīn-i Maʿānī [Tehran: Bunyād-i Farhang-i Īrān, 1348/1969), 179–180]). For a somewhat earlier example, see Eva Marie Subtelny, "The

Poetic Circle at the Court of the Timurid Sultan Husain Baiqara, and Its Political Significance" (Ph.D. dissertation, Harvard University, 1979), 165–166.

49. Ṣā'ib, *Dīvān*, 4:2126.

50. Quoted in Mu'taman, *Taḥavvul*, 76.

51. Sā'ib, *Dīvān*, 2:533. This feeling of helpless incapacity before the masterworks of the past is found more often in the poetry of Naẓīrī of Nishapur.

52. Ibid., 2:475.

53. Ibid., 2:832.

54. Ibid., 3:1160.

55. Ibid., 1:388.

56. Ibid., 4:1628.

57. Ibid., 6:3077.

58. Ibid., 3:1164. For other uses of the trope of the "Shirazi bottle," see Gulchīn-i Maʿānī, *Farhang*, 2:496.

59. Galan, *Historic Structures*, 166 (summarizing J. Mukařovský).

60. For further discussion of Bābā Fighānī and his poetry, see: In'amul Haqq Kausar, *Fughani's* [sic] *Life and Works* (Karachi: Pakistan Historical Soceity, 1964); ʿAlīriẕā Ẕakāvatī Qarāguzlū, "Baḥṣī dar shiʿr va fikr-i Bābā Fighānī," *Maʿārif* 4 (1366/1987): 495–520; Raẕīyah Akbar, *Sharḥ-i aḥvāl va sabk-i ashʿār-i Bābā Fighānī-i Shīrāzī* (Hyderabad: Shālimār Publīkayshinz, 1974); and Ṣafā, *Tārīkh-i adabīyāt*, 4:411–417.

61. Bābā Fighānī, *Dīvān*, 91. Transcription of the Persian text:

1. *sāqī-yā bīdār gardān chashm-i khvāb ālūdah-rā*
   *bādah nush u nuql kun dil-hā-yi khūn pālūdah-rā*

2. *lālah az ḥad[d] mībarad mastī u gul tar-dāmanī*
   *khīz u dar jām-i sharāb andāz mushk-i sūdah-rā*

3. *gar gunāhī nīst dar mastī ṣavābī nīz nīst*
   *ajr chandānī nabāshad kār-i nā-farmūdah-rā*

4. *kishtī-yi may mībarad az varṭah-'i ʿaql-am burūn*
   *var nah āsān chūn ravam'īn rāh-i nā-paymūdah-rā*

5. *ānchah dar ganj-i du ʿālam nīst dar maykhānah hast*
   *tā bi-khvārī na-ngarī īn kahgil-i farsūdah-rā*

6. *ay ṣabā bu-gẕar bi-khāk-i shūr bakhtān-i firāq*
   *īn namak bar dil biyafshān mardum-i āsūdah-rā*

7. *nāmah-'i dard-i Fighānī qābil-i taḥrīr nīst*
   *bahr-i ān bayt al-ʿamal ẕāyiʿ magardān dūdah-rā.*

62. Only the noun *dūdah* ("smoke" or "soot") and the adjective *bīhūdah* ("useless," "futile") appear in this sequence of poems. All other rhyme words and compounds are past participles.

63. I have been able to find only one ghazal written before Fighānī that uses this particular rhyme scheme. This poem, by Amīr Khusraw Dihlavī, is in the somewhat rare meter *rajaz-i muṣamman-i sālim*; see Amīr Khusraw, *Kullīyāt-i ghazalīyāt-i Khusraw*, ed. Iqbāl Ṣalāḥ al-Dīn, rev. Sayyid Vazīr al-Ḥasan ʿĀbidī, 4 vols. (Lahore: Paykījiz Ltd.,

1972–75), 1:134–135. The question of Amīr Khusraw's influence on Fighānī is complex and outside the scope of this essay. Suffice it to say that Fighānī probably had Amīr Khusraw's poem in the back of his mind, but completely changed its theme and tone. Aside from its sonic qualities, Amīr Khusraw's ghazal has little in common with either Fighānī's poem or any of its imitations.

64. For lamp soot as the raw material of black ink, see Ahmad Y. al-Hasan and Donald Hill, *Islamic Technology: An Illustrated History* (Cambridge: Cambridge University Press, 1986), 172.

65. Taqī al-Dīn Kāshī, "Khulāṣat al-ashʿār va zubdat al-afkār," Sprenger 321 (Berlin: Deutsche Staatsbibliothek), ff. 343b-344a.

66. Ibid., f. 344a.

67. In addition to the three poems I discuss below, two other poems are worth noting. The poet Ghazālī of Mashhad (d. 1572–73) uses the same meter as Fighānī's poem, but makes a radīf of *ālūdah-rā*, preceded by the rhyme syllable *āb*; this was probably inspired by Fighānī's opening rhyme *khvāb ālūdah-rā* ("sleepy"). This poem can be considered a "cousin" of the main line of descent from Fighānī's poem. See Ṣafā, *Tārīkh-i adabīyāt*, 5:709. Ḥakīm Shafāʾī of Isfahan (d. 1627–28) also wrote an imitation of Fighānī's poem, using exactly the same meter and rhyme scheme, that has only recently come to my attention. Shafāʾī's response takes quite a different tack from the three poems discussed in this essay and has been excluded from consideration here. See Ḥakīm Sharaf al-Dīn Ḥasan Shafāʾī Iṣfahānī, *Dīvān-i Ḥakīm Shafāʾī Iṣfahānī*, ed. with intro. and notes Luṭf ʿAlī Banān (Tabrīz: Idārah-'i Kull-i Irshād-i Islāmī-i Āẕarbāyjān-i Sharqī, 1362/1983–84), 261.

68. My translation is based on a collation of four different manuscripts of Shāpūr's works: "Dīvān-i Shāpūr," Supp. 756 (Paris: Bibliothèque Nationale), f. 36a-b; "Dīvān-i Shāpūr," Add. 7816 (London: British Library), f. 13b; "Dīvān-i Shāpūr," Add. 7819 (London: British Library), f. 186a-b, margins; and "Dīvān-i Shāpūr," Nb. 73 (Calcutta: Asiatic Society of Bengal Library), f. 39b. Transcription of the Persian text:

1. *az fighān u nālah kāham jān-i gham farsūdah-rā*
   *tā magar bīdār sāzam bakht-i khvāb ālūdah-rā*

2. *ārzū-yi vaṣl bahr-i iẓṭirāb-i dil khush-ast*
   *garchah taskīnī nabakhshad jān-i gham farsūdah-rā*

3. *dar kham-i zulfī parīshān-am kih har tārī az-ū*
   *dar parīshānī kashad ṣad khāṭir-i āsūdah-rā*

4. *az ʿadam bar dūsh-i qismat āmadam sū-yi vujūd*
   *bī qadam paymūdah-'am īn rāh-i nā-paymūdah-rā*

5. *nāṣiḥ az ʿishq-i butān-am tawbah farmūd-ast līk*
   *nīst Shāpūr iʿtimādī tawbah-'i farmūdah-rā.*

On Shāpūr's biography, see Ṣafā, *Tārīkh-i adabīyāt*, 5:1097–1110; and Ẕabīḥ Allāh Ṣafā, "Khvājah Shāpūr-i Tihrānī va khāndān-i ū," *Īrān-nāmah* 1 (1362/1983): 502–510. I am presently editing Shāpūr's works and preparing a study of his poetry.

69. Naẓīrī Nīshāpūrī, *Dīvān-i Naẓīrī-i Nīshāpūrī*, ed. Maẓāhir Muṣaffā (Tehran: Amīr-i Kabīr, 1340/1961), 22–23. Transcription of the Persian text:

1. *tā bi-kay bar khirqah bandam jism-i gham farsūdah-rā*
*sar bi-ṭūfān mīdiham īn musht-i khāk-i sūdah-rā*

2. *dar darūn hamchūn ᶜanab shud khūshah-'i ashk-am girih*
*bas furū burdam bi-dil khūn-hā-yi nā-pālūdah-rā*

3. *gūsh-hā kar gasht u yā rab[b] yā rab[b]-am kārī nakard*
*nīst gūyā rawzanī īn saqf-i qīr andūdah-rā*

4. *Khiẕr ṣad manzil bi-pīsh-am āmad u na-shnākhtam*
*bāz mībāyad zi sar gīram rah-i paymūdah-rā*

5. *vah kih yak qāṣid kih bāshad muḥrim-i īn rāz nīst*
*chand bar kāghiẕ nivīsam ḥāl u shūyam dūdah-rā*

6. *az sharāb-i sūdmand-am bakht-i bad parhīz dād*
*may kih mīkhurdam namīkhurdam gham-i bīhūdah-rā*

7. *gul zi bahr-i ashk-i lu'lu'ī u rang-i kāhī-yam*
*dar balūrīn ḥuqqah dārad kahrubā-yi sūdah-rā*

8. *az kināyat-gāh-i mastī manᶜ-i ān lab chūn kunam*
*mīchakad bīkhvud ḥalāvat qand-i āb ālūdah-rā*

9. *bā Naẕīrī chūn nishastī gūsh bar ḥarf-ash makun*
*dar parīshānī mayafgan khāṭir-i āsūdah-rā.*

For biographical information on Naẕīrī, see Muṣaffā's introduction to the *Dīvān*; Ṣafā, *Tārīkh-i adabīyāt*, 5:896–916; and Shiblī Nuᶜmānī, *Shiᶜr*, 3:112–137.

70. Ṣā'ib, *Dīvān*, 2:646.

71. Ibid., 1:396.

72. Ibid., 1:105. Transcription of the Persian text:

1. *mīkunad pāmāl tan ākhir dil āsūdah-rā*
*mīshavad dāmān kafan īn pā-yi khvāb ālūdah-rā*

2. *juz pashīmānī nadārad ḥāsilī ṭūl-i amal*
*chand paymāyī mukarrar īn rah-i paymūdah-rā*

3. *ān kih dārad ārzū-yi rāh-i bī-pāyān-i ᶜishq*
*kāsh mīdīd īn dil u dast u qadam farsūdah-rā*

4. *mīkashad dar ḥalqah-'i farmān bih andak furṣatī*
*gūshmāl-i āsmān gūsh-i sukhan na-shnūdah-rā*

5. *az dil-i shab mīkunad daryūzah-'i rūz-i siyāh*
*dīd tā māh-i tamām ān rū-yi mushk andūdah-rā*

6. *dil chu ghāfil shud zi ḥáq[q] farmān-pazīr-i tan shavad*
*mībarad har jā kih khvāhad asb khvāb ālūdah-rā*

7. *kay barābar mīkunam Ṣā'ib bih māh u āftāb*
*chihrah-'i bar āstān-i khāksārī sūdah-rā.*

73. Muḥammad Pādshāh Shād, *Farhang-i mutarādafāt va iṣṭilāḥāt*, ed. Bīzhan Taraqqī, 2nd ed. (Tehran: Kitābfurūshī-i Khayyām, 1346/1967–68), 93, s.v. *payālah-'i sharāb.*

74. This technique is considered characteristic of Ṣā'ib's poetry and the poetry of the Safavid-Moghul period generally, although its use is seldom analyzed in the context of the ghazal as a whole; see Ṣafā, *Tārīkh-i adabīyāt*, 5:540–542; Yar-Shater, "Safavid Literature," 234–236; and Qamar-i Āryān, "Vīzhigīhā va mansha'-i paydāyish-i sabk-i mashhūr bi-Hindī dar sayr-i taḥavvul-i shiʿr-i Fārsī," *Majallah-'i Dānishkadah-'i Adabīyāt va ʿUlūm-i Insānī-i Dānishgāh-i Mashhad* 9 (1352/1973): 280–281.

# NOTES ON THE CONTRIBUTORS

**Hassan El-Banna Ezz El-Din** (Ph.D., Ain Shams University, Cairo) is Assistant Professor of Arabic Literature at Zagazig University in Egypt. He has published a series of review articles and translations on contemporary literary theory in the Egyptian journals *Fuṣūl* and *Alif* and is the author of *Al-Kalimāt wa al-Ashyā'* (Beirut: Dār al-Manāhil, 1989), a study of the *aṭlāl qaṣīdah* in pre-Islamic Arabic poetry, and *Al-Ṭayf wa al-Khayāl fī al-shiʿr al-ʿarabī al-qadīm* 2nd ed. (Cairo: Dār al-Ḥaḍārah, 1993), on the apparition of the beloved in classical Arabic poetry. He has recently published an Arabic translation of Walter J. Ong's *Orality and Literacy* (Kuwait: ʿĀlam al-Maʿrifah, 1993) and is currently working on a monograph on orality and Arabic poetry.

**Th. Emil Homerin** (Ph.D., The University of Chicago) is Assistant Professor in the Department of Religion and Classics at the University of Rochester. Among his articles and reviews on Arabic poetry and Islamic mysticism are "Echoes of a Thirsty Owl: Death and Afterlife in Pre-Islamic Arabic Poetry" (*Journal of Near Eastern Studies*, 1985), "Preaching Poetry: The Forgotten Verse of Ibn al-Shahrazuri" (*Arabica*, 1991), and "A Bird Ascends the Night: Elegy and Immortality in Islam" (*Journal of the American Academy of Religion*, 1991). His recent work on the Arab Sufi poet Ibn al-Fāriḍ will be appearing with the University of South Carolina Press.

**Franklin D. Lewis** is a Ph.D. candidate in Persian literature at The University of Chicago, where he has taught Persian. His publications include translations of modern Persian poems and short stories, and encyclopedia articles on Iranian religion. He has also worked with the resettlement of Iranian refugees in the United States. He is currently completing his doctoral dissertation.

**Paul E. Losensky** has just completed a doctorate in Persian literature at The University of Chicago. He has received Fulbright and Whiting fellowships in support of his dissertation work on imitation and influence in Safavid-Moghul poetry. His published translations from the Persian include "Inshallah Ghurbah ast" (God willing, it's a cat), a poem by ʿAlī Akbar Dihkhudā (*Iranian Studies*, Winter 1986), and "The Wolf" by Hūshang Gulshīrī, "The First Story" by Ghulāmḥusayn Sāʿidī, "Hard Luck" by Maḥmūd Dawlatābādī (with Cyrus Amīr-Mokri), and "The Discreet and Obvious Charms of the Petit Bourgeoisie" by Farīdūn Tunakābunī (all in Heshmat Moayyad, ed., *Stories from Iran: A Chicago Anthology 1921-91*, Mage Publishers, 1991). He will be joining the Near East faculty at Indiana University, Bloomington, as Assistant Professor of Persian Literature in 1994.

**Michael A. Sells** (Ph.D., The University of Chicago) is Associate Professor of Islam and Comparative Religions and Chair of the Religion Department at Haverford College. He is the author of *Desert Tracings: Six Classic Arabian Odes* (Wesleyan University Press, 1989) and *Unsaying: Freedom, Meaning, and Mystical Discourse* (The University of Chicago Press, in press), a study of mystical language in Plotinus, Eriugena, Ibn 'Arabi, Eckhart, and Marguerite Porete. His work on Qur'anic language includes "Sound, Spirit, and Gender in *Surat al-Qadr*" (*Journal of the American Oriental Society*, 111.2) and "Sound and Meaning in *Surat al-Qari'a*" (*Arabica*, in press). He is now completing a volume for the Classics of Western Spirituality Series (*The Foundation Texts of Sufism*) and has received an NEH grant for 1993-94 to complete a book of critical studies on the early Arabic qasida. He lives in Haverford, Pennsylvania, with his wife, Janet, and daughters, Ariela and Maya.

**John Seybold** received his BA in English literature from Columbia College and his MA in Near Eastern Languages and Literatures from The University of Chicago. His graduate studies focused on classical Arabic poetry and the literature of Muslim Spain. Other interests include altered states of consciousness, psychic phenomena, and mystical and occult literature. Currently he works as a technical writer in the Boston area computer industry.

**Jaroslav Stetkevych** (Ph.D., Harvard University) is Professor of Arabic Literature at the University of Chicago. He is the author of *The Modern Arabic Literary Language: Lexical and Stylistic Developments* (The University of Chicago Press, 1970) and *The Zephyrs of Najd: The Poetics of Nostalgia in the Classical Arabic Nasīb* (The University of Chicago Press, 1993). He has published in Spanish, English, and Arabic on both modern and classical Arabic literature. Among his recent studies are "Encounter with the East: The Orientalist Poetry of Ahatanhel Krymskyj" (*Harvard Journal of Ukrainian Studies*, 1985), "Name and Epithet: The Philology and Semiotics of Animal Nomenclature in Early Arabic Poetry" (*Journal of Near Eastern Studies*, 1986), and "Arabic Hermeneutical Terminology: Paradox and the Production of Meaning" (*Journal of Near Eastern Studies*, 1989).

**Suzanne Pinckney Stetkevych** (Ph.D., The University of Chicago) is Associate Professor of Arabic Literature at Indiana University, Bloomington. She has published a series of articles in English and Arabic on pre-Islamic and ʿAbbāsid Arabic poetry and is the author of *Abū Tammām and the Poetics of the ʿAbbāsid Age* (E. J. Brill, 1991) and *The Mute Immortals Speak: Pre-Islamic Poetry and the Poetics of Ritual* (Cornell University Press, Myth and Poetics Series, 1993). Her current research on poetic creativity versus Qur'ānic inimitability in the Arabo-Islamic tradition has received support from the Fulbright Foundation, the NEH/American Research Center in Egypt, and the Social Science Research Council.

# INDEX


Abū ʿAmr Ibn al-ʿAlā', 61
Abū al-Faraj Rūnī, x, 206–207, 211
Abū Naṣr-i Fārsī, 205–206
Abū Nuwās, 93–94, 191
Abū Tammām, 110–11
Adīb-i Ṣābir, 208, 211
*akhbār* (historical-anecdotal materials), 2, 4, 5, 17, 21, 23–24, 34, 35, 40, 41–42
al-Akhṭal, 88
al-ʿAlavī, Muḥammad bin Nāṣir, 206
ʿAlī Bayk, Ḥusayn, 210
ʿAlī Ibn Abī Ṭālib (Imam ʿAlī), 63–64, 227
ʿAlqamah ibn ʿAbadah, 2–49, 90–91, 131, 136, 140, 143, 145, 150, 153, 155, 172; al-Faḥl, 2, 20
ʿAmʿaq-i Bukhārā'ī, 203
Amīr Khusraw, 234
al-Anbārī, Abū Bakr Muḥammad Ibn al-Qāsim (son), 91
al-Anbārī, Abū Muḥammad al-Qāsim Ibn Muḥammad Ibn Bashshār (father), 3, 91
ʿAntarah, 77, 107–108, 135–37, 140, 145
Anvarī, 207–208, 211, 234
Arberry, A. J., 174–76
ʿArūẓī, Niẓāmī, 200, 213
*ārzū* (yearning), 251–52
Āshuftah-yi Shīrāzī, 210
al-ʿAskarī, Abū Hilāl, 227
al-Aṣmaʿī, 78
*ātash u āb* (fire and water), 199–226, 228
*athāfī* (hearthstones), 89–105, 108
*aṭlāl* (ruined abodes), ix, 113, 150–52, 155, 157, 165, 182, 184–85, 188
Atsiz, Khvārazm-Shāh, 207, 211
ʿAṭṭār, Farīd al-Dīn, 201, 209, 234
ʿAwfī, Muḥammad, 205, 207
Awḥadī, 234
ʿAyn Ubāgh, 3
*aẓ'ār* (foster-nursing she-camels), 96–98, 104
Azraqī-yi Haravī, 203

*badīʿ* (original, unprecedented), 106, 110–11, 234
Badr-i Shīrvānī, 209, 214
Bahrām Shāh, 207–208
Bakhtin, M. M., 79
*Bānat Suʿād* (the Mantle Ode), 2, 21–49, 137–41, 145, 155
Banū Bakr, 113–14
Banū Kaʿb ibn ʿAwf, 10, 13
Banū Tamīm, 3, 4, 5
Bashāmah Ibn ʿAmr al-Ghadīr, 109
*bayt*, 65, 66, 100
beloved, the, 131, 133–34, 136, 141, 146, 151–52, 156, 252; as gazelle (metaphor), 141; sexual union with, 157
*bīgānah* (unfamiliar, strange), 234
Bint ʿAjlān, 186
Bishr. *See* Ibn Abī Khāzim al-Asadī, Bishr
Bloom, Harold, 201, 212–13
Brockelmann, Karl, 42
al-Buḥturī, 66, 80–81, 91–92, 110
Bujayr ibn Abī Sulmā al-Muzanī (brother of Kaʿb ibn Zuhayr), 21–23
*burdah* (mantle), 42–44
al-Burjumī, Ḍābi' Ibn al-Ḥārith Ibn Arṭāh, 88
Burkert, Walter, 41

Camporesi, Piero, 84
*Chahār Maqālah*, 200
"The Chicago School," vii
Clermont-Ganneau, Charles Simon, 85
*The Concept of Plagiarism in Arabic Theory*, 256n.9
*Il Convivio*, 125n.127
*creatio*, x. *See also* originality
Ctesiphon, 63, 87

al-Ḍabbī, ʿAbd Allāh Ibn ʿAnamah, 109
al-Ḍabbī, al-Mufaḍḍal, 20, 180–89
Dante Alighieri, 125n.127
al-Daqqāq, Abū ʿAlī, 191
*dār/diyār* (abode/s), 61–68, 72–73, 75, 79–80, 92, 94, 100, 108, 113, 117
al-Daylamī, Mihyār, 82, 111–12
Detienne, Marcel, 83–84
Deubner, Ludwig, 121n.44
*Dhakara r-Rabāba*, 146
*dhikr* (memory), 134, 136, 140, 144–45, 152, 154
Dhū al-Rummah, 109, 157, 188
al-Dhubyānī, al-Nābighah, 61–63, 66, 68, 71, 74, 76, 88, 92, 99, 103, 106
Diel, Paul, 118
*dimnah/diman* (dung), 74–88, 89
*Dīvān* (Sayyid Ashraf), 207
*Dīwān*: of Abū Nuwās, 191; of Abū Tammām, 110–11; of al-Buḥturī, 66, 81, 91–92, 110; of Mihyār al-Daylamī, 111–12; of al-Nābighah al-Dhubyānī, 61–62, 66, 69, 71–72, 76, 99, 106–108; of al-Ḥuṭay'ah, 90; of Bishr Ibn Abī Khāzim al-Asadī, 76, 94, 98, 171–72; of ʿUmar Ibn Abī Rabīʿah, 59; of ʿAbīd Ibn al-Abraṣ, 68, 70, 78; of Imru' al-Qays, 59,

75–76; of al-Nābighah al-Ja'dī, 63; of Labīd, 170–71; of al-Sharīf al-Murtaḍā, 82
*diyār.* See *dār*
Douglas, Mary, 137
Duerr, Hans Peter, 73

Eliot, T. S., 119
Empedocles, 202
Eschenbach, Wolfram von, 119
Evans-Pritchard, E. E., 5
exchange, ritual, 4–5. *See also* Kurke, Leslie; Mauss, Marcel

*fakhr* (boast), 1, 19, 157, 167, 171–73, 175–76
Farghānī, Sayf al-Dīn Muḥammad, 209
Farrukhī, 202, 203
Fayzī, 234
al-Fazl 'Alī, Amīr Abū, 203
al-Fazl 'Alī, Sayyid Bū, 203
Fighānī of Shiraz, Bābā, x, 227–55
Firdawsī, 215n.9
"fire and water," ix. *See also ātash u āb*
Frappier, Jean, 118–19
Frye, Northrop, 119, 226n.68

Galan, F. W., 238, 255n.5
Gaster, Theodor, viii, 5–6, 11, 13, 31, 33–35
gazelle, 141–44, 147
generosity, 17, 18
Gesenius, Wilhelm, 60
*ghazal,* 239–40, 242–44, 248, 252
*ghūl* (Ghool), viii, 25, 180–82, 186; guises of the, 130–64
*The Gift,* 4–5
Goethe, Johann Wolfgang von, 82
Greene, Thomas M., 255n.4
Grunebaum, Gustave von, 94, 153, 159n.1, 229, 231, 256n.9

*Ḥadāyiq al-siḥr fī daqāyiq al-shi'r,* 200
al-Ḥādirah, 168–70
Ḥāfiẓ, 209, 213–14, 234–36, 238–39
al-Ḥallāj, 193
*ḥamāmah/ḥamāmāt* (dove/s), 94, 101, 103, 104
Ḥammād al-Rāwiyah, 2–3
al-Ḥārith ibn Jabalah (Ghassanid King), 3–5, 7, 8, 11–13, 15–20; al-Wahhāb ("the Munificent"), 12–16
Havelock, Eric, 19–20
"A Heart Turbulent with Passion" ('Alqamah), viii, 2–49
Hermerén, Göran, 255n.7
Hestia, 100
*hieros gamos* (sacred marriage), 13
al-Ḥijr, 61–62, 87
*hijrah,* 21, 38–39
*Historic Structures: The Prague School Project: 1928–1946,* 255n.5
Hopkins, Gerard Manley, 186
howdah, 141
al-Ḥuṭay'ah, 90

Ibn 'Abd al-Malik Ibn al-Zayyāt, Muḥammad, 110
Ibn Abī Khāzim al-Asadī, Bishr, 76, 78, 94, 98, 101, 169–72
Ibn Abī Rabī'ah, 'Umar, 59, 109
Ibn Abī Sulmā, Zuhayr (father of Ka'b and Bujayr), 23, 43, 61, 94; *Mu'allaqah,* 66, 69, 77–78, 90, 166
Ibn Abī Wahb, Hubayrah, 22
Ibn al-Abraṣ, 'Abīd, 68, 70, 78
Ibn Aḥmad, al-Khalīl, 64–65
Ibn 'Amr al-'Abdī, Tha'labah, 79
Ibn Ḥizām, 'Urwā, 79
Ibn Jandal, Salāmah, 168
Ibn Jinnī, Abū al-Fatḥ 'Uthmān, 196
Ibn Khidhām, 58–59, 61, 75
Ibn Kulthūm, 'Amr, 173–76
Ibn Kurā' al-Uklī, Suwayd, 59
Ibn al-Mahdī al-Ghazzāl, Aḥmad, 115
Ibn Maqrūn, Rabī'ah, 109
Ibn Munqidh, Usāmah, 60, 67, 94
Ibn Muqbil, 170
Ibn Qays al-Ruqayyāt, 'Ubayd, 92
Ibn Qutaybah, 1, 6, 11, 182
Ibn Rashīq, 227–28, 233
Ibn al-Ṣimmah, Durayd, 23
Ibn al-Ṭabīb, 'Abdah, 87
Ibn Ya'fur, al-Aswad, 63
Ibn al-Zaba'rā, 22
*ibtidā'* (original invention), 228
*imitatio,* x, 229–32, 238
imitation, 228–38, 242
Imru' al-Qays, 20, 43, 58, 61, 75
*Influence in Art and Literature,* 255n.7
invigoration, 7, 12–13, 17, 33, 37–39
*iqtidā* (following), 231
Iṣfahānī, Jamāl al-Dīn (father), 208–209, 211, 213
Iṣfahānī, Kamal al-Dīn (son), 209
Isfarangī, Sayf al-Dīn, 208
*istiqbāl* (imitation), x, 199, 211–12, 229, 232–35, 237–38, 255
*istisqā'* (prayer for rain), 18
Iunx, 83–84
al-Iyādī, Abū Du'ād, 94–95

Jacob, Georg, 42
Jacobi, Renate, 153–55
al-Ja'dī, al-Nābighah, 63
Jāhilīyah (Age of Ignorance), 1, 21, 23, 30–32, 36, 39–40, 64, 87, 109
*javāb* (reply), 229, 232
*javāb guftan* (speaking in reply), 234
*javāb-gū'ī* (speaking in reply), x, 231
Jinn (Jinnee), viii, 180
Johnson, Samuel, 199

jubilation, 7, 12, 17
al-Jumaḥī, Ibn Sallām, 3, 166
al-Junayd, 195
al-Jurjānī, ʿAbd al-Qāhir, 229

Kaʿb Ibn Zuhayr, viii, 2, 21–49, 137–41, 145, 155
Kaʿbah, 65
*kahrubā* ("straw robber"), 248
Kamālī, 205
Kāshī, Taqī al-Dīn, 242
*khalīṭ* (tribal medley), 172
al-Khansāʾ, 40
Khāqānī, 234
*khawālid* (immovable rocks), 93–94, 97, 101, 103
*khayāl* (phantom), 181–82. *See also ṭayf*
Khayyam, Omar, 244
Khizr, 245, 247, 252
*Khulāṣat al-ashʿār va zubdat al-afkār,* 242
*khuld* (eternity), 101–103
Khusraw, Nāṣir, 203
Khvājah Aḥmad, 202
Khvājū of Kirman, 234
*Kitāb al-Aghānī,* 43–44
Kotlarevs'kiy, Ivan, 88
Krenkow, F., 168–69
Kulayb, 113–14
al-Kumayt Ibn Zayd al-Asadī, 98–99
Kurke, Leslie, 45–46n.11

Labīd, 33, 59, 78, 108, 112, 119, 151–52, 155, 170–71
*lafẓ* (enunciation), 118
Lāmīyah, 153
Lane, Edward, 180, 188
Laylā, 7, 11, 12
Lewis, Franklin D., 228
*The Light in Troy: Imitation and Discovery in Renaissance Poetry,* 255n.4
*Lubāb al-albāb,* 205
Lyall, Charles James, 14, 167, 169, 181, 185

*madḥ* (panegyric mode), 1
*madīnah* (city), 87–88
Maḥmūd the Ghaznavid, 202
*majlis* (literary salon), 235
Malti-Douglas, Fedwa, 48n.48
*Al-Manāzil wa al-Diyār,* 59–60, 67, 92, 95
mantle (of the Prophet), 42–44
"The Mantle Ode." *See Bānat Suʿād*
Manūchihrī, 202
Masīḥ, Rukn al-Dīn, 235
Masʿūd III (Sultan) (ʿAlāʾ al-Dawlah), 204–207, 211
Mauss, Marcel, viii, 4–5, 7, 16–17, 19, 36, 43; *The Gift,* 4–5
Mayyah, 61, 62, 68, 72, 106, 157
McDonald, M. V., 165
Medina, 22, 23, 38, 88
metalanguage, 34
Mintah (Mint), 83–84
al-Miṣrī, Dhū al-Nūn, 192
mortification, 6, 13, 17, 31, 33, 39. *See also nasīb*
*Muʿallaqah*: of ʿAntarah, 77, 135–36, 145; of Zuhayr Ibn Abī Sulmā, 66, 69, 77–78, 90, 166; of ʿAmr Ibn Kulthūm, 173, 175; of Labīd, 33, 59, 78, 112, 151–52, 155; of Ṭarafah, 141–45, 154, 166
*muʿāraḍah* (competitive imitation), 229, 231, 233
Muʿāwiyah (Caliph), 42
*Mufaḍḍalīyāt,* ix, 181–89; *1* (Ta'abbaṭa Sharran), 185–86; *6,* 181; *21* (Mukhabbal al-Saʿdī), 146–50; *46* (Muraqqish the Elder), 184–85; *55* (Muraqqish the Younger), 150, 182–84; *57,* 181, 186–88; *62* (al-Ḥārith Ibn Ḥillizah al-Yashkurī), 185; *119* (ʿAlqamah), ix, 2–49; *120* (ʿAlqamah), 2, 131–33; poets of the, 109
Muhājirūn, 38, 39
Muhalhil Ibn Rabīʿah, 113–14
Muḥammad, the Prophet (the Messenger of God, Rasūl Allāh), viii, 2, 21–24, 28, 32, 35–38, 43, 86, 89; the mantle of, 42–44
Muʿizzī, 199, 207, 211
*mujtaṣṣ* (meter), 201, 203–210
Mukhabbal al-Saʿdī, 146–52, 154–56
*mukhaḍram* (bridging generations), 87–88, 90, 108
al-Mundhir ibn Māʾ al-Samāʾ (Lakhmid King), 3, 7, 12–13, 17–18
*mundus,* 73–74
al-Muraqqish: the Elder, 90, 109, 167, 184–85; the Younger, 150, 182–84, 186–88
al-Murtaḍā, al-Sharīf, 82, 92
*musābaqah* (poetic competition), 231
*mushāʿarah* (poetic competition), 231
Mutammim Ibn Nuwayrah al-Yarbūʿī, 96
al-Mutanabbī, 194–96
Muʿtazilites, 38
Muzaynah, 23; Banū, 22, 32, 40
mythogenesis, 21–49
mythopoesis, 21–49

*naʿt* (characterization), 130
Najd, 62
*nāqah. See* she-camel
*nasīb,* viii, ix, 1, 6, 11, 17–18, 31, 33–34, 37, 40; of Kaʿb, 30; the seven words of the, 58–129. *See also* mortification
Nāṣif, Muṣṭafā, viii, 58, 166
*naẓīrah-gū'ī* (saying the like), 229, 231, 234
Naẓīrī of Nishapur, 234–35, 243–54
Niẓāmī, 234
Nöldeke, Theodor, 65
al-Numayrī, Abū Ḥayyah, 95
*nu'y* (trench), 68–74, 155, 157

originality, 228–29, 232–38

Paret, Rudi, 43

Paris, Ginette, 100, 126n.133
pearl, 150–51
Peuckert, Will-Erich, 73
plagiarism. *See* sariqah
poesis, 41–49
poets: Ṣūfī, 9; Safavid-Moghul, x, 232–62
purgation, 6, 17
purification, 137, 140–41, 144, 150, 157
purity, 134

Qā'ānī, 210, 214
al-Qāḍī al-Māwardī, 64
*qaṣīdat al-burdah.* See *Bānat Suᶜād*
Qaṭrān-i Tabrīzī, 203
*qawm* (tribal warriors), 63
Qazvīnī, Fakhr al-Zamān, 235
Qur'ān, 18, 28, 31, 36, 38, 39, 64, 67, 87, 101
Quraysh, 2, 23, 166
al-Qushayrī, Abū al-Qāsim, 191
al-Qushayrī, Ṣimmah, 95

*rabᶜ* (vernal encampment), 66–69, 72
Rabāb, 146–47, 151
*radīf* (refrain), 199–226, 228, 240
*raḥīl* (desert journey), 1, 6, 12, 17, 18, 31–34, 40, 150, 157, 166, 173
*rajaz* (meter), 209
*ramal* (meter), 205, 207–208
Rashīd al-Dīn. *See* Vaṭvāṭ, Rashīd al-Dīn
al-Rāvandī, 199
redemption, 38
reincarnation, 14
al-Ribāᶜī, ᶜAwf Ibn ᶜAṭīyah Ibn al-Kharīᶜ al-Tamīmī, 108
rites: of invigoration, 6–7, 13; of jubilation, 6–7; of mortification, 6, 13; of passage and sacrifice, 7; penitential, 15; of purgation, 6
*rithā'*(elegy), 19
Ritter, H., 153–54
Riyāẓ-i Hamadānī, Mīrzā, 210
Rūdakī, 199
Rūmī, Mawlānā, 209, 234–36

*ṣabūḥ* (morning wine), 240
Saᶜdī, 209, 234–35
*ṣaḥw* (waking), 134, 140–41, 144–45, 150, 152, 191
Ṣā'ib of Tabriz, 230–39, 243, 249–54
Said, Edward, 212
Ṣāliḥ, 14
Salmā (Salmah), 40, 132, 134, 167
Salmān, Masᶜūd-i Saᶜd, x, 204–207, 211–12
Sanā'ī, x, 199, 206, 207, 211, 234–36, 250
Sanjar (Seljuk Sultan), 205, 207–208, 211
al-Saqaṭī, Sarī, 192
*sāqī* (Saqi), 239–40, 252
*sariqah/sariqāt* (plagiarism), x, 227–28
Saul, 117
Sayyid Ashraf Ḥasan-i al-Ghaznavī, 199, 207–209, 211–12
"seasonal pattern," 5–7. *See also* Gaster, Theodor
*Seelenvogel,* 14
Seybold, John, ix
Shāh ᶜAbbās, 235
*Shāh Nāmah,* 199
Shakespeare: *Henry V,* 85, 88; *Macbeth,* 97
Shanfarā, 153–54
Shāpūr of Tehran, 234–35, 243–46, 249–54
*sharḥ* (exegetical commentary), 24, 37, 59
Sha's (ᶜAlqamah's brother), 3–5, 11–12, 17
she-camel (*nāqah*), 14, 31–33, 96, 98, 173–75
*she'ōl,* 116–17
al-Shiblī, 195
Shiraz, 236–38
*shu'ūn* (tear lines), 154–55, 157
*siᶜlāh* (ogress, witch), 181
simile, viii; of beloved as gazelle, 154; dissembling, 131–64; as jackal, 154; *talawwun,* 141
Smith, W. Robertson, 104
Spitzer, Leo, viii, 58
Strabo, 85
*Studien zur Poetik der altarabischen Qaṣide,* 153
Suᶜād, 24–25, 30–31, 37, 137, 139–40, 155
*su'āl* (question), 105–119
submission, 35, 37, 43
Suᶜdā, 107
Ṣuḥbat-i Sharar, 210
al-Sukkarī, 37
Surkhāb, Abū al-Muẓaffar, 203
Sūzanī of Samarqand, 208

Ta'abbaṭa Sharran, 14, 185
*taḍmīn* (quotation), x, 229
al-Ṭā'ī, Ḥātim Ibn ᶜAbd Allāh, 69
Takallū, Shānī, 235
*ṭalal* (ruin), 58–60, 64, 109, 113, 117–19
*talawwun* (mutability), 141, 157
Ṭālib, 234, 250
*taqlīd* (imitation), 230, 232
Ṭarafah, 141–45, 154, 166
*tatabbuᶜ* (imitation), 229–31
*tawārud* (unintentional coincidences), 228
*ṭayf,* 150; *al-khayāl* (dream phantom), 165, 180–89
*tāzah-gū'ī* (speaking the new), 234
*taẓmīn* (quotation), 200
al-Thaᶜālibī, 194, 196
Thamūd, 14; people of, 98
*Thespis: Ritual, Myth, and Drama in the Near East,* 5–6
*The 1001 Nights,* 180–81
al-Tibrīzī, 14, 37
*tofet* (place of immolation), 104–105
*The Traffic in Praise: Pindar and the Poetics of Social Economy,* 45–46n.11
*Traufe* (eaves), 73–74

Trotsky, Leon, 224n.62
Ṭufayl al-Ghanawī, 168–69, 171

ʿUmar (Caliph), 44
ʿUnṣurī, 199, 203
ʿUrfī of Shiraz, 234–35, 250
ʿUs̱mān-i Mukhtārī, 206
*utrujjah* (etrog, citron), 131–32, 134, 140, 145, 150

Vaṭvāṭ, Rashīd al-Dīn, x, 200–201, 207–209, 211
Vesta, 100
Vico, Giambattista, 212

*waḥy* (revelation), 112
al-Walīd Ibn Yazīd, 109
*waṣf* (description), 131
Weinraub, Eugene J., 128n.175
Williams, William Carlos, 234
*wiṣāl* (amorous union), 83–84
*Woman's Body, Woman's Word: Gender and Discourse in Arabo-Islamic Writing,* 48n.48

Yaghmā, 210
al-Yashkurī, al-Ḥārith Ibn Ḥillizah, 185

*ẓaʿana* (to depart), 166–67, 170–71
*ẓaʿīnah/ẓaʿāʾin* (departing woman), 62, 165–79
Ẓallāmah, 76
*ẓaʿn* (departure), ix, 131, 170–71
Zephyr, 239, 241, 251–52

www.ingramcontent.com/pod-product-compliance
Lightning Source LLC
Chambersburg PA
CBHW071917160426
42813CB00098B/710
*9780253354938*